OPERATION OVERFLIGHT

A MEMOIR OF THE
U-2 INCIDENT

Series Editors
Walter J. Boyne and Peter B. Mersky

Aviation Classics are inspired non-fiction and fictional accounts that reveal the human drama of flight. The series covers every era of military and civil aviation, is international in scope, and encompasses flying in all of its diversity. Some of the books are well-known best-sellers and others are superb, but unheralded, titles, which deserve a wider audience.

Other Titles in the Aviation Classics Series
Ploesti: The Great Ground-Air Battle of 1 August 1943 by James Dugan and Carroll Stewart
Thirty Seconds over Tokyo by Ted W. Lawson

2020 x

OPERATION OVERFLIGHT

A MEMOIR OF
THE U-2 INCIDENT

FRANCIS GARY POWERS
with Curt Gentry

Potomac Books
An imprint of the University of Nebraska Press

Library of Congress Cataloging-in-Publication Data

Powers, Francis Gary, 1929–
    Operation Overflight : a memoir of the U-2 Incident / Francis Gary Powers with
Curt Gentry.

        p.cm.
    ISBN 978-1-57488-422-7 (alk. paper)
        1. Powers, Francis Gary, 1929– 2. U-2 Incident, 1960. 3. Cold War. I. Gentry,
Curt, 1931– II. Title.

    DK266.3 .P64 2002
        973.921'092—dc21

                                                                            2002071149

Printed in the United States of America on acid-free paper that meets the American
National Standards Institute Z39-48 Standard.

To Sue, who provided the happy ending

To the memory of
Buster Eugene Edens
who died in the crash of a U-2
at Edwards Air Force Base, California
April 1965

CONTENTS

On May 1, 1960—the traditional May Day holiday—an American U-2 spyplane flew high above the Soviet Union photographing strategic targets. It was the twenty-fourth U-2 mission over the USSR since the first overflight almost four years earlier. The pilot of this U-2 was thirty-year-old Francis Gary Powers. A former U.S. Air Force fighter pilot, Powers was the most experienced U-2 pilot in the spyplane program with about six hundred hours at the controls of a U-2. He was also one of the most respected spyplane pilots, for his airmanship and for his integrity.

The calm sky more than seventy thousand feet above the USSR, far above the altitude of any Soviet fighter, was suddenly ripped apart as a surface-to-air missile detonated near Powers's aircraft. Heavily damaged, the plane fell out of control. Unable to use his ejection seat, with great difficulty Powers bailed out of the crippled aircraft as it spun toward earth. He landed safely and was soon captured and flown to Moscow.

The shootdown of the U-2 piloted by Powers had a spectacular impact on the Cold War. In the late 1950s, the United States, under President Dwight D. Eisenhower, and the USSR, under Premier Nikita S. Khrushchev, had been moving toward closer relations. Following a successful summit meeting of the two superpower leaders in Geneva in July 1955, there was some thawing of the Cold War. Khrushchev visited the United States in September 1959, seeing Congress and Iowa cornfields and meeting stars on a Hollywood movie set. He invited Eisenhower, his children and grandchildren to visit the Soviet Union.

This superpower warming ended abruptly with the Powers shootdown. American cover stories about a weather reconnaissance plane straying off course were soon revealed to be boldfaced lies. Khrushchev himself went to New York to denounce the overflights at the United Nations. Powers was put on trial and found guilty of spying. Eisenhower, poorly served by the Central Intelligence

Agency in the affair, personally took responsibility. The long-planned summit meeting in Paris in mid-May was a disaster as Khrushchev demanded an apology from the president.

The revelations that followed about the overflights were both a triumph and an embarrassment for the Soviet Union: One of the acclaimed American spyplanes had been shot down, but for almost four years—since July 4, 1956—the U-2s had overflown Soviet territory with impunity.

The twenty-three successful overflights had been vital to U.S. national security. Penetrating the "iron curtain" that had descended over the Soviet Union and its Eastern European satellite states, the U-2 provided explicit intelligence of the Soviet manned bomber program and then of its intercontinental ballistic missile program. Further, strategic targets that had been known only from German maps of the early 1940s and even older documentation could be located with accuracy.

In *Operation Overflight*, Francis Gary Powers provided un-equaled insights into the U-2 program, the training of U-2 pilots, and of spyplane missions—over the USSR as well as over the Middle East and even certain "friendly" countries. His descriptions are vivid and his writing style engrossing.

This book is a significant contribution to the history of aviation.

Norman Polmar
Author, *Spyplane: The U-2 History Declassified*

Turner Air Force Base, Albany, Georgia
January, 1956

In the service you scan the bulletin board with one eye closed, hoping not to see your name, since its being there means one of two things. You've fouled up in some way, and been caught at it. Or you've been assigned extra duties.

That afternoon I had returned to the base after a routine training flight in an F-84F jet fighter; passing the board, I spotted a new list. On it: Powers, Francis Gary 1Lt.

I was to report to a major in the wing headquarters building at 0800 hours the following morning. No reason given.

There was some consolation. Mine wasn't the only name. A number of other pilots were also listed.

Next morning we met outside the major's office a few minutes before eight. Wracking our collective brains, we couldn't come up with any unusual devilment, at least none of which we were all guilty.

The major came right to the point. Some men were interested in talking to us about a possible job offer.

"Why us?"

Because, he replied, we met certain qualifications: we had exceptional pilot ratings; were reserve officers with indefinite enlistments; had Top Secret clearances; plus having in excess of the required number of hours' flight time in single-engine, single-place aircraft.

We all started to ask questions. The major interrupted. He was sorry, that was all he could tell us; except, if we were interested, when and where to report.

Later, over coffee, we tried to figure it out, agreeing only that it was a flying job. Everything else was decidedly odd.

The Air Force was not in the habit of arranging outside job interviews for its officers.

Even more puzzling, the meetings were to take place individually, at different times, not during duty hours but at night, not on base but at a motel outside Albany, the Radium Springs Inn on Radium Springs Road. In my case, at 1900 hours (seven p.m.) I was to go to cottage 1, knock, identify myself, and ask for a "Mr. William Collins."

Cottage 1 was at the end of the row.

I knocked, feeling more curious than anything.

The man who opened the door was in his mid-thirties, of medium build, about five-feet-ten, with black hair, and, like the two men I could see in the room behind him, in civilian clothes.

"I was told to ask for a Mr. William Collins," I said, feeling a trifle silly.

"I'm Bill Collins," he replied. "You must be—" He paused and waited.

"Lieutenant Powers."

Motioning me inside, he introduced me to the other men.

We shook hands and I took the chair they indicated.

Collins was apparently spokesman for the group.

"I suppose you're wondering what this is all about?"

I admitted I was.

"I'm afraid there's not very much I can tell you, at least at this time. What I can say is this. You, and several other pilots, have been picked to be part of an organization to carry out a special mission. It will be risky, but patriotic. Should you decide to join us, you'll be doing something important for your country. The pay will be more than you are now receiving.

"And that's about all I can tell you now. What we'd like you to do is think about it overnight. Then, if you're still interested, call me here at the motel tomorrow; we'll arrange another meeting."

Despite the sketchiness of the information, everything Collins had said appealed greatly to my sense of adventure. There was no clue as to what the job would be, or for whom I would be working, but it sounded like a Flying Tiger-type operation, such as Chennault had organized in China prior to World War II. I was definitely interested, and told Collins so.

"No," he said, "don't decide now. Think about it overnight. Oh, one more thing. You'll be overseas for eighteen months, and you can't take your family along."

I had been married just nine months, and the marriage had been troubled. I was not at all sure it could survive a long separation.

Barbara and I had no children. That wasn't important. But the future of our marriage was, and I didn't feel we could risk it.

I told Collins that because of this last condition, I'd have to turn it down.

Collins replied that he was sorry, but should I change my mind, I knew where to reach him. As I was leaving, he added that should I want to discuss the offer with my wife, I could do so. He would appreciate, however, my not mentioning it to anyone else.

Returning home, I told Barbara about the mysterious interview and my decision. I also told her how appealing I found the offer, in spite of the fact that I had no idea for whom I'd be working or what I'd be doing. To my surprise, she shared my enthusiasm, but for less adventurous and more practical reasons.

We could use the additional money, she noted. And I had to agree. Although she worked and our combined salaries equaled about seven hundred dollars per month, we were, like most service couples, living above our income. We had recently made payment on a new car; the balance was still due.

She could move in with her mother while I was gone, she suggested, while keeping her secretarial job at the Marine Corps Supply Center. Since the cost of living overseas was almost always less than in the United States and my pay would be more, we could probably save enough money to pay for the car while possibly making a down payment on a home.

"And eighteen months isn't forever."

When she wanted to be, Barbara could be quite persuasive. And I was already more than slightly tempted.

Despite Collins' admonition, coffee the next morning was a gab-fest. Several of the pilots had already rejected the offer because of the separation from their families. The remainder, myself included, were undecided, but highly curious.

Guesses as to the nature of the employment were as varied as they were wild. But they were just that, guesses. Collins had given us just enough information to whet our curiosity. No more.

That afternoon I called to make another appointment, for that evening.

Driving to the motel, I thought about the interviews. Although secrecy appeared to be the major reason for their unorthodox arrangement, I felt sure the psychological effect had not been lost on Collins and his associates. Occurring at night, in an unusual place, set apart from the routine and ordinary—all generated excitement.

But I'd had enough mystery. Tonight I was determined to get some hard answers.

Collins supplied them. More than I'd anticipated, and without my asking.

He began by explaining that he and the other two men were representatives of the Central Intelligence Agency. Should I be accepted, I would be working under contract for that agency.

I knew nothing about the Central Intelligence Agency, except that it was a supersecret branch of the government, most often referred to by its initials, CIA.

Though I was impressed, I tried not to show it.

As for the Air Force, Collins continued, should I wish to return to it following completion of my contract, arrangements would be made so I could do so, with no loss of time in grade or toward retirement. In short, I could reenter at the same rank as my contemporaries, my time in the CIA being counted as service time.

Now the particulars. First, I would be checked out on an entirely new aircraft—

To a pilot who loved flying, as I did, there are few words more thrilling. But Collins went on to add them.

—a plane which would fly higher than any plane had ever before flown.

I was hooked.

My pay, training in the United States, would be fifteen hundred dollars per month. On arrival overseas, it would be upped to twenty-five hundred.

I was so surprised I couldn't reply. Even with combat pay, this was far beyond anything I could ever hope to earn in the Air Force; it was nearly as much as the captain of a commercial airliner received!

Collins appeared to read my thoughts, that I was now contemplating what nature of job would necessitate such a pay scale.

"Once you've completed your training, you will be sent overseas. Part of your job will be to make reconnaissance flights along the border outside Russia, the highly sensitive equipment aboard the plane monitoring radar and radio signals.

"But that's only a part," he continued. "Your main mission will be to fly over Russia."

Stunned, I listened as he described how during these "overflights" special cameras would photograph Russian defenses, missile-launching sites, military deployments. . . .

It is difficult to describe exactly what I felt at that moment. I was one of what I presumed to be a not inconsiderable number who believed that the Cold War was a very real war, with real objectives, and that since the stalemate and compromise in Korea, the free world had been losing that war, and one country after another, to Communism.

The discovery that the government of the United States had conceived an intelligence operation so bold and daring restored much of my faith in the alertness of that government.

I was amazed. And immensely proud, not only of being chosen to participate in such a venture, but, even more, proud of my country itself, for having the courage, and guts, to do what it believed essential and right.

Collins was still talking. Huge areas of Russia were a dark mystery. Since World War II, tremendous industrial and military complexes—whole cities—had grown up beyond the Urals, never seen by outsiders. Except for the limited intelligence received from inside the Soviet Union, there was no way of knowing what Russia was planning militarily, its capabilities, what we must be prepared to meet should war come. At the time of Pearl Harbor, we at least had some comprehension of Japan's military might. This was not the case with Russia. After the Soviets failed to approve President Eisenhower's Open Skies Plan of 1955, "Operation Overflight" had been conceived to close this gap.

"How do you feel about it now?" he asked.

"*I'm in.* I wouldn't miss it for the world. All my life I've wanted to do something like this!"

This was no exaggeration. Had I been asked to do it simply on a volunteer basis, as an Air Force pilot, my enthusiasm and commitment wouldn't have been one whit less great.

"Take another night to think it over," Collins suggested.

"That's not necessary: I've decided."

"We want you to be sure. If you feel the same way tomorrow, call me. We'll talk about it."

He needn't have added the obvious, but he did, that this time I was not to discuss our conversation with anyone, even my wife.

I slept little that night. Early the following morning I called him with my answer.

Our third and last meeting at the motel was quite businesslike. As always, Collins did most of the talking.

It was necessary that I go to Washington, D.C., for briefings and certain tests. The following week, routine Air Force orders would be issued, directing me to report there for several days' temporary duty. These would cover my absence from the base, as well as authorizing travel expenses. Actual orders—where to report in Washington and when—would be issued verbally by the major with whom I had first been in contact. I was to travel in civilian clothes. Hotel reservations would be made for me. My alias, to be used on the hotel register: "Palmer, Francis G."—false last name, correct first name and middle initial. ID, with this name, would be issued to me prior to the trip, identifying me as a civilian employee of the Department of the Air Force.

Again Collins anticipated my question. Wives being naturally inquisitive, I could tell my wife that I would have several months to clear up pending business and to make necessary living arrangements. I could also tell her the amount of my pay, that I would be working as an employee of the government—though under no circumstances was I to mention the Central Intelligence Agency—and that my job would be to make reconnaissance flights along the border outside Russia. Just enough to make her feel she was in on what was happening and to impress upon her the necessity for complete secrecy. Nothing more. As for others—parents and friends—I would be given a separate cover story at a later date. Meantime, I was to say nothing.

Collins also informed me he would be in communication when necessary. If for any reason I had to reach him, there was a telephone number to memorize. There would be an answer at all hours of the day or night.

During our meetings I had several times referred to the Central Intelligence Agency as the CIA. Each time, Collins had winced slightly. When he or the other men referred to it, it was always "the government," or, most often, "the agency." Almost automatically, I fell into the same habit.

I was learning.

Thus, I suppose, spies are made.

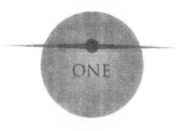

ONE

THE AGENCY

One

I have never thought of myself as a spy, yet in a certain sense this attitude is probably naïve, for Operation Overflight was to change many of the traditional definitions of espionage, providing a bridge between the age of the "deep-cover" cloak-and-dagger agent and that of the wholly electronic spy-in-the-sky satellite.

Although as a boy I had dreamed of myself in many roles, interestingly enough, being a spy was not one of them. Looking back, however, I can see almost an inevitability in the events that led me to that motel door.

Born August 17, 1929, in Burdine, Kentucky, in the heart of the Appalachian coal-mining country, I was the second of six children of Oliver and Ida Powers. The other five were girls. The lone boy was not to follow in his father's footsteps, however. From as early as I can remember, I was to become a doctor, not through any choice of my own but because that was what my father had decided I was to be.

His reasons were simple: doctors made money, their families suffering few hardships. A coal miner most of his years, he had known only the harshest kind of life.

A close call in the mine while I was a child had cemented his resolve. While he was working as brakeman on a "motor," an electric engine used to pull strings of coal cars, another motor had rammed his, the force of the collision pinning him against the roof of the mine. When other miners finally extricated him, his hip was badly injured. Neither the resultant limp nor the recurrent pain kept him out of the mines, however; it was the only work available. One of my first jobs as a boy, in Harmon, Virginia, had been to walk up to the mine each morning to see if there was work that day. These being years of the Depression, more often than not there wasn't. Sometimes at night I could hear my parents talking, not about where the next dollar was coming from, but the next nickel. Many days there wasn't enough money for a loaf of bread.

Fortunately my sisters and I were spared the agonies of envy. None of our friends and neighbors had much more. It was a poor region.

Growing up the only boy in a family of five girls made me

something of a loner. Reading was my main pastime. History, historical fiction—other times, other places—fascinated me. One of my greatest disappointments as a boy occurred when I read of Admiral Byrd's discovery of Antarctica. It seemed there were no new worlds left unfound, that all the great discoveries had been made.

Much of the time that I wasn't reading I spent outdoors. Although, together with the other boys, I swam in the local rivers and streams, did some fishing and a little hunting—rabbit, squirrel, bird—I most enjoyed getting off by myself and tramping the Cumberland Mountains. Best of all was to sit on the edge of a high cliff on the side of a mountain and look out over the valleys. It seemed to give me a perspective I couldn't find in my daily routine.

Green, hilly, with abundant trees, it was beautiful country, the Virginia-Kentucky border territory—or would have been, except for the mines. Their presence poisoned everything, the water in the streams, the hope in the miners' lives. They scarred the landscape, made people like my mother and father old before their time.

Yet even on the mountaintop I couldn't see any other horizons for myself. An obedient son, I had accepted my father's decision that I was to be a doctor, though the prospect interested me not at all.

My father had a second dream—to get out of the mines himself. He tried repeatedly, even enlisting as a private in the Army for three years, at twenty-one dollars per month. But always he returned underground.

I had the same restlessness. Two incidents during my teens contributed to it.

When I was about fourteen my father and I took a short trip through West Virginia, passing an airport outside Princeton. A fair was in progress, a large sign offered airplane rides for two and a half dollars. I begged my father to let me go up. He finally relented. The war was on now, the mines operating at full capacity, and money was no longer quite so scarce.

The plane, which seemed incredibly large to me at the time, was a Piper Cub. The female pilot, viewed from the vantage point of my fourteen years, seemed like an old woman, but was probably about twenty. My enthusiasm was so obvious that she kept me up double time. As my father remembers it, when we returned to earth I told him, "Dad, I left my heart up there." I don't recall saying it, but I probably did, since it came as close to describing my feelings as anything could. There was something very special about it. Like climbing mountains, only better.

Much as I enjoyed it, however, it led to no great decision regarding my future; that was already decided.

In 1945, during my junior year in high school, my father took a job at a defense plant in Detroit and moved the family there. It was a world apart from Appalachia. The patriotic fever of the times was contagious, and everyone seemed to be doing something for his country. Except me. Though I was certain my father would never give his permission, I was determined, on finishing high school the following year, to enlist in the Navy.

But the war ended in 1945, and we returned to the Cumberlands, where I finished my last year of high school, at Grundy, Virginia.

I was keenly disappointed to have missed World War II.

This feeling was compounded when I started college the following fall. The school, Milligan College, near Johnson City, in east Tennessee, was, like all colleges at the time, packed with returning veterans, each with stories of his wartime exploits. I envied them. It seemed I had been born too late for the important things.

I hadn't really wanted to go to college, but was simply going along with my father's intention that I become a doctor. I got through the premed courses, but barely; the interest wasn't there. Too, at home nearly everyone had been poor. At college this wasn't the case. Others had cars, new clothes, spending money. What money I earned—waiting table, washing dishes, scrubbing and waxing floors, all the typical college chores—went toward my expenses. Now in my late teens, I wanted to get out on my own, cut parental ties, be independent.

My youthful rebellion didn't take place all at once, but in stages, the first actually occurring the summer between high school and college, when, knowing I would need money to supplement my father's savings, I took the only work available that paid a decent wage. It was also the one thing my father had vowed his son would never do: work in a mine.

In high school I had played left guard on the football team. At Milligan I went out for track, running the 100-yard dash, 220, broad jump, 440- and 880-yard relays. Caves abounding in the area, I took up "spelunking." It didn't satisfy my yearnings for adventure, only fired them.

Being a church school, Milligan offered less than most colleges in the way of excitement.

There was none, I decided, in premed, at least not for me. To be a doctor required a special type of person. Whatever that was, I wasn't it. My junior year, much to my father's displeasure, I dropped premed, retaining as majors the two subjects which did interest me, biology and chemistry.

Summers, while at home, I worked at various construction jobs: helping build a bridge across a river; laying railroad track; digging a tunnel through a mountain between Virginia and Kentucky; erecting a tipple, a mechanism that grades, washes, and loads coal. None was a job that appealed to me as a possible occupation. More and more I began thinking of enlisting in the service, at least until deciding what I really wanted to do. Although I had not been aloft since, I had never forgotten the excitement of that first airplane ride. During my senior year in college I applied for Air Force Cadets, took the tests, passed them, and was accepted. All that remained was to sign the papers, which I intended to do the moment I graduated.

Finally, it seemed, I was going to make the break.

My father, meantime, had made an important break of his own. Some years earlier he had bought into a shoe-repair shop, in time buying out his partner. While my father was in the mines, my mother kept the shop open, collecting work for him to do when his shift ended. Eventually he was able to make shoe repairing a full-time occupation, finally escaping the mines.

That his only son also wanted to make a change was something he refused to accept.

At this time my family was living in Pound, Virginia, or The Pound, as it is known locally. Ages ago, the river had formed a natural bend, in the shape of a U. The Indians had discovered that by closing the gap at the top with a fence they had a natural corral, or pound, for horses. The first white settlers had turned the same three hundred acres into farmland. My grandfather had owned a small farm there since the start of the century. By moving onto a portion of his land, my parents were able to raise their own produce, supplementing earnings from the shoe shop.

Except for my family, there was nothing in The Pound to keep me there. Realizing this, my father, noting that I had been away from home four long years, argued that I owed it to my mother to remain home for at least a few months.

Again, I was an obedient son, although this time less easily so. Reluctantly I passed up the chance to go into Cadets.

In June, 1950, I received my Bachelor of Science degree from Milligan; the North Koreans moved into South Korea; and, while many of my classmates enlisted or were recalled, I got a job as lifeguard at a swimming pool in nearby Jenkins.

With a war in progress, it now became obvious even to my

father that eventually I would have to go into the service. Changing tactics slightly, he tried to persuade me to wait for the draft. That way I would have to serve only two years in the Army; the shortest enlistment in the Air Force was four.

But I wanted to fly. That October, two months after turning twenty-one, I finally made the break, enlisting in the United States Air Force for four years.

After basic training at Lackland Air Force Base, outside San Antonio, Texas, I was sent to Lowry AFB, at Denver, Colorado, for photo school. On graduation, I was assigned to Westover, Massachusetts, where I worked as a photo lab technician.

While at Lowry I had reapplied for Air Cadets. Approval was finally received, and in November of 1951 I went to Greenville, Mississippi, for training.

Aviation Cadets was rough, intentionally so. But the concentrated work made me able to solo after only twenty hours' flight time. The plane was a T-6, a large, 550-horsepower holdover that had been a first-line fighter plane back in the thirties. For the last ten hours of training, the instructor had rarely touched the controls. Realizing that he wasn't there, that the back seat was empty, and I was completely alone, came as a decided shock—immediately followed by a tremendous feeling of self-assurance: I really didn't need help, I was in full control. One of the real joys of flying, and a feeling that never dissipates but mellows the more you fly, is the satisfaction of total responsibility, of being dependent solely on yourself.

But long before discovering this, on touching down after that first solo, I knew that flying would be my life work.

After completing six months' basic flight training, there followed another six months' advanced flight training at Williams AFB, Arizona, where I checked out on the T-33 and F-80. Graduating from Cadets in December, 1952, with silver wings over my left breast pocket and a shiny new second lieutenant's bar on each shoulder, I was sent to Luke AFB, near Phoenix, for gunnery school with the F-84G, on orders to Korea.

Appendicitis stopped me in the middle of training. Because of lost time in the hospital, I was washed back to the next class. By the time I graduated, signing of the armistice was imminent.

Again I felt I'd lost my chance to fight, to prove myself.

Given as choice of duty assignments peacetime Korea, Maine, or Georgia, I chose the last, and in July, 1953, reported to the 468th

Strategic Fighter Squadron of the 508th Strategic Fighter Wing at Turner AFB, near Albany, Georgia.

Survival school at Hazlehurst, Georgia, and advanced survival school at Stead AFB, outside Reno, Nevada, followed. In addition to regular survival training, such as how to live with minimum provisions in a desolate area, and simulated parachute jumps from a fifty-foot tower, there were additional lessons, gathered from experiences of the Korean War, for use in the event of enemy capture. We were briefed on brainwashing techniques and we were given the task of compiling a list of questions that could be used to establish a positive identification if, for instance, we were captured and there was a prisoner exchange. These were personal things the enemy would be unlikely to know, such as mother's maiden name, family birthdates, the position I played on the high-school football team, the name of my coach. At the time, with no war in sight, it seemed unlikely I would ever have occasion to put much of this to use. Some of the training I was given, I hoped I'd never have to use. In October, 1953, I was put on special orders to report to the top-secret Sandia Base in New Mexico, for Delivery Course DD50. This was a deceptively simple title for the actual instruction—how to load and drop atomic bombs from fighter aircraft. The course, which included lectures on how atomic bombs were made and detonated, of necessity gave us not only glimpses into the extent of our nuclear preparedness but also a very clear idea of U.S. operational plans in the event of war.

It was more than just a glimpse. Should a certain alert be called, I was assigned a place to report, where an aircraft, complete with nuclear payload, would be gassed up and waiting. As preparation, I was given navigational charts so I could memorize the route I was to take. And I was thoroughly briefed on my specific assigned target, on the other side of the Iron Curtain.

In July, 1954, I made first lieutenant, bringing about a good increase in pay, enough to justify a big step the following April, when I married Barbara Gay Moore.

Barbara and I had met in August, 1953, one month after I reported to Turner AFB, introduced by her mother, a cashier in the PX cafeteria.

Barbara was a very pretty, impetuous girl of eighteen. The courtship that followed was long and erratic, with one or the other of us breaking off the engagement a half-dozen times. Although I was twenty-five, presumably old enough to know better, we decided that once we were married our problems would cease. It didn't happen that way.

I had been hoping, when my enlistment expired in December, 1955, to become a pilot for one of the commercial airlines. On checking, however, I found that at twenty-six-and-one-half I was at the upper edge of the age limit, and therefore not eligible. Considering the other alternatives—there were few, if I wanted to fly—I signed an indefinite enlistment.

There was no reason to be dissatisfied, I suppose. Though our marriage was less than ideal, we had good friends, enjoyed many of the same things. Most of our vacations were spent in Florida, swimming and water-skiing. As for my job, I was doing what I most enjoyed, flying. My pay, over four hundred dollars per month take-home, was the most money I had ever earned in my life and was supplemented by what Barbara made. I was visiting parts of the world I had never seen before: I had flown an F-84G to England, and prior to my marriage, I'd spent three months on temporary duty in Japan. Periodically, as a break from routine, there was the excitement of the Air Force gunnery meets, my team taking several top command prizes. I had the satisfaction of knowing that my job was important, not only in the future, if war ever occurred, but now, as a small but necessary part of a collective defense effort in itself a deterrent to war.

There was no reason to be dissatisfied, yet I was. The vague restlessness since boyhood remained—not so much of an ache now, but a bother nonetheless. To date I hadn't really proved myself, contributed anything.

This was my frame of mind when I was approached by "the agency."

Two

Late in January, 1956, as Francis G. Palmer, a civilian employee of the Department of the Air Force, according to the official identification in my wallet, I signed the register at the Du Pont Plaza, Washington, D.C., went to my room, and waited for a telephone call, all the while feeling more than a little foolish. Such antics belonged in the realm of spy stories.

When the call came, the voice was that of Collins, informing me we were to meet in another room. Most of the other pilots were already there. Except for one man busily looking behind picture frames, back of dresser drawers, under beds, and whom I took to be an employee of the agency, everyone was familiar. A number of the men were from Turner AFB.

Collins handled the briefing, more informal and relaxed than any of those at the motel. Yet in its way, more serious.

This would not be the first attempt to photograph Russia from the air. Following World War II, modified B-36s and, later, RB-47s, had been used. These had a great advantage—the capacity to carry large quantities of sophisticated photographic and electronic equipment. But disadvantages were also great. Because the altitude at which they flew was well within the range of Russian radar, they were vulnerable to both missiles and fighters and therefore couldn't be risked on anything other than short-range penetration missions. The most important targets, however, those in which Intelligence was most interested, were deep inside Russia. And, though unarmed and carrying only cameras and electronic gear rather than bombs, they were still, to the uninformed observer, bombers. As such, they could cause an incident.

Then something different had been tried—huge camera-carrying balloons. Set adrift at various points, these were picked up by prevailing winds and carried across the Soviet Union to Japan, where U.S. planes were sent up to shoot them down. Although this had netted some valuable footage, the limitations were obvious, and the Russians, who had shot down more than a few balloons themselves, had protested.

As far as using planes was concerned, there was one big problem—altitude. There had been no solution to it until recently, when Clarence L. "Kelly" Johnson, design genius at Lockheed, had advanced plans for an entirely new aircraft capable of flying well above the range of all known rockets and interceptors.

After some delay, occasioned by the familiar "it can't possibly fly" objections of other engineers, Johnson had been authorized to build the plane. With men working hundred-hour weeks, the first model had been completed in less than eight months. In August, 1955, it had made its first flight. The plane did everything Johnson had claimed for it, and more.

While Collins talked, one could feel the excitement generating in the room.

Reaching into his briefcase, he extracted a photograph.

It was a strange-looking aircraft, unlike any other I had ever seen. Although the picture was a long shot and gave little detail, it obviously had a remarkably long wingspan. A jet, but with the body of a glider. Though a hybrid, it was nevertheless very individual, with a beautiful symmetry all its own.

It was also a single-seater. I liked that. Whenever possible, I preferred flying alone.

We had a thousand technical questions. Collins told us to save them for our training.

"What do you call it?" someone asked.

"No one calls it anything publicly yet," he replied. "This project is so secret that, other than those involved in the operation, only top-level government people know about it. But for your information, it's been dubbed the Utility-2, or U-2."

The radio was on; I was having trouble hearing Collins. Reaching over, I snapped it off.

Not only did the music stop. But as if he were plugged into the set also, Collins' voice stopped too. Silently he glared at me.

Red-faced, I turned the radio on again. The moment the music resumed, Collins resumed speaking.

Slowly, bit by bit, I was losing my naïveté. You learn as you grow up, I suppose. And I was growing up.

The other agency man called one of the pilots into the bedroom, closing the door behind him. When he returned, with an odd look, another pilot was summoned. Later he too returned, looking strange.

"Palmer," he said. "Your turn."

Entering the room, I saw, on top of the bureau, what looked like an elaborate tape recorder. Only I knew, suddenly, it wasn't.

"Ever see one of these before?" he asked.

"No," I answered, "but I think I can make a pretty good guess as to what it is."

"Any objection to taking a lie-detector test?"

Though I had a great many, I didn't voice them, shaking my head. If this was a condition of the job, I'd do it. But I didn't like it.

"Sit down. While I'm strapping you in, you can look over this list of questions."

Knowing what he's going to ask in advance should make it easier, I thought. Except that the opposite psychology was used. Awareness that a disturbing question was upcoming served only to increase the tension.

I had never felt so completely exposed, as if there was no privacy whatsoever. If at that moment someone had handed me a petition banning polygraphs forever from the face of the earth, I would gladly have signed it. When I was asked the last question and the straps were taken off, I vowed that never again, no matter what the circumstances, would I undergo such an insult to my integrity.

Apparently we all passed the test, for the same men attended the rest of the meetings. These took place in various Washington hotels—the Mayfair, Roger Smith, etc.—at irregular intervals over the next three months. At no time did we meet in a government building. "Covert," as opposed to "overt," employees, we never saw inside headquarters of the Central Intelligence Agency.

Turning up the radio and careful inspection of the room were only two of the precautions against "bugging," I soon learned. By changing hotels and randomly selecting different pilots' rooms, we avoided establishing a pattern.

Our travel arrangements were also carefully planned so that no routine could be detected. Sometimes we traveled singly, sometimes in groups of two, three, or four, sometimes with an agency representative along, sometimes not. Usually, when accompanied, it was by Collins, who was becoming as omnipresent as the radio in each of our hotel rooms.

When I got to know him better, he confirmed what I had long suspected, that "Collins" was just as native to him as "Palmer" to me. I learned his real name, but, the pseudonym having become habit, never used it.

With one exception, aliases presented no problem, since, being a generally friendly lot, pilots aren't given to much use of last names. The exception was a pilot whose surname began with Mac, which, of course, was also his nickname. The agency, however, had given him the cover name of Murphy. Fortunately no one ever asked Murphy why he was called Mac.

More troublesome were the phony addresses we had been instructed to use on hotel registers. I suspect more than a few men have encountered the same dilemma, although under different circumstances. Trying to make up an address on the spot, the mind suddenly blanks. We learned, after a few curious looks from desk clerks, to manufacture our cover addresses in advance.

As covert agents, we probably left a great deal to be desired. Although we all had Top Secret clearances, and our time in the Air Force had made us security-conscious, we considered ourselves pilots, not spies, and at times the cloak-and-dagger precautions tickled our funny bones.

Orders directed us to report to Omaha, Nebraska. Inasmuch as this was the headquarters of the Strategic Air Command, to which we were all assigned, it was nothing out of the ordinary. Arriving in Omaha, however, we were given a number to call. To no one's surprise, Collins answered. Greeting us at the airport, he asked us to resume our covers, whereupon he gave us tickets for the next flight to St. Louis.

We managed, though with some effort, to suppress our laughter. St. Louis had been one of the stops en route to Omaha.

From St. Louis we caught a flight to Albuquerque, which we now learned was our actual destination, checking into the Lovelace Clinic for a week-long physical examination.

It was incredibly thorough. I had been unaware that many of the tests given us even existed, and commented on this to one of the doctors. They hadn't existed before, he laughed; many had been especially designed just for us. Many of the tests which we pioneered were later made a part of the astronauts' physicals. All of the Mercury personnel went through Lovelace Clinic.

Occasionally, if we asked, we were told the purpose of a set of tests. For example, a number were designed to determine any tendency toward claustrophobia. I couldn't understand, at the time, why these were so important.

Other tests defied guessing, until we discovered that they had nothing to do with our physical. For some time doctors had been aware that pilots as a group apparently age more slowly than other people. Lovelace was working on a government grant to determine why. We just happened to be handy guinea pigs.

At Lovelace we had our first washout. One pilot, though perfectly capable of flying for the Air Force, did not meet the rigid specifications required for this particular project.

He was the only washout in our group. As far as we knew, no one was eliminated because of a security check. To be more accurate, we were not even sure such an investigation had been made.

When a serviceman or potential government employee is given a background check for security clearance, the FBI usually questions former employers, neighbors, associates. Often some word of the investigation gets back to the individual. If the agency conducted a separate security check on us, we were unaware of it; this meant either that we were accepted on the basis of our Air Force clearances or that the investigation was more discreet than usual. Considering the extreme sensitivity of the project, I strongly suspect the latter to be the case. It is also possible the investigation occurred before we were ever approached.

As we later learned, our initial selection was less random than it first appeared.

Only reserve officers had been interviewed, no regular officers. This was because there were apt to be fewer questions asked when a reserve officer resigned.

Also, the choice of a number of pilots from the same unit was not accidental. Our wing was being dissolved, its personnel assigned elsewhere. In such a transition, with everyone moving, there was less chance the disappearance of a few pilots would evoke comment.

In April, on instruction from Collins, I submitted my letter of resignation to the Secretary of the Air Force.

Under ordinary circumstances several months would have been required for the request to be approved. It was back in less than one. On the thirteenth of May, 1956, I became a civilian again.

Within a few days I signed my contract with the Central Intelligence Agency. The document was brief and covered my terms of employment—eighteen months from the date of signing, fifteen hundred dollars per month while in the United States, twenty-five hundred per month overseas, with five hundred taken out each month and held in escrow, to be paid upon satisfactory completion of contract. This last provision, it was explained to us, had been added to make the tax bite easier.

There was also a security clause, containing the regular national security agreement that everyone in the service and most government employees must sign, prohibiting the revelation of any information adversely affecting national security, the penalty for so doing being a ten-thousand-dollar fine and/or ten years in jail.

There was only one copy of the contract, which the agency kept. Nor was I given a copy of any of the several other documents I signed. One, already cosigned by the Secretary of the Air Force, Donald A. Quarles, promised that upon completion of my contract I would be permitted to return to the Air Force at a rank corresponding to that of my contemporaries and with no time lost toward retirement. This was especially important to me, because already I had nearly six years in, and, on finishing the assignment, planned to return to the Air Force.

Following the signing of the contracts, we flew to a secret base on the West Coast to begin training.

Three

Watertown Strip was one of those "you can't get there from here" places. Located in a desolate portion of southern Nevada desert, it was almost completely isolated: there were no towns in the vicinity, not even a ghost town, only miles of flat, uninhabited land. The only convenient way to reach it was by air, as we had, flying in from Lockheed's Burbank, California, terminal.

As a place to live, it left much to be desired. As a secret training base for a revolutionary new plane, it was an excellent site, its remoteness effectively masking its activity, such as the U-2 crash the week before we arrived, the first fatality on that aircraft.

Pilots are always quick to deny they are a superstitious lot. Be that as it may, I'm certain each of us was hoping and praying the same thing—that this was in no way a portent of things to come.

It was silver. But the altitude at which it would fly was so high as to render it invisible from the air and ground below.

Its wings, as the photographs had indicated, were its most startling feature. Except that the photograph hadn't prepared us for the actuality. In proportion to the length of the fuselage, which was some forty feet, they stretched out to more than eighty. Like the wings of a giant bird, they drooped slightly when on the ground; in turbulent air they flapped noticeably.

This was the U-2, basically a powered glider, jet engine inside a glider frame, only it was capable of things no glider or jet had ever accomplished before: it could reach, and maintain for hours at a time, altitudes never before touched.

But at a cost.

To achieve this height, carry a pilot, as well as a variety of electronic and photographic gear, plus enough fuel to keep it aloft for periods in excess of nine hours, it had to be extremely light. In aerodynamics there are certain balances. To achieve lightness, something else must be sacrificed. With the U-2 it was strength.

Each piece of structure was a little thinner than a pilot would have liked. Where there was usually extra support, such as joints and junctures, in the U-2 there was none. It was not a plane for heavy or drastic maneuvers.

In short, it had not been built to last. The intention was to go in, get the job done, get out. Even the eighteen months called for in our contracts seemed a highly optimistic measure of the plane's probable life span. It was even rumored that the original concept of Operation Overflight had been a one-shot, single flight over the Soviet Union for each plane: the plane to take off without wheels, make the flight, return to its base, and belly-land.

Since both Lockheed and agency personnel were extremely tight-lipped when it came to matters of planning, this remained an unconfirmed rumor among the pilots.

We badly underrated the U-2 and its maker, "Kelly" Johnson.

One place where Johnson had eliminated weight was the ejection seat. There was none. To bail out, a pilot had to climb out.

Another economy was the landing gear. Rather than the tricycle type, with a gear under the nose and another under each wing, the U-2 had one under the nose and one under the tail, a bicycle arrangement. To support the wings while on the ground, a "pogo," or extension with a small wheel on the end, was set in a socket underneath each wing. These kept the wings level while taxiing, but dropped off on takeoff.

Or were supposed to. On the fatal flight the week before our arrival, one of the pogos had failed to release. Coming back over the field, the pilot had flown in low, attempting to shake it off. Heavy with fuel, he had miscalculated, stalled, and crashed at the end of the runway.

Except for a rare accident of this sort, it was obvious just from looking at the arrangement that takeoff should present no special problems, but landing—without the pogos—would be tricky. Like riding a bicycle; only, with the ground roll finished, the plane would tilt over onto the heavy wing, the wing tip acting as part of the landing gear.

As for what it would be like in the air, it was a safe guess it would be extremely difficult to handle.

My hands itched to get onto the controls.

But that had to wait until we learned something very basic. How to breathe.

It now became apparent why we had been given some of the tests at Lovelace Clinic.

One of the risks of high-altitude flight is danger of sudden loss of pressurization in the cockpit. For safeguard, a special partial-pressure suit had been designed. Airtight, of rubberized fabric with almost no give or elasticity, it fit snugly around the body, so snugly that the slightest movement—bending a knee or arm, turning the head—would rub the skin, leaving bruises. Wearing long johns helped, but not much; even when worn inside out, the seams pressed into the skin.

A hermetic seal at the neck fastened the helmet into place. Once on, it felt exactly like a too-tight tie over a badly shrunk collar. On long flights, counting preparatory time, we would have to remain in the suit for up to twelve hours. Anyone with the slightest touch of claustrophia would have gone mad.

Nor were these the only discomforts.

Since there was no way to unfasten the suit without losing oxygen, we had to learn to curb our appetite.

Early in the program some of the pilots would occasionally loosen the face plate to take liquids. In April, 1957, Lockheed test pilot Robert L. Sieker was killed in a U-2 crash near Edwards AFB, California. It was later determined that Sieker had done this, lost pressurization, and was unable to resecure the face plate. After this the pilots kept their face plates fastened when flying.

We also, rather late in life, had to learn new bathroom habits. This wasn't quite as bad as might be imagined. Not drinking coffee or other fluids prior to a flight lessened the need. Too, because there was no ventilation in the suit, no way for the skin to breathe, perspiration was constant, with much moisture eliminated this way, rather than through the kidneys. But this also meant there was no way for perspiration to evaporate. Following a flight, you wrung the water out of the long johns; during the flight, you had to live with it.

Before each flight we put on the suit and helmet and began what was called prebreathing. This was a denitrogenization process during which we were given pure oxygen, under slight pressure, to avoid getting the bends.

In normal breathing it takes a little effort to inhale, while exhaling is automatic. Under pressurization this is reversed. Inhaling is automatic, while exhaling is an effort. It was literally necessary to learn to breathe all over again.

As if the process weren't tiring enough, the long use of pure oxygen often had as side effects painful head and ear aches. After two hours of prebreathing before each flight, plus actual flight time, a pilot was so exhausted that he wasn't allowed to fly again for two days.

Each aircraft has its pecularities, most of which can be simulated in a trainer. Because the U-2 was so new, however, some phases of the testing still in progress, many of these had to be first experienced in actual flight. And, as a unique aircraft, designed for the specific purpose of high-altitude flights, the U-2 had some decidedly unusual characteristics.

Ascent was rapid and spectacular. The U-2 required very little runway for takeoff; a thousand feet would suffice. Within moments after the pogos dropped, you could begin climbing—at better than a forty-five-degree angle. (On the first couple of flights, you were sure you were going to continue right over on your back.) Within minutes, in the time most planes took to reach a few thousand feet, the U-2 had disappeared from sight.

Once in flight, other peculiarities manifested themselves. One was that at maximum altitude the fastest the plane could go was very close to the slowest it could go. This narrow range was known as the "coffin corner"; a slight miscalculation either way, and you were in trouble. If you went too slow, the plane would stall; if you went too fast, it would go into "Mach buffet" and could become unmanageable. To keep the plane at the exact speed required a great deal of attention and personal control. Although it was equipped with an autopilot, you couldn't place too much reliance on it because of what could happen if it malfunctioned.

There was also—especially before the technical bugs were worked out—the problem of flameouts, which occurred with some regularity. During a flameout the jet engine loses its fire, and the pilot must bring the plane down to a lower altitude to restart it.

Navigation was also a challenge. Since we couldn't depend on the Russians to provide radio fixes, we had to learn to navigate completely on our own, without radio aids of any kind.

Landing the U-2 was even more difficult than we had guessed. There was an either/or situation. A regular airplane can land while still flying. The U-2 had to be through flying to stay on the ground, as a result of which it was necessary to stall it before touching down. If you stalled it a little high, it would drop down. If you hit the ground before it stalled, it would bounce back up in the air. You had to gauge it exactly.

Once touched down, however, one problem remained. Because of the bicycle landing gear and the long wings, the plane had a strong tendency to ground-loop. Should you start turning, however slightly, the plane would try to keep turning.

These were only a few of the special problems of flying the U-2.

The pleasures were far greater.

Whatever initial worries we had about the plane soon vanished. It was not an easy plane to fly, but it was not dangerous. Once its idiosyncrasies were mastered, so long as you stayed alert, the plane behaved beautifully, so much so that you looked forward to each new flight.

And there was the excitement of pioneering a new frontier, something I had wanted to do all my life.

On August 29, 1955, British Wing Commander Walter F. Gibb, piloting a Canberra B. Mark II, had set an international record for altitude, reaching 65,889 feet.

We broke that record every day. And could stay higher for hours at a time.

If the weather below was good, the view from this altitude was unsurpassed, the country a huge map come to life. On one flight, while crossing the Colorado River in Arizona, approaching California, I could see clearly from Monterey Peninsula on the north, halfway down Baja California on the south.

Being so high gave you a unique satisfaction. Not a feeling of superiority or omnipotence, but a special aloneness.

There was only one thing wrong with flying higher than any other man had ever flown.

You couldn't brag about it.

Like the U-2, Watertown hadn't been built to last. Everything about it was temporary. The pilots lived in house trailers, four to a trailer. There was no PX, no club. As if to compensate for the lack of other creature comforts, there was an excellent mess, the food exceptional by any standard. But recreation consisted of a couple of pool tables and a 16-mm nightly movie. It is probably unnecessary to add that we played a lot of poker.

Weekends we deserted the base en masse, via shuttle flight to Burbank on Friday afternoon, returning on Monday morning.

Off base we used our real names and carried our own identification, plus a card identifying us as employees of Lockheed on loan to the National Advisory Committee for Aeronautics (NACA). This enabled us to cash checks or establish credit. Arrangements had been made to verify our employment.

On returning to the base, we turned in our identification and resumed our cover names. Since we would revert to our own names once training was finished, it was a further security measure, since many of the personnel at Watertown wouldn't be going overseas with us.

On flights we carried no identification, this being unnecessary inasmuch as we took off and landed at the same base.

Just as we had learned never to call the Central Intelligence Agency the CIA, but "the agency," Watertown Strip became "the ranch."

We were an unlikely-looking bunch of cowboys.

Much later, for reasons which will become obvious, it would be widely reported that the U-2 pilots were largely uninformed about the specialized equipment they carried, that they were merely "airplane jockeys" who, at points designated on the map, snapped on and off switches with no real knowledge of what they were doing.

Our job would have been simpler, had this been true, but it wasn't. We were thoroughly checked out on all the equipment. It was essential, since if a piece of equipment broke down in flight we had to do what we could to get it working again. With a radar signal recorder, for example, we might shut it off and recycle it, this sometimes correcting the condition. Having attended photo school and worked as a photo lab technician in the Air Force, I was especially interested in the cameras and other photographic apparatus, and studied them whenever I got the chance.

Throughout our training, equipment tests continued. One piece was especially exotic. This was the destruct unit.

If it became necessary to abandon the aircraft over a Communist country, the plane carried a two-and-a-half-pound explosive charge. This would not have totally obliterated the aircraft, only the portion of it containing the cameras and electronic equipment. There was some doubt as to whether it would have even completely succeeded in this, since it is almost impossible to destroy a tightly wound reel of film or recording tape. Nor was there a worry that if the Russians captured the plane they would copy it or steal valuable technical secrets. It was common knowledge that Russian aviation was quite far advanced, equal to, in the opinion of some, if not better than our own. The only danger of having the U-2 captured intact was that it would constitute physical proof of our spying.

The destruct mechanism was arranged so that once activated by the pilot it would allow him a small but supposedly sufficient margin of time to bail out before the explosion occurred.

Testing to see how long it would take us to get out of the aircraft, we decided to try seventy seconds on the timer. We could have given ourselves longer, up to one and one-half minutes, but we wanted to make absolutely sure the plane exploded in the air. Should it crash, there was always the possibility that the charge would not go off, or if it did, that the earth would cushion some of the blast.

The destruct unit was operated by two switches. One, marked ARM, activated the circuits. To trigger the unit, however, a second switch had to be flipped. Marked DESTRUCT, this started the timer. At any time during the seventy seconds the switch could be flipped back and the whole process halted. Once done, however, the timer couldn't be reset to compensate for the lost time. So we were instructed not to flip either switch until the last possible moment.

There was one more complication. Testing the timers on the different units by stopwatch, we discovered they did not work uniformly. On some there was a variance of as much as five seconds. This made testing the timer prior to each flight a must.

While we were at Watertown, the destruct unit was of minor interest, since the charge itself would be placed in the plane only when we arrived overseas, and then only on the actual overflights.

There was, however, during our training, some discussion as to switching from the pilot-actuated-type mechanism we were using to an impact device, to explode automatically when the plane hit the ground.

It was a short discussion. Pilots are leery of impact devices, for good reason. On returning to base, if there were some problem with the landing gear and it was necessary to belly-land, the result could be disastrous.

We quickly ruled out the proposed switch, preferring to stay with the pilot-actuated type.

One question was never asked, one subject never discussed.

It was approached only two times, and then obliquely, never directly.

The first time was when we were briefed on the destruct device. The second occurred toward the end of our training, when a group of us were flown to the East Coast and put up in one of the agency's special facilities.

This was my first introduction to a "safe house," a carefully guarded, maximum-security residence, from the outside resembling an ordinary home or estate, but inside manned entirely by agency personnel. In this instance, the cover was a farm, though unlike any farm I had ever seen. Its fences, some fourteen feet high, and some electrified, were identical to those found along the borders of all Communist countries. We were taught how to get through or over or under the fences. Some of its fields were mined, some weren't. We were taught how to spot the ones that were and circumvent them. Even its ordinary plowed fields were special, similar to the plowed strips along the borders; we were taught how to walk through them without leaving telltale footprints.

It was strictly evasion training, no survival training being given, the presumption apparently being that our Air Force training was sufficient.

It was also a quickie course, lasting less than a week, and was, I suspect, intended more than anything else to build up our self-confidence.

And it was also the closest anyone actually came to mentioning the unmentionable: What were we to do if for some reason we did come down in Russia?

There was, at this time, little concern about being shot down. We knew the altitude at which the U-2 flew. Agency Intelligence sources were firm in their assurances that the Russians possessed neither aircraft nor rocketry capable of reaching us. But an airplane is a complicated piece of equipment. One loose electrical connection, one stalled engine, one unforeseen malfunction . . .

No one from the agency briefed us on what procedure to follow if we were forced to come down in Russia.

None of the pilots, to my knowledge, asked for such a briefing, nor, as if to do so would be to tempt fate, did we discuss it among ourselves.

It was a bad mistake.

One thing not ignored was actual flying. While at Watertown we flew the U-2 far more than we would have if we'd been in the Air Force and checking out in a new aircraft. As a result, on completing our training we had the utmost confidence in its reliability. It was a remarkable piece of equipment; perhaps it was this, more than anything else, that rendered less immediate whatever doubts we had.

Our group, the second to go through Watertown, was fortunate. We came through "clean." No washouts, all pilots qualifying on the aircraft. No accidents, no crashes.

Three U-2 groups went through Watertown. The last class, which followed us by some months, had a fatality. A pilot, taking off on a night mission, apparently was confused by the bright lights at the end of the runway and flew directly into a telephone pole.

Another class there at the same time as we were fared less well. Shortly after our arrival at Watertown the agency brought in four Greek pilots to be checked out on the U-2.

Presumably they were mercenaries, in the program on their own and without the knowledge of their government. At least this was what it seemed to be. We were never told otherwise. There was some speculation that, being Mediterraneans, they could pass more easily and attract less attention than Americans in some of the countries from which we would be flying. And there were other theories. But all were merely speculation; we were never informed as to why they had been included.

Whatever the reason, it didn't work out. Inconspicuous they were not, at least not in Hollywood, where they spent most of their weekends, always with an agency escort. It was no secret that none of the CIA men relished the escort job. Like playing nursemaid to four Zorbas, each intent on his own devilment. Their zest for enjoying themselves was epic.

At flying they did less well. Without exception, they failed to qualify on the aircraft. Not wanting them to return to Greece with their knowledge of the U-2 project, the agency was forced to keep them in the United States. Two, we heard later, were sent to college, at government expense, while one, it was rumored, had attempted to blackmail the agency. Unsuccessfully.

The U-2 was much too distinctive an aircraft, either on ground or in flight, to be kept completely secret. Too, with the movement of the various groups overseas, some leak was inevitable. To forestall comment and speculation, a series of cover stories was released.

The first appeared late in April, 1956, in the form of a NACA press release announcing that "a new type of airplane, the Lockheed U-2," had been developed, which, with the logistical and technical assistance of the Air Weather Service of the USAF, would be used to study turbulence and meteorological conditions. Although indicating the U-2 was capable of high-altitude flight, the release gave no particulars. It did state, however, that initial flights were made from "Watertown Strip, Nevada."

The first U-2 group, which had completed its training early in April, a month before our arrival at Watertown, and which had been officially designated the Weather Reconnaissance Squadron, (Provisional), had been sent to Lakenheath, England.

The second release, covering this, announced that NACA was extending its weather program to Europe. Again the release was long on rhetoric, short on details. There was no mention of the U-2's altitude, its range, its duration of flight. Nor were photographs of the plane released.

The cover story was not entirely fictitious. Some of the U-2s were being used for weather research, and doing a superb job of it.

They were also, at this time or very shortly after, being used for purposes the news releases didn't mention.

Our unit, which was officially designated the Second Weather Observational Squadron (Provisional), and, more informally, Detachment 10-10, completed its training early in August, 1956. Our destination, Incirlik AFB, Adana, Turkey, was mentioned in no press releases, however.

While the U-2s we would be using were disassembled and flown to Incirlik, we were given two weeks' leave.

Before it began we were provided with new identification, in our real names, as civilian employees of the Department of the Air Force, GS-12. We were also given a card which stated that we worked for NACA, that we were authorized to fly Air Force aircraft, but that we were not subject to Air Force flying regulations. The latter stipulation was important, because it would permit us to take off from Air Force bases when regular Air Force pilots would be grounded by weather minimums.

As cover story for parents and friends, we could say that we would be going overseas as a part of NACA's program for studying weather phenomena in various parts of the world. If we felt it necessary, we could also drop some comment that this was tied in with the forthcoming scientific International Geophysical Year.

Two weeks was barely enough time to care for the minor business matters I couldn't handle once overseas; however, the agency had taken care of many details, including supplying a mailing address and a twenty-four-hour agency number in Washington, D.C., which Barbara could use for emergencies.

We did manage to work in a brief visit to The Pound. My father asked quite a few questions, more, in fact, than I had anticipated. But I got around them fairly well, or so I thought.

At the airport, before taking off for overseas, I called home to say good-bye.

When my father came on the line he said, "I've figured out what you're doing."

"What do you mean? I told you what I'm doing."

"No, I've figured it out," he stated emphatically. "You're working for the FBI."

Hanging up, I had to laugh. He was far more perceptive than I'd realized. But I suspect parents usually are. His guess was close. At this time few people had heard of the CIA.

May 1, 1960, I regret to say, would change that.

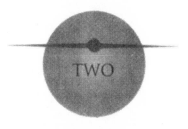

TWO

OPERATION OVERFLIGHT

One

Geographically, Adana was an excellent choice as takeoff point for the overflights. Situated in the southern portion of Turkey, near the Mediterranean, it was sufficiently distant from the USSR for the Russians to have no radar coverage of the site, yet close enough for a plane to make the flight without too great an expenditure of fuel.

There were other advantages. Though a Turkish base, Incirlik already housed a small USAF detachment and was functioning primarily as a refueling stop for American planes on trips across the Middle East. From the point of cover and logistics, this was ideal, since it meant the fuel and equipment required for the U-2 flights could be brought in without attracting undue attention.

Presumably there was still another reason for the choice. Since little of what occurred at diplomatic levels made its way down to the pilots, we could only guess whether the government of Turkey knew our real mission and had granted approval for such use of the base. It was our presumption—perhaps erroneous—that they were at least aware of the border-surveillance flights, though possibly not of the overflights. For a weather unit, Detachment 10-10 had suspiciously tight security, something obvious to any Turk who worked on other portions of the base.

If we did have approval, tacit or otherwise, we were one up on the first U-2 group. Shortly after arrival at Lakenheath, the British government, learning their mission was something more than the collection of weather data, requested them to leave, in the interim restricting them to training flights. Kicked out of England, the unit had been transferred to Wiesbaden, Germany, from which the first U-2 overflight took place.

Although a combined military-agency operation (USAF providing logistics, the agency planning and operations), Detachment 10-10 was patterned after a regular squadron. There was a commanding officer (USAF) and an executive officer (agency), who together ran the outfit. In addition to the operations officer, who had under him the flight planners, navigators, and weather personnel, there was an administrative officer, intelligence officer, security men, flying-safety officer (one of my extra duties), pilots (seven of us at this time), ground crews, medics, and radio, radar, and photographic personnel. About all that was missing was an actual, legitimate representative of NACA. Briefings and debriefings were conducted similarly to those in the Air Force. Even the size of the unit, close to one hundred members, was of squadron strength.

But there was one great difference. Each person, from crew chief to pilot, had been especially picked for the operation. Too, since most of us had been together at Watertown, we were already functioning as a well coordinated team before arriving overseas. As a result, 10-10 was run with an efficiency rarely if ever, encountered in service.

Each man was a specialist in his field. As pilots, the seven of us had been assigned a specific job. We were aware of its importance. And were anxious to get on with it.

This had to wait, however, for additional training.

Although we had flown some of the same U-2s at Watertown, each had to be checked out again after they were reassembled. The U-2 was not a mass-produced, stamped-out-of-sheet-metal aircraft. Each was custom-made, with its own peculiarities. One might fly heavy on one wing, another might consume an inordinate amount of fuel, while still another might be a bastard to land. Since there was no assurance that a specific plane might be available for a particular flight, the pilots had to know the characteristics of each.

Much time was spent studying maps of Russia. These were, for the most part, badly outdated. Part of our assignment would be to act as cartographers—in seeing a new city, a new military or industrial complex, an unmarked airdrome, to jot it down. We would be making our own maps as we went along.

Because we could depend neither on available maps nor on radio contact with our unit, we also spent considerable time listening to Russian civil broadcast stations. Intelligence provided lists of stations, showing their locations and ranges. These were annotated on the maps. With the use of a radio compass, we could home in on them while in flight, establishing navigational fixes.

As new equipment was developed and shipped over—and it was a continuous process—we would have to be thoroughly checked out. It was also necessary to check out personal equipment we would be carrying, such as survival gear.

Most of this was contained in the seat pack. Its contents included a collapsible life raft, clothing, enough water and food to sustain life for a limited time, a compass, signal flares, matches, chemicals for starting fires with damp wood, plus a first-aid kit, with such standard items as morphine, bandages, dressings, APCs, water-purification tablets.

The clothing was heavy-duty winter hunting gear. It occurred to me on first sight that it not only didn't look Russian but was probably of better quality than even the best-dressed Russian hunter would wear. And it was definitely not the type of clothing you would put on if you wanted to blend inconspicuously into a crowd.

Also included was a large silk American-flag poster, bearing the following message: "I am an American and do not speak your language. I need food, shelter, assistance. I will not harm you. I bear no malice toward your people. If you will help me, you will be rewarded." This message appeared in fourteen languages.

In addition, the pack contained 7,500 Soviet rubles; two dozen gold Napoleon francs (it being presumed that even though we couldn't speak Russian, gold was a universal language); and, for barter, an assortment of wristwatches and gold rings.

Like the seat pack which was strapped onto the pilot and carried on all flights, no matter what their objective, two other items were also standard—hunting knife and pistol.

The hunting knife was usual survival gear, for use, for example, in severing parachute lines if caught in a tree, ripping up the chute to make a sleeping bag, shaving wood for a fire.

The pistol was especially made by High Standard. It was .22 caliber and had an extra long barrel with a silencer on the end. Although rated Expert in the service, I was out of practice and tested it periodically on the range. While the silencer obviously decreased the velocity, it was far more accurate than I had expected. Not completely silent, it was quiet enough that if you were to shoot a rabbit you could do so without alerting the whole neighborhood. Only .22 caliber, however, it wouldn't be a very effective weapon of defense.

In addition to what was in the clip, there were about two hundred rounds of extra ammunition in the seat pack.

It was September before I flew my first electronic surveillance mission along the borders outside Russia, the specialized equipment monitoring and recording Soviet radar and radio frequencies. Routes on such flights varied. We usually flew from Turkey eastward along the southern border of the Soviet Union over Iran and Afghanistan as far as Pakistan, and back. We also flew along the Black Sea, and, on occasion, as far west as Albania, but never penetrating, staying off the coast, over international waters. While our territory was the southern portion of Russia's perimeter, the U-2 group in Germany presumably covered the northern and western portions.

Since these "eavesdropping" missions were eventually to become fairly frequent, there was a tendency to minimize their importance, but in many ways they were as valuable as the overflights, the data obtained enabling the United States to pinpoint such things as Russian antiaircraft defenses and gauge their effectiveness.

Of special interest were Soviet rocket launches. For some reason, many of these occurred at night, and, from the altitude at which we flew, they were often spectacular, lighting up the sky for hundreds of miles. When they were successful.

Many never made it off the pad, and some exploded immediately after doing so.

But there were no "failures."

When the United States planned a major launching, they ballyhooed it in advance, even permitting television coverage. When it failed, the whole world knew it. But the Russians never publicized their launches until after they had occurred, and then only if they were successful and if it served their purposes to do so. As a result, it appeared that the United States had a lot of failures, Russia none.

Because of our flights, we knew better.

At this time our intelligence on the rocket launchings was exceptional. We knew several days in advance when one was scheduled to occur. Although intelligence did not discuss its sources with us, it was our guess that in the monitoring—both by the U-2s and ground-based units—we were picking up the actual countdowns, which at this time took several days.

The equipment we carried on such occasions was highly sophisticated. One unit came on automatically the moment the launch frequency was used and collected all the data sent out to control the rocket. The value of such information to our own scientists was obvious.

There was a cardinal rule on all such flights—don't penetrate, even accidentally. When the time came to cross the border and violate Russian air space, it was for a purpose.

There were numerous other flights, including weather research. Far more than just cover, these provided much heretofore unavailable information on atmospheric conditions. Also, on occasion, such as after a Russian nuclear test, we did atomic sampling. The information gathered from this, together with other intelligence, made it possible to determine the type of detonation, where it occurred, its force, fallout, and so forth.

Because of our location in relation to wind patterns, however, we did less of this than the U-2s flying above Alaska and, later, Japan and Australia.

And there were other "special" missions.

It was important work; we knew it. But it was not the work we had come over to do.

Living arrangements at Incirlik were similar to those at Watertown, with one important exception: the food was much worse.

Again trailers provided housing, two pilots to a unit. Each had a tiny living room, kitchen, bathroom, and one small and one medium-size bed (I won the toss). There was a small PX on the base, but it stocked few items. As a change of pace, occasionally we would go into Adana at night for drinks and dinner. There was only one place you could eat safely, a restaurant located above a hotel. Tales of throat cutting and robbery being common, we did little wandering around the streets at night, and then only in groups.

Even so, there were a few close calls. About one hundred miles from Adana was what must be one of the greatest trout streams in the world. On one trip—which I'm happy to say I missed—the men awoke to find that during the night they had been visited by Kurds, the nomadic tribesmen who wander the crescent from the Persian Gulf up into Turkey. Great thieves, they had taken not only fishing gear, cameras, food, and clothing, but also the blankets off my friends' backs. Fortunately no one woke during the raid, the Kurds having a rather cavalier attitude toward human life.

Late one afternoon I saw, not more than a mile or two away from the base, one of their caravans, a string of some hundred camels traveling along a ridge silhouetted against the sunset. Ancient Persia come to life, it provided a vivid contrast to our twentieth-century electronic gadgetry.

As transportation, most of us bought small motorcycles, which we used for excursions through the countryside. Not far from Adana, there were crusader castles, mostly in ruins—shepherds used them as pens; Roman aqueducts; the remains of a sunken Roman bath; and a huge area of old tombs, which we spent much time exploring. The beaches along the Mediterranean were beautifully virgin, much like those in Southern California once were, before the days of population explosion and oil slicks. During the long warm season, which stretched from spring well into fall, we swam, skin-dived, snorkled. As for hunting, there were ducks on the lakes and on occasion an expedition in search of wild boar, the latter less than successful, at least from our point of view. The Turks, who acted as guides, were highly excitable; as soon as they saw a boar they began firing. Most of us never got a shot.

But, except for these occasional activities, the social life was decidedly limited. The poker games frequently lasted three days. Leave was set up on a military basis, thirty days per year. With little to do in Turkey itself, R&R (rest-and-recuperation leave) was established. For each weekend spent in Turkey, compensatory time was accrued that could be spent in Greece or Germany. Since planes frequently landed at Incirlik for refueling, there was little trouble catching a hop. We saved up the time, to make the trips worthwhile.

In the interim, we had to create our own diversions.

In an attempt to provide a touch of much needed domesticity, one of the pilots bought a box of cake mix at the PX and invited us all over for coffee and cake.

Not wanting to be remiss socially, I decided to bake some cakes too.

I baked one, but extended no invitations. As a cook, I decided, I made an excellent pilot.

We were restless, for several reasons. One was that none of us was flying as much as he wanted to.

Among pilots it is proverbial that the more you fly, the more you enjoy it. But when you lay off awhile and then go up again, you approach it with hesitation; everything a little strange, you're not as sure of yourself as you should be.

We were flying the bare minimum to preserve the plane. The U-2 was too fragile to last, the engineering experts reiterated; its life span was limited; it wouldn't stand up under prolonged stress and strain.

Although we saw little evidence of this ourselves, a tragedy occurred not long after our arrival overseas which seemed to bear this out most graphically.

In September, 1956, Howard Carey, a contract pilot I had known at Watertown, was killed in a U-2 crash in Germany. There was some confusion as to what actually happened, initial speculation ranging all the way to sabotage. It was later determined, however, that while in flight Carey had been buzzed by two curious Canadian

Air Force interceptors. Caught in their wake turbulence as they passed him, his U-2 had apparently simply disintegrated.

With sad irony, Carey had not started with the first class at Watertown but had come in late, to replace the pilot killed in the first crash.

Not considering that this might be a freak accident, the experts cited it as further proof of the U-2's fragility. As a result, we were flying the bare minimum; so far as most of us were concerned, it wasn't nearly enough.

Nor was it the flying we had been told we would do.

By November we still hadn't made our first overflight.

Although the 10-10 detachment had its own section of the base, closed to all except authorized personnel, within those boundaries some sections were even more tightly restricted. The photo lab was one. By far the most secret, however, was the communication section, which housed not only the radio apparatus but also the cryptographic unit. It was through here that the orders would come, when they came. After a while we began, almost unconsciously, to study the faces of the personnel who worked there, as if expecting clues.

When the order came, it was a surprise. Stopping me as I was walking through the area one day, the detachment commander, Colonel Ed Perry, said simply, "You're it, Powers."

"When?"

"If the weather holds, a couple of days."

I'd been picked for the first overflight out of Turkey.

This was to be the pattern.

Target priorities were established in Washington. It was our understanding that the White House then approved "packages," or series, of flights. Once approval was given, the orders were relayed to Incirlik in code via radio. With one later, and quite important, exception, which will be mentioned.

Weather usually determined when the flight occurred. Almost always we would be briefed several days in advance of the actual flight in order to have time to study maps of the various routes and work out the navigation. Alternate targets were provided on each flight so that if we went up and found clouds covering one area, we could switch to another without sacrificing the mission. Approval, it was reiterated over and over, was difficult to obtain. When it came, we were to make the best of it.

At times intelligence would tell us what they were looking for: an airfield here that isn't on the map; a complex of new buildings there to watch out for. Usually, however, we weren't told anything, our only instructions being when and where to switch on what equipment. The equipment itself, however, was sometimes a clue. A camera with a telescopic lens pinpointing a tiny area, for example, meant an entirely different type objective than one which photographed a strip 100 to 150 miles wide.

We were aware that when we returned, the photographs would undergo intensive scrutiny by experts, the pictures providing information on things we knew nothing about. While we might be instructed to photograph a missile-launching site and the area around it, thinking intelligence was most interested in the missile on the pad, their real interest might lie in the railroad tracks leading away from the site, which, if followed, might lead to factories where the missiles were assembled.

We didn't try to second-guess. We followed instructions.

Briefings were concerned primarily with navigation, and little else. I had anticipated that once overseas the question we had been avoiding would be asked and answered. It wasn't. Nor did the pilots discuss it among themselves. Perhaps, almost unconsciously, we thought that to do so would bring bad luck.

The intelligence officer did mention in one briefing session that cyanide capsules would be available if we wanted them. Whether we did or did not choose to carry them was up to us, but, in the event of capture we might find this alternative preferable to torture.

The lessons of Korea were still fresh in mind.

The last item put on the plane before each overflight and the first taken off on its return was the destruct unit.

Easily the most enduring myth about the U-2 flights concerns this mechanism, which has engendered an apocrypha so vast it seems a shame to blow it up.

First advanced by the Russians, and later picked up and made much of by certain American writers, was the claim that U-2 pilots were worried that if the device had to be used the CIA had rigged it in such a way that it would explode prematurely, thus eliminating, in one great blast, *all* incriminating evidence, plane *and* pilot.

One simple fact quite thoroughly dispels this imaginative fiction. Prior to each and every overflight, maintenance personnel tested the timer. It was a standard part of the preflight check.

Pilots could supervise the testing if they wished to; usually we didn't bother. We knew and trusted our ground crews. More often than not, these men were close friends (some remain so today). Had such a thing as rigging of the device even been suggested, they were not the type of people to remain quiet about it.

That the device was tested was not because of any suspicion that our employers intended to do us in, but because, as previously noted, there was a slight variance in the allotted time on some units. We were never sure which unit would be used. In a situation where a few seconds could mean life or death, it was imperative not only that we be sure that the timer was working properly but also that we know the exact seconds' leeway between flipping the switches and the actual explosion.

As for the pilots being nervous about the device, this was quite true. We had also been nervous in the Air Force when flying with payloads. In each case there were a number of safeguards to forestall accidental detonation. But in both we were still flying with a bomb, and there was always the possibility—whether real or imagined, the fear existed—that a small electrical spark might accidentally bypass the most carefully planned circuitry. Neither was especially conducive to peace of mind.

The evening before the flight, I went to bed early. Although it was November, Turkey, being situated on the Mediterranean, had a warm climate almost year round. Made uncomfortable by both the temperature and the unusual hour, I tossed and turned.

The only difference between this and other flights I had already flown, I told myself, was that this would take a little longer and I'd be seeing a different country.

I wasn't fooling myself. Sleep came hard, even with a couple of sleeping pills.

At five A.M. I was awakened and went to breakfast, after which I reported to Prebreathing to "get on the hose" and suit up. Because of the bulkiness and tightness of the suit, the latter required assistance. During the next two hours I restudied my maps. The routes were color-coded, in blue, red, and brown. Blue indicated the general route, along which some deviation from course was permitted. Red lines marked target areas and were to be flown exactly on course if possible. Alongside were marks indicating where specific photographic and electronic equipment was to be switched on and off. Brown lines denoted routes to alternate bases, if for some reason I couldn't return to Incirlik.

Following a last-minute briefing on the weather, the intelligence officer asked me if I wanted to carry a cyanide capsule.

I shook my head. Not for any profound reason, rather one that in retrospect sounds a trifle silly. I was afraid the capsule might break in my pocket, and I wanted to avoid the risk of accidental contact.

The plane was already on the runway.

The suit was so cumbersome I had to be helped up the ladder into the cockpit. Once in, it was as snug as always. There was little room for movement.

After the ladder was pulled away, I started the engine. The U-2 has a whine all its own; no matter how many times heard, it thrilled me. This time the feeling was not unmixed with nervousness.

Checking the oil, fuel, hydraulic pressures, the EGT, the RPM, I closed the canopy, locking it from the inside, and turned on the pressurization system.

On signal, I began moving down the runway, pogos falling away the instant the plane left the ground. The ascent, sharp, rapid, started moments later and continued until the base was a tiny speck on the landscape below.

Reaching assigned altitude for this particular flight (it varied), I leveled off.

Periodically I checked the instruments, warning lights and gauges, the clock on the instrument panel.

Exactly thirty minutes after takeoff I reached for the radio call button.

Too close to Russia for voice contact, we had devised a code.

If everything was going well and I planned to continue the flight, I was to give two clicks on the radio.

Since I was still within radio range, this would be picked up back at base.

As acknowledgment, they would click once, indicating message received, proceed as planned. Or they would click three times, indicating that the flight had been scrubbed and I was to turn around and return to base immediately.

This would be the last radio contact until my return.

I clicked twice.

After a moment there was a single click in acknowledgment.

I continued the flight, crossing the Turkish border between Black and Caspian seas and penetrated Russian air space.

Two

There was no abrupt change in the topography, yet the moment you crossed the border you sensed the difference. Much of it was imagination, but that made it no less real. Knowing there were people who would shoot you down if they could created a strange tension. I'd never flown combat; perhaps the feeling was the same. But I thought not. In combat you knew what you were up against. Here you were apprehensive of the unknown. It was the not knowing that got to you.

Were they even aware that I was up here? At this altitude the U-2 couldn't be seen from the ground, and, above ninety percent of the earth's atmosphere, conditions were such that jet contrails usually did not form. As for Russian radar, we were, at this time, skeptical of its capabilities, doubtful that it could even pick us up at this height.

Were they, at this very moment, trying to bring me down? The view from the U-2 is restricted. Although you can see miles in front and to the sides, to look down, immediately below, you have to use a view sight, similar to an inverted periscope. From what I could see of the air and ground below, there were no clues. No signs of rockets. No jet condensation trails. Nothing that resembled unusual activity.

Fortunately, just piloting the aircraft and fulfilling the requirements of the mission was a full-time job. Checking the RPM, the EGT, the compass, the fire warning lights, the artificial horizon; watching the ever-critical air speed; homing in on Soviet radio stations; compensating for drift; flipping switches on and off: these were clear and sharply defined things. This was the reality. But the uneasiness remained, like the overlay on a map.

And it would remain throughout this and all other overflights.

By the time you returned to the base you were physically and emotionally exhausted. You told yourself it was because you had been wearing your helmet and breathing pure oxygen for twelve hours, because you had been in a tight-fitting suit in a cramped cockpit for ten.

But that wasn't all of it.

As I was soon to learn, tension was not the exclusive property of those actually making the overflights. Each time a plane was out, there was a changed feeling in the squadron. The personnel went about their duties as usual, but with less comment. The good-natured joshing vanished, along with the horseplay. Remarks were spare, clipped. It was quieter. Everyone was waiting. As the hours passed, the silent tension increased. Navigation on the U-2 was so exact that you knew, almost to the minute, where the plane should be, could time almost exactly when it should reappear on the radar screen. But this only made the waiting, especially during the last minutes, more intense.

The returning pilot got no clue of this, not until the next time, when he was among those waiting.

The moment he touched down, the squadron was alive with activity.

While the pilot was being debriefed, equipment was unloaded, film and recording tape rushed to the photo lab. Once the film was developed, a copy was made of the negatives. The recording tape was also reproduced. One set of films and tapes was then flown to the United States for study.

The duplication was essential; if the courier aircraft went down, the mission itself would not have been wasted.

Occasionally pilots were shown the films, but not often. Nor were we usually told how important a specific mission had been. But there were indications. When the agency couldn't wait for the transfer of films to Washington, but flew photo interpreters over to examine them the moment they were processed, we knew they were looking for something out of the ordinary. When, at a later date, the "big wigs"—both military and civilian—began visiting the base, they were less careful than agency personnel in hiding their enthusiasms. From their reactions we could often tell when there had been a major breakthrough.

One occurred late in 1956, although it wasn't until later that we were filled in on its ramifications.

In the United States a battle had long raged in military and congressional circles over how much of our defense effort should be allotted to bombers, how much to missiles. It was not only a matter of "keeping up with Russia" in retaliatory strength; also at stake was whether our defenses were or were not geared to the actual threat.

There was considerable evidence the Russians had chosen to concentrate on production of heavy bombers, in particular one similar to the U.S. B-52. On Soviet Aviation Day in July, 1955, a mammoth air spectacular had been staged over Moscow. On a "fly-by," flight after flight of these planes had passed over the reviewing stand, in numbers far greater than our intelligence had believed existed. From other intelligence sources throughout Russia came supporting evidence, reports of a squadron sighted here, another there.

The U-2s revealed this "bomber buildup" for what it was, an elaborate hoax, one which had already cost the United States millions of dollars and could conceivably in time have cost millions of lives.

There was only one squadron of these planes, reappearing periodically in those places Westerners were most likely to spot them. As for the fly-by, it was now surmised that having once passed overhead, the same planes had flown out of sight, circled, and returned again and again.

The U-2s revealed more than this. Evidence accumulated proved that while the United States was busily manufacturing bombers, the Russians had shifted their major emphasis to missiles. And from photographs of their launching sites and other data, such as that picked up on the electronic surveillance flights, U.S. intelligence was able to determine how far Soviet technology had progressed in both missile development and production.

Bit by bit, mission after mission, the U-2s were penetrating, and dissipating, a cloud of ignorance which had for decades made the Soviet Union a dark and shadowy land, revealing for the first time a composite picture of military Russia, complete to airfields, atomic production sites, power plants, oil-storage depots, submarine yards, arsenals, railroads, missile factories, launch sites, radar installations, industrial complexes, antiaircraft defenses. Much later, *The New York Times* would call the U-2 overflights "the most successful reconnaissance, espionage project in history," while Allen Dulles, head of the Central Intelligence Agency during this period, would observe that the U-2 "could collect information with more speed, accuracy, and dependability than could any agent on the ground. In a sense, its feats could be equaled only by the acquisition of technical documents directly from Soviet offices and laboratories. The U-2 marked a new high, in more ways than one, in the scientific collection of intelligence."

The U-2 pilots were denied this broad overview. We caught only glimpses.

That was enough, however, to convince us of the importance of what we were doing.

And to make us aware of the risks involved.

Still no one asked the big question.

Returning from one of the "special" missions, I was handed a message from Colonel Perry. Exhausted, still mentally involved in the flight just finished, I couldn't understand it, even after reading it several times.

The colonel explained it to me, his tone something less than happy.

"Your wife called the Washington number you gave her, Powers. To tell us she's on her way to Athens, determined to see you."

The agency didn't want her in the vicinity. But they couldn't order her to return home. I'd have to persuade her.

But Barbara had already made up her mind and wasn't about to change it. She was going to stay in Athens and get a job. Nothing I could say would dissuade her.

And, I must admit, I didn't try very hard. At this time we were not at all sure the overflight program would last the full eighteen months. There was the possibility we would be returning to the United States much sooner. In the interim, although I was quite aware it would displease the agency, I couldn't see any good reason why she shouldn't stay.

One thing bothered me, though: Barbara was given to impetuous acts. When she wanted to do something, she did it, regardless of consequences. In the States, living with her mother, there had been some check on her wilder impulses. In Athens, away from home for the first time, and separated from me except for occasional visits, she would be on her own. Yet there was the possibility this was just what she needed, to be out from under the parental roof, where she could learn self-control.

We rented an apartment in Athens. She found a steno-clerk job in one of the Air Force offices. And by arranging my off-duty time, I was able to fly over and be with her almost every other weekend.

Although Operation Overflight settled into an established routine, the flights themselves never became routine.

After a while, for example, there was no need to mention in briefings that under no circumstances was radio contact to be attempted while over "forbidden territory," or that in the event of a bail-out or forced landing the pilot should do everything he could to see that the aircraft was not captured intact. Since we all knew this, we could take such things for granted and eliminate mention

of them from the briefings, instead concentrating on the most important thing, navigation. The procedures became familiar; as for the
flights, however, each was new.

There were no "milk runs." Although there were return flights
to a few specific targets, because of continuing interest in what
was happening there, the route was changed each time. We did
not believe the Russians yet had the capability of shooting us down;
the easiest way to find out, however, would have been to make
the same trip twice. We avoided any semblance of establishing a
pattern. We went out of our way to avoid passing over known
radar or antiaircraft installations. But in so doing we also ran another
risk, inadvertently passing over installations which intelligence
knew nothing about.

It was only a matter of time, we knew, before Russia would
have the capability. The only question was when.

Because this risk existed on every flight, the overflights never
became "old hat."

Whether awaiting its return, or flying it, we sweated each overflight.

Three

D uring 1957 there was a step-up in activity in the U-2
program.

After the third and last class completed its training at
Watertown, a new U-2 base was opened, this one in the Far East,
at Atsugi, fifteen miles west of Yokohama, Japan.

Having received too much attention at Wiesbaden, the first U-
2 group moved to a more isolated location, Giebelstadt.

It wasn't isolated enough.

On takeoff, pilots frequently noticed a long, black limousine
parked at the end of the runway. Checking license plates, agency
security discovered it was registered by one of the Iron Curtain em-
bassies.

Giebelstadt had been "compromised." Shortly afterward, the first
and second U-2 groups combined, at Adana. Although special flights
were to continue to be made from West German bases, major
emphasis in Europe now shifted to Turkey and its environs. By
this time we were flying not only out of Adana but also, on occasion,
from two bases in Pakistan: Lahore and Peshawar. There were two
major reasons for the change. Being closer to targets in the Soviet
Union in which we were most interested, this cut down flying

time and fuel consumption. And, because of the ruggedness of the terrain, with its fierce mountains, it was one of the least defended portions of the Soviet border, decreasing odds on flights being spotted.

During 1957 there were modifications of the plane. Its silver coloration was changed to blue-black, making it even harder to spot when in flight. And an ejection seat was installed. Prior to this time, there had been few successful bail-outs from the U-2. If the plane became disabled and went into a spin, the g forces pinned the pilot in the cockpit, making it extremely difficult for him to climb out. The ejection seat was supposed to remedy this hazard.

It merely substituted another.

It was discovered that at high altitudes the plastic canopy over the cockpit, normally broken by the top of the seat when it ejected, froze and became like steel. Tragically, this wasn't discovered until a pilot tried to escape using the ejection seat. Though he had hit the canopy with tremendous force, it hadn't budged. He went down with the plane.

Following this, the explosive charge was increased and sharp breaker points installed on top of the seat, positioned in order to hit the canopy at its points of greatest stress, causing it to shatter.

Like many another pilot, I remained leery, hating to ride in a plane with an ejection seat. It was comparable to sitting on a loaded shotgun. There had been instances, though not yet in the U-2, where, because of some mechanical failure, pilots had been ejected while their planes were taking off, landing, or still aground.

There was a "safety pin" to keep the seat from ejecting. Pilots were supposed to remove this before takeoff. I never did, always waiting until reaching an altitude where I knew the chute had some chance to open.

Today successful ejections may be made from most aircraft while still on the ground. This was not the case during the period of Operation Overflight. Any altitude below two thousand feet was considered marginal.

In one respect our luck held. There were no incidents over Russia, not even a close call.

The year 1957 brought more changes, ramifications of which are still felt.

On August 26 the Soviet Union announced it had launched its first successful intercontinental ballistic missile, or ICBM.

On September 4 a new age opened with the successful orbiting of the first space satellite, Sputnik.

One month later, less one day, Sputnik II was in orbit, with the dog Laika aboard.

Russia was busy. So were the U-2s. With these events, the over-flights gained a new and far greater importance. That the government of the United States was pleased with our efforts became evident when we were told that, although civilians, each of us had been awarded the Distinguished Flying Cross, our military records having been changed to show the award.

Another significant event during this period was a revision of attitude toward the aircraft itself. By now it was apparent the engineers had badly misjudged the reliability of the U-2. It had proven to be an extremely capable plane, able to withstand a great deal of abuse and still perform beautifully.

The number of flights increased. And, as we neared the eighteen-month expiration date of our contracts, we were asked to renew for another twelve months.

I had mixed feelings. My commitment to the program was total. I believed in what we were doing, feeling it was not only vital to our national security but that the information gathered might someday be a determining factor in our survival.

My reservations were personal.

Sometime earlier Barbara had obtained a transfer from Athens to a job at Wheelus Air Force Base, Tripoli, Libya. Occasionally it was necessary to ferry one of our T-33 instrument trainers to Wheelus for inspection; whenever possible, I would try to get the assignment. But our marriage was badly floundering and in the fall of 1957, when Barbara and I returned to the United States, we discussed the idea of a divorce.

I did not talk over my personal problems with the agency (they would not be mentioned here except for their relevance to what followed), but I did indicate that in November, when my contract expired, I might not renew.

Nor was I the only one who had made this decision. Several other married pilots had decided that an eighteen-month separation from their families was more than enough.

Having little choice, the agency capitulated. If we extended, they would let us move our families to Adana.

I gave the matter much thought. It seemed to me that many of Barbara's and my problems could be attributed to long separations. Perhaps were we together we could still salvage our marriage. We

could at least give it one more try. I did not believe in divorce—
it seemed like giving up.

After taking another physical at Lovelace, I renewed my contract
and brought Barbara back to Adana in time to celebrate Christmas
in Turkey.

With the arrival of the wives, social life at Incirlik improved
immeasurably, as did the food.

The married couples rented houses in town. Parties were frequent. Because the job was not without its tensions, when we got the
chance to relax we made the most of it. This included considerable
drinking. Enjoying liquor, I did my share. Barbara, I soon realized,
was doing more than hers. There were arguments, incidents. Not
really facing up to the fact that we had problems, I convinced
myself that once she adjusted to the changed way of life, things
would go more smoothly.

Because there was little to do in Turkey, the R&R leaves became
much-anticipated events. We had a C-54 transport to bring in supplies from Germany. Arrangements were made for it to drop off
families there one week, pick them up the next. On occasion,
shopping-sight-seeing trips were set up for the wives, to Athens,
Beirut, Paris, Naples. Many of the pilots bought cars and had them
shipped to Adana. The detachment obtained a small boat with
outboard engine. There was a reservoir not too far away. To our
activities we added water skiing. Also, on one of our trips to Germany, we acquired a German shepherd, whom we named Eck.
With the growing number of conflicts in the Middle East—Suez in
1956, Lebanon in 1958—Incirlik became strategically important, as
both a military base and a staging area. With the increase in permanent military personnel stationed there, a few more "creature comforts" were added, including an officers' club, which, while primitive
compared to those on most modern bases, added to our social life.

The pilots made a conscious effort to separate "squadron business" from their personal lives. While it's possible some told their
wives what they were actually doing, I'm inclined to doubt it.
Overriding the question of security was one other consideration:
we didn't want our wives to worry; had they known what we were
doing, they would have done so.

Whether any of them suspected is, of course, another matter.
As intelligence gatherers, wives rival anything ever dreamed up by
the agency or the KGB.

No secret can be kept indefinitely. Despite elaborate security measures, that of the U-2 was leaking out bit by bit.

Although there had been veiled references to the U-2's "other uses" by aviation writers in several American newspapers—including *The Los Angeles Times* and the New York *Journal American*—the most startling disclosure appeared in one of the most unlikely places. *Model Airplane News,* in its March, 1958, issue, carried a short article on the aircraft, complete with drawings. The article observed: "An unconfirmed rumor says that U-2s are flying across the Iron Curtain taking aerial photographs."

We also learned, through intelligence, that *Soviet Aviation,* official newspaper of the Red Air Force, had published a series of articles mentioning the U-2. They had dubbed it "the black lady of espionage." Although much of the information in the articles was incorrect or outdated—for example, the statement that U-2s were flying out of Wiesbaden—we weren't lulled into any false sense of security.

The U-2 was a distinctive aircraft, spectacular in its takeoffs, like none other in the air. The overflight program was two years old; in addition to the two main bases, Adana and Atsugi, U-2s were also, on occasion, flying out of bases all around the globe.

Such flights couldn't long escape notice.

How much did the Russians actually know about our outfit, Detachment 10-10? Talking it over with the intelligence officer we concluded that they probably knew a great deal. It was an unusual unit, set off by itself, flying an easily identifiable aircraft. Spying was an ancient, if not honorable, profession in Turkey. If Russian intelligence was as good as our own intelligence repeatedly told us it was, it seemed likely they not only knew how many planes we had but how many pilots, plus our names.

Of one thing we were sure. There was no longer any doubt they knew about the overflights. Our evidence of this was of the most conclusive kind. Although none of the pilots had actually seen them, electronic equipment on returning U-2s indicated the Russians were now sending up rockets attempting to bring us down.

In the fall of 1958, another country—knowingly or otherwise— became involved in the U-2 program.

That September, the Soviet Union, after a six-month suspension, resumed nuclear testing, with several large detonations north of the Arctic Circle. Flying out of Bodö, Norway, U-2s collected atomic samples and other data on the tests. We remained in Bodö for about three weeks; grounded by the weather much of the time, we got in a lot of fishing. We presumed—strictly presumption—that some understanding had been reached with the Norwegian government regarding our presence there. A Norwegian military officer acted as our liaison. Similar arrangements pertained in Pakistan.

To my knowledge no intentional overflights were made from Norway. On returning a U-2 to Adana, one pilot did accidentally stray over the border into the USSR. Recrossing uneventfully, he was more fortunate than two U.S. Air Force planes that earlier made the same mistake.

In June a C-118 transport, hauling freight from Turkey to Iran, had inadvertently crossed into Soviet Armenia during a bad storm and was shot down. The nine crew members, who had escaped injury in the crash, were released by the Russians little more than a week later. According to a strongly worded U.S. State Department protest, Russian MIGs had continued firing at the plane even when it was in flames and trying to land. Some crewmen had been badly beaten by the peasants who captured them, and one was almost lynched from a telephone pole before police rescued him from the irate mob.

Early in September another unarmed transport plane, this one a turboprop C-130, also crossed over into Soviet Armenia from Turkey and was shot down. This time the Russians returned the bodies of six crewmen, but ignored inquiries as to the fate of the other eleven men aboard.

The significance of these incidents wasn't lost on us.

At our altitude we weren't too worried about MIGs, but we were beginning to be concerned about SAMs, surface-to-air-missiles.

By this time a few of the "unknowns" were disappearing from U-2 overflights.

We now knew that the Russians were radar-tracking at least some of our flights; it was possible that they had been doing so from the start. Equipment on board recorded their signals; from their strength it was possible to tell whether they were "painting," that is tracking the flight. However, this could only be determined after returning to base and studying transcriptions. There was still no way, while in flight, to know for sure.

We also knew that SAMs were being fired at us, that some were uncomfortably close to our altitude. But we knew too that the Russians had a control problem in their guidance system. Because of the speed of the missile, and the extremely thin atmosphere, it was almost impossible to make a correction. This did not eliminate the possibility of a lucky hit. In our navigation we were careful to ensure our routes circumvented known SAM sites.

We were concerned, but not greatly. In retrospect—from which everything always seems crystal clear—we should have been damn worried. The truth is, we were growing complacent.

As defense against air-to-air missiles, those fired from another aircraft, a new piece of equipment called a "granger" was installed in the tail. As explained to us, should an aircraft lock onto a U-2 with his radar and launch a missile, the granger would send out a faulty signal to break his radar lock. Whether it actually did this or not, we had no way of knowing, since we had never been threatened by aircraft.

The U-2 had a problem shared by many Americans. It was overweight. From the day of its birth, it had been gaining extra pounds, each new piece of equipment adding more, at the same time lowering the altitude at which the plane could fly.

In 1959 a more powerful engine was developed to compensate for this extra weight, lifting us back into the higher altitudes. One of the first U-2s so adapted was sent to Atsugi, where it promptly made its share of unwanted headlines.

As flying-safety officer for the detachment, I received reports on all U-2 accidents around the world, a great many of which were never publicized. By this time, U-2s had made flights not only from Turkey and Japan but also from California, Nevada, Alaska, Texas, New York, Brazil, Okinawa, Formosa, the Philippines, Australia, England, West Germany, Norway and Pakistan. Most of these, of course, were not overflights, but for collection of weather data and atomic sampling.

The Japan incident, in September, 1959, was much too well publicized. It especially interested me because the plane, number 360, had one of the new engines. Also it had set two new records, on the same day: it had flown the highest, and the lowest, any U-2 had ever flown.

Rumor had the accident as pilot error, or, to be more precise, pilot goof. Testing the new engine, he had decided to see if he could set a new altitude record. He did. He also used up more fuel than anticipated. Less than ten miles south of Atsugi he ran out of fuel and was forced to make an emergency landing at a glider-club strip.

Mired deep in mud, he set his second record that day: having flown the U-2 lower than anyone else in history.

Remaining in the cockpit, he radioed the base for assistance. Meantime, the Japanese, with their ever-present cameras, had surrounded the plane, happily taking pictures. When U.S. military police arrived, they ordered them away at gunpoint, cordoning off the area.

It was not exactly the way to avoid publicity. Japanese newspapers and magazines picked up the story and the pictures, their editorials asking why, if the U-2 was being used strictly for weather research, it bore no identification marks and occasioned such extreme security.

Still, it was a minor incident, or seemed so at the time.

I had no idea then how well I would come to know plane number 360. Nor did anyone foresee the kind of headlines it would soon make.

The original concept of Operation Overflight had been short-term, something less than the eighteen months called for in our contracts.

In November, 1957, we had extended for another year.

We had done the same in November, 1958, and 1959.

In the interim, the Russians had made spectacular strides in missile and space development.

We could not shake the feeling that time was catching up with us.

Not long after the installation of the granger, the intelligence officer introduced us to another new piece of "equipment."

We couldn't figure it out. It looked like a good-luck charm. It seemed to be an ordinary silver dollar, with a metal loop at one end so it could be fastened onto a key chain or a chain around the neck.

Obviously enjoying our puzzlement, he unscrewed the loop. Inside the dollar was what appeared to be an ordinary straight pin. But this too wasn't what it seemed. Looking at it more closely, we could see the body of the pin to be a sheath not fitting quite tightly against the head. Pulling this off, it became a thin needle, only again not an ordinary needle. Toward the end there were grooves. Inside the grooves was a sticky brown substance.

It was curare, the intelligence officer explained. Just one prick would suffice.

From now on, we could carry this, if we wanted to, instead of cyanide.

The majority of pilots had decided, individually, against carrying cyanide. I had never carried it.

But we were fascinated with the dollar-pin-needle device. Passing it around, quite carefully, leaving the needle in the sheath, we each examined it. It was ingenious. Who would ever think of looking inside a silver dollar for something like this?

We were again champing at the bit. Most of 1958, all of 1959, and thus far in 1960, there had been a drastic reduction in the number of overflights. Months would pass without one. Although never told the reason for the severe cutback, we presumed it was because of the political climate. We were quite capable of making many more flights than was the case, in fact were anxious to do so. We were not inactive; we continued to make border-surveillance missions, and the "special" missions, but were definitely restive. The longer the layoff, the greater the tension. The fewer the overflights, the more apprehensive we became about the next one.

Then, suddenly, after a long pause, two flights were scheduled for the same month, April, 1960.

I was to be "backup" on the first and to fly the second.

Use of a backup, or substitute, pilot was a comparatively recent change in procedure, occurring after we had started making overflights from bases other than Incirlik. Along with the lead pilot, the backup pilot went through all preflight stages, from briefings up to and including prebreathing. Should the lead pilot have a heart attack (or, considering the food, a much more common occurrence, the GIs), the backup could take over.

Some accounts, apparently confused over the role of the backup, state that on each overflight two U-2s would take off simultaneously, one to fly along the border, throwing off Russian radar, while the other made the actual mission. To my knowledge, this was never done, nor probably was it ever considered, since Russian radar was quite capable of picking up more than one plane at a time.

The backup pilot was simply a substitute for the lead pilot in the event he was unable to fly.

It was some weeks prior to the first April flight, when we were studying routes, that I finally asked the question.

It had been put off much too long. There had been no mention of it in our contracts. It had never been brought up in our briefings.

We had never discussed it among ourselves. Yet I knew we had thought about it—or, at least, I knew one pilot had.

Though Operation Overflight was nearly four years old, we were totally unprepared for an "accident." It didn't necessarily have to be a missile. One loose screw, in just the right place, could bring an aircraft down.

The silver dollar had provided the obvious opening, and I had presumed someone would ask it then. But no one had done so. Now, as we were preparing to resume overflights, I decided to put it directly to the intelligence officer.

"What if something happens and one of us goes down over Russia? That's an awfully big country, and it could be a hell of a long walk to a border. Is there anyone there we can contact? Can you give us any names and addresses?"

"No, we can't."

While it was not what I wanted to hear, his answer was at least understandable. If we had agents in Russia, as we presumably did, release of their names could place them in jeopardy also.

I persisted. "All right, say the worst happens. A plane goes down, and the pilot is captured. What story does he use? Exactly how much should he tell?"

His exact words were, "You may as well tell them everything, because they're going to get it out of you anyway."

As if anticipating our concern, and perhaps hoping to set it to rest before such questions were asked, the agency had set up a survival exercise the previous summer—excluding the little bit of evasion-training on the East Coast at the start of the project, the first such for most of us since we had been in the Air Force. Divided into several groups, we were driven out into the desert, with only parachute and minimal rations, and left there.

Our group managed fairly well. When our supplies finally ran out, we stumbled onto a farmer's sugar-beet patch.

Only later, thinking about it, did we consider that had he appeared with a shotgun, and been inclined to use it, a good portion of the U.S. U-2 program in Turkey could have been wiped out.

Surviving a bad thunderstorm, we found a little village, were treated to an excellent but native meal, and, renting donkeys, rode back to the pickup point in style.

Another group was not so lucky. Some of the natives, claiming they had seen men parachuting out of planes, called the Turkish police, who arrested them as Russian spies.

If the intention was to buoy up our self-confidence, the exercise was decidedly less than a success.

Overseas, possibly because it is so limited, you consume news. What newspapers you can get, such as *Stars and Stripes*, you read from beginning to end.

During April, 1960, we were aware of the upcoming Summit Conference, scheduled to take place in Paris the following month; like other topics of the day, we discussed the talks, hopeful that something good would come out of them. But not optimistic. There still seemed to be no solution to the problem of Berlin; according to everything we read, Khrushchev was determined to make trouble over the issue.

But it was a minor topic. We were equally interested in Senator John F. Kennedy's win over Hubert Humphrey in the Wisconsin Presidential primary; De Gaulle's visit to the United States; the orbiting of a navigational satellite from Cape Canaveral. We didn't connect it with our work, or with the sudden increase in the number of overflights.

We had our own explanation for that.

No one told us this, it was just a presumption, but we had a feeling that intelligence, suspecting the Russians were close to solving their missile-guidance problem, was trying to crowd in as many important targets as possible while time remained.

The feeling, correct or not, didn't lessen the tension.

However, the first April flight, on the ninth, went off as smoothly as its predecessors.

There was no reason to suppose that mine, scheduled for late in the month, would go otherwise. Yet we were a little more apprehensive about it than usually would have been the case, since it would differ from all previous overflights in one respect.

Taking off from Peshawar, Pakistan, I was to fly thirty-eight hundred miles to Bodö, Norway.

It would be the first time we had attempted to fly all the way across the Soviet Union.

Four

The main reason we had never tried to fly all the way across the Soviet Union was not fuel but logistics. Previously all the overflights had returned to their originating base. Taking off from one base and landing at another required two ground crews, doubling personnel, preparation, and risk of exposure.

But it was considered worth the gamble. The planned route would take us deeper into Russia than we had ever gone, while traversing important targets never before photographed.

Since arriving in Turkey in 1956, Detachment 10-10 had changed commanding officers several times. The latest, who had joined us only a short time earlier, was an Air Force colonel, William M. Shelton. Shelton handled the briefings for the flight, conducted at Incirlik, prior to our leaving for Pakistan.

As usual, they were concerned primarily with navigation.

Taking off from Peshawar, Pakistan, I was to overfly Afghanistan and cross the Hindu Kush range, an extension of the Himalayas. Once in the Soviet Union, my route would take me over or near Dushambe, the Aral Sea, the Tyuratam Cosmodrome (Russia's Cape Canaveral), Chelyabinsk, Sverdlovsk, Kirov, Archangel, and, on the Kola Peninsula, Kandalaksha and Murmansk, from which I was to fly north to the Barents Sea and along the northern coast of Norway to Bodö. This way I would avoid overflying Finland and Sweden.

The flight would take nine hours, cover approximately 3,800 miles, 2,900 within the Soviet Union itself. With an early-morning takeoff, and considering the time changes, I would be in Bodö about nightfall.

I was thinking about this as, early on the morning of Wednesday, April 27, I packed a bag for the trip. Should I stay in Bodö a day or two, I'd need a shaving kit, civilian clothes, ID, and money. Checking my wallet, I found I had some German marks, Turkish lira, and about one hundred dollars in U.S. currency. Estimating that should be sufficient, I tossed the wallet into the traveling bag along with the other items.

With a refueling stop at Bahrein, the trip to Pakistan would take about seven hours. Barbara, fixing a lunch for the flight, asked if I'd be back in time for the party.

It took me a minute to remember which one. In the fall of 1959 the married couples had moved from town back onto the base, our trailers forming a small community at the end of the base housing area. Proximity had rendered the parties all the more frequent. Unfortunately, the drinking problem not only remained, but had grown worse. I'd miss one recent party because of being scheduled for an early flight the next morning. Barbara had gone anyway, fallen down while dancing, and broken her leg; it was still in a cast. Nevertheless, she continued to insist she had no problem with alcohol.

She did, however. But because I had never encountered it before in someone I knew, I didn't know how to handle it. Although on flights I'd learned to leave personal concerns behind and to concentrate on the job at hand, I worried about her when I had to be gone for several days on trips of this sort. I worried not only about her excessive drinking but also about what she was apt to do when left alone.

Then I remembered. This was to be a special party. The communications chief was returning to the States; an appropriate sendoff had been planned.

I checked the calendar.

If the flight took place as scheduled, on Thursday the twenty-eighth, I should be back in plenty of time.

The party wasn't until Sunday evening, May 1.

More than twenty of us made the Turkey-Pakistan trip, aboard a Lockheed C-130 turboprop transport. It took that many to handle each flight. In addition to the detachment commander, navigator, intelligence officer, doctor, crew chief, mechanics, and photographic and electronic specialists, radio personnel were required to pick up the O.K. for the flight, transmitted from Washington through Germany to Turkey and from there to Pakistan via radio code.

Accommodations at Peshawar were primitive. Our hangar was set off from the rest of the base; we slept there on folding cots and cooked our own food from rations.

There was one departure from routine. Rather than bringing the U-2 over and leaving it at Peshawar until the flight took place, we were trying something new. Chiefly for security, to reduce plane exposure, we were ferrying it to Peshawar the night prior to flight, then, should the flight not take place as scheduled, for weather or some other reason, we would ferry it back to Incirlik.

It was the best plane we had, which was comforting. Aside from the long layoff, and the fact that this flight would be going all the way across Russia, there was nothing else to distinguish this overflight from its predecessors. Nor did the thought of an overflight in itself make me nervous. Of the original group of pilots at Adana, I was the only one who hadn't transferred elsewhere or returned to the States. As a result, simply by being there so long, I had accumulated more spy flights—overflights, eavesdropping missions, and "special" missions—than any other pilot. One other pilot and I tied on the total number of overflights. However, I could later claim the totally uncoveted distinction of having made the last.

Yet because this was to be the first flight all the way across Russia, I felt an additional touch of excitement and some apprehension. However, my complete trust in the aircraft helped.

The schedule called for a six-A.M. takeoff. Wednesday afternoon I went to bed about four o'clock. It was hot and noisy in the hangar; as usual, I tossed and turned, sleeping only sporadically. At two A.M. I was awakened by someone from message center. I had washed and was dressing when I received another message: due to bad weather, the flight had been postponed twenty-four hours.

This left me with a full day of nothing to do.

Thursday afternoon I again went to bed early, to be awakened at two A.M. This time I had finished breakfast and was "on the hose" when the second order came through: another twenty-four-hour postponement.

Friday afternoon, shortly before I was to go to bed, word came that there would be no flight on Saturday. A night of poker and a day of reading and loafing relieved some of the tension built up by the two false starts. But not all. For I also discovered that I wouldn't be flying the plane I'd hoped.

The departure from routine had turned out to be less than a good idea. Periodically, after a certain number of hours' flight time, an aircraft has to be grounded for maintenance check. Flying back and forth from Turkey to Pakistan, time on the plane I'd counted on flying had run out.

As substitute, on Saturday night U-2 number 360 was flown over.

Following its emergency landing on the glider-club strip in Japan, number 360 had been returned to Lockheed's Burbank, California, factory for repairs. Inasmuch as we were at that time short a U-2 at Incirlik, one of our planes also having been returned to Lockheed for maintenance, number 360 was sent to us.

It was a "dog," never having flown exactly right. Something was always going wrong. No sooner was one malfunction corrected than another appeared. Its current idiosyncrasy was one of the fuel tanks, which wouldn't feed all its fuel. But not all the time, just occasionally. So the pilot was kept guessing.

Saturday afternoon I again went to bed early, again to be awakened at two A.M. With my backup pilot, I had a good substantial breakfast—two or three eggs, bacon, toast. It was to be the last food I'd have until reaching Norway, some thirteen hours from now. The doctor checked me over, finding me in good shape. During prebreathing my backup and I were joined by the pilot who had ferried number 360 over the night before, a good friend whom we'll call Bob.

Bob had flown the April 9 overflight on which I was backup, and had been present when I finally asked the intelligence officer the long-avoided question. On this particular mission he would act as mobile control officer. Among his other duties, he would acknowledge when I used the radio code: single click indicating proceed as planned; three clicks meaning return to base.

There was no need for additional briefing. I had studied the maps, knew the route. There had been a slight wind change, meaning navigation had to be corrected; otherwise the weather looked good. Because of 360's fuel-tank problem, however, Colonel Shelton suggested that if, just before reaching Kandalaksha, I discovered I was running low on fuel, I could take a short cut across Finland and Sweden, thereby saving a few minutes' time. As for alternate landing fields, he told me I could land in Norway, Sweden, or Finland—the first being preferable, the second less so, the third to be used only in dire emergency, but added, "Anyplace is preferable to going down in the Soviet Union."

As I was suiting up, I remembered that traveling bag, with wallet and clothing, and asked that it be put in the cockpit.

"Do you want the silver dollar?" Shelton asked.

Before this I hadn't. But this flight was different. And I had less than complete confidence in the plane.

"If something happened," I had previously asked the intelligence officer, "could I use the needle as a weapon?"

He couldn't see why not. One jab, and death would be almost instantaneous. As a weapon, it should be quite effective.

"O.K.," I replied. Shelton tossed it to me, and I slipped it into the pocket of my outer flight suit.

Though with more than sufficient time to think about it since, I'm still not sure why this time I chose to take it.

Could it have been premonition?

About 5:20 A.M., with Bob's assistance, I climbed into the plane, the personal-equipment sergeant strapping me in.

It was scorching hot. The sun had been up nearly an hour.

Bob took off his shirt and held it over the cockpit to try to shield me from its rays.

Takeoff was scheduled for six A.M. I completed my preflight check and waited. And waited. Six o'clock came and passed with no sign of a signal.

The long underwear I was wearing was already completely soaked. Beneath the helmet, perspiration was running down my face in rivers. There was no way to wipe it off.

Finally Colonel Shelton came out to explain the delay. They were awaiting approval from the White House.

This was the first time this had happened. When Presidential approval was necessary, it usually came through well in advance of the flight.

Because I would be without radio contact, I had to depend heavily on the sextant for navigation. But since all precomputations had been made on the basis of a six-A.M. takeoff, the sextant would be useless. At this point I was sure the flight would be canceled, and was looking forward to getting out of the sweat-drenched suit, when, at 6:20 A.M., the signal came: cleared for takeoff.

Bob had been holding his shirt over the cockpit for a full hour. As he closed the canopy, I yelled my thanks and locked the canopy from the inside. Once the ladder was pulled away, there was no delay in getting started and taking off.

At top altitudes, the temperature outside the aircraft dropped to sixty degrees below zero. Some of the chill began to penetrate. Although the suit would remain damp and uncomfortable throughout the flight, at least I was no longer sweltering.

Switching on the autopilot, I completed my flight log. I had already filled in the Aircraft Number, 360, and the Sortie Number, 4154. Now I added takeoff time, 0126 Greenwich Mean Time, 6:26 A.M. local time, with the notation "delayed one-half hour." I also filled in the date: "1 May 1960."

Five

After the single-click acknowledgment from Bob, only silence. A lonely feeling, knowing you'd broken radio contact. Approaching the border, I could feel the tension build. It happened on every overflight. Once across the border, you relaxed a bit. For some reason you felt that anything that was going to happen would happen there.

The weather below was worse than expected. On the Russian side, the clouds came right up to the mountains, a solid undercast.

As far as intelligence was concerned, this wasn't important, there being little of interest in this area. But it didn't make the navigation easier. Without visual observations, I needed the sextant, but couldn't use it, my celestial computations having been made on the basis of a six-A.M. takeoff. Instead I had to rely on time and headings. The sextant was usable, however, as a check to see if the compass was working correctly. It was.

After about one and one-half hours I spotted the first break in the clouds. I was southeast of the Aral Sea. Slightly right of course, I was correcting back when some of the uncertainty came to an end.

Far below I could see the condensation trail of a single-engine jet aircraft. It was moving fast, at supersonic speed, paralleling my course, though in the opposite direction.

I watched until it disappeared.

Five to ten minutes later I saw another contrail, again paralleling my course, only this time moving in my direction. Presumably it was the same aircraft.

I felt relieved. I was sure now they were tracking me on radar, vectoring in and relaying my headings to the aircraft. But it was so far below as to pose no threat. Because of my altitude, it would have been almost impossible for the pilot to see me. If this was the best they could do, I had nothing to worry about.

Odd, but even before reaching the border I had the feeling they knew I was coming.

I wondered how the Russians felt, knowing I was up here, unable to do anything about it. I could make a pretty good guess.

For four years the U-2s had been overflying the USSR. Much of this time, if not all of it, the Russian government had been aware of our activities. Yet, because to do so would be to admit that they could do nothing to stop us, they couldn't even complain. I could imagine their frustration and rage. Imagining it made me much less complacent.

Ahead, about thirty miles east of the Aral Sea, was the Tyuratam Cosmodrome, launching site for most of its important ICBM and space shots.

This wasn't our first visit to the area, nor was it a major objective of this particular flight. But since I was to be in the vicinity, it had been included. Due to the presence of some large thunderclouds, I couldn't see the launch site itself but could see much of the surrounding area. I switched on the cameras. Some intelligence was achieved, though not one hundred percent.

The clouds closed over again and remained solid until, about three hours into the flight, they began to thin; I could see a little terrain, including a town. With my radio compass I picked up the local station. In regard to this particular station, intelligence had indicated that their information might not be accurate; the call sign, the frequency, or both, could be incorrect. The call sign was wrong, the frequency right. Again slightly off course, I corrected back.

About fifty miles south of Chelyabinsk, the clouds disappeared. To my left I got a good view of the Urals. Once the traditional boundary between Europe and Asia, as mountains they were not very high. Still snow-topped, on either side the land was green. It was spring in Russia. It was also a beautiful day, and now that I was back on course, the clouds behind me, I began to relax a little.

Predictably, number 360 chose this moment to be unpredictable. The autopilot began malfunctioning, causing the aircraft to pitch nose-up. To correct the condition, I had to disengage the autopilot, retrim, and fly the plane manually for a few minutes. When I reengaged the autopilot, the plane flew fine for ten to fifteen minutes, after which the pitch controls again went to the full nose-up position. The aircraft couldn't take much of this. Again I went through the same procedure. With the same result. This time I left the autopilot disengaged.

Should I go on, I'd have to fly the plane manually the rest of the way.

It was an abort situation, and I had to make a decision: to turn around and go back, or to continue the flight. An hour earlier the decision would have been automatic; I would have gone back. But I was more than thirteen hundred miles inside Russia, and the worst of the weather appeared to be behind me, while ahead visibility looked excellent.

I decided to go on and accomplish what I had set out to do.

Normally, without this complication—having to navigate, compute ATAs and ETA, turn on the switches at the designated points, pay constant attention to the instruments to keep from exceeding the mach limitation on the high side and stalling the aircraft on the low side, the variance in speed also affecting fuel consumption— my work was cut out. Having to fly the plane manually called for an extra pair of hands.

Spotting a huge tank farm, I noted it on my map. Observing a large complex of buildings, which could have been either military or industrial, I marked them down also, with the notation "big outfit" as a reminder for debriefing.

Sverdlovsk was ahead. Formerly known as Ekaterinburg, it was here, in 1918, that Czar Nicholas II and his family were assassinated by the Bolsheviks. Once a small village, isolated from the mainstream of Russian life, in recent years it and the surrounding area had grown as astronomically as Southern California. Now an important industrial metropolis, Sverdlovsk was of special interest; I flipped the appropriate switches.

This was the first time a U-2 had flown over the area.

Once past Sverdlovsk, my route would take me northwest to Kirov, whence I would fly north to Archangel, Kandalaksha, Murmansk, and, finally, Bodö, Norway.

About thirty to forty miles southeast of Sverdlovsk, I made a ninety-degree left turn, rolled out on course, and lined up on my next flight line, which would go over the southwestern edge of the city.

I was almost exactly four hours into the flight.

Spotting an airfield that did not appear on the map, I marked it down. My route would take me directly over it.

Following the turn, I had to record the time, altitude, speed, exhaust-gas temperature, and engine-instrument readings. I was marking these down when, suddenly, there was a dull "thump," the aircraft jerked forward, and a tremendous orange flash lit the cockpit and sky.

Time had caught up with us.

Knocked back in the seat, I said, *"My God, I've had it now!"*

The orange glow seemed to last for minutes, although it was probably gone in seconds. Yet I had time enough to think the explosion was external to the aircraft and, from the push, probably somewhere behind it.

Instinctively I grasped the throttle with my left hand, and keeping my right hand on the wheel, checked instruments. All readings normal. Engine functioning O.K. The right wing started to droop. I turned the wheel, and it came back up. Fine. Now the nose, very slowly, started to go down. Proper correction for that is to pull back on the wheel to bring it up. I pulled, but it kept going down. Either the control cable had severed or the tail was gone. I knew then I had no control of the aircraft.

As it kept nosing down, a violent movement shook the plane, flinging me all over the cockpit. I assumed both wings had come off. What was left of the plane began spinning, only upside down, the nose pointing upward toward the sky, the tail down toward the ground. All I could see was blue sky, spinning, spinning. I turned on the emergency oxygen supply. Sometime earlier—I hadn't felt it at the time—my suit had inflated, meaning I'd lost pressurization in the cockpit. The suit was now squeezing me, while the g forces were throwing me forward, out of the seat, up toward the nose.

I reached for the destruct switches, opening the safety covers, had my hand over them, then changed my mind, deciding I had better see if I could get into position to use the ejection seat first. Under normal circumstances, there is only a small amount of clearance in ejecting. Thrown forward as I was, if I used the ejection seat the metal canopy rails overhead would cut off both my legs. I tried to pull my legs back, couldn't. Yanking at one leg with both my hands, I succeeded in getting my heel into the stirrup on the seat. Then I did the same with the other heel. But I was still thrown forward, out of the seat, and couldn't get my torso back. Looking up at the canopy rails, I estimated that using the seat in this position would sever both legs about three inches above the knee.

I didn't want to cut them off, but if it was the only way to get out . . .

Thus far I had felt no fear. Now I realized I was on the edge of panic. "Stop and think." The words came back to me. A friend who had also encountered complications trying to bail out had told me of forcing himself to stop struggling and just think his way out of his predicament. I tried it, suddenly realizing the obvious. The ejection seat wasn't the only way to leave the plane. I could climb out! So intent had I been on one solution, I had forgotten the other.

Reaching up—not far, because I had been thrown upward as well as forward, with only the seat belt holding me down—I unlocked and released the canopy. It sailed off into space.

The plane was still spinning. I glanced at the altimeter. It had passed thirty-four thousand feet and was unwinding very fast. Again I thought of the destruct switches but decided to release my seat belt first, before activating the unit. Seventy seconds is not a very long time.

Immediately the centrifugal force threw me halfway out of the aircraft, with movement so quick my body hit the rear-view mirror and snapped it off. I saw it fly away. That was the last thing I saw, because almost immediately my face plate frosted over. Something was holding me connected to the aircraft; I couldn't see what. Then I remembered the oxygen hoses; I'd forgotten to unfasten them.

The aircraft was still spinning. I tried to climb back in to actuate the destruct switches, but couldn't; the g forces were too great. Reaching down, I tried to feel my way to the switches. I knew they were close, six inches away from my left hand at most, but I couldn't slip my hand under the windscreen to get at them. Unable to see, I had no idea how fast I was falling, how close to the ground . . .

And then I thought: I've just got to try to save myself now. Kicking and squirming, I must have broken the oxygen hoses, because suddenly I was free, my body just falling, floating perfectly free. It was a pleasant, exhilarating feeling. Even better than floating in a swimming pool, I remember thinking.

I must have been in shock.

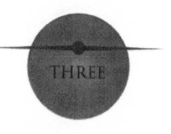

THREE

USSR

One

I was thinking, I should pull the ripcord, when a quick jerk yanked me upward. The chute had opened automatically.

Suddenly my thoughts were sharp and clear. The chute had been set to open at fifteen thousand feet, which meant I was somewhere below that. And under fifteen thousand feet I didn't need the emergency oxygen in my seat pack and could take off my face plate.

I was immediately struck by the silence. Everything was cold, quiet, serene.

The first thing to do when the parachute opens, I had been taught in Air Force survival school, is to look up and make sure the chute has billowed correctly. This I was reluctant to do, since, having only one chute, I was not anxious to discover whether it had failed. But I looked up. The orange and white panels blossomed out beautifully. But against the vast expanse of sky, the chute looked very small.

There was no sensation of falling. It was as if I were hanging in the sky, no movement at all.

Part of the aircraft passed me, twisting and fluttering like a leaf. I thought it was one of the wings. Yet I had no way to estimate size or distance. It could have been a small piece up close or a large piece some distance away.

Looking down, I saw I was still quite high, probably ten thousand feet.

Below were rolling hills, a forest, a lake, roads, buildings, what looked like a village.

It was pretty country. A typical American scene. Like parts of Virginia.

As if by wishing it I could make it so.

It was odd. Under other circumstances it would have seemed amusing. A country as large as the Soviet Union, so vast, with huge sections almost totally uninhabited, and I had to pick a populated area in which to go down.

Remembering a map in my pocket, which showed alternate routes back to Pakistan and Turkey, I took off my gloves, took it out, carefully ripped it into little pieces and scattered them. One piece of incriminating evidence was gone.

I also remembered the silver dollar and took it out. Looking at it at this point, I realized the coin cover wasn't such a good idea after all. What better souvenir of the capture of a capitalist American pilot than a bright new U.S. dollar? It was one of the first things they would take. Unscrewing the loop at the end, I slipped out the poison pin and dropped it into my pocket, where there was a chance it would to unnoticed, then tossed away the coin.

I recall thinking: That's probably the first dollar I've ever deliberately thrown away.

I also recall wondering what some Russian farmer would think when he came upon this years from now—an American dollar in the middle of a Siberian field!

My mind seemed to be perfectly sharp and clear, though incapable of dwelling on a single thought for any length of time. It kept jumping from one thing to another.

Occasionally I would start to swing, but mostly I fell straight, without oscillation, without any real sense of falling.

I thought again of the pin, wondering whether I should use it. Recalling the crash of the C-118 and how the local populace had almost lynched one of the crew, for a moment I seriously considered it. Yet I was still hopeful of escape.

The forest was to my right. I tried to maneuver the shroud lines in order to float down into the trees, thinking that if I could reach them I might at least have a chance of getting away. But the winds were variable. I'd drift toward the woods, then back toward the lake. That worried me, since I knew that tangled in the chute, with all the equipment I was carrying, swimming would be impossible.

Only a few hundred feet remained. I spotted a small car moving along a dirt road. It seemed to be following my course. I watched as it stopped near the village and two men got out.

I also saw, almost directly under me, a plowed field, a tractor, and two men. One was on the tractor, the other standing alongside piling brush.

By now I was too far away to reach the trees. I had also missed the lake. But now a new worry emerged: power lines.

Suddenly the earth rushed up to meet me. I missed the lines by about twenty-five feet, coming down about an equal distance from the tractor, hitting hard, the weight of my seat pack causing me to fall, slamming my head against the ground.

While one of the men collapsed the chute, the other helped me to my feet. Soon joined by the pair from the automobile, they assisted in removing the parachute harness and helmet. My head ached and my ears rang from the sudden descent.

The village was less than one hundred yards away. There must have been a school there, for suddenly there were twenty or thirty children running toward us, followed by almost as many adults.

Escape at this point looked impossible. I still had the gun, but the knife was attached to the parachute harness they had removed.

Everyone was questioning me at the same time. Because I couldn't speak Russian, I could neither understand them nor reply. They seemed solicitous, but also curious. When I didn't answer— I didn't even know the words for "Thank you"—I could see that they were puzzled.

One of the men held up two fingers, pointed at me, then at the sky. Looking up, I could see, some distance away and very high, a lone red and white parachute. There had been no second chute on my plane. Unable to see whether there was a man below the chute, I guessed this to be in some way connected with the explosion. Had they used a rocket, it was possible this was the way they recovered the missile's first stage. I shook my head no, indicating I was alone.

With my continued silence I could see the puzzlement changing to suspicion. A man on either side, I was helped to the car. One, spotting the pistol on the outside of my suit, reached over and took it. I didn't try to stop him. By now the crowd numbered more than fifty.

It was a small compact car. Loading my parachute and seat pack in the trunk, they motioned for me to slide into the front seat beside the driver. The man with the pistol slid in on my right. Three or four other men crowded into the back.

Driving through the village, I made motions indicating I was thirsty. It had been six or seven hours since I had had anything to drink, eat, or smoke. Also, sure they were taking me to the police, I wanted to delay confrontation as long as possible.

It occurred to me that had I been able to speak Russian, I could have pretended to be a Soviet pilot and commandeered their automobile. I probably wouldn't have gotten far—knowing a plane had crashed and its pilot had bailed out, there would be search parties, roadblocks—but certainly it would have been better than my present situation.

Stopping in front of a house, one of the men went in and returned with a glass of water. Gratefully I drank it, but my mouth remained dry. I suspected I was in a state of mild shock. I was terrifically tense, extremely tired. Pilots are unusually conscious of their hearts. Mine was racing, at well over ninety beats per minute.

I could only estimate this. Because of the difficulty of slipping the band over the pressure suit, I didn't wear a watch when I flew. I could only guess at the time. I had been four hours into the flight when the explosion occurred. Nearly a half-hour had passed since then.

Too early for them to miss me at Bodö.

One of the men offered me a cigarette. I accepted, noticing the picture of a familiar dog on the package. "Laika," he said. I nodded, indicating understanding. The brand had been named for the Russians' Sputnik II passenger. A filter cigarette, it tasted very much like its American counterparts.

There was a package of Kents in my flight-suit pocket. I left them there.

The man who had seized my pistol now had it out of the holster and was examining it. I saw what he saw at exactly the same instant: on the barrel the initials USA. I hoped he didn't understand their meaning. But with one finger he traced the letters in the dust on the dashboard, asking in Russian what could only have been: Are you an American?

Inside the trunk was my seat pack. In it, among other easily identifiable items, was the American-flag poster, with "I am an American . . ." printed on it in fourteen languages, including Russian. It seemed useless to deny it. I nodded and the conversation around me suddenly grew very animated. Fortunately it didn't seem hostile. Rather they appeared to be congratulating themselves on having made such a prize catch.

The road was muddy, either from spring thaw or recent rains, and we bounced and slid over the ruts. It was important that I think clearly, decide what my course from this point should be.

The problem: I was completely unprepared. I presumed that once it was known I was missing a cover story would be issued. Unfortunately, no one had ever bothered to inform us pilots what it would be.

I decided that when questioned I would say I had been piloting a weather plane, en route from Pakistan to Turkey, when my compass had gone out, and that apparently I had accidentally flown in the wrong direction. I doubted that they would believe me; I was over thirteen hundred miles inside Russia; but it was all I had to work with.

We were totally unprepared for the crash possibility. I could not speak Russian, had no one to contact. In the four years I had worked for the agency, only once had I received instructions on what to do in the event of capture. And that, brought out by my own questioning, had been the single remark of the intelligence officer: "*You may as well tell them everything, because they're going to get it out of you anyway.*"

I was damned if I was going to do that. Although not sure how, or if, I could manage it, there were some things I was determined to keep from them at any cost.

After driving for about thirty minutes we came to another village, larger than the first, with paved streets. Later I learned that I had landed on a large state farm. The second village was its headquarters; the building to which I was taken was the Rural Soviet. Pulling in front of the building, one of the men went in and brought out a man in uniform, whom I assumed to be a policeman. Making me stand alongside the automobile, he made a cursory search, finding and keeping my cigarettes and lighter, but missing the poison pin.

Taking me to one of the offices in the building, they indicated I was to undress. This time the search was more thorough, even the seams of my clothing examined.

On completion, they kept the pressure suit but gave me back the outer flight suit. While putting it back on, I casually ran my hand down the outside of the pocket. And felt it. Again they had overlooked the pin.

Several of the men in the office wore military uniforms. As one took down the statements of the men who had apprehended me, another tried to question me in German. I shook my head. Apparently no one spoke English.

A doctor arrived, to my surprise a woman, about thirty. She checked my heartbeat and pulse; noticing some scratches on my right leg, she painted them with antiseptic. When I indicated I had a headache, she gave me two small pills that looked and tasted like aspirin.

Perhaps I imagined it. Perhaps I was so desperate for some hopeful sign that I created it in my mind. But I was sure the look she gave me was sympathetic, as if she understood my predicament and wished she could help me.

Individually and in small groups people began arriving bearing pieces of equipment or wreckage from the plane. I could see English lettering—manufacturers' names, maintenance instructions, serial numbers—on some of them.

I cringed inside. One man was carrying a reel of seventy-millimeter film.

What little credibility my cover story possessed disappeared at that moment.

As the people came in, some took out small cards and proudly showed them to the officers. There was much examining and comparing. It was only a guess, but I thought they must be Communist-party membership cards, the lowest numbers perhaps indicating their owners having been party members longer than the others.

During all of this I seemed to be largely forgotten.

But I knew that was wishful thinking. There was also much telephoning. I didn't have to speak the language to surmise the subject.

After we had been there about two hours, I was escorted out of the building and placed in a military vehicle similar to, but a little larger than, the U.S. jeep. In the front seat were a military driver and civilian. I was in the middle of the back seat, between an officer and an enlisted man. Across the lap of the latter was an automatic weapon with a huge clip. It could have been a carbine but looked more like a submachine gun. He kept his finger in the trigger guard. A second car followed. Once on the road, a third car joined the procession.

Had my flight proceeded uninterrupted, I would have been about two hours from Norway.

Our destination was Sverdlovsk. From the flags, banners, and crowds on the street, it was obvious something was being celebrated. Not until then did I recall the date and remember that May 1 was a Communist holiday.

The building in front of which we stopped—three story, with a severe stone façade—was unmistakably a government building, and would have been recognizable as such in either the United States or Russia. I was taken to a busy office on the second floor. There was no mistaking it, either. Although there were no bars on the windows, and some of the men wore military uniforms, and the others wore civilian clothes, they were far more authoritative and sure of themselves than any of the people previously encountered. They were police of some kind, presumably KGB. At this time I knew nothing about the KGB, other than its initials and that it was some form of Russian secret police. Later I would learn a great deal more than I wished to know. Its full name is Komitat Gosudarstvennoi Bezopasnosti, or Committee for State Security; it is the current descendant of the Cheka, NKVD, and MVD.

These men were professionals. There was another search. And this time they didn't overlook the pin.

The man who found it, however, one of the civilians to whom the others seemed to defer, didn't seem greatly interested. Examining it cursorily, he slipped it into his briefcase.

I was determined to keep that briefcase within sight.

My ears were still ringing. I stuck my finger in one and shook my head, trying to stop the buzzing.

One of the men reached over and slapped my hand down.

It seemed uncalled for and made me mad, although I tried not to react.

A few minutes later I tried to clear my ears again, and again he knocked down my hand. Then I realized they were probably worried that I had a poison capsule in my ear and was trying to get at it.

From their careful examination of both my person and my clothing it was obvious they expected to find some sort of poison on me.

"Are you an American?" one man asked.

Hearing English for the first time startled me. I admitted I was.

Apparently he was the only one who spoke the language, as he acted as translator whenever any of the others asked questions. His English was very poor.

As convincingly as possible, I explained how I had lost my bearings and had flown over the border by mistake.

It was obvious they didn't believe a word of it.

I hadn't really expected that they would. Evidence indicated otherwise. As they brought in items from the wreckage, I had spotted my maps, which I'd hoped had been destroyed in the crash of the plane. Most hadn't. There were even maps I hadn't known were aboard, duplicates someone back at Peshawar had thoughtfully stuck in my pack or on the plane. My route, from Pakistan to Norway, was clearly marked on the set I had been using for navigation. And, from what I could see of them, these seemed to be intact.

Nor was this all. Not only did they have wreckage from the plane, and contents of the seat pack, including the Russian rubles, gold coins, watches, and rings, they also had my flight bag with my shaving kit, clothing, and wallet.

Carrying that had been a mistake, I realized. It showed how complacent we had become. Thinking only of what I would need in Norway, I hadn't considered the possibility that I might not reach my destination. Nor had anyone else thought to stop me from carrying it.

I tried to recall exactly what the wallet contained. There was a Defense Department card, identifying me as a civilian employee of the Department of the Air Force, authorizing medical care and PX privileges, and, I was sure, listing my outfit as Detachment 10-10; a NASA certificate (the National Aeronautics and Space Administration had succeeded NACA in 1958); instrument rating cards; U.S. and international driver's licenses; a Selective Service card; a Social Security card; American, German, and Turkish currency; some U.S. postage stamps; pictures of Barbara; and I wasn't sure what else.

The Social Security and Selective Service cards had been issued in Pound, Virginia; the U.S. driver's license in Georgia. Just from these items, they could put together a pretty accurate profile, provided their intelligence didn't already know just about everything there was to know about the U-2 pilots.

I stuck to my story, untenable as it was.

Occasionally I'd glance at the unbarred windows. Always there was someone standing in front of them. When one man left, another replaced him. They were professionals. They knew the way a prisoner thought.

One thing about the questioning especially disturbed me. Again and again they tried to make me admit I was military, not civilian. I wondered why. Did they think the nature of my mission was something other than espionage? By trying to make me admit I was military, were they trying to establish that my purpose was not spying but aggression, that I was in fact the forerunner of an American invasion of Russia?

I now realized why the agency had hired civilians to fly the missions. It was important that I prove to them that I wasn't military.

Pointing out the card which identified me as a civilian employee of the Department of the Air Force didn't help. Ignoring the word "civilian," they fastened onto "Air Force," repeating it over and over. This was proof I was military!

Possibly it was a trick. But I thought not. The ramifications of what they were maintaining seemed to be far more dangerous than admitting the truth. I dropped my spur-of-the-moment cover story and told them I was a civilian pilot employed by the CIA.

They seemed aware of the organization. But it didn't change their thinking.

During the questioning there had been a number of incoming

and outgoing telephone calls. Because the tone of voice used was becoming increasingly respectful, I assumed my case was being passed up the chain of command. After one call they stopped the questioning and held a hurried consultation.

One of the men took out a pair of handcuffs; after some additional discussion, however, he put them back in his pocket. Someone brought in a poncholike raincoat, and the interpreter told me to slip it on. Since it wasn't raining, I could only presume it was intended to cover my flight suit and make me less conspicuous.

We went downstairs, got into a large limousine, and drove to an airport, stopping by a gate that led out onto the field. One of the men flashed his identification, the guard opened the gate, and we drove right onto the runway, where a jet passenger plane was waiting. From the car, we ran up the ramp, one of the men prodding me in the back so I would move faster. As soon as we were inside, the door was shut, the ramp pulled away, and the engines started.

Four men got on the plane with me; the interpreter, a major, and two civilians, one with the briefcase that held the poison pin. There were no guards as such, although the major had a pistol strapped on his belt.

I asked the interpreter where we were going; he replied, "Moscow."

Although we were alone in the front part of the aircraft, with a curtain shutting off our compartment from the one behind it, there was a stewardess, and when she came through the curtain I could see other passengers and presumed this was a regular commercial flight to Moscow which had been held up pending our arrival.

I was offered some fruit and candy, but had no appetite. Two of the men passed the time playing chess. I eyed the major's pistol, but gave up the idea. Even if I got it, and the holster was fastened, I could do nothing but complicate the situation.

There was no questioning on the plane, and I was grateful for that. I needed the time to plan.

It was while we were en route that I decided upon the course of action I would follow in subsequent interrogations. It was entirely my own idea, and I was not at all sure it would work. But I had to try.

Although unsure of the time, I knew that more than nine hours had passed since my takeoff. They would give me another half-hour, because I had carried that much extra fuel, but after that they would know, beyond a doubt. I could imagine the panic among the crew at Bodö and, after the word was relayed, at Adana.

I wondered how and what they would tell my wife and parents. I had many worries, not only regarding Barbara but also regarding my mother, who had a heart condition.

I was exhausted, more so than I could recall ever having been before, but I couldn't sleep. My wife, my family, the people at Bodö and Adana occupied all my thoughts.

Worrying about them was, I suppose, an escape mechanism, preferable to thoughts of my own predicament.

As for what lay ahead, I knew for sure only one thing. Sooner or later they were going to kill me.

Two

The flight from Sverdlovsk to Moscow took over three hours. After the other passengers had deplaned, I was rushed down the ramp into a waiting limousine.

The frenzy of rushing seemed designed less to hurry than to make sure no one got a good look at me.

The automobile, similar to older-model Buicks, had curtains on its windows so that occupants could look out but outsiders couldn't see in. Again a guard sat on either side.

Our route took us from the outskirts into the capital. Reaching downtown Moscow, we pulled up in front of a pair of large iron doors. The driver blew his horn, someone looked out a peephole, there was a consultation, the doors swung open, and we drove into a courtyard. Behind us the doors closed with a solid sound.

I was inside Lubyanka Prison, headquarters of the KGB.

We stopped alongside a guarded door, and I was escorted through it into an elevator.

It was no ordinary elevator, but divided into two compartments; the back and smaller section was a metal cage. Placed inside this, facing forward, the plate-steel doors slid shut inches in front of my face, leaving me alone in the darkness. It was both light- and soundproof. Although I could feel the elevator's movement, I could neither see nor hear the people in the front compartment.

Thus it was possible to transport two prisoners at the same time, without either being aware of the other.

I began to wonder after all if I had really passed the claustrophobia tests at Lovelace.

From the elevator I was taken down a long, brightly lighted hall into a small room, where I was again stripped and thoroughly searched. Only this time my clothes were kept and I was given a double-breasted black suit several sizes too large, underwear, shirt, socks, shoes. The clothing was all old and worn. The pants were beltless, the shoes loafers, without laces, so I'd have nothing with which to hang myself.

From there I was taken to a large room where some dozen people were waiting. A few wore uniforms, but most were in civilian clothes. There was no doubt they were "big shots." It was interesting how you could distinguish rank, even when never mentioned. I was seated at one end of a long table; a different interpreter and two other men sat alongside. The others remained behind me, out of sight.

There were no harsh light in my eyes, the chair was not uncomfortable, but the interrogation atmosphere was unmistakable.

What was my name? My nationality? My parents' name? My birthplace? What was my military rank? Why had I flown over Russia? On whose orders was I carrying out this act of aggression? What type aircraft had I been flying? Was I alone, or were there other planes? What people was I to contact if I went down? What was my takeoff point? Where had I intended to land? How many times had I flown over Russia?

The tactic I had decided upon was simple. When questioned, I would tell them the truth.

Up to a point. And with definite limitations.

Should the question concern something I was sure they already knew (such as my route, which was on the maps), or something they could easily find out (such as the commanding officer of Detachment 10-10), I would tell them the truth. Establishing a foundation of truthfulness on little things, I could risk lying on the big ones.

The limitations were also important. Although I was prepared to admit having made a number of border-surveillance flights, which were not illegal, I intended to maintain this was my first overflight. If I could convince them of this, vast areas of questioning would be cut off: where the other flights had originated, how many there had been, where they had gone, their intelligence objectives. As a further limitation, I decided to stress, in whatever ways I could, that I was only a pilot, not an intelligence agent or spy, paid only to fly a plane along a certain route, flipping switches on and off at points designated on the map; that I was unfamiliar with the special equipment carried in the plane; nor had I ever been told the intelligence results of my border flights.

As for the "special" missions, I had no intention of mentioning them, knowing that this information could be far more damaging to the United States than any other I possessed.

There was no denying they had captured a U-2 pilot. This didn't mean he had to be particularly knowledgeable or experienced.

My tactics were improvised. No one had briefed me on how to handle such a situation. And I was not at all sure they would work. But I had to try. Too much was at stake to do otherwise.

"Why was this flight flown so close to the Summit meetings? Was this a deliberate attempt to sabotage the talks?"

That caught me off guard. The Summit hadn't even crossed my mind.

I replied that I was sure the flight had nothing to do with the Summit, that had the United States wanted to wreck the talks they needed only not to show up, that sending an airplane over Russia was certainly a roundabout method.

From the way they repeatedly returned to that question, it was obvious someone was obsessed with this explanation. I could make a fairly good guess who.

They refused to believe this was not one of the purposes of the flight.

Just as they refused to believe I was not military.

"At what altitude were you flying when your flight was terminated?"

This was, as far as I was concerned, one of the most important questions they could ask. Having already given it a great deal of thought, I replied, "At maximum altitude for the plane, sixty-eight thousand feet."

This was not one, but two, lies.

The maximum altitude of the U-2 was highly relative. Stripped down, it could reach heights greatly different from those it reached when it carried a variety of equipment and a full fuel load. Sixty-eight thousand feet was not the maximum altitude for the plane in either case.

Nor was it the altitude at which I had been flying during this particular flight.

It was an arbitrary figure I had chosen, close enough to my actual altitude to be credible, I hoped; far enough away so that if the overflights continued, and the Russians used it as a setting for their missiles, they would miss their targets.

This was my greatest fear: that we might resume the flights.

Following the crash of the C-130 in 1958, the Communists had returned the bodies of six men. There had been no mention of the eleven others known to be aboard.

The United States knew the C-130 had been shot down, but they would not necessarily know what had happened to me. Should the Russians choose to say nothing, the agency might well conclude I had developed engine trouble or, considering number 360's fuel-tank problem, run out of fuel and crashed unnoticed in an isolated area.

After a time, hearing nothing, they might well resume the over-flights.

Should they do so, I did not want my fellow pilots to end up as I did.

It was important that they believe me. This was the main reason I decided to answer their questions rather than remain silent. Despite instructions of the intelligence officer ("You may tell them everything because they're going to get it out of you anyway"), all my service training inclined me toward silence.

Yet, as I was well aware, it was a dangerous gamble. It was possible their intelligence had already ferreted out the exact altitude. I was inclined to doubt this: this was one of the most closely guarded secrets of the U-2. Even more dangerous were their radar plots. Everything depended on their accuracy, or rather, lack of it. Previously we had felt their height-finding radar was inaccurate at the altitudes at which we were flying. If we were wrong, they would quickly pinpoint the lie.

The alternative made the risk imperative.

My interrogators were, unfortunately, professionals. From their set expressions I couldn't tell whether they believed me or not.

I was exhausted. As the questioning continued, I had to watch my answers, weighing each carefully to make sure not to make a slip. Just the use of the plural rather than the singular—"overflights" instead of "overflight"—could give away everything.

The biggest problem with lying, I realized, is that you have to remember your lies.

Yet I discovered something else that worked to my favor. Each question and each answer had to be translated. And this not only eliminated the possibility of a barrage of rapid-fire questions, it also gave me extra time, time in which to think, to try to determine the direction of the line of questioning and, if possible, prepare myself.

Also, so long as I didn't do it too often, I found I could interrupt the interrogation, by asking questions myself.

Could I see a representative of the U.S. Embassy?

Not permitted.

The Red Cross?

Not permitted.

Looking around, I suddenly realized that the man with the briefcase had left the room. I had been afraid of this.

Immediately I told the interpreter to warn him to be extremely careful with the pin.

One of the men hurried out to relay the message.

I knew that on closer examination the secret of the pin would be discovered. But I didn't want it to be found through a pricked finger and an accidental death. My situation was bad enough without adding a killing.

And I didn't want to be responsible for the death of any human being, KGB or not.

The man who appeared to be in charge of the interrogation was middle-aged, heavyset, puffy-faced, wore glasses. Later I learned he was Roman A. Rudenko, procurator-general of the USSR, and that following World War II he had been chief prosecutor for the Union of Soviet Socialist Republics in the Nazi war-crimes trials at Nuremberg.

After about three hours the questioning took an unexpected turn. Rudenko offered me a cigarette. I accepted, noticing it was a Chesterfield. He then asked me if I had ever visited Moscow before. I told him no.

"Would you like to take a tour of our capital city?" he asked.

"Yes, I'd like that very much," I replied. I didn't add that anything would be preferable to the questioning, and, although I was not greatly hopeful, that this might provide an opportunity for escape.

"It might be arranged," he said cryptically.

Something had changed. It was hard to define, but for some reason there had been a subtle shift in atmosphere. Everyone became a little friendlier. Realizing that my cigarettes had been confiscated, one of the men gave me a package. At first I thought this was a trick to throw me off guard, that, once I had relaxed, they would throw an unexpected question at me. But there were no more questions. The interrogation was over for the night, the interpreter told me.

I was taken back down the hall and locked into a tiny room. It had no windows, the only furniture a wooden bench built into the wall. Presuming this to be my cell, I lay down and tried to sleep. But a few minutes later a doctor and two guards entered. Again the doctor was a woman. Tall, pleasant-faced, middle-aged, she wore a white smock, stethoscope sticking out of her pocket.

Indicating I was to remove my shirt, she listened to my heart, still beating very rapidly, took my pulse, examined my mouth and throat, checked my breathing, then motioned for me to drop my pants. Embarrassed, I hesitated. One of the guards gruffly barked an order; I complied. She gave me a fairly thorough examination and then indicated I was to dress.

After they left I tried again to sleep, but the guards returned, taking me down another hall into a room obviously a doctor's office. There was an examining table, dentist's chair, heat and solar lamps, medicine cabinet, and table with all the standard paraphenalia—cotton swabs, bandages, antiseptic, distilled water—but with one surprising addition: a huge jar of leeches.

I hadn't realized that in this day and age they were still used.

Another doctor, also female, motioned for me again to take down my pants, as she prepared an injection. My first concern was that the shot was penicillin, to which I was allergic. She seemed to recognize the word and shook her head negatively. My second concern, which I didn't voice, was that it might be truth serum or some sort of drug.

Following the injection, I was taken to a cell about eight feet wide and fifteen feet long. The door appeared to be solid oak, reinforced by plate steel. After another search, the guard went out, slamming the door and locking it.

I was alone. But still under surveillance. There was a small peephole in the door, at eye level, while a light bulb over the door illuminated the room as brightly as if it were day.

Exhausted, my only interest was the bed. It was simple, consisting of a metal frame with crisscrossed iron stripes, each about two inches wide, in place of springs. There were two Army-type blankets and a mattress, the latter very lumpy and thin, in places no thicker than two layers of cloth. It seemed designed to be as uncomfortable as possible, and was.

Though extremely tired, I slept only fitfully. I kept waking, looking around the room, as if to assure myself that it was only a bad dream. But the harsh glare, the stark walls, the locked door, were always there. It was all too real.

Three

The opening of my cell door awoke me. I was surprised to see a little old lady come in. Greeting me in Russian, she set a large tin tea kettle, a cup, and a box of sugar cubes on the table. The guards stood in the doorway, watching.

All appeared curious. I could sense no hostility.

After they left, I poured out some of the liquid, tasted it, found it was hot tea. Although worried about being drugged, my mouth and throat were parched.

As I dressed I realized I felt no ill effects from the shot, which apparently had been for sleep, or perhaps a general immunization given all new prisoners.

The night before, I had been too tired to examine my cell.

The floor was concrete, painted a rusty red, the color extending halfway up the wall. The balance was gray, the ceiling off-white.

At the end opposite the door was a single window. Of opaque glass, reinforced with wire, it opened inward about twenty degrees at the top, providing the only ventilation. Looking at the window up close, I saw it was double. Behind the first pane was a dead-air space of perhaps six inches, probably to retain heat during the winter, then another identical pane. Through it I could see the outline of bars.

Standing in just the right position, I could see out the gap at the top. But my view was limited to a small rectangle including two windows plus a piece of the wall of the building across the courtyard.

As I faced the window, with my back to the door, my bed was on the left. On the right, in the corner nearest the window, was a small table and chair. Along the right wall was a narrow shelf and, below that, pegs on which to hang clothing. There was a light bulb in the ceiling, of the same wattage as the night light over the door. It was on now, the night light off.

These comprised the furnishings.

Although I could find nothing to indicate it, I assumed the cell was bugged. But it would do little good since I was alone and, so far as I knew, didn't talk in my sleep.

The guards returned and took me down the hall to the toilet.

There were two tiers in the cellblock, each with sixteen cells, eight on one side, eight on the other. My cell was on the bottom level, the fourth cell on the right as you entered through the doors that separated the cellblock from the rest of the prison. The guards' desk was in the center of the hall, almost opposite my cell door.

There were two guards on duty. Each wore a pistol. Since they were holstered, I couldn't see what type.

The floor was carpeted, explaining why I could occasionally hear voices from inside my cell but no footsteps.

The toilet was located under the stairway leading to the upper tier, at the end of the hall opposite the entrance.

Handing me a package, the guards locked me in. Although alone, privacy was absent here too. Like the cell door, this one also had a peephole.

The package contained a small towel, a soap dish and soap, toothbrush and powder, a comb, and some coarse toilet paper.

The toilet itself was of the European, that is, stool, type. There were three wash basins, with very cold and extremely hot water. The soap had a sweet strawberry smell. I looked for a mirror, to comb my hair, but there was none. Nor had there been one in my new abode.

On being returned to my cell, I noticed a cover over the outside of the peephole. The guards could look in whenever they chose; I couldn't look out.

Shortly afterward the elderly lady returned with breakfast—a slice of black bread, a boiled egg, and a tiny cube of meat. Having no appetite, I didn't touch it.

Then the guards took me back to the interrogation room.

Many of the same people were there. And most of the questions were exactly the same as those asked the previous night. But there was a difference. Now the questioning was frequently interrupted for conferences, which were not translated. Although unable to understand the words, I got the distinct impression they were unsure as to what they were going to do with me, and debating the various alternatives. This was later borne out when I was shown the interrogation transcripts. Only this session was missing. For the first time since my capture I began to feel a little bit of hope.

After only sporadic questioning, the interpreter told me I was to be taken for a tour of Moscow that afternoon.

Lunch consisted of potatoes and cabbage soup. I was still not hungry.

Following lunch, accompanied by the interpreter, two guards, a driver, and two officials, I rode out of the prison in the same limousine which had brought me there from the airport.

But the relief I had expected to feel once outside the gates wasn't as great as anticipated. Surrounded as I was, my only chance for escape would be to make a run for it when we stopped, but we didn't stop. Still it was good to have the questioning over, even if only temporarily.

For some reason, although I knew better, whenever I thought of the Russian people it was as in Tolstoy's day, the men bearded, the women in black shawls. The streets of Moscow quickly dispelled this notion. Although the clothing was much more drab than in America, the people looked very much the same.

Our route took us past the Kremlin, Moscow University, a large stadium, an immense ski jump located right in the city. But their enthusiasm was less for these things than for the great amount of construction going on, particularly the rising apartment houses. Although they didn't say it, it was clear that housing was scarce.

Their pride in their capital city was obvious. They answered my questions eagerly, as if anxious for me to get the best impression possible. And they had numerous questions of their own, thankfully not about my flight, but the United States. Every aspect of life there seemed to fascinate them.

The mood was definitely easier than it had been, and, sensing it, an idea began to form in my mind. Perhaps I wouldn't be shot after all. Perhaps they were trying to impress me, both with their city and their kindness, because they were soon going to release me.

Maybe it was fantasy, born out of the desperateness of my situation, but it occurred to me that when the Summit talks took place in Paris on May 16, Khrushchev might bring along a surprise. Taking me by the scruff of the neck, he might say, "Here, Ike, is something that belongs to you!"

I would be a great embarrassment to Eisenhower, but a tremendous publicity coup for Khrushchev. See how humane the Soviets are! You send a pilot to spy on us. Do we shoot him? No, we return him unharmed to his family.

Not a single word indicated that this would happen. But the scene was so real I began to believe it would.

Returned to my cell, I could barely contain my elation, not even minding the thorough search, which was already becoming almost routine.

As the hours passed, the fantasy began to dissipate and depression set in. With nothing to read, nothing whatsoever to do, my thoughts began to close in on me.

Although I still had no appetite and left it untouched, supper was a welcome interruption, as was a trip to the toilet.

But after that I was alone.

It was odd. Earlier, out of boredom and curiosity, I had gone to the door and tried to look out the peephole, to see an eyeball staring back at me. It shook me. Yet, even knowing I was being watched, I felt totally alone, in a way I had never felt before, bereft of family, friends.

No one knew where I was. Quite possibly they presumed me dead. There was nothing anyone could do to help me.

In my mind I had already reviewed the possibilities of escape. Even if I succeeded in getting the gun away from one guard and disposing of the other, I would still be locked in the cellblock. There were a half-dozen doors, each locked, each guarded, between me and the street. To escape I would need help, and this was when I felt the loneliness most, for there was no one, absolutely no one, who could—or would—offer that help. I couldn't count on the other prisoners aiding an American spy.

My earliest feelings again became certainty. Although thus far I hadn't been mistreated, there was no reason to feel this situation would continue, and every reason to expect it wouldn't.

I had been a fool to think they would believe my lies. They were experts at this sort of thing; I wasn't even as good as an amateur. Sooner or later they would see through the fictions in my story. Even if they didn't, the end result would probably be the same: I would be tortured and shot, without anyone outside the Soviet Union even knowing what had happened to me.

The day light went off, the night light came on. I had no idea of the time.

Tying my handkerchief around my head like a blindfold to try to keep out at least a little of the light, I lay down, momentarily expecting the guards to come in and tell me this was not permitted. But they didn't. I was left undisturbed.

Though not given to dreams, I had one that night.

I was in The Pound, on my father's farm, walking down the road toward the house with Barbara, my mother, father, and all five of my sisters, when suddenly I felt a severe pain in my leg. As it grew worse, I began falling back, unable to keep up with them. Slow down, I wanted to yell, but for some reason couldn't. Finally the pain became so acute I had to sit down on the edge of the road and watch as my family walked away from me, seeming not to know or care that I was not with them.

I awoke. The pain was real. Because of my lying in one position too long, one of the iron strips had pressed through the thin mattress into the flesh of my leg.

When the guards and the little old lady arrived with the tea, I was already up and dressed. I had been anticipating their arrival, eagerly awaiting it, in fact.

She greated me with *"Zdravstvuite"*; I replied with "Good morning." Pointing to the tea kettle, I asked what it was called, managing to make myself understood. It was a *chænek*.

"Chænek," I repeated.

I'd had my first lesson in Russian.

I felt better than the night before. Whether intentional or not—and I felt sure everything my captors did was for a purpose—leaving me alone had a definite psychological effect. It made me anxious to talk to someone, anyone. I'd have to guard against this, I realized.

But it was, in a way, an unnecessary worry. For that morning, May 3, the interrogations began in earnest. Morning, afternoon, evening, averaging eleven hours per day, seven days per week, they were to continue without pause for nineteen days, then, after a single day's recess, start all over again.

The indecision as to my fate I had sensed on the second day was gone now. As was the friendliness. From this point on everything was quite businesslike, with one objective, to get as much information as possible from the prisoner.

Although the cast occasionally varied, technical experts sometimes sitting in with questions of their own, five people were usually present at the interrogations:

A stenographer. I had expected them to tape-record the sessions. Instead, each word was laboriously transcribed, typed in Russian, then, later, translated and retyped in English. Not too surprisingly, in the process words and phrases changed, whole sentences got lost, meanings distorted. In some instances, intentionally. Thus, questioned about the Defense Department certificate in my wallet and asked if this meant I was an Air Force pilot, my reply, "It means that I was a civilian employee of the Department of the Air Force," became in transcript, "It means that I served in the United States Air Force as a civilian." A small but quite important change.

The interpreter. In his mid-thirties, only he "appeared" to know English. I was never sure about the others.

Two majors, Kusmin and Vasaelliev. Both about thirty, my age, which I suppose was more than coincidence. They handled the bulk of the questioning, working as a carefully rehearsed team. I'd read in detective stories of how American policemen would sometimes grill a suspect, utilizing a Mutt and Jeff routine. While one would be impatient and threatening, his partner would be sympathetic and kind, the prisoner naturally hating the former, but warming to and cooperating with the latter. Although I recognized the tactic, this didn't keep me from succumbing to it, halfway. I hated Major Vasaelliev. But, quite aware that his purpose was exactly the same, I didn't allow myself the luxury of thinking Major Kusmin meant me well.

A colonel. At one point I asked if I could have an attorney present during the questioning. In the United States, I noted, an accused person has that right. The interpreter had pointed to the colonel. As a representative of the prosecutor's office, he was present to see that the interrogation proceeded in accordance with the law. Supposedly an observer, the colonel frequently asked questions himself, including some of the most incriminating. Later, examining transcripts of the interrogations, I would find every one of his questions attributed to someone else.

Although present during the first two interrogations, Rudenko was absent from most of those which followed. During one session, which was conducted by a general rather than the two majors, a short, thin, chain-smoking man of about forty monitored the proceedings. Later I learned his name. He was Aleksandr N. Shelepin, his official title chairman of the State Security Committee under the Council of Ministers of the USSR, or head of the KGB.

(Shelepin was head of the KGB from 1958 to 1961, at which time he was elevated to the Presidium. A Khrushchev protégé and one of the premier's most trusted advisers, later he would betray him, helping arrange his downfall.)

At what altitude was the U-2 flying when the rocket hit you?

About sixty-eight thousand feet, but I'm not sure it did hit me. It could have been a near-miss.

You were hit on the very first shot. You didn't see any other rockets, did you?

No, but then neither did I see this one.

How many flights have you made over Russia?

This was my first.

How many?

Just one.

What is your unit called?

Detachment 10-10.

Where is it based?

Incirlik.

Where is Incirlik?

Adana, Turkey.

How many U-2s are there at Incirlik?

Four or five.

How many U-2 pilots are stationed there?

Seven.

What are their names?

I'm not going to tell you that.

We know them anyway, so you might as well tell us.

Fine, if you already know them, then there's no need for me to tell you.

Did any high-ranking officials ever visit Incirlik?

Occasionally.

Who were they?

General Thomas D. White was one.

Who is he?

I think he's Chief of Staff of the United States Air Force.

Did he visit your detachment?

No, only the base.

Who were the others?

General Frank F. Everest, Commander-in-Chief of the United States Air Force in Europe.

The others?

I can't remember anyone else.

Think. Who else?

Cardinal Spellman.

Did he visit your detachment?

No, neither White nor Spellman did. They only visited the base.

What is the name of the commanding officer of Detachment 10-10?

Colonel Shelton.

Who ordered you to make this flight?

Colonel Shelton.

Who was in charge of planning such flights?

All I know about is the one flight I took. Colonel Shelton handled that.

Who briefed you?

Colonel Shelton.

Who marked the route you were to follow on the maps?

Our navigator.

What was his name?

Major Dulak.

How many navigators are there in the detachment?

Just one.

How many pilots?

Seven.

What are their names?

I told you I wasn't going to answer that.

Where did you learn to fly the U-2?

In the United States.

Where in the United States?

A base on the West Coast.

What is it called?

Watertown.

Who was in charge of your training?

A Colonel Perry.

When did you first arrive at Incirlik?

In 1956.

Who was your commanding officer then?

The same Colonel Perry.

What were the names of your other commanding officers?

The only other one I can remember was a Colonel Beerli.

What is this piece of equipment? What does it do?

I don't know. I told you the pilots were never shown the equipment. (It was part of the radar recording apparatus.)

You said that the purpose of your flight was intelligence. Now—

No. I didn't say that. I said I *presumed* that was its purpose. As far as my own knowledge goes, I don't *know* that to be the case.

You could surely guess?

Yes, I could. But it would be only a guess.

When you were hit by the rocket, did you radio your base and tell them you were bailing out?

I don't intend to answer that question.

Why not?

Because I don't think it to my advantage to do so.

Under Soviet law, complete cooperation, which includes answering all questions truthfully, can be an important factor in mitigating punishment.

That may be so. But I still refuse to answer.

What are the names of the other pilots at Incirlik?
(Silence.)
How many flights have you made over the Soviet Union?
This was my first and, presumably, my last.

The detachment number appeared on my identification; Incirlik was shown on my maps, as well as listed on the U-2 radio channel-ization chart in the aircraft. The visits of generals White and Everest were parts of well-publicized European base-inspection tours, Cardinal Spellman's visit only a stop on his regular Christmas tour— all had been written up in *Stars and Stripes.* Other visitors, unpubli-cized and of far more interest to the Russians, I left unmentioned. NACA had issued a press release identifying Watertown; it was no longer in use as a training base. As for Detachment 10-10's commanders, I presumed it would be relatively easy for the Russians to discover their names, if their intelligence didn't already know them. By crediting each with far more duties than he was actually responsible for—training, planning, operations, intelligence, etc.— I was able to avoid revealing the names of more than a dozen others. Nor was Major Dulak the only navigator.

I didn't want to mention any names. If I had to do so, to make my story seem truthful, I wanted them to be as few as possible.

As for the number of U-2s at Incirlik, I couldn't be sure whether they had the base under surveillance. The number I chose was the number they were likely to see should this be the case. It was not exact. Nor was the number of pilots in the detachment.

Toward the end of the evening interrogation session on May 3, the interpreter asked me why I wasn't eating. I told him I simply had no appetite. Could they get some other food? he asked. They would order anything I wanted, if I would just eat it.

Although not interested in food, I told him I would like something to read.

Noting that there were a number of English books available in Moscow University library, he asked what I wanted.

A Bible, I answered, curious as to whether they would supply it.

He promised to try to obtain one. In the meantime, he had some paperback mysteries, his own personal collection, also a copy of *Gone with the Wind.* He could lend me these if I was interested. I was, definitely.

Deciding to tempt my luck, I also asked if I could have some paper and a pencil. After consulting with the majors, he gave them to me, without asking why I wanted them.

That night I made a calendar. I don't know why—I was not serving out a sentence; on the contrary, each day I checked off might well be my last—but it seemed important to know what day it was. It was a small link with the outside world. One of the only ones I had.

"Yesterday you refused to tell us whether you had radioed your base, reporting you were bailing out. We didn't press you for an answer then, wanting to give you time to consider the benefits of complete cooperation. But you must tell us now."

"I still refuse to do so."

My reasoning was thus: If the Russians thought the United States already knew I had bailed out and was probably alive, they would be much more likely to release the news of my capture than if they were positive my fate was unknown.

On the other hand, I was unsure whether the radio had survived the crash. If it had, by examining it their experts could determine that its maximum range was three to four hundred miles.

It seemed definitely to my advantage to refuse to answer either way.

I wanted my presence here known. I presumed that when I failed to reach Bodö my wife and parents would be notified that I was missing on a flight. I was desperately afraid that, worrying about me, my mother would have a heart attack. Knowing that I was alive and well, even though in a Russian prison, would be easier on her, I felt, than not knowing. The same would be true of Barbara.

Neither way would be easy, but I was powerless to do anything about that.

Just as I had loaded Colonel Shelton with more chores than he could possibly have handled, so did I do the same with "Collins," who became my only CIA contact, something the Russians were inclined to believe, since in their own espionage apparatuses, rarely did an agent know more than one immediate superior.

Actually, in four years I had met a great many agency people, including some of the top planners of the U-2 program, such as Richard M. Bissell, deputy director of the CIA for plans, one of the unmentioned visitors to Detachment 10-10.

By citing Collins, however, I had another, far more important purpose.

"Collins" was a pseudonym. I also knew Collins' real name. And Collins knew I knew it, as did others in the agency.

If the Russians released a story linking me to the CIA, I could be fairly sure the name of my contact would be mentioned. That I referred to him as "Collins," and not by his actual name, should alert him, and the agency, to the fact that I wasn't telling everything.

It had to. It was, as far as I could see, the only way I had of getting the message through.

Asked the time of my takeoff from Peshawar, I told them, 0626 local time. It was on my flight log.

Asked the air speed of the U-2, I told them that, also. On this particular flight it averaged about four hundred miles per hour. Knowing the time and place of my takeoff, the time and place my flight terminated, and the exact number of miles in between the two points, a child could have computed it.

On all such easily traceable details, I was exact.

Asked questions I felt I could safely answer truthfully, I did so. But I didn't volunteer information. There were some things about the aircraft they could learn neither from the wreckage nor from the records of this particular flight. I had no intention of supplying them. Though they knew from the notation on my flight log that takeoff had been delayed one-half hour, I didn't volunteer the reason: that we were awaiting White House approval. One of the last things I wanted to do was give the impression the President himself knew and approved of the overflights. Nor when they were laboring under a misapprehension did I go out of my way to correct it. For example, realizing they had jumped to the conclusion that all our flights out of Pakistan had been made from Peshawar, I saw no reason to recall Lahore.

I told them everything they wanted to know about my childhood and schooling.

I told them when I enlisted in the Air Force, where I was stationed, what planes I flew. But I skipped quickly over my photo-school training and my work as a photo-lab technician, not wanting them to wonder why, with this background, I showed so little interest in the cameras I was carrying. Nor did I find it necessary to mention some other things, such as the secret training at Sandia, where I learned about the construction of atomic weapons, how to load and check them out, different methods of delivery. Nor the target assigned to me behind the Iron Curtain.

As for SAC's operational plans and preparedness in the event of war, I was sure these things had been changed greatly in the past six years. At the same time, though what I knew was probably outdated, I had no desire to fill any possible gaps in their knowledge.

As for when I joined the CIA, I told them, truthfully, in May, 1956—not mentioning the four months of secret meetings in Washington hotel rooms which preceded the actual signing of the contract, or several of the trips which followed.

As for Watertown, though I was quite truthful in describing my flight training, some of the things that would have interested them far more went undiscussed. Such as the number of classes that went through the base and the number of pilots in each, the Greek washouts, the "safe" house on the East Coast and the training given there.

And I said nothing about the "special" flights. This, above everything else, I was determined to keep from them at all costs.

Each night, on return to my cell, I would go over the questions again in my mind, trying to fit together, bit by bit, a composite picture of what they actually knew.

I'm quite sure they were doing the same thing.

It was like a poker game. Each side with its hole cards, hopefully unknown to the other.

Could they tell when I was bluffing? And, equally important, could I tell when they were?

Only it wasn't a game. No poker session ever had such high stakes.

Asked if I had made the overflight on April 9, which they had apparently radar-tracked, I replied that I hadn't. Which was true.

Asked if I knew what its intelligence objectives were, I replied that I didn't. Which was not true. I'd been backup pilot on the April 9 mission.

Asked about the RB-47 flights, I told them I knew only about the U-2s. The RB-47s had, on occasion, flown out of Incirlik.

Asked what I knew about U.S. missiles in Turkey, I told them I had never seen one. Which was not true.

Asked when the first U-2s were shipped to Europe, I replied I had no idea.

Asked when the first U-2 overflight took place, I gave the same, and equally erroneous, reply.

All these were safe bets. They might doubt my answers, but there was no way they could disprove them. So long as I kept my stories straight.

When had I first been told by the CIA that I would not only be flying along the borders but also over Russia? Some months after signing my contract.

When had I been told I would be making the May 1 flight? The night before.

How had I felt about it? Scared.

As much as possible, I wanted to eliminate the element of premeditation.

Had I ever been stationed at Atsugi, Japan?

No, only at Adana, Turkey.

Was I aware that U-2s were stationed at Atsugi?

I had heard that, but didn't know it from personal knowledge.

They showed me articles, in Japanese, on the U-2 that had crash-landed on the glider-club strip. Had I heard about this?

Yes, I admitted, I had, but I didn't know any of the details. I didn't find it necessary to tell them that they were now the proud possessors of that same aircraft. Or what was left of it.

Did I know of any U-2 bases in West Germany?

Yes.

Which bases?

Wiesbaden and Giebelstadt.

Had I ever flown out of either?

I had flown a T-33 trainer to Wiesbaden once. And in 1959 I had ferried a U-2 nonstop across the Atlantic, to a base in New York State, from Giebelstadt.

From the limousine incident, we knew that Giebelstadt had been compromised. From the articles in *Soviet Aviation*, that they also knew of Wiesbaden. Neither base was still in use; it seemed safe to mention both.

Bodö, Norway, was marked on my maps as the destination of my May 1 flight. Who would have met me there?

A ground crew.

Were they from Incirlik?

I didn't know. All I was told was that a crew would be waiting.

Had I ever been to Bodö before?

Yes, in 1958.

Possibly telling them this was a mistake, an unnecessary admission. However, it had been a regular trip, with passports, and clearance through customs, and if their intelligence had the resources we had been told they had, I felt sure they could probably find out.

How long was I at Bodö?

About two or three weeks.

Had I made any flights from there?

No, I replied. I was about to explain that this was due to bad weather but—as would happen far more often than I would have imagined—they interrupted, jumping to their own conclusions.

If I hadn't made any flights, then I must have been there for another reason. And the only possible reason was that I had been sent there to study the landing field in preparation for my May 1, 1960, landing!

It was a ridiculous assumption. How long do you need to study a landing field? If you have a radio, and the operator tells you the field is clear, you land. And even if it were of some benefit to study it in advance—two years? Everything about it could change.

This was really establishing premeditation. I tried to set them straight, but didn't try too hard, not wanting them to examine too closely the related and quite basic fallacy in my own claim that this was my first overflight.

I had stuck to this, through repeated questioning, although, to me at least, its weakness was all too apparent.

If I had arrived in Incirlik in 1956, and hadn't made my first overflight until 1960, it certainly appeared someone was wasting the taxpayers' money.

At least this was the way I was afraid the Russians would look at it. The irony of this was that there were some pilots on the program—in the group which transferred from Japan late in 1957— who had never made a single flight over Russia. Why, I never knew, but some were never assigned overflights.

To make the story more believable, I had stressed the "eavesdropping" missions along the border. Though vague as to exactly when these occurred, or how many there had been—as best I could remember, I told them, I had made one or two in 1956, maybe six to eight in 1957, ten to fifteen each in 1958 and 1959, and several in 1960—I had tried to indicate that they were my primary job. It would have helped make my one overflight story more convincing had I been able to mention the atomic-sampling missions, but, unsure as to whether the Russians knew of these, and not expert enough myself to gauge their importance, I didn't dare risk it.

Their tendency to jump to conclusions also caused them to fall into still another error regarding Bodö, one I made no effort to correct.

In going through the wreckage of the plane, they had discovered, in the cockpit, a large black cloth.

Explain this, they said.

I told them, truthfully, that Colonel Shelton had handed it to me just before I took off and had said to give it to the ground crew at Bodö.

Then this flag was to be used as a sort of password, they interrupted, a way to prove your identity!

Tired from the long questioning, I noted, somewhat sarcastically, that under the circumstances, having a U-2 strapped to my back, it hardly seemed necessary to prove my identity.

But they had already made up their minds. And, in a moment of whimsy, I decided that if they wanted to go on believing it, I'd let them do so, although it was their own conclusion, not mine.

Actually the "mysterious black flag" did have a specific purpose. There was a series of camera windows on the underside of the aircraft. When a U-2 was outside the hangar, where someone might see it, we put metal covers over them. Colonel Shelton hadn't been sure the crew which had been sent to Bodö (every member of which I knew quite well) had remembered to take the covers along and so had given me the cloth and a roll of tape to give them.

It was a tiny little deception. But for some reason, every time it was brought up it gave me a special inner satisfaction, knowing how wrong they could be.

The deceptions were by no means one-sided. I fell into more than a few traps myself. In one of the early interrogations I had noticed one of the majors examining a sheaf of papers. One, which was sticking out, was obviously my flight log.

"Tell me what all these symbols mean on your flight log," he said.

Thinking he was trying to test my truthfulness, since all the symbols were standard flying abbreviations—ETA, ATA, etc.—I tried to recall, item by item, what had been on the log.

Only some days later did I chance to see the flight log again, out of the sheaf, and discover that the bottom half was missing, apparently destroyed in the crash.

There was nothing on it they couldn't have surmised from my maps.

But knowing I had been tricked made me much less complacent.

Ironically, the times they seemed most convinced I was lying, I was telling the truth.

They refused to believe the CIA hadn't provided me with a list of names, addresses, and letter drops to be used to contact the underground in Russia.

They were convinced I must have made short practice flights over the Soviet Union prior to May 1, although my reply—if we were going to take the risks, then why not do the real thing?—seemed self-evident.

They refused to believe this had been my first parachute jump. Their own pilots made actual jumps in training; we must do likewise.

And there were some surprises.

"Are you a good boxer?"

Puzzled, I replied that I wasn't a boxer.

"Then how did you get a black eye?"

Up to this time I hadn't known I had one. Apparently I had blacked it in the crash. Not having seen a mirror, I hadn't realized.

The absence of mirrors was, of course, intentional. You get into the habit of seeing your face each morning. Whether you look well or ill, young or maybe just a trifle older, helps shape your day. Without that reflection, you begin to lose a little of your sense of identity.

It's amazing how much you miss a simple thing like a mirror.

There were other psychological tricks. The unbarred window in the interrogation room was one. It was always there, offering the tantalizing possibility of escape, even if only a seven-story plunge to the courtyard. Yet, no sooner would the man in front of it step away than another man would replace him, as if to say, much more effectively than in words: For you there is no escape.

Little things. No mirrors. An unbarred window. But they got to you.

"Were you nervous about your earlier flights over Russia?"

"I told you, this was my first such flight. And, yes, I was nervous."

"Even if this was your first flight, surely the pilots talked among themselves, discussed their experiences, mentioned what they had seen?"

"No, we had been ordered never to discuss our flights. And we obeyed orders."

Again and again they returned to the question, as if hammering on a locked door, knowing that if they could succeed in opening it a treasure trove awaited them on the other side.

They wouldn't give up. Neither would I.

In law, ignorance is no excuse.

In interrogation, it can be a godsend.

Time after time my safest refuge was the simple phrase "I don't know."

Using it, I could deny knowing who in Washington authorized the U-2 overflights; in what manner the flight orders were transmitted to Incirlik; what happened to the intelligence data once a flight returned; how many U-2s there were and where based.

And—of prime importance—I could deny knowing how many flights there had been before May 1, the dates on which they had taken place, and what their target objectives were.

Some of the most valuable information I possessed concerned these earlier flights. If the Russians learned it, a great deal of what we had accomplished through the U-2 program could be negated. For the value of intelligence lies not only in knowing what the enemy is doing; often of equal—and sometimes even greater—importance is their not knowing that you know.

If the Russians thought we had made ten overflights, and we had actually made more, we possessed an advantage.

If they thought we had made ten, and we had actually made fewer, the advantage was still ours.

The same was true if the number were a hundred or a thousand.

It was possible they had radar-tracked all of the overflights. But I couldn't risk making that assumption.

Repeating "I don't know" so often probably made me seem stupid, uncurious, unobserving.

For once I was quite happy to give that impression.

Yet one lie, exposed, could bring down the while structure.

Even worse was the realization that, once it was discovered, they might not even bother to confront me with it.

That the walk might not be to the interrogation room but to some soundproof courtyard.

No, it was not a game.

Four

W ith the crossing off of May 7, I finished my first week in Lubyanka Prison. By now the days had developed into a routine, some of the strangeness had worn off, and I began to observe things missed earlier.

If the wind was right, I could hear the Kremlin clock strike six A.M. This was also the time the night light went off, the day light came on, and I was to get up.

Hot tea was followed by a trip to the toilet, then breakfast.

Several times I tried to eat. I would pick up the food, taste it, and put it down. I did drink the tea, however—hot in the morning, cold the rest of the day.

As utensils I was given a fork and spoon but, for obvious reasons, no knife.

After breakfast a doctor or nurse would arrive. Did I realize I had eaten nothing for a whole week? Yes. Was it because I didn't like the food? No, I just had no appetite. This quite obviously worried my captors. They were anxious that I not ruin my health. At least not yet.

Without access to a scale I couldn't tell how much weight I had lost, but it was a good amount, since I had to knot my pants at the waist to keep them up. I was far more worried about my heart. It would beat irregularly, all at once stop, then a big beat, and back into sequence again.

It was ironic. I was convinced that sooner or later they were going to shoot me. At the same time, I was worried about an irregular heartbeat, which might take me off flying status.

After the doctors left I would be allowed to shave. There was an electrical outlet outside the cell. The guard would plug in the electric razor, hand it to me, then stand in the door watching until I was through. Without a mirror I had to learn to do it through feel.

Then I would be escorted to the morning interrogation.

I never saw another prisoner. Elaborate precautions had been taken to ensure that there were no chance encounters. The elevator cage was just one such precaution. In each of the halls, in both the prison and the administration building, was a series of three lights—white, green, red. The white light was strictly for illumination, since it was on all the time. The green light indicated the passageway was clear. When the red light was on, however, it meant another prisoner was being escorted down the hall. Whenever this happened, I was quickly placed in an empty cell until after they had passed.

Occasionally, en route or returning, I'd pass a cell whose door was open, indicating its occupant had been taken out. Looking inside, I could see clothing, the kettle on the table, books on the shelves. For some reason all the beds looked more comfortable than mine.

Morning interrogation always began the same way. I was asked to initial each page of the interrogation record of the previous day.

But they're in Russian, I argued, and I can't read Russian.

That does not matter. It is required.

Finally, seeing my argument was without effect, I gave in, at the same time pointing out that with no knowledge of the language it was a ridiculous, meaningless procedure, certifying nothing.

That might be. But it was required.

They were incredibly bureaucratic. Many things were done not because of necessity but because these were the rules. And they were not about to question them. Even if they made no sense.

After the first several days there had been a welcome addition to the routine. Following lunch I would be taken up onto the roof for about fifteen minutes of exercise.

The roof, which I estimated was on about the twelfth floor of the prison, five stories above my cell, was divided into tiny courtyards about fifteen by twenty feet each. High walls separated them. Atop the walls a lone guard patrolled with a submachine gun.

The adjacent administration building was three or four stories taller than the prison. From the antennae on the roof, I guessed the upper floors to be the KGB's communication center. Sometimes I'd see people standing in the windows looking out.

One thing struck me as unusual. Along the side of the building, workers were scraping paint off the storm gutters. Although it was a high building and the work looked very dangerous, all were women.

It reminded me a little of the old WPA. No one seemed in any great hurry to get the job done—a typical government project.

Up here, where I could see the open sky, my thoughts were often on escape. Yet the more I thought about it, the more hopeless it seemed. The walls were too high to climb. The guard and his submachine gun remained well out of reach.

Occasionally, although talking was forbidden, the guard would speak to someone in one of the other courtyards. The replies were always in Russian, never English. Were there any other Americans here? I wondered. And if there were, how could I get a message to them? I'd already ruled out one possibility—leaving a note. The guard would spot it.

There were two things in my courtyard that especially interested me.

The walls were covered with tin. One rusty piece was loose. Each time I came up, I checked to make sure it was still there. If things got really bad, I intended to wait until the guard was looking the other way, then break it off. Since I was searched after each walk, getting it to my cell would be a problem. I had noticed, however, that during the searches the guards were frequently lax, not bothering to make me take off my shoes.

I'd have to wait until the same day I intended to use it because my cell was searched also. One morning I'd arranged my paper and pencil in such a way as to tell if they had been moved during my absence. They had. Apparently they were interested in learning what I was writing, and must have been disappointed to find only doodling and a calendar.

I'd asked for permission to write letters. It had been denied.

The other thing in my walk area which interested me greatly was my "garden." The prison was an old building. Over the years thousands of feet had paced these courtyards, wearing down the cement, leaving dirt in the cracks between the slabs. Carried by the wind, seeds had lodged in the crevices and, now that it was spring, had sprouted and begun to grow into weeds. After a rain the water would accumulate in little puddles. The problem was getting it to my garden. Then I devised a technique. I'd stand in the puddles until the soles of my shoes were wet, then flip the water on the weeds as I walked by.

Each day I'd watch their growth. When several days passed with no rain, I'd become very despondent, afraid they were dying.

Occasionally, rather than taking the elevator, the guard would walk me back down the stairs from the roof. It was this way I discovered that most of the prison was not in use: there were guards on only a few of the floors.

There was one other break from routine. Every five days I would be allowed to take a shower, and issued clean underwear and socks.

The water was scalding hot. I luxuriated in it, remaining until the guard ordered me out. The soap was of the homemade variety, like the kind my grandmother used to make on the farm.

The first time I was taken to the shower room, the guard had pointed to a large tub. It was filled with something greenish-brown and slimy. Not understanding what he meant, I had ignored it, but later asked the interpreter what it was. He roared with laughter, as did the others when he translated my question.

It was seaweed, he explained. Russians used it as a washcloth.

I tried it once; it *was* slimy, and thereafter I decided to forgo this particular native custom.

Afternoon interrogation; supper; toilet; evening interrogation, toilet; than I was alone and could read. The mysteries were American paperbacks, by Agatha Christie, Ellery Queen, Rex Stout, and others. I'd finish one each night; then, when I had gone through all, I would go back and read them over again. And again.

I owe those authors my sanity.

At ten P.M. the light in the ceiling went out and the light over the door came on. There was no attempt to regulate my activities within the cell. Often I'd read until the streets were silent and I could hear the Kremlin clock.

Thus were my days and nights spent.

Hour after hour, session after session, the interrogations continued. As the experts studied the wreckage, there were new questions. Usually, however, they were the same old ones, rephrased, approached from a different direction, in an attempt to catch me off guard, or simply repeated, over and over:

"Your identification says you work for the Air Force. Your maps are stamped 'Confidential: U.S. Air Force.'" Among the items in my survival pack was a set of maps of the Soviet Union. Originally stamped "Confidential" and "U.S. Air Force," someone had thoughtfully scissored out these identifying marks. Someone else, however, had apparently stuck another set in the cockpit, identical to the first, but with the marks left on them.

They'd go on: "You were flying an Air Force aircraft: half the parts are labeled 'Department of Defense.' You took off from an Air Force base. Your detachment commander was an Air Force colonel. Why do you continue to maintain that you are a civilian?"

If I wanted to stop the interrogation and think a bit, I would ask them a question about the Soviet Union. They would usually take time to answer it. And often such questions led to inquiries about the United States.

Mostly these were easy to answer, and bought me more time. Occasionally, however, a question would stop me cold. One such was: "What is the difference between the Democratic and Republican parties?"

I had to confess that I didn't know the answer, that it stumped even the political scientists.

As other delaying tactics, I could request a glass of water or ask to be taken to the toilet. Realizing that they could interpret these interruptions to mean that I was avoiding answering a question, I used them sparingly, not to avoid a particularly bothersome query but when I was concerned about the direction in which a line of questioning was heading.

Occasionally they came close to extremely sensitive subjects, then veered away.

Often I led them off. I was surprised how easy it was to change the subject. The safest way was to begin talking about something related and interesting. Usually they would get back to the original topic, but often it would be a day or two later, after they had had time to reread the interrogation records.

But what amazed me most were the questions never asked. For example, although they knew I had been assigned to the Strategic Air Command, it never seemed to occur to them I might have had training in the use of atomic weapons.

I had worried about this question, trying to foresee ways they might trap me into an unintentional admission. Instead, it never came up, while some areas even touchier were passed over quite casually.

In many ways their thinking was highly parochial. I was never asked, for example, about U-2 flights over Communist China, Albania, or other Eastern European countries. Had I been, I could have answered, quite honestly, that I had no personal knowledge of such flights. But that they never asked was indicative of their single-mindedness. And on these and other areas, I wasn't interested in expanding their horizons.

One session, they brought in an American road map and asked me to point to Watertown. They already knew its location, they warned me. They just wanted to see if I was telling the truth.

I pointed to a spot in the desert, neglecting to mention that the map was of Arizona, not Nevada.

Such slips on their part made me question seriously the quality of their intelligence.

Perhaps they intended it that way. But I think not. It was to their advantage to have me believe them omnipotent.

Thinking this over, I began to wonder if we weren't greatly overrating their espionage skills.

As the interrogation continued, this conviction grew.

We had presumed the Russians knew a great deal about the U-2 program. Our intelligence officers had assured us that they probably not only had spies who noted every time we took off and landed, but that the KGB might well have a file on each of the pilots.

"They probably know more about you than you know about yourself," was one comment I recalled.

In attempting to get me to reveal the names of the other pilots, they had claimed already to know them. Yet the one thing that would have convinced me—the mention of a single name other than mine—was never tried. Which convinced me they didn't know.

Overrating an enemy can be just as serious an error as underrating him. Because I had been led to believe that the Russians knew more about us than they probably did, I undoubtedly told them things they didn't know, gave them information which, had we been realistic as to their capabilities, need never have been mentioned.

In retrospect, I regret most having named Colonel Shelton. Not because the information mattered one way or the other to the Russians, but because following the release of the news, he was transferred to an obscure duty assignment at a base in upper Michigan.

That what I told the Russians was a great deal less than I had been told to tell them, and that I withheld the most important information in my possession, was not the point. We should have known better.

From an intelligence standpoint, this was another bad mistake.

I'd known the moment was coming. But I had hoped it could be postponed just a little longer.

"Our technical experts have been studying the radar plots of your flight. And they have some questions about your altitude."

It was obvious they had already been given considerable study. Someone had even transposed my coordinates onto a map. Looking at it, I felt a flicker of encouragement. They had me off course far more often than I actually was.

But it was the height-finding radar that most worried me.

All the measurements were in meters. Nervously I waited as they translated them into feet.

As they read the figures, I began to disbelieve them. Surely this was some cruel hoax, designed to throw me off guard. No one could be so lucky. Not only was their height-finding radar off—the figures were up, down, above, below—but some were actually at sixty-eight thousand feet!

It took a tremendous effort to hide my relief. This part of my story had been verified and proven true by their own evidence.

And it was a lie!

Reading, I would see the words, follow the lines, turn the pages. But my thoughts were elsewhere.

If I hadn't made the flight that day, what would I be doing now?

Probably drinking an icy cold drink rather than lying here imagining one.

But this was no good, I knew. Because if I hadn't made it, someone else would have. And there were none of my friends on whom I would wish this.

For a few more minutes I'd read, really concentrating on the words. Then a wave of depression would sweep over me. And I'd again think the forbidden thoughts, the ones I tried so hard to avoid.

Like imagining what Barbara was doing now.

Or, subtracting eight hours, picturing what was happening at home in Virginia.

Or, worse, I would visualize the base, and see a pilot, someone I knew, being awakened by the message center and getting ready to report to Prebreathing to prepare for a flight. Unaware that the Russians now had missile capability.

Convincing the Russians that the U-2s flew at sixty-eight thousand feet wasn't enough, I realized. It might save someone from flying into a preset trap. But I had been shot down, and I had been at my assigned altitude.

Some way I had to get word back to the agency that Russia did have a rocket capable of reaching us.

From what I had been taught about brainwashing, I had anticipated certain things: I would be lectured about Communism, given only propaganda to read. Food would be doled out on a reward-punishment basis: if I cooperated, I would be fed; if I didn't, I wouldn't. Interrogation would be at odd hours, under bright lights. No sooner would I fall asleep than I would be awakened, and it would start all over again, until eventually I lost all track of time, place, identity. And I would be tortured and beaten until, finally, I would beg for the privilege of being allowed to confess to any crime they desired.

None of this had happened. And yet, more than anything else, the loneliness began to get to me. When in the cell. Even in the interrogation room, surrounded by people.

Later, after having asked some questions about Communism as a stalling tactic during an interrogation, I was given a book on the subject. It was a Penguin paperback, published in England, and written by a British M.P.

One day in the midst of questioning I suddenly interrupted myself in mid-sentence and said, "Why should I talk to you? You're going to kill me anyway. Why should I bother answering your questions, when, as soon as you have everything you want, you're going to take me out and shoot me? Why should I even open my mouth when there's no way out of this for me?"

"There may be a way," one of the majors said.

"If there is, I can't see it," I replied. "As far as I can see, my situation is hopeless."

"There may be a way."

"Then tell me what it is!"

"You just think about it."

"I have, for hours at a time. And I can't see any way out except death."

"There may be another way. You go back to your cell and think about it."

I did. And I knew it had to be one of two things. That I defect to Russia or that I become a double agent.

At our next session the major asked me if I had thought about the matter we had discussed. I said I had, and that I still couldn't figure out what he meant.

With that the subject was dropped.

Obviously they didn't want to make the suggestion themselves. If made, it would have to be my idea.

I hoped they were holding their breaths.

Torture, I decided, would be better than not knowing.

On Tuesday, May 10, on being taken to the morning interrogation, I told my inquisitors that I would refuse to answer further questions, on any subject, until I had proof the American government had been informed I was alive.

Refusing to back down, I was returned to my cell. That afternoon, when the guard unlocked the door and motioned me out, I had the feeling this might be my last walk.

Instead I was taken to a larger interrogation room. Rudenko and a number of other people were present. The interpreter had a copy of *The New York Times*, dated Sunday, May 8, only two days ago. He then read from a speech purportedly made by Khrushchev in which he said: "We have parts of the plane, and we also have the pilot, who is quite alive and kicking. The pilot is in Moscow, and so are the parts of the plane."

"Can I see the paper?" I asked.

"Not permitted."

"You could be making that up. Or you could have had that paper printed right here in Moscow."

They brought out other U.S. papers, quoting from interviews giving the reactions of my wife and both my parents to the news. My wife, the articles said, had been flown back to Milledgeville, Georgia, where her mother lived. The comments of my mother and father were so typical that I couldn't doubt their veracity. "I'm going to appeal to Mr. Khrushchev personally," my father said, "to be fair to my boy. As one old coal miner to another, I'm sure he'll listen to me."

I couldn't help it. I broke down and cried.

My interrogators didn't know what to make of this. But they weren't experiencing the relief I felt.

Just knowing that my family knew I was alive and thinking of me, I was suddenly no longer as alone.

Back in my cell, realizing that Khrushchev had released the news of my capture, that it had appeared on the front page of *The New York Times* and other papers, I began to sense for the first time that in the outside world this was not being treated as just another instance of a plane being shot down. That this was to be no ordinary case.

Five

The release of news of my capture marked a turning point in the interrogations: they became tougher. Now I had to try to outguess not one adversary but two: Russian intelligence, and the American press.

"You lied to us!"

The blunt accusation stunned me. "What do you mean?"

They had caught me at something, but what? The actual altitude of the U-2, the number of overflights I'd made? These and a dozen other possibilities ran through my mind as I waited for the interpreter to translate the reply.

"You told us you had never taken a lie-detector test. But it says right here, in *The New York Times*, that you did!"

I *had* lied about that: I didn't want them suggesting that inasmuch as I had already taken one such test, I certainly couldn't object to another.

At the time it had seemed a safe lie. It was the kind of information I felt sure they would have no way of checking. I hadn't counted on a newspaper giving it to them, for ten cents.

"It says here that all the CIA job applicants are required to take polygraph tests."

"That may be true of the agents," I replied. "But we were pilots. Hired to fly airplanes."

From then on each familiar question became charged with a hidden meaning. Why were they asking that again? Did it mean they had learned something?

Often it did.

"You told us the U-2's maximum altitude is sixty-eight thousand feet. Yet this newspaper says the plane 'can actually rise to close to one hundred thousand feet'! How do you explain that?"

"The writer of that article has never flown a U-2. I have."

There was one saving grace. Given two contradictory statements, they had to make a choice. Although I couldn't be sure, I felt they were often inclined toward accepting my version, since I had proven truthful on the things they could verify. Nor was this particular contradiction a dangerous one: other newspapers and magazines gave the U-2's maximum altitude as ninety, eighty, seventy, sixty-five, sixty, and fifty-five thousand feet.

Yet, in my particular situation, the incorrect information was often as dangerous as the correct, especially since it was often attributed to "an authoritative government source." If they were getting their questions from the newspapers, a fantastic amount of misinformation was being published. While much of it was undoubtedly conjecture, I wondered whether some of it might have been intentionally "leaked" by the agency. But from the way they quizzed me, in bits and pieces, never letting me see the papers themselves, it was impossible to discern the background pattern. All I knew was that the U-2 had become world news.

While I was most anxious to read the newspapers, I came to dread the sight of them.

"See," Major Vasaelliev would say, brandishing a paper, "there's no reason for you to withhold information. We'll find it out anyway. Your press will give it to us."

Often they did. From American newspapers they learned that Watertown was in Nevada, not Arizona; that flights had been made from English bases; that the U-2s were used to measure fallout from Soviet hydrogen-bomb tests.

"Did you know that President Eisenhower personally authorized the flights over Russia?"

"No, I didn't. Is that true?"

A trick? Or had the incident become much bigger than I suspected?

With the release of the news, there was another change: gradually nature took over, and I began to eat again. At first it was only a cup of yoghurt at breakfast and lunch, but before long I was even trying the foul-smelling fish soup. Though I never found any pieces of fish in it, from the aroma it was obvious a very ripe one had at least swum through.

I estimated my weight loss to be between ten and fifteen pounds. The heart palpitation remained, however, and that worried me.

As did what was going on in the United States.

Toward the middle of May, I received additional clues. I was taken out of the prison for the second time, to examine the wreckage of the plane. A display had been set up in a building in Gorky Park. On the walls were large signs in Russian and English, the latter reading: THIS IS WHAT THE AMERICAN SPY WAS EQUIPPED WITH; POWERS FRANCIS GARY THE PILOT OF THE SHOT AMERICAN PLANE; AMMUNITION AND OUTFIT OF THE AMERICAN SPY. Below the signs were displays with my maps; identification; parachute, helmet, pressure suit; survival gear—knife, pistol, ammunition, first-aid kit.

The poison pin was prominently displayed. As were the gold coins and flag reading "I am an American . . ." in fourteen languages.

Accompanied by an interpreter, stenographer, and a dozen technical experts, I was questioned about each piece of equipment. If it was a standard aircraft part, such as the tachometer, I'd identify it readily. But if part of the special equipment, I'd examine it curiously, as if seeing it for the first time.

And in a sense I was. Never before had I realized how identifiable everything on the plane was. The engine was stamped "Pratt & Whitney"; the camera bore, in addition to its model number, focal length and other specification, the name plates of its U.S. manufacturers; the destruct device was labeled "DESTRUCTOR UNIT, Beckman and Whitley, Inc.," with the penciled-in date on which it had been received at Incirlik—August, 1959; the radio parts had the trademarks of General Electric, Sylvania, Raytheon, Hewlett-Packard, and others.

Nor was it surprising that they kept insisting I was military. The granger was stamped "MILITARY EQUIP." A sign under the fueling hatch read: "Fuel only with MIL-D-25524A. Permission to use emergency fuel and climb limitations must be obtained from Director of Matériel."

No effort had been made to disguise the nationality of the plane. Yet, had the destruct device been used, only a small portion of the aircraft, that containing the surveillance equipment, would have been destroyed. Again it seemed no one had really considered the possibility the plane might go down in hostile territory.

The aircraft itself was a mess, some parts missing entirely. The instrument panel revealed indications of a fire in the cockpit, but apparently a small one, since the maps and other papers were merely singed. The wings and tail were displayed separately from the battered fuselage. I was especially interested in examining the tail, to determine whether there was evidence it had been shot off. But there were no scorch marks, and the paint was intact.

Everything I saw confirmed my belief that the aircraft had not been hit, but disabled by a near-miss.

Seeing the display, I no longer had any doubt that the Russians were exploiting the incident for maximum propaganda value.

From being worried that no one knew I was alive I had gone full circle to being much too well known. I was not at all sure it was a desirable change.

Shortly after this I was informed I would be tried for espionage under Article 2 of the Soviet Law on Criminal Responsibility for Crimes Against the State. Maximum penalty, seven to fifteen years' imprisonment, or death.

This aroused no great hope. Before, they could have killed me and no one would have been the wiser. Now they would have to observe the amenities. But the end result would be the same. After a secret trial, I would be shot.

Could I see an attorney now? The investigation is not yet completed. When will it be completed? When we have learned everything we wish to know.

With the press each day adding to their knowledge, I knew that sooner or later they would succeed in trapping me in one or more lies. Should that happen, they would question everything I had already told them. Thus far I had succeeded in withholding the most important information in my possession. But this didn't mean I could do so indefinitely. There were other ways to make me talk.

One reason I was so concerned was an incident that had occurred a few nights earlier.

Because the bed was so uncomfortable, I always slept fitfully. Very late that night I had rolled over and opened my eyes, to find one of the guards in my cell. It startled me. Seeing I was awake, he picked up my ashtray, indicating it was smelling up the cell. Another guard was standing in the doorway. After handing it to him to empty, the first guard then returned it to the table, closed and locked the door. I returned to sleep, only to reawaken sometime later, in a haze, seeing him there again. This time he left without explanation.

Nothing like this had happened before. Once locked in my cell at night, I had been left alone. It bothered me. Had I dreamed it? No. There was the empty ashtray. Perhaps his excuse was true. But if so, why had he returned? Since, so far as I knew, neither guard spoke English, the idea that I was talking in my sleep and they were trying to listen seemed unlikely, as did the possibility that they feared I had obtained a weapon or some other contraband and were searching my cell. Still another explanation occurred to me. That I might have been drugged. For the first time, I seriously wondered.

The incident remained unexplained. But it made me more anxious than ever that they not doubt my story.

My interrogators now held most of the cards. They knew what had happened since my capture. I didn't. Each new question increased the possibilities of contradiction, exposure. In some way I'd have to further limit those possibilities.

Notification of the pending trial gave me the excuse I needed. Since I was to be tried for my May 1 activities, I now refused to answer any questions, of whatever kind, on anything happening prior to that date.

This would count against me in the trial, they warned. Reading the appropriate section of their criminal code, they pointed out, as they had on many previous occasions, that the only possible mitigating circumstances in my case were: (1) voluntary surrender; (2) complete cooperation; and (3) sincere repentance.

I had surrendered voluntarily. But as for the last, I had already repudiated that.

Earlier in the questioning, they had asked me if, having it to do over, I would have made the flight. Yes, I replied, were it necessary for the defense of my country.

Since I was unrepentant, the only things now in my favor were my voluntary surrender and complete cooperation.

I stuck to my resolve. I would discuss nothing that happened prior to May 1.

Perhaps it was in an attempt to change my mind that they now decided to make a radical departure.

For the first time since my capture more than two weeks before, they raised the Iron Curtain, giving me a glimpse at what had happened outside Russia.

It was much too good a story to keep to themselves. They had to brag about it. Thus I finally learned from my interrogators what the rest of the world had long known.

On May 2 the public information officer at Incirlik AFB, Adana, Turkey, had released the news that an unarmed weather reconnaissance aircraft, of the U-2 type, had vanished during a routine flight over the Lake Van area of Turkey and that a search for the missing plane was in progress. During his last radio communication, the pilot—a civilian employee of Lockheed on loan to NASA—had reported trouble with his oxygen equipment.

This was the cover story the CIA had prepared for such an eventuality.

Nobody had ever bothered to share it with the pilots.

The next several days brought further details from NASA, including information that all U-2s had been grounded to have their oxygen equipment checked.

On May 5, in a speech before the Supreme Soviet in Moscow, Premier Khrushchev had announced that on May Day an American plane, in "an aggressive provocation aimed at wrecking the Summit Conference," had invaded Soviet territory and, on his personal orders, been shot down by a missile.

Just that. Nothing more.

The trap had been baited.

The same day NASA announced that the U-2 previously reported missing from Incirlik might have strayed across the border on automatic pilot while its pilot—now identified as thirty-year-old Francis

G. Powers, of Pound, Virginia—was unconscious from lack of oxygen.

On May 6 a U.S. State Department spokesman uncategorically stated to reporters that "There was no—N-O—deliberate attempt to violate Soviet air space, and there has never been." The suggestion that the United States would try to fool the world about the real purpose of the flight was "monstrous."

While a formal note of inquiry was sent to the Soviet government, requesting additional information as to the fate of the pilot, various U.S. senators and congressmen waxed indignant over the shooting down of the unarmed weather plane. That Khrushchev could order such action so close to the Summit was a clear indication of bad faith.

Apparently it was presumed by almost everyone, including the agency, that I had not survived the crash.

On May 7 Premier Khrushchev sprang his trap. "Comrades, I must tell you a secret," he confided to the Supreme Soviet, and the world. "When I was making my report, I deliberately did not say that the pilot was alive and in good health and that we have got parts of the plane. We did so deliberately, because had we told everything at once, the Americans would have invented another version."

The pilot was "quite alive and kicking," he had confessed that he was an agent of the Central Intelligence Agency, and, acting on orders of his detachment commander, a United States Air Force colonel, had flown on a spying mission over Russia, taking off from Peshawar, Pakistan, intending to land at Bodö, Norway. Only en route, when over Sverdlovsk, he had been brought down by a Soviet rocket. Flying at twenty thousand meters (65,000 feet), he had thought himself to be safe from rockets. But his capture had proven otherwise.

With great glee Khrushchev debunked "official" U.S. statements about the plane:

"If one believes the version that the pilot lost consciousness owing to oxygen trouble and that the aircraft was subsequently controlled by the automatic pilot, one must also believe that the aircraft controlled by the automatic pilot flew from Turkey to Pakistan, touched down at Peshawar Airport, stayed there three days, took off early in the morning of May 1, flew more than two thousand kilometers over our territory for a total of some four hours."

Nor was Khrushchev finished setting traps. He noted it was possible President Eisenhower was unaware of the flight. But if so, that meant the militarists in his country were actually "bossing the show."

Thus Eisenhower was left with two choices, neither pleasant: to admit he had authorized espionage, an unprecedented admission for a President to make, or to deny knowledge of the flights, with the clear implication that he wasn't in charge.

In reaction, the U.S. State Department then admitted that the U-2 had probably made an information-gathering flight over Soviet territory, but stressed that "there was no authorization for any such flight" from authorities in Washington.

What happened behind the scenes—the setting up of a scapegoat to be blamed for the whole incident; CIA head Allen Dulles' offer to resign and take responsibility for the flight; President Eisenhower's vacillation, finally culminating in his unprecedented decision—I was not to learn until much later.

What I was told, however, was that on May 11, two days after Secretary of State Christian Herter stated that specific U-2 missions were not subject to Presidential authorization, the President of the United States himself admitted he had personally approved the flights. Espionage was, he said, "a distasteful but vital necessity," mandatory because of Soviet secrecy, the rejection of his Open Skies Plan of 1955, and to avert "another Pearl Harbor."

The President of the United States had pleaded guilty for me.

Yet, because I had no doubt as to my ultimate fate, this concerned me far less than one other thing my interrogators told me.

Both Secretary of State Herter and Vice-President Nixon had stated publicly that the flights over Russia would continue.

To me this was the most incredible thing of all. They now knew I had been shot down, that Russia did indeed have missile capability, yet other pilots were to be sent on overflights anyway!

I was still reacting from the shock of this, when, on May 16, I received some news more current.

The Summit talks had collapsed. And I was responsible.

Lacking a meeting point on the Berlin question, no one had anticipated much from the Summit. But there had been a slim chance something would come of it, that the world might move just a little bit closer to peace.

That I was responsible for destroying this possibility shook me, hard. It still does.

With this revelation, the Iron Curtain again descended. Whatever was happening beyond the borders of my very small world, I wasn't told about.

But I had been left with more than enough to think of.

Although greatly depressed by the news, at least one portion of it was encouraging. I now knew that by May 7, the day on which Khrushchev announced my capture and details of my flight, my interrogators had bought my story, believed I was telling the truth, even to altitude, Khrushchev's use of twenty thousand meters being the closest approximation to the sixty-eight-thousand-feet figure I had used.

From this alone the CIA should know I hadn't told everything.

The problem, however, was that the Iron Curtain worked both ways. It not only denied me knowledge of what was happening in the rest of the world; it also kept the agency from knowing exactly how much I had told the Russians.

There were things I knew which, if revealed, would create a far greater incident than had taken place. That this hadn't happened should indicate to them I was still withholding the most important information. Yet, in consideration of Khrushchev's trap, they couldn't be sure. Maybe I had told everything, with Khrushchev only awaiting a more opportune time to reveal it.

There were at this moment, I was sure, some very nervous people in the United States government.

There was no way I could set their fears at rest.

On Sunday, May 22, I awoke with a bad cold, so hoarse I could barely speak. Interrogation was canceled.

It was my first day off after twenty-one days of questioning. Despite the cold, I thoroughly enjoyed the respite.

I was treated with the sun lamp and given extra time on the roof. My weed garden was thriving. All day I was able to rest and read. On Sunday the head guard was off; the other guard and the old woman who brought the meals came into my cell and tried to converse with me. We managed only a few words, but that they even ventured such a thing was encouraging.

Small pleasures all, but greatly appreciated.

The next morning the interrogations resumed.

Now, with a trial in the offing, there was a greater effort to shape my answers.

They were determined to make me say I had been hit on the first shot—so insistent that I seriously doubted it was true.

The granger also became a matter of dispute. Hadn't my detachment commander assured me that it would break the radar lock on both air-to-air and surface-to-air missiles?

No, only those fired by aircraft. Nothing had been said about SAMs.

I could see what they were getting at. Here the Americans used their foremost scientific know-how to create an electronic device to thwart all our rockets—and their best still wasn't good enough.

I was not about to give them that satisfaction.

Two other pieces of "equipment" also received an undue amount of attention.

One was the destruct device. Why hadn't I activated the switches? Why had I climbed out, rather than using the ejection seat? Had I been afraid the CIA had linked the destruct device to the ejection-seat mechanism to make it explode if I tried to use it?

They returned to this so often it seemed less to get a positive answer than to plant the seed of doubt.

And there was the pin. They had tested the poison on a dog. It had died in ninety seconds. Had I used it, the same thing would have happened to me. But it would have been a horrible minute and a half. Because, according to expert analysis, the poison caused paralysis of the respiratory system. Unable to breathe, the dog had suffocated. Since such a death would resemble death from lack of oxygen, had it occurred to me that this might have been the reason for the U.S. releasing the story of my having trouble with the oxygen equipment?

It hadn't occurred to me until they mentioned it. Then it made a certain amount of sense. But I wasn't about to admit anything of the sort.

One day they brought in the device, now devoid of poison. Had I noticed how poorly it was constructed? The sheath covering the needle, supposedly to make it look like an ordinary straight pin, didn't even fit tightly against the head.

Examining it, I had to agree. It was badly made. Given time and tools, I probably could have done a better job of it myself. Obviously it had been designed to be used, not closely examined. But these thoughts I kept to myself.

Why had I disobeyed orders and failed to use the pin?

I had never been given any such orders. On the contrary, I didn't even have to carry it. The decision was mine alone. And, since carrying it was optional, use was optional too.

They returned to this subject many, many times.

"The story is now circulating in Washington, D.C., your capital, that you were not shot down at the altitude you mentioned to us, but that after either engine trouble or a flameout you descended to thirty thousand feet, where the rocket reached you."

That bothered me. If U.S. authorities really believed that, there would be no reason not to continue the overflights.

"They also say they knew this because you radioed such information to your base."

Now that the news of my capture had been released, there was no need to withhold information as to whether I had or hadn't used the radio. I told them I hadn't, that it would not have transmitted that distance, that this was simply conjecture on someone's part. I had encountered neither engine trouble nor flameout. During training I had experienced the latter, on several occasions, and there was no comparison. Nor had I descended to thirty thousand feet. Whatever happened to my plane had occurred at my assigned altitude.

I had already convinced the Russians of this. Now, ironically, I was faced with the problem of convincing my own government.

Unbeknownst to me, I had become a pawn in the missile-gap controversy then raging in the United States.

"You will be permitted to write two letters, one to your wife, the other to your parents." With this they gave me a fountain pen and several sheets of paper.

The letters were extremely difficult to write. Not wanting my family to worry any more than they already had, I tried to be as cheerful as possible—emphasizing that I had been well treated, that I was taking walks, even sunbaths, that I had been given cigarettes and books to read—but found it impossible to eliminate the hopelessness I really felt.

"Barbara, I don't know what is going to happen to me. The investigation and interrogation is still going on. When that is over, there will be a trial. I will be tried in accordance with Article 2 of their criminal code for espionage. The article states that the punishment is seven to fifteen years' imprisonment and death in some cases. Where I fit in, I don't know. I don't know when the trial will be, or anything. I only know that I don't like the situation I am in or the situation I have placed you in. . . .

"I was told today that I could write letters to you and my parents. That was good news. I was also told that there appeared in one of the U.S. papers a statement that my father had made that he would like to come here and see me. I was told that if the U.S. government would let any of you come that you would be allowed to see me. I would rather you waited until the trial or after so that

I could tell you what the results were. But I will leave the decision of when to come up to you. . . ."

The following day both letters were returned to me. Certain remarks were unacceptable and had been crossed out. Words had been changed, sentences and paragraphs transposed. I was to re-copy both letters, as indicated, also wording them in such a way that it appeared I was alone in my cell while writing them.

Since there was no pattern in the content of the deletions, this meant only one thing: they were watching for a code, and were using this method to frustrate it.

Also, rewritten, the letters gave no indication of censorship.

There was no need for such niceties when it came to the letters I received, toward mid-June. They were butchered. Not just single lines or paragraphs, but half-pages cut out. A code, as the Russians well realized, can work both ways.

There was little in the way of encouraging news, except that both my wife and my parents wanted to come to Moscow, if they could get visas. My father had written to both Premier Khrushchev and President Eisenhower, asking them to help me. My mother urged me to be a good boy and read my Testament.

A photo of her was enclosed. She was in bed, obviously ill.

I could have done without that.

From the moment I had been told I would be allowed to receive mail, I had anxiously awaited its arrival, asking each and every day if any letters had come.

Now that they had, the loneliness became even more acute.

Earlier, the evening interrogations had been discontinued. Now, as June passed and spring turned to summer, there were no more Sunday interrogations; then I was given Saturdays off too; and occasionally, without warning, there would be no questions for a whole morning or afternoon.

I learned a new way to tell time. From the gap at the top of my cell window I could see two office windows across the courtyard. They were opened each weekday morning at nine, then closed each evening at six. On Saturdays they were opened at nine, closed at two. Sundays they remained closed all day. But on Sunday the streets outside the prison were quiet, and I could hear each hour as the Kremlin clock tolled the time.

It hung very heavy.

Often I'd wondered whether there were other Americans in Lubyanka. Maybe even as I took my walks there was someone in one of the adjoining courtyards, waiting for a signal.

Desperate for communication of any kind, I hit upon a way to make my presence known. Although I was forbidden to speak, no one had said anything about whistling.

As I walked, I'd whistle American songs.

Finishing one, I'd listen for a reply.

That there wasn't one today didn't mean there mightn't be one tomorrow, or the day after.

On June 30 I was informed that the investigation was officially completed. There would be no further interrogations.

My first reaction was relief. After sixty-one days the questioning was finally over. Despite all their tricks, I had succeeded in keeping from them the most important things I knew.

The self-congratulatory feeling lasted only until I was returned to my cell. Then I realized that except for reading and walks, there was no way to fill my days.

Another realization followed. Now that the investigation was finished, I was that much closer to the trial. And whatever came after.

Six

On July 9 I had a visitor.

Mikhail I. Grinev was a small, balding man in his early sixties, with horn-rimmed glasses and a wispy goatee. His English was so poor as to be nearly unintelligible—he had studied it in school, used it little since—but as interpreter he had brought along an English teacher from Moscow University.

Grinev informed me that he was a member of the Moscow City Collegium of Lawyers and had been appointed my defense counsel.

I had been hoping for a lawyer of my own choice, an American. Not permitted.

For seventy days I had been held in solitary confinement. Except for a few heavily censored letters, no communication with the outside world had been allowed. Repeated requests to see a representative of my own government had been denied. Albeit involuntarily, I was learning a few of the differences between Soviet and American law. Grinev would teach me quite a few more.

This was a courtesy visit, he explained. We could not actually start work on my defense until we received a copy of the indictment.

When would that be?

Sometime before the trial; the date was not yet set.

I was curious to know whether the trial would be open to the public. My wife and parents had applied for visas; if granted, would they be allowed to attend?

Grinev didn't know, or so he said. I was to be tried before the military division of the Supreme Court of the USSR. Often in cases involving state security, as did mine, such trials were closed to the public. The military division, he went on to explain, consisted of three generals—Lieutenant General Borisoglebsky, chairman; Major General Vorobyev, of the Artillery; and Major General Zakharov, of the Air Force—who acted as judges.

I was civilian, I noted, not military.

That was not important, Grinev said. In the USSR all espionage cases came under jurisdiction of the military division of the court.

Would there be a jury?

There were no jury trials in Russia. I should realize, he added, I was being tried before the highest court in the land. And the procurator general himself, Roman Rudenko, would act as prosecutor. Remembering Rudenko from the interrogations, I wasn't surprised at this.

Procurator general, Grinev explained, was a position corresponding to that of Attorney General of the United States.

The following background piece on Rudenko appeared in *The New York Times* on August 18, 1960, the second day of the trial. Although I was not to read it until much later, it bears reprinting here for its insight into his character and motivations:

"Traditionally, there is only one side of criminal law in the Soviet Union that offers the attorney opportunities for fame, stature, and high office. That is the right side, the prosecution side. It is the side that Roman Andreyevich Rudenko, meticulously and without ostentation, as traveled for thirty years. He revealed his traits again yesterday in prosecuting Francis Gary Powers, the American reconnaissance pilot. Mr. Rudenko appeared in court as chief prosecutor, not because he is an unusually brilliant lawyer or because he is a particularly striking performer in public, like the late Andrei Y. Vishinski. He apparently holds the office of prosecutor general because he has been a faithful and thorough executor of whatever law was decreed by his superiors in the worst days of Stalin as well as in the best days of Premier Khrushchev.

"He has purged and he has purged the purgers. He has helped to concoct false confessions and fantastic indictments, and he has dealt affably and studiously before a tribunal run in the Anglo-Saxon manner.

"He has stretched the law as ordered, to arrange secret and unconstitutional proceedings, and he has presided over efforts to reestablish the law against the former 'abuse.' "

Reviewing his career, *The New York Times* characterized this adaptable man as "careful, capable, and colorless."

I had the distinct feeling that Grinev expected me to feel grateful for these honors. But he went on to add the liabilities. Since I was to be tried before a branch of the highest court, there could be no appeal of the sentence. While technically possible to appeal to the full bench of the Supreme Court, such requests were almost always refused. Of course, a personal appeal could be made to Premier Khrushchev or to President Brezhnev.

It was interesting. I felt, that we were discussing appeals even before we got around to a defense.

I was fortunate, Grinev continued. In 1958 Soviet criminal law had undergone a tremendous reform. Previously the penalty for espionage had been twenty-five years' imprisonment, with death in some cases. Now maximum imprisonment was fifteen years.

But still death in some cases?

Yes, he admitted.

Was this one of them? In short, what were my chances?

He couldn't tell me that, not until after he had seen the indictment. Also, a great deal would depend on my testimony in court.

We wouldn't have to worry about that factor, I told him, because I didn't plan to testify. Since there was no question of my guilt, my intention was to plead guilty and let the court sentence me.

That was not the way the law worked in the Soviet Union, he explained. Even should I plead guilty, a trial would still follow, with the prosecution introducing its evidence. As for not testifying, the prosecution would simply read the transcripts of all my interrogations into the record.

Also, my refusal to testify would be held against me.

The explanation that followed was highly technical but boiled down to this: in the Soviet Union there was no such thing as the right to remain silent, no privilege against self-incrimination. They could not force me to testify. But if I didn't, the judges could draw unfavorable inferences from my refusal. Too, this would show that I was uncooperative and did not feel sincere repentance. And these mitigating circumstances were my only chance to reduce the sentence.

If I had no further questions, he would see me again when he received the indictment.

I had one, though I suspected his presence was in itself the answer. Was he a member of the Communist party?

He nodded affirmatively.

I observed that in my particular circumstances, being both defended and tried by Communists, I could see no prospect of having a fair trial.

On the contrary, he replied, the state guaranteed every accused person a defense. And it was his job to supply it.

Escorted back to my cell, I thought about another important difference between American and Soviet law. In the United States there is a confidential relationship between attorney and client. You can tell your lawyer things you do not wish the prosecution to know, things instrumental in shaping your defense. In short, you can trust your attorney. I couldn't trust mine.

Perhaps it was fortunate that I did not learn, until much later, the track record of my so-called "defense counsel."

Mikhail I. Grinev specialized in losing important state cases. When Lavrenti Beria, head of Stalin's secret police, was tried for treason, Grinev defended him. Beria was executed. In 1954 and 1956 Grinev defended twelve of Beria's former secret-service officials following purges. All twelve were convicted; four were given stiff sentences, eight executed.

Nor was this the first time he had worked in tandem with Rudenko. During the Nazi war-crime trials at Nuremberg, Grinev had been a defense counsel, Rudenko a prosecutor.

Such knowledge, however, would have made little difference. I knew my captors wouldn't appoint someone to defend me who would not act exactly as they wanted.

Maybe I was wrong, but I had the strong feeling that everything had already been decided, that even Grinev knew what the sentence was to be.

Grinev's visit on July 9 was the first time I had seen anyone other than my guards and the serving woman in nearly a week.

That previous occasion had come as a surprise. A few days after the first of July, I had been taken back to the interrogation room.

What did I know about the RB-47 flights?

I gave the same answer as in the earlier interrogations. Nothing. Which was not true.

Although they approached the subject from a number of different directions—Did I know any of the pilots? Had I ever flown the plane? Was there an arrangement whereby the RB-47s covered certain areas, the U-2s others?—I continued to plead lack of knowledge.

I knew something had spurred their interest. I had no idea what.

When the interrogations were in progress, I had dreamed of the day they would be over. Now, left alone in my cell, I missed them. Deceiving my captors had been a challenge; even that stimulation was gone, and with it any semblance of human companionship. This was the way they intended it, I was sure. No beatings, no torture except that inflicted by the mind. Only an all-pervading emptiness that made you desire even the company of your enemies.

Even visits to the doctor became welcome events. Possibly because of the ten days when I hadn't eaten, or the changed diet, I was still losing weight and having considerable stomach trouble. Had I known what was coming, I would have said nothing, for the result was the ultimate indignity, a proctoscopic examination, made even more unpleasant by an audience of doctors, nurses, guards, and interpreters.

Ten days after Grinev's visit, I was informed that my trial would begin on August 17.

My thirty-first birthday. A hell of a birthday present!

I was also allowed to write two more letters. Again I was to reiterate that I was being well treated; "very nice" was the phrase they wanted me to use. I was also to state that I had conferred with my defense counsel several times. This wasn't true; I had seen him only once, and I still hadn't received the indictment, but I went along because it was a small point and I didn't want my mail privileges revoked. Although my incoming letters were censored, and my outgoing letters edited and rewritten, this was my only link with the outside world.

Again the letters were hard to write. I knew that my family wanted to come to Moscow for the trial. More than anything, I wanted to see them. But it would be cruel to raise false hopes. I made it clear that "there is no doubt in my mind that I will be found guilty. . . . It will be more of a trial for determining the degree of guilt and the degree of punishment."

I didn't add that I felt sure I knew what the latter would be.

Monotony formed the shape of my days, loneliness their substance. About three hours were spent on the roof, walking, sitting in the sun, or tending my garden. To have something growing—alive, green—in the midst of this bleakness meant a great deal to me. One weed had grown very tall. I was afraid one of the guards would pull it. But on each visit to the roof it was still there.

As was the piece of tin.

Most of the rest of the time I read. In addition to the mysteries, *Gone with the Wind,* and the Bible (for the first time I read it all the way through), I'd received a few books from Moscow University Library, including Mikhail Sholokhov's *And Quiet Flows the Don* and *The Don Flows Home to the Sea.*

This was not all my reading matter. I read the few letters I had received, over and over and over again.

But there was still time—much too much time—for thought.

From the moment of my capture I had been certain of eventually being taken before a firing squad. My captors had never stated positively that this would happen; since telling me I was to be tried, they had noted two possibilities—imprisonment or death; but I had brainwashed myself into expecting the latter.

And yet just the word "trial" contained the element of hope.

I had to keep reminding myself that I was thinking in terms of American justice, not Soviet, that whatever was decided here would be in the best interest of the state.

Sometimes it occurred to me that maybe I wouldn't die, that with the whole world watching the outcome of the trial, the Soviets would have to be lenient.

Yet the whole world had been watching the Rosenberg case. And we had executed them anyway. Except for the fact that their crime was treason, mine espionage, there was no reason to suppose the Russians would be any less severe with me. The more I thought about it, the more likely it seemed they would give me the strictest possible punishment, as an object lesson to dissuade others from attempting the same thing.

I gave a great deal of thought as to whether I should or should not testify.

The prospect of having the interrogation records read in open court bothered me. Not only would it stretch out the trial for weeks. Many of the things I had told the Russians were meant for their ears alone; an astute newspaperman, with good sources in Washington, was bound to spot some of the lies immediately. Exposing them would be an opening of Pandora's box. Other statements I had made would be reexamined. Subjects carefully avoided would be scrutinized minutely. And once they began digging . . .

Yet, alone in my cell, with only my thoughts for company, there were moments when I was tempted, when my imagination engaged in the heroic fantasies of a young boy. Not only would I refuse to testify, when it came time to plead I would stand and deliver to the court a ringing declaration, in the manner of Nathan Hale or Patrick Henry. Every man would like to be remembered as a hero. This would be my chance to play the part.

What would it accomplish?

It would ensure Francis Gary Powers a place in history books, thought he would not be around to read them. For I could be fairly certain it would remove any slight element of doubt as to my sentence.

And it might well negate everything I had succeeded in doing thus far.

I knew some things about the U-2 project which, brought out, would make the headlines already published seem microscopic. That I had remained silent about them did not mean that, given enough clues, the Russians couldn't draw their own conclusions.

Although I debated the question for hours, in a way my decision had been made long before, after my capture and on the flight to Moscow. I had decided then what course of action to follow during interrogations. If it appeared to the world I had told everything, it was a risk I'd have to take. I knew that the President, the CIA, and others involved in the U-2 program would know better. And maybe, someday, someone would set the record straight.

There was more mail from home. Containing good news— and bad.

The visas had been granted. But some sort of misunderstanding had arisen between my wife and my parents. Exactly what occasioned it was not clear, but they would be traveling to Russia separately.

I could only imagine the pressures they had been under. Yet I couldn't help feeling let down. At this, of all times, I wanted them to be united.

Having this to worry about, as well as the trial, did nothing to help my frame of mind.

On August 10 Grinev brought me a copy of the indictment. Drawn up by Shelepin, had of the KGB, on July 7, Rudenko, as prosecutor, had approved it on July 9, the same day as Grinev's first visit: yet they had waited more than a month—until just seven days before the start of the trial—to show it to me. Grinev claimed to have received his copy only that day. Although I said nothing, I frankly didn't believe him. I later leaned it had been released to Reuters on August 9 and appeared in most newspapers before I saw it.

Typewritten, single-spaced, it ran to seventeen pages. As a legal case it appeared to this layman as sound as any could possibly be. It contained quotes from my interrogations, President Eisenhower's admission that he had authorized the flights for espionage purposes, testimony from the rocket crew who shot down the plane and the people who detained me. It itemized such physical evidence as maps, photographs of important installations, recordings of Soviet radio and radar signals. It cited Soviet and international law, making it clear that espionage and unauthorized intrusion into the airspace of a sovereign country were crimes in any land.

But it went beyond that. It was, from the first page to the last, a propaganda attack on the United States. It accepted as fact what was in reality conjecture: that the flight had been sent to wreck the Summit talks. It used prejudicial terms such as "gangster flight" and "brazen act of aggression." It quoted in detail the official lies told by the United States before Khrushchev revealed the capture of the pilot and plane, extraneous material that would be inadmissible in any Western court. It drew unwarranted conclusions, as when it spoke of my "espionage activities" as "an expression of the aggressive policy pursued by the government of the United States."

Once finished reading it, I realized the trial would not be the USSR v. Francis Gary Powers, but the USSR v. the US and, incidentally, Francis Gary Powers.

But only one defendant would be in the dock, facing the prospect of a death sentence.

And for legal defense he would be completely at the mercy of a man he couldn't trust.

Exactly what would my defense be?

Grinev was vague. That would depend in large part on the prosecution's case. Since, from the indictment, this appeared quite solid, he would have to rely heavily on those mitigating circumstances which, he hoped, might cause the court to lessen punishment. Reading from the appropriate code, Article 33 of the 1958 Fundamental Principles of Criminal Law, he cited these. Many were not applicable to my case; the relevant ones included truthful cooperation during interrogation and trial, voluntary surrender and admission of guilt, and "sincere repentance."

This phrase had been drummed into me even during the interrogations. It was extremely important, Grinev said. I would be asked during the trial whether I was sorry for my action. Upon this answer alone could depend the severity of my sentence.

I thought about it. I *was* sorry—sorry I had made the May 1 flight; sorry I had been shot down; sorry I was a prisoner having to undergo trial; sorry that as a result of my flight the Summit talks had collapsed. Eisenhower's visit to Russia had been canceled, and the United States placed in an embarrassing position; sorriest of all that the flight had not been successful, in which case none of this would have happened.

Yes, I could say it, if my life depended on it, as long as I did not have to define too closely what I meant.

Grinev had been given transcripts of the interrogations. We went over them, checking the references in the indictment. I had expected him to ask me a number of questions. But there were very few, either in this or later sessions.

Back in my cell, I reread the indictment carefully, the first time just to see what news I could glean about happenings in the world outside.

But there was little there beyond what I already knew. Though the collapse of the Summit was mentioned, there were no details as to exactly what had occurred.

Both Herter and Nixon were quoted as indicating that the overflights would continue. There was, in the indictment, no statement otherwise. This disturbed me greatly. In some way I would have to get over in the trial that I had been hit while flying at my assigned altitude, that all talk of engine trouble and descending to a lower altitude was false.

I was struck with the sixty-eight-thousand-foot figure. However, maybe I could use that advantageously. If given the chance, I decided to stress that I had been hit at "maximum altitude, sixty-eight thousand feet," hoping the CIA would realize by "maximum altitude" I meant I was flying exactly where I was supposed to when the explosion occurred. For me to say I was flying at my "assigned altitude" would imply the plane could fly higher, which was true.

If I could get that message across, the trial, for all its propaganda value, would have served one positive purpose. It could be the means for saving the lives of other pilots.

There was no mention of "Collins" in the indictment. Nor had there been in the excerpt from Khrushchev's speech read to me. That was one of the first things I'd hoped would come out, but apparently it hadn't. Somehow I would have to get that in too, as a message to the CIA that I hadn't told everything.

Shouldn't we rehearse my testimony, go over what I should or shouldn't say?

That wouldn't be necessary, Grinev said. The same questions asked during the interrogations would be asked during the trial. So long as I stuck to my earlier answers, there would be no problem. However, we would have to work on my "final statement."

I didn't like the sound of that.

Unlike American law, which permitted the prosecution the final summing up, Soviet law allowed the accused the last word in his own defense. This would be a short statement, which I could read. The important points to be made, Grinev noted, were: I realized I had committed a grave crime; I was sorry for having done so; and I asked the court to realize that the real criminals responsible for my flight were those persons who formulated the aggressive, war-making policies of the United States.

I told him that I would admit to committing a crime, since under the law I had; that I would say I was sorry, if that was essential to my defense. But I refused to denounce my own government.

It would help my case greatly if I did this, he observed.

I didn't care.

Despite his arguments, I stuck to my resolve.

It seemed to me we were overlooking some other possibilities. I was not an attorney, but wasn't there a difference between attempting to commit a crime and actually committing one?

What did I mean?

I was guilty of violating Soviet airspace. Granted. But since none of the data I collected had ever left the Soviet Union, was I guilty of espionage?

Grinev rejected the argument, for what were probably valid legal reasons. All the same, I wanted that point in the statement: none of the information collected during the flight had reached a foreign power, the Soviets had seized it all, and therefore no one had been harmed by my act.

After some grumbling, Grinev let me add it. We worked over the wording of the statement for some time. In fact, we spent almost as much time on those few lines as the rest of my defense.

Both prior to and after the trial there was considerable discussion in the United States as to whether I was actually guilty of violating Soviet airspace, the argument being that as in maritime law, with its twelve mile limit, there must be some boundary beyond which airspace no longer belongs to a single country, that the U-2, flying at sixty-eight thousand feet, or nearly thirteen miles above the earth, might well be considered outside this invisible border. Unfortunately, not having my own attorney, and denied access to U.S. newspapers and magazines, I wasn't aware of this as a possible defense. However, in all likelihood the court wouldn't have even considered this argument, since Soviet law is quite firm in claiming sovereignty over all air above the Soviet Union.

Considering the space satellites soon to take over many of the espionage functions of the U-2, it was, and remains, an interesting question. To parody a popular song title: How High the Spy?

My last meeting with Grinev took place on Tuesday, August 16, the day before the trial. And Grinev had some news. Barbara and my parents were in Moscow. He had conferred with them the previous evening. My mother was accompanied by a physician, but wanted to assure me she was feeling fine. The trial would be open to the public, and Barbara, she, and my father would be there. I wouldn't be allowed to see them privately, however, until after conclusion of the trial.

They had sent me something. Grinev handed me a package. Inside were several handkerchiefs and a birthday card.

Just before leaving, Grinev sternly warned me that if I made a demonstration in the courtroom it would be held against me.

Prior to the trial I had four meetings with my defense counsel, for a total of not more than five hours.

As I figured it, the prosecution had used well over a thousand hours of my time in the preparation of their case.

It didn't seem a fair balance.

Knowing that my family was in Moscow, so close and yet so completely separated from me, was rough. I slept little the night before my thirty-first birthday.

Seven

Blinded by the flash bulbs and TV lights, with a guard holding either arm, I was escorted into the wooden prisoner's dock. Only then was I able to make out my surroundings.

This was no courtroom, but an immense theater. Tall white columns flanked all four walls. Hanging between them and from the ceiling were more than fifty chandeliers, all brilliantly lighted.

The major participants, myself included, were at one end of the auditorium, on an elevated stage. Grinev occupied a desk before the prisoner's dock. In a corresponding spot on the opposite side loomed Rudenko, wearing what looked like a streetcar conductor's uniform. Center stage, on a raised dais, were the three judges, all in military dress. Above and behind them, on the wall, rested a mammoth state seal, with large gold hammer and sickle in the center.

The audience, which filled the rest of the auditorium and its several balconies, numbered close to a thousand.

Grinev had given me no warning. This was like being tried in Carnegie Hall!

As a boy in school I had suffered stage fright. Despite my attempts to hide it now, I was extremely nervous. The previous day I had been issued a double-breasted, blue pinstripe suit, again several sizes too large. The poor fit didn't make me any more comfortable.

I looked intently for my family, but could not find them in the crowd.

The presiding judge was speaking to me. The trial was to be conducted in Russian but simultaneously translated, via a headset arrangement, into English, French, German, and Spanish. Did I have any objections to the interpreters? I replied no.

There was a bench built into the dock. Noticing that everyone else was seated, I sat down.

"Defendant," observed the presiding judge. "You are obliged to stand when the Court addresses you."

While I was still smarting from the rebuke, the judge asked my name, nationality, date and place of birth, family status, occupation, and whether I had received a copy of the indictment.

Four witnesses were then introduced. I recognized them as the men who had helped me when I had landed in the field. Following this, some dozen "expert witnesses" came forward. I had never seen any of them before.

Presiding Judge: Defendant Powers, you also have the right to challenge the selection of experts.

I hesitated before answering. Having no idea as to who they were, their qualifications, or the nature of their testimony, how could I challenge them? This was my defense counsel's job. But Grinev remained silent.

Defendant Powers: I have no objections.

The secretary of the court then read the indictment, in full. Aloud, it became even more a propaganda attack.

Presiding Judge: Defendant Powers, you have heard the reading of the indictment against you. Do you understand the charge brought against you? Have you understood?

Defendant Powers: Yes.

All too well. This was no trial, but a show. And I wanted no part of it.

Presiding Judge: Accused Powers, do you plead guilty of the charge?

Defendant Powers: Yes, I plead guilty.

The judge then ordered a twenty-minute recess. As I was being led out, I spotted Barbara, waving from a box in the rear of the courtroom, and saw my family for the first time. Neither of my parents had ever been outside the United States before. They looked so alone, so alien in this strange land, that I choked up.

I was thankful for the break. I didn't want a thousand people to see the tears in my eyes.

Hundreds of foreign journalists were attending the trial, an interpreter effused during the recess. Interest was so great, he said, that crowds had to be turned away. Television crews were photographing the entire proceedings, so they could be shown on Soviet television and in movie theaters.

As for the auditorium in which the trial was being held, he went on, it was known as the Hall of Columns. Built in the first year of the reign of Catherine the Great, it had been the setting for many historic events. While a concert hall, its performers had included Liszt, Tchaikovsky, and Rachmaninoff. For a time a private club, it had numbered Pushkin and Tolstoy among its members. And both Lenin and Stalin had lain in state here following their deaths.

He neglected to mention that it was here that the infamous purge trials of the 1930's had taken place, also before the military division of the Supreme Court of the USSR.

I was not in any frame of mind to appreciate the fact that a new chapter was being added to the history of the Hall of Columns.

Returned to the dock, I learned another difference between U.S. and Soviet courtroom procedures. The first witness against the accused was to be the accused himself.

Prosecutor Rudenko asked the questions.

Q. Defendant Powers, when did you get the assignment to fly over the territory of the Soviet Union?

A. On the morning of May 1.

If a representative of the agency was present, and I was sure there must be at least one in the huge crowd, he would know this was a lie. Thus alerted, I hoped he would listen carefully to my further replies, especially if the altitude of the flight was mentioned.

Additional questions established that the order for the flight had come from Colonel Shelton, that he was commanding officer of the 10-10 detachment at Adana, Turkey, that the flight had taken off from Peshawar, Pakistan.

Q. How did the U-2 plane get to the Peshawar airfield?

A. It was brought to the airfield the night before, April 30.

Q. By another pilot?

A. Yes.

Q. But it was brought for you to fly in it into the Soviet Union?

I spotted his trap. All through the interrogations I had maintained I had learned of having to make the flight only a couple of hours before takeoff. He was attempting to make me admit otherwise.

A. At the time, I didn't know I had to make the flight, but, apparently, the plane was brought there for that purpose.

Q. Were you the only one prepared for the flight, or were there other pilots prepared too?

A. There were two of us being prepared at the same time.

Q. Why?

A. I had no idea why. . . .

This was typical of the dilemmas that had confronted me during interrogation. How much was it safe to tell them, how much safe to hold back? I was unsure what information the United States would release concerning the flights. If I failed to mention the backup pilot, and the United States did, the Russians would know I was intentionally withholding something. On the other hand, mention of him might set them to wondering about the other flights. If there was a backup pilot on each mission, why hadn't I ever served my turn? Maybe I had, and was lying when I claimed to know nothing about the earlier overflights. Trying to straddle both sides of the fence, I had indicated that, as far as I knew, having an extra pilot sit in on briefings seemed to be a new practice.

Rudenko asked about the U-2. "Is it a reconnaissance military plane?"

Again the attempt to make me military.

A. Well, I wouldn't call it exactly a military plane, but it is an airplane of the type which is for reconnaissance as well as research work at high altitudes.

Q. And for military purposes?

A. Well, as I said, I don't know whether it was military or not.

Q. But it did belong to your detachment?

A. Yes.

Q. That is, the 10-10 detachment?

A. Yes.

Q. Is this a military detachment?

A. Well, it is commanded by military personnel, but the main part of the personnel were civilians.

Having failed in court to get me to say the unit was military, they found a much easier way. In the "official" Soviet transcript of the trial, published both in the USSR and the United States in English translation, "Well" was changed to "Yes."

The transcript contains a number of such changes. That each involved an important point, such as the above, proves that the cause was not simply poor translation.

Fortunately, several of the reporters present did not depend on the authorized text released by the Soviets but kept their own shorthand notes.

Q. Did you see any identification marks on the U-2 before the flight?

A. Well, I could not inspect the plane because I was wearing my special flying suit, and hence I do not know if it had any markings. It was hard for me to look at all the sides of the plane.

Q. But did you see any identification marks?

A. No, I did not observe the plane at close range.

Q. But at any time, Defendant Powers, did you see any identification marks on the U-2?

A. All the planes based in Turkey had identification marks.

Q. But I ask you about this U-2.

A. I personally did not see any identification marks on this plane, but all the other planes which I have seen did have identification marks.

Rudenko was getting exasperated.

Q. It is important for me to establish that the plane on which Defendant Powers flew did not have identification marks. Why were there not any identification marks?

A. I cannot be positive that there were none.

Q. But you just informed this court that you did not see any identification marks.

A. I did not look for any.

Q. You further stated that the absence of the identification marks was for the purpose of hiding the national identity of these planes.

A. Would you repeat the question?

Although the length of the stage separated us, I was sure Rudenko's face had turned livid.

Q. In the preliminary investigation you stated that the absence of identification marks was for the purpose of hiding the national identity of these planes.

Rudenko was lying, and we both knew it.

A. I do not remember.

Q. You do not remember. We will leave it to the experts to prove that there were not any identification marks. . . .

Realizing that flying an aircraft without identification marks was in violation of international law, and not sure whether such an admission would worsen the case against me and further compromise the United States, I had insisted during the interrogations that all the U-2s at Adana bore national identity marks. This was true, at least part of the time. Such marks appeared on the tail. Prior to each overflight, the markings were removed. But I had no intention of admitting this. Nor, since I had stuck to that story throughout the interrogations, had I any intention of changing it now.

When I originally told them this, of course, I had been unsure how much of the plane had survived the crash. That was why I had qualified my statement, saying that prior to this particular flight I hadn't noticed the markings. It was not until seeing the wreckage in the Gorky Park exhibit that I realized those portions of the plane on which the markings should appear had come through relatively intact.

As with many of my statements during interrogation, this particular fiction was tied in with several others. If I had admitted that sometimes the planes bore markings, sometimes not, the Russians could have asked how often I had seen the planes without markings, and when—giving them at least a clue as to the number and timing of the overflights.

It may well be that I credited their questions with far more subtlety and deviousness than was actually the case. But at the time, each one had seemed a potential trap.

After questioning me about the time of my takeoff and the time I crossed the Soviet border, Rudenko asked the big question. I had been waiting for this, afraid he might not ask.

Q. At what altitude were you supposed to fly?

A. At the maximum altitude. Altitude varies with fuel load. As the fuel burns out, the plane climbs higher.

Q. To what altitude?

A. The maximum altitude is sixty-eight thousand feet.

A few minutes later, after asking questions about my flight chart, reserve fields, landing arrangements at Bodö, air speed, etc., he returned to it.

Q. At what height did the flight occur?

A. The flight began approximately at sixty-seven thousand feet and as the fuel burned out I rose to sixty-eight thousand feet.

Rudenko was obviously anxious to get the point across, to prove that the USSR did indeed possess rockets capable of reaching the higher altitudes.

For a change, we were in complete accord.

Q. On your plane there was aerial-reconnaissance photo equipment. What instructions were you given?

A. I was not given any special instructions to operate the equipment. I was to turn switches on and off as indicated on the chart.

Q. With what purpose did you switch on the equipment.

A. I was instructed how to do this. It was indicated on the map that the equipment was to be turned on.

Q. Defendant Powers, you probably know the purpose for which you had to turn off and on the equipment?

A. I could very well guess the purpose for which I turned on and off the equipment. However, to be very exact, I would have to say no.

Q. Surely Defendant Powers knew of this equipment?

A. Not at first. But now that I have seen its results, I now know better what this equipment is for.

Q. I think that Defendant Powers did not doubt that this was a reconnaissance plane from the moment he started his flight.

A. No, I didn't doubt it.

Q. On your plane were found radio intelligence equipment, tape recordings of various Soviet radar stations. Is that so?

A. I have been told that there were tape recorders, but I don't know. However, much of the general equipment, I do not know what it looked like except what I've seen here.

Q. But you, Defendant Powers, were trained enough to know that such equipment is designed for special spying flights?

A. I didn't know anything about the equipment before.

Q. But you were sufficiently informed that this flight had espionage aims?

A. I saw no other reason for such a flight. I ask that the lights of the cameras be taken away. They are blinding my eyes.

PRESIDING JUDGE: I ask that the lights be taken away. . . .

What most of the audience couldn't know was that this was an old battle, one which, like those of the Civil War, had been verbally fought over and over again.

At the interrogations, I had insisted I had never seen the special equipment, wasn't sure exactly what it did, had never been informed that the purpose of my flight was espionage, though my suspicions were another matter.

An affirmative response to any of these points would have opened the door to questions I didn't want to answer.

In short, I was just an airplane jockey, not a spy, paid to fly along an assigned route flipping on and off switches as indicated on a map, with little knowledge of the results of my actions, and even less curiosity.

During the interrogations, I had succeeded, I felt, in making this sound plausible, even convincing. Out of context, however, as it was now, it sounded extremely dubious.

Yet, having stuck to this story during more than a thousand hours of intensive grilling, I wasn't about to change it now to give Rudenko a perfect case.

I wondered what my parents were thinking. How confused and frightened they must be, seeing their only son on trial for his life in a Moscow courtroom, charged with spying! And Barbara, with all her problems and weaknesses, what was going through her mind? More than anything, I wanted to make it easier for them. But there was no way I could do so, nothing I could say or do to help. Most of all, I was worried about the effect of the verdict. The longer I remained on the stand, the more helpless the situation appeared.

There followed an attempt to make me verify that the granger was supposed to deflect SAMs as well as air-to-air missiles; another

Dubbed "The Black Lady of Espionage" by the Soviets, the U-2 for four years provided the United States with invaluable intelligence data on Russia's nuclear testing, missile and space launches, and other war-making potentials.

Designed to reach altitudes never before touched by man, and to remain there for more than nine hours at a time, the U-2 spy plane was part jet, part glider. Its unusual 80-foot wing span was twice the length of its fuselage.

Defense Atomic Support Agency

Sandia AFB, New Mexico, where in 1953 U.S. Air Force pilot Francis Gary Powers received top secret training in the handling and delivery of atomic weapons.

Incirlik AFB, Adana, Turkey, from which U-2s made many of their overflights of the Soviet Union. Most of the "special missions" originated from here as well.

The allegedly "plush" accommodations used by the pilots and their families in Adana, Turkey. Later they were moved to the relative comforts of trailers at the base.

First in a series of bogus cover stories that helped create the "credibility gap." The United States, unaware that Premier Khrushchev had set a trap, initially claimed the U-2 was a weather plane which had accidentally drifted across the Russian border.

Khrushchev springs the trap, revealing that Russia had captured both the pilot and the plane. The U.S. cover stories were then repudiated by President Eisenhower's unprecedented admission that he knew and approved of the espionage flights over Russia.

Tass from Sovfoto

"Comrades, I must tell you a secret . . ." Khrushchev confiding to the Supreme Soviet, and the world, that "we have parts of the plane and we also have the pilot." Brandishing a photograph of the gold coins found on Powers, Khrushchev gleefully denounced "official American lies."

Sovfoto

On display in Gorki Square in Moscow, the wreckage of the American spy plane drew crowds of curious Russians. In the foreground is the center section of the U-2.

The tail section of the U-2 on display in Moscow.

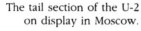

San Francisco Chronicle

Refusing to participate in the talks unless President Eisenhower apologized for the U-2 overflights, Premier Khrushchev forced the collapse of the 1960 Summit Conference.

The trial of Francis Gary Powers in Moscow's Hall of Columns, August 1960. Prosecutor Roman Rudenko, chief Soviet prosecutor during the Nazi war crimes trials in Nuremberg, is seated at the desk to the left; the three judges of the Military Division of the Supreme Court occupy the raised dais in the center; seated at the first desk on the right is Powers' defense counsel, Mikhail Grinev, a specialist in losing important state cases. Standing in the prisoner's dock immediately behind him is defendant Powers, charged with espionage against the USSR. While the world watched, Russia tried the U-2 pilot, and the United States in absentia.

Anxiously awaiting the verdict and undergoing their own long ordeal were three foreigners to this strange land: Francis Gary Powers' mother, father, and wife.

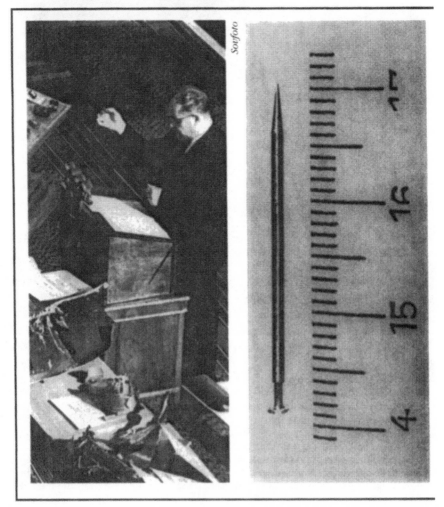

Professor V. I. Prozorovsky, one of the prosecution's "expert" witnesses, testifying regarding the lethal effect of the poison on the pin Powers carried. Dipped in curare, it could kill a man in 90 seconds. Note the ill-fitting sheath. Also included in the evidence was the controversial 2½-pound destruct unit, carried on each overflight. It required being activated by the pilot and could destroy only a small portion of the U-2's secret gear. The prosecution also introduced this phony "U-2 photo," which pictured out-of-date Soviet aircraft. The Russians did not dare risk revealing real U-2 photos which they possessed.

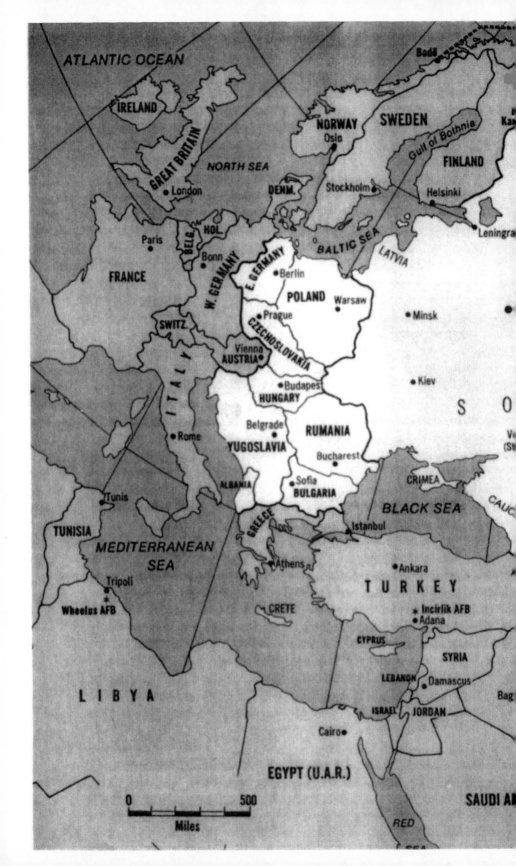

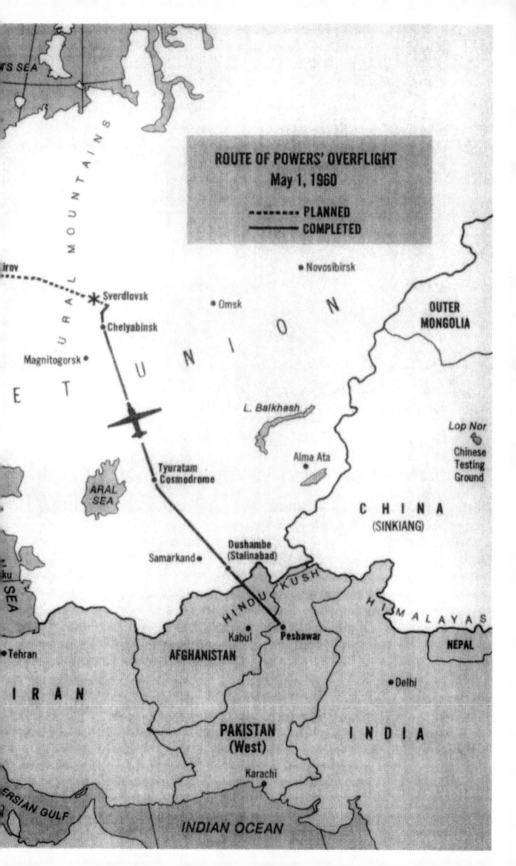

Tass from Soufoto

Expecting the death sentence, thirty-one-year-old American U-2 pilot Francis Gary Powers of Pound, Virginia, hears the verdict: ten years in a Soviet prison.

United Press International, Inc.

Lubyanka Prison in Moscow, the notorious headquarters of the KGB. Powers went through his ordeal of questioning at Lubyanka Prison and was held there until his trial was over. He was taken to Vladimir Prison once he was sentenced. There are no pictures available of Vladimir Prison.

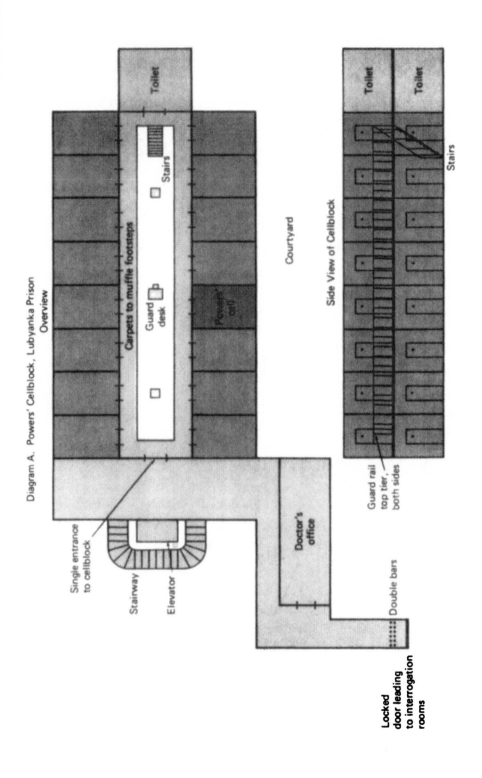

Diagram A. Powers' Cellblock, Lubyanka Prison
Overview

Single entrance to cellblock

Stairway

Elevator

Doctor's office

Locked door leading to interrogation rooms

Double bars

Carpets to muffle footsteps

Guard desk

Toilet

Stairs

Powers' cell

Courtyard

Side View of Cellblock

Toilet

Toilet

Guard rail top tier, both sides

Stairs

Diagram B. Powers' Cell, Lubyanka Prison, Moscow, USSR

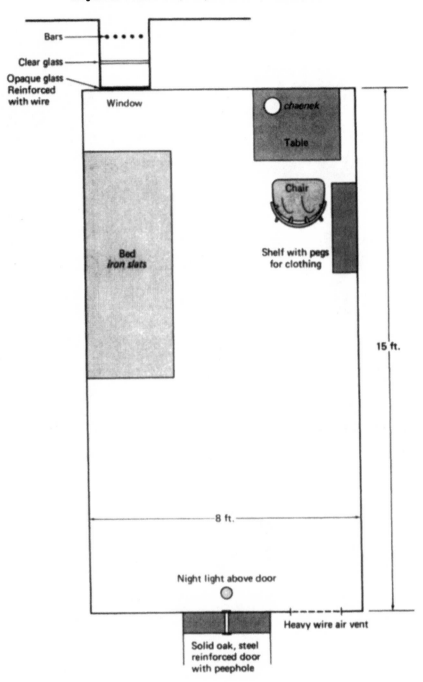

Diagram C. Vladimir Prison, USSR

Walls brick, over 15 ft. high, patrolled by guards with submachineguns and searchlights

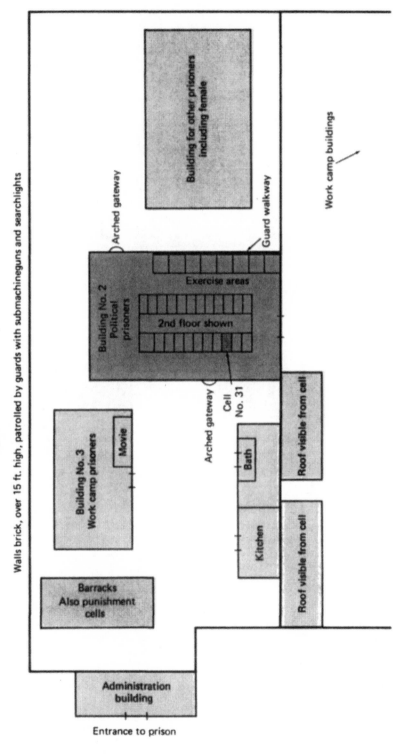

Diagram D. Cell No. 31, Vladimir Prison

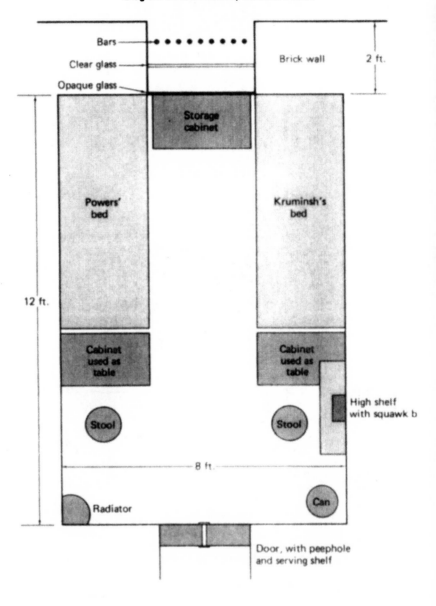

Francis Gary Powers, Vladimir Prison, USSR, November 1960. The haircut was pure Russian. The attempted smile, for the benefit of his family, wasn't altogether successful.

Zigurd Kruminsh, Powers' cellmate during his incarceration at Vladimir Prison. At first Powers was unsure whether the Latvian was a former British Secret Service agent as he said he was, or a Soviet "plant."

U-2 PILOT FREED
Russia Swaps Powers for Red Spy

One year, nine months, and ten days after his ill-fated U-2 flight, Powers was dramatically exchanged for Soviet spy Colonel Rudolph Abel, in the first Cold War spy exchange.

Exchange Is Made in Dramatic Meeting on German Bridge

Following his release from a Russian prison, Powers was held incommunicado for another twenty-four days by the CIA in "safe" houses in Maryland, Pennsylvania, and Virginia. Powers' own story of the U-2 incident was suppressed for eight years, until the publication of this book.

SUNDAY, FEBRUARY 11, 1962

Powers Returning Secretly;
U. S. 'Plays Down' Exchange

Reds Show Abel, U-2 Pilot to See Claim Act Was Family Before Humanitarian Official Quiz

For the first time since his release, the press was allowed to photograph Powers during his appearance before the Senate Armed Services Committee hearing in Washington on March 6, 1962.

The Intelligence Star, one of the Central Intelligence Agency's highest awards. Francis Gary Powers was originally scheduled to receive it in 1963; the award was postponed, for political reasons, until 1965.

Clarence L. ("Kelly") Johnson, left, vice-president of Lockheed's Advanced Development Projects. With him is Francis Gary Powers, who became a Lockheed test pilot following his return from Russia. The plane in the background is the U-2.

Francis Gary Powers, his wife Sue and their children, Claudia ("Dee") and Francis Gary Powers, II, on the patio of their home in Southern California, 1970.

to make me admit that in marking down the unlisted airdrome and other observations on my map, I was, knowingly and intentionally, committing espionage.

Q. With what purpose did you make these marks?

A. I was instructed to record everything that was not shown on my map. This is a "pilot's habit."

Q. A habit which has espionage purposes?

A. I would have done it over the territory of the United States, too.

Q. But I asked you about the flight over the territory of the Soviet Union. Consequently, it was an intrusion for espionage purposes?

A. I suppose it was.

Q. You do not deny that you invaded Soviet airspace in violation of the law.

A. No, I do not deny it.

To do otherwise, considering the evidence, would have been ridiculous.

Q. Therefore, this intrusion pursued intelligence espionage aims?

A. I suppose so.

Having failed to get an unqualified admission, Rudenko approached from another direction.

Q. You stated here, and during the primary investigation as well, that you switched the equipment on and off at definite points.

A. I did what the chart indicated.

Q. Not knowing what the special apparatus was?

A. I never saw the apparatus.

Q. With the same ease, you could have pulled a switch and released an atom bomb?

A. It could have been done. But this is not the type of plane for carrying and dropping such bombs.

Touché, Prosecutor Rudenko.

I'd caught that one. But Rudenko had been questioning me for more than two hours. And I had been standing every minute. I was extremely tired, mentally as well as physically. And the tiredness was rapidly changing into depression. I had to force myself to stay alert, to listen and consider carefully each question and answer, in order not to make a slip.

Still again: Q. At what altitude was your plane when it was struck by the rocket?

A. It was at the maximum altitude, at about sixty-eight thousand feet.

If the agency hadn't gotten the message by now, they never would.

Rudenko then switched to the destruct device. I was sure he was going to imply that I didn't use it because I feared my own destruction also, but he didn't. Instead he moved on to my survival equipment.

Q. For what purpose were you given the noiseless ten-shot pistol?

A. For hunting.

Q. And for that they also gave you 205 cartridges?

A. Yes.

Q. As far as we know, it is the custom to hunt with hunting rifles.

A. It is difficult to carry hunting rifles on this plane.

Q. Yes, especially on this plane, which has espionage purposes.

A. I think that the pistol that was given to me had nothing to do with the purpose of the flight.

What was he getting at with mention of the pistol? Whatever it was, I wanted to forestall it.

Q. Who gave you the poison needle?

A. It was given to me by Colonel Shelton during the briefing at Peshawar.

Q. For what purpose?

We were back on familiar ground. I knew exactly what he wanted to imply.

A. In case I was captured, tortured, and couldn't stand the torture and would rather be dead.

Q. This means your superiors directed you in this flight not to spare your life?

A. It was more or less up to me whether to use that pin.

Q. But they gave you that needle with poison?

A. Yes.

Q. They wanted you to blow up the plane, kill yourself, and wipe out all trace?

A. No, they didn't tell me to kill myself.

Q. But they gave you the needle to kill yourself?

A. If I was tortured.

Q. You were told torture would be used in the Soviet Union?

A. I don't remember being told, but I expected it.

Q. Were you tortured?

A. No.

Q. How did the interrogation authorities treat you?

A. I have been treated very nicely.

Compared to what I had expected, this was quite true.

It was then established that the U-2 shown to me in Gorky Park was the same one I had flown from Peshawar, though, as I noted, not in exactly the same condition. From here Rudenko went back in time to the particulars of my contract with the CIA, such as my pay and duties.

A. I was told that my main duties would be to fly along the Soviet border and collect any radar or radio information. I was also told there would possibly be other duties.

Q. Did you sign the contract?

A. Yes.

Q. Who signed on behalf of the Central Intelligence Agency?

Finally!

A. I don't exactly remember, but it was a Mr. Collins. I think he signed in my presence, but there were others who signed it too.

"Collins" hadn't signed it. But this was the only way I had found thus far to get his "name" in.

Rudenko then attempted to get me to admit that I knew I would be making overflights when I signed the contract. Failing in this, he moved on to Incirlik and Detachment 10-10. And again the attempt to make the operation military:

Q. What were the purpose and aims of the detachment in which the defendant was assigned?

A. In general, to gather information along the borders of the Soviet Union. We likewise conducted weather-research reconnaissance to determine radioactivity.

Q. Who was immediately in charge of the 10-10 detachment?

A. The immediate supervision over the 10-10 detachment was under a military commander, but to whom he was responsible, I did not know.

Q. But it was a military commander?

A. The head of the detachment was a military man.

Q. I understand.

A. But the bulk of the detachment were civilians.

Rudenko didn't appreciate the qualification.

Who were some of the visitors to the base? he asked. I repeated the names I had given in interrogation.

Q. So Cardinal Spellman interested himself in military bases?

A. I would say that he was interested in military personnel, not bases.

Q. Would Cardinal Spellman give his blessings to persons engaged in spy operations?

A. He was a well-known church figure. I think he wouldn't think so much of what a person does as what he is.

Following a long series of questions which established that although I carried NASA identification I had no actual relationship to that agency, the presiding judge announced, "We will take a recess until the afternoon session."

From the hall I was taken to a comfortably furnished anteroom. There was a couch, permitting me to lie down if I cared to. And lunch included the first fresh fruit I had seen since my arrival in Russia—bananas and a piece of watermelon.

Next to my chair was a news magazine called *New Time*. Published in English in Moscow, it was an obvious imitation of the American *Time*. I was leafing through it, hopeful of picking up some outside news, when one of the guards, through the interpreter, ordered me to put it down.

"Why?" I asked.

"Because," he explained, "reading while eating is bad for the digestion."

The irony of his concern gave me my first laugh of the day.

But it was momentary. My depression intensified. The first session had begun at ten A.M. and lasted nearly four hours, the major part of which I had been on the stand. The emotional strain weighed greater than at any time since my capture. Several times I had been on the verge of screaming: I'm guilty! Sentence me to death and end this farce!

I hadn't expected a showcase trial. In a sense, my replies didn't even matter. I was present merely as a symbol. And they were using that symbol to embarrass the United States, to put it on trial by proxy in the court of world opinion. I wanted no part of it. I wanted to bring the trial to an end, get it over with.

When taken outside after lunch, I got my chance.

Seated on a bench in the sun, the guards alongside and behind me, I saw in front of us an empty parking lot, beyond that the open street.

For the first time since my capture there was an opportunity for escape.

The longer I sat there, the more appealing the idea became. It had been years since my college track days, yet, looking at my musclebound guards, I *knew* I could outrun them.

Would they try to shoot me? Probably. Yet that would be an escape too, an end to the trial. And it was just possible, considering the propaganda use to which the trial was being put, they would hesitate, fearing what their superiors would say. And that hesitation, brief though it might be, would be all I'd need for a head start.

I had no plans as to what I would do on reaching the open street. But that wasn't important. What was important was that after more than one hundred days of captivity I had an opportunity.

I tensed my legs, learned forward slightly.

A guard put his heavy hand on my shoulder. Time to go back in.

I was surrounded again. I'd waited too long, and lost my chance.

With the start of the second session, at four P.M., Rudenko resumed his questioning.

It was a stacked deck. Rudenko, holding all the cards, was dealing them out one by one.

He concentrated now on my surveillance flights along the border.

Had I been in an American court, with an American attorney, he would have immediately objected to such questions as irrelevant and prejudicial, since they bore no connection to the charge against me.

But Grinev said nothing. He had yet to make a single objection. He too was a symbol, his presence giving the appearance of my being represented by counsel. Thus far, where my defense was concerned, he might as well have stayed home.

Rudenko then switched to my earlier use of Peshawar, Giebelstadt, Wiesbaden, and Bodö. He was building up to something, I felt, but I couldn't discern what, when suddenly, without warning, he announced he had no further questions at this time.

It was now Grinev's turn.

When my parents had consulted with him prior to the trial, they were accompanied by Carl McAfee, a lawyer whose office was located above my father's shoe-repair shop in Norton, Virginia. McAfee had prepared a set of photographs of my parents' home and The Pound, to show the poverty of the area and, hopefully, gain the sympathy of the court. After introducing these into evidence, Grinev began his questioning, establishing that I came from a working-class family: that my parents were poor, my father not a capitalist, that is, did not employ any labor in his shoe shop but did all the work himself; and that the money offered me by the CIA was the most I had ever received, and had enabled me to pay my debts and live in relative prosperity for the first time in my life. Further questions brought out that I was not political, had never even voted in a U.S. election, knew very little about the Soviet Union except for what I had read in the American press.

I could see what he was trying to do. Though not at all sure this was the best possible defense, it was the only one I had, and, like it or not, I had no choice but to go along with it.

In our brief preparatory sessions, however, I had insisted that certain matters be included in my defense. Though Grinev seemed less convinced than I that they were important, he went into them now.

Q. Was the flight of May 1 your only flight over Soviet territory?

A. Yes, it was the only flight.

Q. Were you consulted about the program of spy flights over the Soviet Union?

A. No, I knew of no such program.

Q. Were you acquainted with the special apparatus on the plane?

A. No, I have never seen any of the special equipment loaded or unloaded. It was never done in my presence. My knowledge of the special equipment was to follow instructions on my map.

Q. Did you know any of the results of your reconnaissance flights?

A. I was never informed of the results of my missions and did not know whether the equipment worked properly, except as indicated by signal lights in the cockpit.

At the interrogations I had admitted some hesitation when it came to renewing my CIA contract. I hadn't given the reasons, which were strictly personal, but had let my interrogators assume I found the job too nerve-racking and exhausting.

Grinev now asked me: Q. Were you sorry you renewed your contract?

A. Well, the reasons are hard to explain.

Q. Why are you sorry now?

A. Well, the situation I am in now is not too good. I haven't heard much about the news of the world since I have been here, but I understand that as a direct result of my flight, the Summit Conference did not take place and President Eisenhower's visit was called off. There was, I suppose, a great increase in tension in the world, and I am sincerely sorry I had anything to do with this.

And I was.

One by one Grinev was establishing the mitigating circumstances.

Q. Did you resist detention or did you contemplate resisting?

A. No, I did not.

Voluntary surrender.

Q. Have all your statements till now been truthful?

A. Yes, it is impossible to deny what I have done. Once in a while I will change my mind in some little details on this or that question.

Complete cooperation.

And, again, sincere repentance.

Q. What is your present attitude toward work in the CIA, and do you now understand the danger the flight entailed?

A. I understand a lot more now than I did before. At first I hesitated as to whether I should renew the contract. I did not want to sign. If I had a job, I would have refused to sign, now that I know some of the circumstances of my flight, though I don't know all of them, by any means. But as indicated a few moments ago, I am profoundly sorry I had any part in it.

DEFENSE COUNSEL GRINEV: I have no more questions for today.

PRESIDING JUDGE: The court will adjourn until ten A.M. tomorrow, the eighteenth of August.

Like a well-coordinated team, my so-called "defense counsel" and the judge had arranged for this to be the last question. Now the headlines for the first day of the trial could read: POWERS "PROFOUNDLY SORRY" HE HAD ANY PART IN SPY FLIGHT.

Eight

Prior to the conclusion of the trial's first day I had given Grinev messages for my family. I told him to tell Barbara that I was anxious for the trial to end so I could see her. I thanked my parents for the birthday present of the handkerchiefs; kidded my father about his natty bow tie—the first time I had seen him wearing one; and asked that my mother not attend the second day, but remain in her hotel room and rest.

As I was escorted back into the dock next morning, I noticed she wasn't present. Despite my instructions, this worried me. Maybe she was really sick and no one had told me. But then I saw my sister Jessica in her place. I hadn't realized she also had made the trip to Moscow. I knew that if she was here, my mother was all right; otherwise Jessica would have been with her. Her presence would, I knew, make the ordeal much easier for my parents, as she had a way of teasing that put them at ease.

These concerns out of the way, I had to concentrate on my own fate.

The session began promptly at ten A.M. Grinev asked half a dozen more questions, then turned me over to Rudenko for reexamination.

This time there was no question what he was attempting to establish.

Q. When you took off from Peshawar on May 1 for your flight, what countries did you fly over?

A. A part of Pakistan, a small part of Afghanistan—I do not know how much—and the Soviet Union.

Q. In other words, you violated the airspace of Afghanistan?

A. If there were no permission obtained by the authorities, then I did.

Q. No Afghan authorities gave you their permission?

A. They did not give me permission personally.

Q. Your superior officers did not say anything?

A. No.

Q. You thereby violated the sovereignty of the neutral state of Afghanistan?

A. If no permission was given to my detachment, then yes.

Q. But did your detachment ever get any permission to make flights along the borders of the Soviet Union?

A. I have no idea.

Still not a single objection from Grinev, though the introduction of such evidence was damning.

During the interrogations I had felt safe in mentioning the border-surveillance flights. Presuming there was nothing illegal about them, I had even emphasized them, to take attention off my "one-overflight" story. Now I could see this had been a mistake. If no permission had been obtained from the countries overflown, these flights were also illegal. And this being the case, I was not a "first-time offender," but a man guilty of a number of previous "crimes."

The dialogue immediately following was ridiculous enough to bring laughter from the spectators. But it was important to Rudenko's case.

Q. And did your detachment ever get any permission to make penetration flights over Soviet territory?

A. I would assume not.

Q. You assume. Perhaps you can tell us something more definite?

A. If any permission would have been obtained, it would have concerned higher authorities, and I would not have known anything about it.

Q. If there would have been such permission, you obviously would not be in the prisoner's box today.

A. That is why I assume we had no such permission.

Again Rudenko established my altitude as sixty-eight thousand feet, then asked, "It was at that altitude that you were struck down by a Soviet rocket?"

A. It was at that altitude that I was struck down by something.

Q. You say you were struck down by *something*?

A. I had no idea what it was. I didn't see it.

Q. But it was at that altitude?

A. Yes.

The report of a Major Voronov, said to have been in charge of the rocket crew, was read. According to the report, "As the plane entered the firing range at an altitude of over twenty thousand meters, one rocket was fired and its explosion destroyed the target."

Rudenko and I then reached a draw on the subject of my radio, his contention being that I didn't use it because of fear of detection, mine because of its limited range.

Then my maps got a going-over, the alternate routes through Finland, Sweden, and Norway drawing extra attention.

With the mention of Bodö came a special pleasure, one of the few thus far, the "black flag."

Q. Before your flight on May 1, 1960, Colonel Shelton handed you a piece of black cloth. For what purpose was this cloth?

A. I don't know. I was already in the airplane when I got it from Colonel Shelton. He ordered me to give this piece of black cloth to the representatives of the 10-10 detachment who were to meet me in Bodö.

Q. In the event of your successful flight over the Soviet Union?

A. At that time he thought it would be successful.

Q. This was your point of destination, and you were to have been met by representatives of the 10-10 detachment?

A. Yes.

Q. And you were to have handed them this piece of black cloth which was given to you by Shelton before your flight to the USSR?

A. Yes.

Q. In other words, this cloth was something in the nature of a password?

A. I have no idea.

Q. But what do you think?

Thus far I had resisted the temptation to get smart with Rudenko, knowing it could be held against me. But he had led himself up this blind alley.

A. I did not think I would need a password; the plane itself was proof who I was.

Q. The plane itself and Powers himself. But why this piece of cloth?

A. I don't know. This was the only instruction I received on this.

Plainly exasperated, Rudenko said, "Let's leave this subject."

Unimportant though it seemed, this exchange marked a turning point. Realizing that I could occasionally shake up Rudenko, I was no longer completely on the defensive. From now on I was determined to make him work doubly hard for his answers.

He immediately stumbled into another thicket, with the duplicate maps.

As noted earlier, I had been given a set of survival maps, which, in the event I went down, were to enable me to find the borders of the USSR. These had originally been stamped "Confidential" and "U.S. Air Force," but someone had thoughtfully scissored out the words. Someone else, however, had stuck a second set in the plane, words still intact. A typical service snafu. But Rudenko was incapable of seeing that. He had to provide an explanation.

Q. This is quite clear, Defendant Powers. The two maps with these identifications cut out were in your possession and were to assist you, as you said, in getting out of the Soviet Union, but the other two maps were in the plane which you were to have destroyed on the orders of your masters.

That the explanation was nonsensical did not seem to occur to him. Apparently I had brought along an extra set of maps just so I could destroy them.

We came now to the watches and gold coins: Q. All these things were for bribing Soviet people?

A. It was to help me in any way to get out of the Soviet Union.

Q. I ask, for bribery?

A. If I could have done it, I would have resorted to bribing. If I could have bought food with the money, I would have bought it, for I would have had to make a fourteen-hundred-mile walk. In other words, the money and valuables were to be used in any way to aid myself.

Q. But you, of course, found that you were unable to use the money for bribing Soviet citizens. The very first Soviet citizens whom you met disarmed you and handed you over to the authorities.

A. I didn't try to bribe them.

Rudenko had no further questions. I was not finished testifying, however. It was now the turn of the presiding judge to examine me. I was getting a course in Soviet courtroom procedure, one which I could very well have done without.

PRESIDING JUDGE VIKTOR V. BORISOGLEBSKY: Defendant Powers, I ask you to answer my questions. What was the main objective of your flight on May 1?

A. As it was told to me, I was to follow the route and turn switches on and off as indicated on the map.

Q. For what reason?

A. I would assume that it was done for intelligence reasons.

In the transcript this was edited to remove Borisoglebsky's second question and revise my reply as follows: "As it was told to me, I was to follow the route and turn switches on and off as indicated on the map. It stands to reason that this was done for intelligence reasons."

Q. You testified in this court yesterday that Colonel Shelton was particularly interested in rocket-launching sites.

A. Yes, he did mention one place on the map where there was a possible rocket-launching site.

Q. Would it be correct to say that the main objective of your flight on May 1 was to discover and register on the map all rocket-launching sites?

A. I can only express my opinion on this matter. I feel sure that the experts who studied the film from my camera know what interested the people who sent me, but in my own opinion Soviet rockets interest not only us but the whole world as well. And I assume a flight like this would be to look for them, I suppose. But I repeat, I do not know, and I'm only expressing my own opinion.

As previously mentioned, the rocket-launching site, Tyuratam Cosmodrome, was not a primary target on this particular overflight but had been thrown in since I would be in the vicinity. I had emphasized it in the interrogations in the hope, successful I felt, that the Russians would focus on this rather than our major objectives.

Q. Defendant, did you realize that by intruding into the airspace of the Soviet Union you were violating the sovereignty of the USSR?

A. Yes, I did.

Q. Why did you agree?

A. I was ordered to do so.

Q. Do you think now you did your country a good or an ill service?

A. I would say a very ill service.

Q. Did it not occur to you that by violating the Soviet frontiers you might torpedo the Summit Conference?

A. When I got my instructions, the Summit was farthest from my mind. I did not think of it.

Q. Did it occur to you that a flight might provoke military conflict?

A. The people who sent me should have thought of these things. My job was to carry out orders. I do not think it was my responsibility to make such decisions.

Q. Do you regret making this flight?

Grinev had warned me the question was coming. I had expected it from him or Rudenko, not the presiding judge. If I had entertained any doubts that they were working as a team, this settled them.

A. Yes, very much.

I didn't add that I regretted it only because it was unsuccessful.

Another of the judges, Major General Alexander I. Zakharov of the Air Force, now had his inning. As might be anticipated, his questions dealt with my flight training, details of the May 1 mission, instrumentation, and so forth. Except for a query about the granger, in which I managed to make clear it was designed for air-to-air rockets, none were loaded questions. Most of those which followed, from Major General Dmitry Z. Vorobyev of the Artillery, were. Vorobyev tried to trap me into saying I was familiar with the special equipment, but failed.

It was interesting how the questions dovetailed. What Rudenko left out, Grinev or one of the judges put in.

Finally I was allowed to sit down. Counting the previous day, I'd been on the stand nearly six hours.

Looking exceedingly uncomfortable in suits and ties, and obviously nervous about appearing before such a large audience, the four men from the state farm (who were later decorated by the USSR for heroism) related the details of my "capture."

Something was missing from their testimony, but not until the last one had finished did I realize what it was. None of the four had mentioned the second parachute we had seen.

Why?

At the time, I had assumed the parachute was in some way

connected with the rocket. Now I began to wonder if, in addition to the U-2, the Soviets had also shot down one of their own planes.

With that same "first shot."

Asked if I had any questions for them, I said, "I want to express my thanks for the help that was shown to me by all these people on that day. This is the first opportunity I have had to thank them. I am happy to thank them."

Since "voluntary surrender" was one of the mitigating circumstances, I wanted it clearly established that I had not resisted capture and felt no antagonism toward them.

It was now the turn of the "expert witnesses." Functioning as a committee, each group had been assigned for study a certain portion of the evidence.

The first group, after examining the various documents found on me or on the plane, concluded that "the pilot Francis Powers belongs to the Air Force of the United States of America."

Grinev didn't object. But by now I had given up expecting him to. The court seemed to accept their finding as fact.

The next group had been given the task of examining the wreckage and determining whether there were identification marks on the aircraft. They concluded that there were not and had never been.

I knew better. Given a chance to question their spokesman, I asked whether the identification marks could have been placed on top of the paint and then removed. Though he conceded the possibility, the presiding judge made clear that he accepted the original testimony. I realized it was useless to persist.

Other witnesses, after lengthy examination of the special equipment—cameras, exposed film, radio receiving instruments, magnetic recorders, etc.—concluded that they had been used for reconnaissance and that the purpose of the flight was espionage.

After this, there was a break for lunch. This time the guards kept me surrounded. Apparently they had sensed that I was ready to bolt and were determined to give me no second chance.

With the start of the second session at 4:30 P.M. there was no longer any doubt as to why Rudenko had earlier emphasized the pistol.

The expert witness, a lieutenant colonel in the Engineers, stated: "The pistol is designed for noiseless firing at people in attack and defense."

I was now to be made a potential assassin, even though my weapon was only a .22.

But he didn't stop at that. Examining other portions of my survival equipment, he observed: "The above-mentioned vials represent an incendiary means consisting of a packing, combustible substance and a friction-type ignition device. On the exterior surface of the packing there is a brief instruction for use of the vials written in English. Such vials are manufactured for special use when it is necessary for flame to act for a comparatively long time on the object to be set on fire."

The implication was obvious. If I was shot down and succeeded in escaping, I was to act as an agent, either assassinating people or engaging in sabotage, using these "incendiary vials" to burn down important buildings, and similar acts.

I couldn't let this pass.

DEFENDANT POWERS: Would it be possible for me to see one of those things referred to as a vial?

After being handed one, I asked if the interpreter could read aloud the instructions on the cover.

INTERPRETER: "Ignition vial M-2, combustible. To ignite, break open red lid with pin, pull wire from inside. Do not handle red section. Use thin piece of dry wood as shown in drawing." And there is the illustration of a campfire. Defendant Powers claims that this substance is used to light campfires, and in particular, with damp wood.

DEFENDANT POWERS: As regards the pistol, it was given only for hunting, and I took it for this purpose. Unfortunately, nobody but myself knows that I cannot kill a person even to save my own life.

PRESIDING JUDGE: Defendant Powers, you are aware that at an altitude of sixty-eight thousand feet it is difficult to hunt game.

DEFENDANT POWERS: Yes, I know. This was to be used only in case I had a forced landing.

Other experts had examined the destruct mechanism. Again there were implications. "The elements of the remote-control circuit were not found. . . . The safety catch may be connected mechanically with any part of the aircraft that separates when the plane is abandoned by the pilot, for example with the cockpit ejector system."

In short, they were implying that had I tried to use the ejection seat, I would have been destroyed with the plane.

Since the elements of the remote-control circuit were missing (or rather, I suspected, simply hadn't been introduced into evidence), there was no way for me to prove otherwise.

On coming to the poison pin, they stated that it had been "found at the place where the plane, piloted by Powers, fell." Obviously they didn't want to admit the truth: that it had been missed in three separate searches, being discovered only after I had been taken to Sverdlovsk.

Well aware of its effect on the audience, they got maximum propaganda value out of the pin. An expert testified: "An experimental dog was given a hypodermic prick with the needle extracted from the pin, in the upper third part of the left hind leg. Within one minute after the prick the dog fell on his side, and a sharp slackening of the respiratory movements of the chest was observed, a cyanosis of the tongue and visible mucous membranes was noted. Within ninety seconds after the prick, breathing ceased entirely. Three minutes after the prick, the heart stopped functioning and death set in."

As if this weren't gory enough, he went on to describe similar experiments with a white mouse, finally concluding: "In view of the extremely high toxicity and the nature of the effect of the poison on animals and also the relatively large amount of it on the needle, it can be considered that if a person is pricked with this needle, poisoning and death sets in just as quickly as in animals."

With this they had their headlines for the second day. Shortly afterward, the court adjourned until the next morning.

Nine

The first sentences of Rudenko's speech were typical of his whole oration: "Comrade Judges! I begin my speech for the prosecution in the present case fully conscious of its tremendous importance. The present trial of the American spy-pilot Powers exposes the crimes committed not only by Defendant Powers himself, but it completely unmasks the criminal aggressive actions of United States ruling circles, the actual inspirers and organizers of monstrous crimes directed against the peace and security of the peoples!"

And on it went. "The Soviet people, the builders of a communist society, are engaged in peaceful creative labor and abhor war." The ruling circles in the United States "are stubbornly opposing measures for universal disarmament and the destruction of rockets and nuclear weapons. . . ."

Peace v. War. The USSR v. the USA and Francis Gary Powers.

"Powers became a staff pilot, ready to commit any crime to further the interests of the American military who are in service of the monopoly capital. . . . Here we have the bestial, misanthropic morality of Mr. Dulles and company which for the sake of that yellow devil, the dollar, disregards human life. . . . If the assignments received by Powers had not been of a criminal nature, his masters would not have supplied him with a lethal pin. . . ."

There were only two surprises in the early portions of Rudenko's speech. One was that in May President Eisenhower had given assurances "that spy flights by American planes in the Soviet airspace would be stopped."

But Rudenko immediately damned Eisenhower for going back on his word.

Had the overflights stopped or hadn't they?

There was another brief and tantalizing reference. After tracing the history of the U-2 incident, Rudenko stated: "A great wave of indignation swept the world when it became known that new perfidious acts had been committed by the rulers of the United States who sent an RB-47 military reconnaissance bomber on a criminal provocative flight into the Soviet Union on July 1, 1960."

This explained why shortly after July 1 I had been quizzed again on the RB-47 flights. Obviously there had been another "incident," but how serious? Rudenko gave no details.

"Defendant Powers, whose crimes the American intelligence service paid for so generously, is not an ordinary spy, but a specially and carefully trained criminal. . . . Such is the true face of Defendant Powers. And had his masters tried to unleash a new world war, it is precisely these Powerses, reared and bred by them in the conditions of the so-called free world, who would have been ready to be the first to drop atom and hydrogen bombs on the peaceful earth, as similar Powerses did when they threw the first atom bombs on the peaceful citizens of the defenseless cities of Hiroshima and Nagasaki. . . ."

So I was to be blamed even for that.

Listening to him, I felt sick at heart, knowing I was at least in part responsible for giving him the opportunity to mount his harangue. Yet, as he continued—he had passed the two-hour mark by now—not only stating his case but overstating, magnifying, distorting, and exaggerating, raving rabidly about the "American aggressors" being "newly baked imitators of Hitler," I began to wonder if maybe he wasn't going too far, carrying Soviet propaganda to such extremes it might backfire, precipitating a reverse reaction.

Suddenly the hall grew quiet. Rudenko was reaching the end.

"The hour when the criminal is to hear the sentence of the court is near.

"Let your sentence serve as a strict warning to all those who pursue an aggressive policy, criminally trample underfoot the generally recognized standards of international law and the sovereignty of states, who declare their state policy to be one of cold war and espionage. Let this sentence also be a strict warning to all other Powerses who, by orders of their masters, might try to undermine the cause of peace, to encroach upon the honor, dignity, and the inviolability of the great Soviet Union.

"Comrade Judges, in full support of the state indictment against Powers, in accordance with Article 2 of the Law of the USSR 'On Criminal Responsibility for State Crimes,' I have all grounds to ask the court to pass an exceptional sentence on the defendant. . . ."

I had been right. They were going to make an example of me.

"But, taking into account Defendant Powers' sincere repentance, before the Soviet court, of the crime which he committed, I do not insist on the death sentence being passed on him, and ask the court to sentence the defendant to fifteen years' imprisonment."

My immediate feeling was elation. It was as if I had been suffocating and was suddenly able to take a big, deep breath. I wasn't going to be shot!

I looked for my family. There was a disturbance in their box, but because of the popping flash bulbs and crowds of reporters, I couldn't see what was going on. Upon hearing the sentence, my father had stood up and angrily shouted, "Give me fifteen years here, I'd rather get death!"

The presiding judge declared a thirty-minute recess.

During the adjournment, Grinev tried again to persuade me to amend my statement. I didn't even bother to answer him.

After the intermission Grinev began his summation for the defense.

At first I couldn't believe I was hearing him right.

"I shall not conceal from you the exceptionally difficult, unusually complicated position in which the counsel for the defense finds himself in this case.

"Indeed, Defendant Powers is accused of a grave crime—intrusion into the airspace of the Soviet Union for the purpose of collection espionage information and photographing from the air industrial and defense installations and also of collecting other intelligence data. . . .

"The Constitution of the Soviet Union, which, irrespective of the gravity of a crime, ensures every accused the right to defense, makes it our civil and professional duty to render help in exercising this right to those defendants who avail themselves of this right. . . ."

He was defending himself for having to defend me!

But he didn't stop there. He went on to observe that "the defense challenges neither facts of the charges preferred against Powers or the assessment of the crime given by the state prosecutor."

Powers was guilty as charged, he emphasized. And then it became clear, for the first time, what his defense was to be: "I shall be right if I say that the Powers case is of international importance, inasmuch as besides Powers, one of the perpetrators of a perfidious and aggressive act against the Soviet Union, there should sit and invisibly be present here, in the prisoner's dock, his masters, namely, the Central Intelligence Agency headed by Allen Dulles and the American military and with them all those sinister aggressive forces which strive to unleash another world war."

Powers was, he stated, "only a pawn"; though "the direct perpetrator, he is not the main culprit."

Since I had refused to denounce the United States, Grinev was doing it for me.

I could barely contain my disgust. On one thing I was determined: when the trial was over, by some manner or means, to make it clear I had no part in this.

There were extenuating circumstances, he asserted: the poverty of Powers' family; "mass unemployment in the United States"; Powers, "as every other American, was taught to worship the almighty dollar"; "influenced by these ethics, Powers lived under the delusion that money does not stink. . . ."

Interspersed among justifications were more denunciations: "The ruling monopoly circles of the United States could not reconcile themselves to the existence of a socialist country in which the social system is based upon the principles of social justice, on love and respect for the dignity of man."

Grinev was trying his best to outdo Rudenko. It was as if each time he defended me he had to backtrack, to prove again he was only doing his job, that his feelings and sympathy were with the prosecution.

To those mitigating circumstances we had discussed, he added others: Powers was still young, he had just turned thirty-one; when signing his contract with the Central Intelligence Agency, he did not know the real purpose of the task set before him; poisoned by the lies in the American press, he had been misinformed about the USSR.

With these considerations in mind, Grinev asked the court "to mitigate his punishment" and "to apply to Powers a more lenient measure of punishment than that demanded by the state prosecutor."

"Your verdict," he concluded, "will add one more example to the numerous instances of the humaneness of the Soviet court, and will offer a sharp contrast to the attitude to man on the part of the masters of Powers—the Central Intelligence Agency, the ruling reactionary forces of the United States who sent him to certain death and wanted his death."

Grinev was done. There remained only my final statement and the verdict.

PRESIDING JUDGE: Defendant Powers, you have the word for the last plea.

I stood, facing the judges. The lights of the television cameras were so bright that I had trouble reading the statement. But we had gone over it so often that I knew the words. Some went against the grain; some were deeply felt. I could only hope that in reading them the American people could distinguish among them.

"You have heard all the evidence of the case, and you must decide what my punishment is to be.

"I realize that I have committed a grave crime, and I realize that I must be punished for it.

"I ask the court to weigh all the evidence and take into consideration not only the fact that I committed the crime but also the circumstances which led me to do so.

"I also ask the court to take into consideration the fact that no secret information reached its destination.

"It all fell into the hands of the Soviet authorities.

"I realize the Russian people think of me as an enemy. I can understand that, but I would like to stress the fact that I do not feel nor have I ever felt any enmity whatsoever for the Russian people.

"I plead the court to judge me not as an enemy but as a human being who is not a personal enemy of the Russian people, who has never had any charges brought against him in any court, and who is deeply repentant and profoundly sorry for what he has done.

"Thank you."

PRESIDING JUDGE: The court retires to determine the verdict.

It was 12:50 P.M. I was taken directly to lunch, but couldn't eat. Learning that I would see my family directly after the verdict gave me something to look forward to. But my anger with Grinev remained, overwhelming any sense of relief I otherwise would have felt about knowing I wasn't going to die.

Grinev had gone out of his way to "make" the state's case. What Rudenko couldn't prove, Grinev had freely conceded.

Several times he had negated my own testimony. With great care I had thwarted each attempt to extract a so-called "admission" I had been ordered to kill myself. Ignoring this, Grinev had stated that I had been so ordered as if it were an established fact.

He had gone further, implying in closing that the CIA knew I would be shot down, thus setting the stage for the Summit's collapse.

He had introduced into evidence statements never made. One— "I was deceived by my bosses; I never expected to find such a good treatment here"—wasn't even the way I talked. Bothering me even more, however, was one statement I *had* made which, taken out of context of the interrogations, gave an entirely false impression. At one point I had indicated that if I returned to the United States I would probably be tried there also, for revealing the details of my CIA contract. I didn't really believe this, but had said it to make my answers and my hesitations about answering appear more believable. However, I had gone on to add, "But this worries me little, because I am not likely to return home."

By this I had meant I was sure of being executed.

Grinev made it sound as if I intended to remain in the Soviet Union.

But worst of all, speaking as my representative, he had given the impression that I authorized and agreed with his attack against the United States.

But I was not without a voice now. I would be seeing my family. And they could convey to the press my entire repudiation of my "defense counsel" and his charges.

Should I go beyond that, try to give them a verbal message for the agency?

Though hopeful we would be left alone, I doubted that we would be. I had managed to get across, in my trial testimony, most of the things I wanted the agency to know. And, no matter how carefully worded, such a message could place my family in jeopardy. That was the last thing I wanted. I decided against it.

My anger with Grinev had at least one positive effect. It helped pass the time. At 5:30 P.M., four hours and forty minutes after the judges went out, I was summoned back into the courtroom.

While I stood, my hands gripping the wooden railings on either side of the prisoner's dock, the presiding judge read the verdict. It was a lengthy document, so long in fact that I suspected it had been written well in advance and not during the few hours the judges were out. That it was available to reporters, in printed form, immediately upon conclusion of the trial, would appear to confirm this. Again there was a recitation of the charges, during which it became obvious that the judges had not only accepted the prosecution's case in its entirety, including the testimony of the "expert witnesses," but that they had, in some instances, even gone beyond Rudenko, as when they stated that "subsequent events confirmed that the aggressive intrusion of the U-2 intelligence plane into the airspace of the Soviet Union on May 1 was deliberately prepared by the reactionary quarters of the United States of America in order to torpedo the Paris Summit meeting, to prevent the easing of international tension, to breathe new life into the senile cold-war policy. . . ."

I was guilty not only of espionage but all this too.

As, in absentia, was my co-defendant, the United States of America.

The judge was now nearing the end. It came across in his tone, and was communicated to the whole auditorium, which became very still.

Having heard all the testimony, and having examined all material evidence, the judge said, "the military division of the USSR Supreme Court holds established that Defendant Powers was for a long time an active secret agent of the U.S. Central Intelligence Agency, directly fulfilling spy missions of this agency against the Soviet Union, and on May 1, 1960, with the knowledge of the government of the United States of America, in a specially equipped U-2 intelligence plane, intruded into Soviet airspace and with the help of special radio and photographic equipment collected information of strategical importance, which constitutes a state and military secret of the Soviet state, thereby committing a grave crime covered by Article 2 of the Soviet Union's law 'On Criminal Responsibility for State Crimes.'"

The photographers moved into place. I was determined to show no emotion, whatever the sentence. But my fingers gripped the railing even tighter.

"At the same time," the judge continued, "weighing all the circumstances of the given case in the deep conviction that they are interrelated, taking into account Powers' sincere confession of his guilt and his sincere repentance, proceeding from the principles of socialist humaneness, and guided by Articles 319 and 320 of the Code of Criminal Procedure of the Russian Soviet Federated Soviet Republic, the military division of the USSR Supreme Court *sentences*:

"Francis Gary Powers, on the strength of Article 2 of the USSR Law 'On Criminal Responsibility for State Crimes,' to *ten years of confinement.* . . ."

I didn't hear the rest. I looked for my family, but in the confusion couldn't see them. All over the hall people had stood and were applauding. Whether because they felt the sentence suitably harsh or humanely lenient I did not know.

From the moment Rudenko had said he would not ask for the death sentence, I had expected the full fifteen years.

Only as I was being led from the courtroom did the full impact of the sentence hit me.

Ten long years!

My mother, father, sister Jessica, Barbara, and her mother were already in the room when I was ushered in. I couldn't help it. Seeing them, I broke down and cried. They were all crying too.

My hopes for a private meeting were overly optimistic. Besides four guards, two interpreters, and a doctor, there were also, for the first few minutes, a half-dozen Russian photographers.

A table had been set up in the center of the room, with sandwiches, caviar, fresh fruit, soda, tea. None of us touched it. We just looked at each other. For three and a half months we had been awaiting this moment, fearful that it might not occur, but still saving up things to say. Now that it was here, they were all forgotten. There would be long silences; then everyone would try to talk at once. I hadn't realized how much I'd missed hearing a Southern accent, until hearing five of them.

It was mostly small talk, but I'd had very little of that. Family news. Messages from sisters, nephews, nieces. A report on how our dog, Eck, was adjusting to Milledgeville. Decisions—whether to sell the car, rent or buy a house, ship the furniture from Turkey.

I now learned the rest of my sentence, which I had not heard in the courtroom. "Ten years of confinement, with the first three years to be served in prison." This meant, one of the interpreters explained, that after three years in prison I might be assigned to a labor camp in some obscure part of Russia. With permission, my wife could live nearby and make "conjugal visits." There was also the possibility, one of the American attorneys had told my father, that I could apply for the work camp when half my prison time was served, in other words in a year and a half. And my sentence started from the moment of my capture, which meant I had served over three and a half months of it already. Of course, there were still other possibilities. They were appealing to both President Brezhnev and Premier Khrushchev. They had tried to see the premier, but he was vacationing at the Black Sea, although his daughter, Elena, had attended the trial.

We grasped and held tightly like precious things the little bits of hope in the sentence. But the words "ten years" hung over the room.

We tried to make plans, but too much remained unknown. Barbara wanted to stay in Moscow, possibly get a job at the American Embassy. I was against that. There was no assurance they would let her visit me, and I would soon be transferred to a permanent prison outside Moscow; I hadn't been told where or when.

I learned another bit of news. The Russians had shot down an RB-47 on July 1, somewhere in the Barents Sea. The Soviets said it had violated their territory; the United States declared it hadn't. The pilot had been killed; the two surviving crew members—Captains Freeman B. Olmstead and John R. McKone—were being held by the Russians. There was no word yet as to whether they would be brought to trial.

I knew neither man. But I knew how they felt.

My mother had brought me a New Testament. One of the guards took it; it would have to be examined, the interpreter explained. Barbara brought a diary, which I'd asked for in one of my letters. That was taken too. I wondered whether my captors were worried about hidden messages or whether they thought my own family was trying to smuggle poison to me.

Noticing I was without a watch, my father offered me his. No, I told him, they probably wouldn't let me keep it, and if they did, I'd only be watching the time.

My mother was concerned about my loss of weight. I was concerned about their health. All showed the tremendous strain they had been under, Barbara especially. Her face was very puffy, as if she had been crying or—I hated to think it—drinking heavily.

The friction between Barbara and my parents was obvious,

though the cause remained a puzzle. I was determined that if allowed to see them again—the interpreter had said this might be possible—I would try to arrange separate visits.

The interpreter warned us that our hour was nearly up.

I had a message for the press, I told them. Grinev's denunciation of the United States had come as a shock to me. I had not known what arguments he would use, until hearing them in court. I repudiated them, and him, entirely. As for his statement that I might remain in the Soviet Union, I would leave Russia, and gladly, the minute they let me do so. I was an American, and proud to be one.

The hour was up. The guards led me away.

That evening the guards brought me the New Testament and the diary. The latter was a five-year diary. I would need two of these, I realized, before my sentence was completed.

My first entry was brief, purposely. I was afraid that once starting to write, I would release a well-spring of pent-up emotions.

August 19, 1960: "Last day of trial. 10 yr. sentence. Saw my wife and parents for one hour."

The nineteenth was a Friday. Saturday and Sunday were very hard. Everything went on as usual in the prison, yet, knowing I had ten years to look forward to, everything was subtly, immutably changed.

Looking back, I could see I had brainwashed myself into anticipating the death sentence. Perhaps it was a trick of the mind, an escape device. Perhaps unconsciously I had realized all along that for me the worst possible punishment would be a long imprisonment.

On Monday, August 22, I was taken to the Supreme Court Building in central Moscow for my last meeting with my mother, father, and sister, during which my father several times referred cryptically to "other efforts" being made to secure my release.

I had no idea what they were. But he obviously did not wish to elaborate, with my jailers present.

He was extremely angry with Grinev. McAfee had sent him, weeks ago, a detailed brief with suggestions for my defense. He had given no indication of having read it.

I said that I was not exactly happy with his "defense" myself, that Grinev had made it through the trial with a perfect score—not a single objection, not one statement which contradicted the prosecution.

As my father had already told the press, he was convinced that the Russians wouldn't make me serve my full sentence. If for no other reason, they wouldn't want the expense of feeding me.

I hoped he was right, but was afraid it wouldn't be quite that simple.

It was a difficult parting: my parents leaving their only son in this hostile land; I was not sure, considering their age and health, whether I would see either of them again.

After they left, Barbara and her mother came in. They brought along a United States Embassy "News Bulletin," with quotations from President Eisenhower's last press conference. The President regretted "the severity of the sentence," noted that the State Department was still following the case closely and "they do not intend to drop it," and added that there was no question of my being tried on my return to the United States. As far as the government was concerned, I had acted in accordance with the instructions given me and would receive my full salary while imprisoned.

The Moscow embassy personnel had been very helpful, Barbara said. Although they had failed in all their attempts to see me, they had collected over fifty paperback books for me from their private libraries. And they would handle arrangements for my monthly package.

Under Soviet law, each prisoner could receive one seventeen-pound package from home each month. On receiving the money and being informed what I needed, the Embassy would purchase the items and see that I received them. Although not sure what was and wasn't permitted, we made up a list of items I most wanted: American cigarettes, shaving gear, instant coffee, sugar, canned milk (to go over the boiled oats sometimes served for breakfast), news magazines, books, and more books. Asking the interpreter what I would need in the way of clothes—he suggested heavy shoes, work clothes, a warm topcoat, winter underwear, a fur cap with earflaps—Barbara promised to obtain them before leaving Moscow. She intended to stay until Friday, hoping to see Khrushchev on his return.

Thoughtfully, Barbara's mother then left, so we could be alone. As alone as you can be with an interpreter and two guards.

Through the use of guarded phrases, I was able to piece together a number of things. Arrangements had been made by the "U.S. government," by which I assumed she meant the agency, for her to receive five hundred dollars from my pay each month, the balance to be banked pending my return. My "employers" had also paid her way to Russia and arranged for two lawyers, members of the Virginia Bar Association, to accompany her. Their major task, I gathered from her remarks, was to interview me for the agency, but they had been refused permission to see me.

My father has arranged with *Life* to pay his and mother's expenses. And this, apparently, was what had caused the schism between my wife and my parents. The agency had offered to pay their fares also, but my father had refused, wanting to remain a free agent. Barbara, quite bitterly, declared that she wasn't. She couldn't speak to the press without permission. Everywhere she went, she was followed.

Time was up, the interpreter said.

After Barbara had been escorted out, the interpreter returned and said, "There's an American here who would like to see you."

Though I had dreamed for months of just such words, actually hearing them startled me.

"An American? Who?"

I thought perhaps it was someone from the embassy.

"An American tourist who has been given permission to visit you. Do you wish to see him?"

"Of course."

While I was waiting, another thought occurred to me. Maybe the agency had managed to get someone in.

Although his clothing obviously marked him as an American, the man wasn't familiar. Middle-aged, florid faced, he seemed very nervous. Pumping my hand, he told me his name and said, "Perhaps you've heard of me?"

I had to admit I hadn't.

This seemed to deflate him somewhat; reaching inside his wallet, he extracted a sheaf of clippings. "These are all about me," he said, "when I was a candidate for the Presidency of the United States, in 1956."

Looking at the clippings, I saw that he had run as the candidate of the Progressive party. But the name, Vincent Hallinan, still meant nothing to me.

He was an attorney, he explained, and had attended the trial as a guest of the Soviet government. The trial, in his opinion, was absolutely fair—

I was more than tempted to interject a dissenting opinion, but he gave me no chance.

—and my sentence very lenient. Now, as for ways of spending my time, I should start by learning the language.

I agreed with that. In fact, this had been one of my intentions, although I was put off a bit by having a stranger tell me what to do.

Then I should spend my time studying the Communist form of government. It was a remarkable system. If I approached it with an open mind, realizing that the American system had grave flaws, I would learn a great deal.

Pausing only to light one cigarette after another, he gave me no time to reply, but after listening to him for a few minutes I had no inclination to do so.

If the Soviet Union had a Chamber of Commerce, I decided, Mr. Hallinan could easily win its presidency.

When he finished his spiel, he pumped my hand again and asked if there were any messages he could take to the United States for me.

There were a number of things I was anxious to tell the CIA. But I didn't think Mr. Hallinan was the man to serve as courier. Thanking him, I declined his offer.

It was only after he left that the full irony of it hit me.

During all the time I had been in the Soviet Union only one person had tried to indoctrinate me in the Communist form of government.

And he was an American.

I had thought my visits were over. On Wednesday, August 24, I had a surprise.

My parents and sister were leaving for the US today; Barbara would be leaving Friday. I was on the roof, having my afternoon walk, thinking about their going, when the interpreter arrived with two guards.

This was the first time I had seen the interpreter here, and it surprised me.

"Would you like to see your wife again?" He paused, waited a moment, and added, "Without guards?"

"You know the answer to that!"

"Come with us."

I was driven across town to another prison and taken to a cell. Although there were bars on the windows, it was arranged like a sitting room, with an easy chair, a table with fruit and soda on it, and a couch. On the end of the couch, neatly folded, were blankets and sheets.

Left alone, I inspected the room, looking for hidden microphones or peepholes, but could find none.

Barbara was ushered in a few minutes later. She hadn't expected the meeting either. Two Soviet officials had arrived at her hotel only a few minutes before and brought her here.

Seeing her up close, I was shocked at how much she had changed. Somehow I had missed it in our earlier meetings. She was drinking heavily, I was sure. Her speech was slurred, the strong smell of alcohol on her breath. I was extremely worried about her, but this was neither the time nor the place for a lecture or an argument.

We were left alone three hours.

The last time I saw her, she was walking down a long hall with the interpreter and a major. She didn't look back.

I didn't realize it then, but, in her own way, she was walking out of my life.

Diary, August 26, 1960: "I was told that Barbara and her mother left this morning. Feel all alone once more."

Letter to Barbara, September 5, 1960:

"So far my life has not changed much. I am still in the same cell, but I have more time on my hands, since there is no interrogation and no preparation for a trial. I am glad all that is over. I hope I never have anything like that to go through again.

"I am very despondent today. I don't know why so today more than any other day, but that is the way it is. Just the thought of spending ten years in prison is getting to me. . . . The way I feel now, I would much rather have stayed with the airplane and died there than spend any time in a prison.

"I can't help wondering if there will be a pardon of some kind or an exchange of prisoners, or maybe something will happen through diplomatic channels to set me free. I realize that any of these things could happen, but I cannot count on them. There is only one thing that is sure, and that is—my sentence is for ten years.

"I doubt if I will ever be able to go to a zoo again—that is, if I ever get out of here—without having the desire to set all the animals free. I have never, before this, thought very much on the subject, but I think all men and animals were born to be free. To take away one's freedom is worse than to take one's life."

Unexpectedly, the following day I was taken back to one of the interrogation rooms. Several KGB officials and an interpreter were present. Their faces were stern.

"On his return to the United States, your father told the American press that you did not believe you had been shot down at sixty-eight thousand feet."

Oh, God! All through the trial I had wanted to get one message across: that I had been flying at my assigned altitude when knocked down, that if other pilots were sent over it would be at the risk of their lives. And I had, I felt, succeeded in conveying this.

Suddenly it was as if it had all been in vain.

Ten

Father of Powers Says Pilot Doubts U-2 Was Shot Down

The story, which appeared on the front page of *The New York Times*, quoted my father as telling the Overseas Press Club: "He (Francis) said 'if I were shot down, there would have been an explosion behind me and an orange flash around me.' He didn't believe he was shot down."

Had I told my father this?

No. Obviously he had been confused by the testimony in court: the orange flash and the acceleration from behind were what convinced me there had been an explosion.

Would I be willing to write a letter to *The New York Times* clarifying the matter?

I hesitated just long enough not to appear too anxious.

It was the first letter I had been allowed to write anyone other than my family. I spent some time on the draft, relating details of the crash; reemphasizing "I was at maximum altitude, as stated in the trial, at the time of the explosion. This altitude was sixty-eight thousand feet"; and observing that while my father apparently misunderstood me on this matter, he "did not misunderstand me when he stated that when this was all over that I was coming home. I do intend to come home, and I pray that I will not have to stay in prison for ten years."

For reasons known only to the Russians, the letter, written September 6, was redated September 18, 1960, and mailed with a Moscow return address. By this time I was no longer in Moscow.

The reference to "maximum altitude" was not overlooked. On

the contrary, it got too much attention, almost giving the show away. As I learned later, *The New York Times*, in printing the letter, observed: "Military experts here said that sixty-eight thousand feet—the altitude at which Soviet reports have consistently said the plane was downed—was substantially under the maximum altitude of the plane, a fact that should have been known to Mr. Powers."

I couldn't blame my father for being confused. Apparently a great many others were also.

By now it was obvious that I had become the pawn in some sort of top-level power play, that there were some highly placed people in the United States unwilling to admit that Russia now had an effective defensive surface-to-air missile.

If what the Russians had told me was true—and I could see no reason for them to deceive me on this—many newspapers and magazines in the United States, including aviation journals, had accepted the fiction that I had experienced oxygen and/or engine trouble, radioed my base, then descended to thirty thousand feet, at which point I was shot down.

One of the most influential in spreading this nonsense, I later learned, was Representative Clarence Cannon, Democrat, Missouri, chairman of the House Appropriations Committee. Cannon had told the press on May 11 that Khrushchev had lied when he said the U-2 was shot down, that its capture had resulted from either a mechanical defect of the plane or some "psychological defect of the pilot."

I could only conclude the lower-altitude story was a "controlled leak," something someone in a high position, either in the military or the government, wanted disseminated and believed.

Why?

There were a number of possible explanations. The information I had conveyed was important intelligence. And perhaps that was the trouble. It was too important: it wreaked havoc with preconceptions, its implications extending far beyond the U-2 program itself.

Accepting the hard fact that Russia's defenses were much better than we had supposed meant reevaluating our own offensive capabilities, and, inevitably, spending more money for missiles, less for bombers. The United States was currently committed to the B-52 bomber. If the Soviets could down a high-flying U-2, the low-flying B-52 was a sitting duck.

Too, it was impossible to discount the human factor. Someone in our intelligence apparatus had goofed, maintaining that Russia did not have missile capability, while Russia obviously did; quite

possibly, face-saving was involved. Or it could be plain stubborn-
ness, the refusal to accept any information contrary to one's fixed
preconceptions.

Still another possibility occurred to me. While I didn't like to
think about it, I had to admit its existence—that this fiction was
being told to bolster the self-confidence of other pilots and flight
crews.

What was most frustrating was the knowledge that so long as I
remained a captive of the Russians there was nothing I could do
to dispel the lie. Anything I said—whether in my trial testimony or
my letters—was suspect: Powers is a prisoner of the Communists,
either by torture or drugs or brainwashing, they can make him say
anything they want.

In time, I was sure, my story would be verified by other evidence.
And the United States would have to face up to the unpleasant fact
that Russia had effective SAMs. I could only hope the delay wouldn't
prove dangerous or that the supporting evidence didn't consist of
downed planes and dead pilots.

Early on the morning of Friday, September 9, 1960, accompanied
by two guards, a lieutenant colonel, a major, a female interpreter,
and a driver, I rode out the gates of Lubyanka Prison. A second
car, containing three additional guards plus my few personal effects, followed.

In a short time we left "modern Russia" behind. The roads were
narrow, primitive, and in bad repair, necessitating frequent detours.
The occasional villages did not seem to have changed much since
Tolstoy's day, their inhabitants still living in log cabins. But, though
the day was overcast, the countryside was green, the horizons vast,
after so long between four walls, and I saw *trees*, the first in over four
months. I wondered how long it would be before I saw them again.

It was a pleasant drive. I wished it could have gone on forever.
But in a little more than three hours we reached our destination,
Vladimir Prison, located near the Trans-Siberian railroad, about 150
miles east of Moscow.

The approach to Vladimir Prison was deceptive. All you saw
was the large gray administration building, and no walls.

Once inside, I was turned over to prison officials. Whether a
country is Communist or democratic, there are common denomina-
tors—bureaucracy and red tape. More than an hour of answering
questions and filling out forms was required before my assignment

to building number 2. Exiting from the other side of the administration building, I could have no doubt where I was: the walls were better than fifteen feet high, brick; guards with machine guns and searchlights were stationed in towers at the corners.

As we walked through the long empty courtyard, past several buildings, then through an arched gateway, they watched our every step.

Surrounded by its own walls, building number 2 was a prison within a prison. Four stories high, its outside red firebrick, it looked all too secure.

The building superintendent was a roly-poly little major named Dimitri. Quite jolly, he seemed an unlikely jailer. Shortly after my arrival in his office, another man entered. He was about my height, but fairly thin, with a gaunt face that made it difficult to guess his age. He wore a black beret. I thought perhaps he worked in the prison.

"My name is Zigurd Kruminsh," he said in English, shaking my hand. Since handshaking was something my Russian captors never did, this should have been a clue. But I missed it.

I tried to pronounce his name, failed. "Sorry," I apologized, "but I'm still having trouble with these Russian names."

"*I'm not a Russian,*" he barked. "*I'm a Latvian!*" He said it less in anger than in pride.

The major said something, pointing to Zigurd's beret. This time his reply *was* angry, and defiant. I asked him what the major had said.

"He told me to remove my beret. I refuse to do so. They have cut off all my hair, and until the day they let me grow it back, I shall wear this. Because of my self-respect."

I liked him immediately.

While still at Lubyanka I had been asked whether on arrival at my permanent prison I wished to remain in solitary confinement or to have a cellmate. Knowing all too well that loneliness was my worst enemy, I had replied that most definitely I would like a cellmate; then, tempting my luck, I had requested one who spoke both English and Russian. This would eliminate the need for an interpreter, and I could learn Russian at the same time. My request had been granted. Zigurd Kruminsh (pronounced Zoo-gurd Crew-mage) I now learned, was to be my cellmate. He not only spoke and read English and Russian, but Latvian and German, knew considerable Esperanto, some French, and was currently studying Spanish.

After I had been searched by one of the guards, the two of us were taken to the second floor of the building to our cell, number 31.

It was twelve feet long, eight feet wide. The floor was wooden. The walls were painted a dark gray on the lower part, the upper portion and ceiling white.

Having become "stir wise," one of the first things I checked, once the guard had locked us in, was the window, to see if there was any way to look out. There were two. The glass in the upper section of the window was clear. From the floor you could see a bit of the sky. Standing on one of the beds, or the cabinet directly in front of the window, you could see a great deal more. But this, I presumed—correctly—was *zahpretne*, forbidden. However, in the lower section, there was a narrow crack, with a tiny hole in the end. Looking through, I could see the tops of several buildings passed on the way from the administration building, the wall separating our building from the rest of the prison, and the arched gateway. It wasn't exactly the kind of view one would pay a high rent to enjoy, but it had a distinct advantage. I would be able to see at least some of the other prisoners, whenever any were escorted through the gate. And that in itself was a big improvement over Lubyanka.

Looking through the hole, I noticed a few other things. The first sheet of glass was opaque. Behind it was a dead-air space about six inches deep, another window, this one clear glass, another space of about six inches, heavy bars, then about a foot to the outside. From this I was able to estimate that the brick walls were at least two feet thick.

In front of the window was a small cabinet. We could store our bread ration and extra food there, Zigurd told me.

The beds stretched alongside the two walls, separated by a space of about two and a half feet. I tried mine, the one on the left. Had I checked into a hotel in the United States and been given such a bed, I would have complained immediately. But compared to the iron slats at Lubyanka, it was comfort personified. I was rapidly learning that pleasures are relative.

At the foot of each bed was a cabinet and small wooden stool. The top of the cabinet could be used as a desk or table, the inside as storage space for underwear, socks, towels, cigarettes, toothbrush, toothpaste, shaving gear—which just about completed the inventory of our personal possessions.

At one corner near the door was an old-fashioned radiator. At the other, on Zigurd's side, a five-gallon can. I didn't have to ask what it was for.

The lighting arrangement was similar to that at Lubyanka—the night light an unshaded hundred-watt bulb over the door, the day light an identical bulb in the ceiling. But we had one item in our cell not in the earlier prison. On a shelf on the right-hand wall was a squawk box. From six A.M. to ten P.M., with a silent period between 2:30 and four P.M., it broadcast Radio Moscow. It offered music— folk, opera, classical; news; and lots of propaganda. You could turn the volume down but not off.

The door, complete with peephole, was similar to the one at Lubyanka, with the exception that in the lower portion there was a smaller door, about a foot square. At suppertime I learned its purpose: unlocked from the outside, it folded down into a shelf; when we slid our tin plates and bowls out, the serving woman would ladle our meals from a huge vat, and pass them back.

Supper the first night consisted of one item—boiled potatoes.

You could hear the serving woman moving the food cart from cell to cell. Later I counted them. There were ten on our side of the cellblock, twelve on the opposite side.

Of the four floors in our building, Zigurd told me, there were cells on the first and second, the third vacant, the doctors' and dentists' offices and the hospital on the fourth. Until a few days prior to my arrival, Zigurd had occupied a cell on the first floor. Building number 2 housed the worst political prisoners—those who had committed serious crimes against the state: for example, writers and intellectuals who had dared criticize the Soviet regime publicly, and people who had attempted to overthrow it.

Zigurd belonged in the latter category. Convicted of treason, he had received the maximum prison sentence, fifteen years. Of this, he had already served more than five, the first three in solitary confinement.

He was not reluctant to tell me his story. Rather, he seemed excited at the prospect of having someone to talk to.

What did I know about Latvia?

Very little, I admitted.

He described it—its forests and trees, its little villages, its people, their fierce nationalism—with an eloquence that could arise only out of deep love for one's homeland.

In 1940 Latvia had been overrun by the Russians, who had incorporated it as the Latvian Soviet Socialist Republic. Only thirteen at the time—he was now thirty-three, two years older than I—

Zigurd had, like many of his countrymen, nurtured a hatred for the Russians stretching back through centuries of invasion and annexations. In 1941 Germany had invaded Latvia, driving the Russians out. To many of the Latvians, to whom German was a second language, this seemed less a conquest than a liberation. In 1944, when Russia again attempted to reclaim Latvia, Zigurd had joined the German Army, over the opposition of his parents, in order to fight the Russians. What followed was one continuous retreat, while the Red Army pushed their unit back into Poland, then all the way into Germany. By this time it was apparent even to the troops that Germany had lost the war. Many conscripts from Latvia, Poland, and other occupied countries were willing to battle the Russians, but they felt no animosity toward France, Britain, or the United States. Ordered to fight the Allies, they deserted in great numbers, Zigurd among them. Knowing that if he was caught by the Russians he would be shot as a traitor, he headed west, trying to make his way to the American lines. Before reaching them, however, he was captured by the British and placed in a POW camp. There, and later, in a displaced persons' camp, he had learned English, which enabled him to get a job as guard at one of the British bases. While working there, he had been recruited by British intelligence, who flew him to England and put him through a special agents' school. Trained to operate and repair radio transmitters, he was eventually returned secretly to Latvia by boat, where he went to work in the underground, transmitting messages, helping to smuggle people in and out of the country, and working to overthrow the Soviet puppet regime in Latvia.

The group did not engage in sabotage. Its primary functions, apparently, were to provide intelligence from behind the Iron Curtain and to form a nucleus of partisans that could be of assistance in the event of war.

Though in the Latvian underground for over a year and a half, he did not attempt to contact his parents. Erroneously, he had been reported killed in Germany. Not wanting to endanger them because of his activities, he had allowed them to believe that he was dead.

In summer his group had camped in the forests. Winters were so severe, however, that they had to have shelter. The underground hid them on a farm. One night they received warning that the secret police were closing in on the transmitter. A guide arrived, to take them to safety. After walking some distance, he left them by the side of a road while he went for a transport.

Since he had the radio strapped to his back and didn't want it to be seen, Zigurd had left the others, retreating into the woods about one hundred feet, out of sight of the road, where he sat down on a log.

That was the last thing he remembered. On opening his eyes, he found he was staring at the checkerboard pattern in a wooden floor. He had been nearly frozen; now he was warm. Only then did he discover that he was bound to a chair in an interrogation room.

Though he had thought about it often, he was not sure how many hours or days had passed since his capture, nor exactly how it had occurred. He was sure he had been betrayed, however, and suspected the guide had been an informer. That he had been picked up so far back from the road, moments after arriving at the spot, indicated the secret police had been lying in wait.

After what he described as a "farce of a trial"—he was allowed no defense, the judge simply listened to the charges, then gave him the maximum prison sentence—he had been held in solitary confinement for almost three years, while they attempted to break him and make him identify others in the underground. Failing in this, they had transferred him to Vladimir.

When he arrived, his jailers had suggested that he write to his parents, giving them his new address. He had refused to do so. Rather than have them live under the stigma of a son in prison, he preferred that they believe him dead. But the Russians had written for him. His parents had come all the way from Latvia for a visit. And now they sent him letters and packages regularly.

That was Zigurd's story, as he first told it. Not until much later would I learn how much he had left out.

He apologized for his rough English. There had been more than five years since he had had an opportunity to use it.

We made a deal: I'd help him with his English if he would teach me Russian.

Several times during our talk I had heard tapping from the adjoining walls. Was it a code? I whispered. He nodded. What were they saying? "They're asking, 'Is Powers there?' "

Zigurd hadn't replied to the tapping. Not sure whether the cell was bugged, I didn't question him further. I guessed that having spent three years in solitary he was not willing to risk being returned there for a minor infraction of the rules.

Only on going to bed did he remove his beret.

There was another difference between Lubyanka and Vladimir. Here, after ten P.M., when the lights changed and the radio went off, you weren't allowed to remain up or to read.

Zigurd fell asleep almost immediately. I lay awake for several hours, thinking about my new world, wondering when, or if, I would ever adjust to it.

Insofar as first impressions went, I liked my cellmate. As he told it, his story sounded believable. But I knew I couldn't risk trusting him. There was always the possibility he was a Soviet "plant."

At first everything was strange. Within a few days it became routine, then, all too soon, monotonous.

At six A.M. the squawk box blared the musical call sign of Radio Moscow. I started to get up, but my cellmate told me to remain in bed. He had to do his exercises and needed the floor space. These completed, he swept the cell. I offered to do it; he insisted it was part of his exercises. In prison, I soon learned, work of any kind is coveted. Though it required less than two minutes, Zigurd retained the right to sweep the floor, and no matter how many times I protested, he refused to let me do it.

Once dressed, we were escorted to the toilet, taking along the bucket, which Zigurd emptied and then rinsed with a strong disinfectant. Only two trips to the toilet were allowed each day; in the interim there was the bucket. Zigurd insisted on carrying and washing it; this too was part of his exercise, he said. On this I stood firm. We reached a compromise, he taking it one trip, I the next.

The toilet was located at the far end of the cellblock. On opening the door, the smell was almost overpowering. The window was left open permanently in an attempt to air the room. It was not successful.

The toilets were of the Asian, that is, bombsight, type, consisting of open holes in the floor. Learning to squat over them took some getting used to.

There was only one washbasin, with Spartan cold water. Following my cellmate's example, I stripped to the waist and washed myself thoroughly. After that I was wide awake.

When we returned to our cell, I sorted out my new impressions. There was only one door to the cellblock, located midway down our row. There was also, for the whole cellblock, only one guard, who didn't wear a gun.

About seven o'clock he brought the *chaenek*, filled with hot water. We used part of it to shave. I was surprised to find Zigurd not only had a razor but also a small piece of broken mirror. With the rest of the water we made tea.

Between seven-thirty and eight, breakfast was served. We received the same food as the other prisoners, soup or porridge, ladled out of the huge kettle. There were two kinds of soup, one smelling strongly of fish and the other made primarily from dried peas. We received whichever kind was available that day. When porridge was served, it was one of several varieties—manna (similar to Cream of Wheat), boiled oats, barley, millet, or buckwheat. I liked the manna best. I couldn't stomach the fish soup; even when I held my nose, it smelled bad. At breakfast we were also issued our bread ration for the day: a good-sized piece of black or rye bread, about five inches long and three inches thick. Occasionally a lighter whole wheat was served instead. Delicious, fairly fresh white bread could be purchased from the commissary, as could margarine and, on rare occasion, butter. These extra items were available to anyone with money to buy them. Fortunately, before leaving Moscow, Barbara had left twenty-six hundred rubles (about $260) on deposit in my name, to cover such purchasable items, postage, and duty on packages. I was not too fond of black bread and usually gave Zigurd my ration.

There was a labor camp connected to the prison, with about 150 prisoners. Their barracks—which also housed the cooks and other service personnel—was one of the buildings I'd passed on the way from the administration building, and from the window I could see its upper floors, as well as the tops of the buildings in the work area itself. At eight each morning I'd peek through the crack in the window to watch some sixty to eight of the prisoners as they were marched through the arched gateway, around our building, and—on the other side, out of sight—through another gate into the work camp. Most wore prison-issue clothing, gray coat and pants, but some wore combinations of prison issue and their own.

I knew nothing about their life, and only a little about their work—apparently they worked with lumber, possibly making boxes or something similar, as I could hear a sawmill and hammering—but I envied their being outside and having something to do. I had already counted my time. It would be fifteen months before I could apply for transfer to a work camp, and even then there was no assurance the request would be granted.

After washing our breakfast dishes with newspapers, not a very sanitary method but all we could manage, there was about an hour and a half before our walk. We usually spent the time reading.

Zigurd was as happy as a child at Christmas when he saw all the American paperbacks I'd brought from Lubyanka. Otherwise, we'd study Russian. Finding it hard to concentrate, I was a slow pupil, but Zigurd was patient. In a remarkably short time, just from our conversations, his English improved greatly. He had a natural flair for languages and had given up the study of French only because, having no one to practice it with, he was afraid of developing bad pronunciation habits. It wasn't long before he had thoroughly indoctrinated me in one of his beliefs: every child in every country should be taught Esperanto. With all people able to converse in a common tongue, he was convinced that many of the world's problems would disappear.

About ten o'clock we were taken out for our walk. And I made some additional discoveries, negating those made earlier. Although our guard had keys to all the cells, he did not have a key to the door connecting our cellblock to the rest of the building. This had to be opened by a guard on the other side. So, even should we succeed in overpowering our guard, there still remained the problem of getting out of the cellblock.

The green, red, and white light arrangement wasn't used at Vladimir. But chance encounters were prevented by taking out only the occupants of a single cell at one time. According to my cellmate, this was of greater concern in our building than in others, because it housed political prisoners, that is, conspiring types. Some of the political prisoners had cellmates; many didn't. Those who did were carefully paired in order to prevent their spending their time plotting. In the work camp, there were five to seven men in each room.

Our cell faced east. The walk areas were on the opposite side of the building, at ground level. To reach them we were taken downstairs, then out and around the building. Set some distance away from the building, up against the wall, there were about seven of these courtyards. From his guardwalk, one man could watch them all.

Our courtyard measured twenty by twenty-five feet. It took ten seconds to make a complete circle. To break the monotony—we had two hours—we would sit in the sun and do pushups. Feeding the pigeons we enjoyed most of all. It wasn't long before I had several favorites and would watch for them each day.

From our courtyard we could see the windows of some of the cells on the west side of our building. Prisoners were forbidden to stand on their beds and yell out at those in the courtyards below. Some ignored the injunction. Zigurd would translate. For the first several days the messages were all the same.

"Is that Powers?" they would ask.

"Yes," Zigurd would yell back.

"Give him our best wishes."

I had wondered how other prisoners would react to the presence of an American spy. They were friendly, and curious.

They weren't the only curious ones. Cadets studying to be prison officials would visit Vladimir for practical experience. Often we could hear them outside the cell, whole classes lining up for their turn to look through the peephole at the American.

We could always tell when the building superintendent was making his rounds. The Little Major, as we dubbed him, was so fat that his belt buckle scraped against the door.

There was even less privacy than at Lubyanka. However, whenever we heard a sound outside—someone yelling, or, on one occasion, a gunshot—we devised a way to look out the top of the window without being observed. One of us would stand in front of the door, the back of his head covering the peephole, while the other looked out. It had to be quick, because if the guard looked in and saw the peephole blocked, he'd immediately open the door.

Lunch was the best meal of the day, consisting of an excellent soup and a plate of either cabbage, noodles, rice, manna, or mashed potatoes. We were also given two hundred grams, or about half a tin cup, of milk. This was a special privilege, Zigurd informed me; milk was usually reserved for convalescent patients in the hospital. Possibly it was due to the fact that I was still having some stomach trouble. On warm days the milk was usually spoiled, but by letting it stand until it turned to clabber and mixing in a little sugar, we made a passable yoghurt.

We were accorded still another special privilege, although several days passed before we were informed of it. I would be allowed to keep my hair, and since we were in the same cell, Zigurd would be allowed to grow his again. This pleased me as much as it did him, although for quite different reasons. The hair rule appeared to be arbitrary. Of those prisoners I could see from my window, most had their hair clipped short, but a number didn't. Among the latter, however, were apparently those shortly due for release. It was a small thing, perhaps entirely meaningless, but letting me keep my hair seemed to indicate that there might be some possibility of an early release. Of such fragmentary hopes are a prisoner's day made.

Actually, in retrospect, I suspect letting me keep my hair was intended less as a privilege than because it suited Soviet propaganda purposes. When, later, pictures were taken of me, which I was actually urged to send to my family, I looked healthier and far better-treated than would have been the case had I been scalped.

Masters of propaganda, the Russians carefully considered such things.

The afternoon passed slowly, and was spent in napping, reading, or studying. Supper, the worst meal of the day, was invariably potatoes or cabbage. After supper we took our second and last trip to the toilet. The evening was spent in much the same manner as mornings and afternoons.

One night we decided to test how far our "privileged state" extended. Using cardboard from a package, we made a shade for the night light, to keep it from shining directly in our eyes. Our privileged state didn't extend that far. Yelling "*Nyet!*" the guard rushed in and made us take it down.

Usually I would not fall asleep until after the changing of the guard, at midnight. Often much later. This was the very worst time for me. It seemed that the moment I was ready to go to sleep my mind would be filled with thoughts I couldn't suppress. During the day our conversation served to hold the most depressing of these in abeyance. In the still of the night they would sometimes rebound with nightmare intensity.

Nearly all concerned Barbara. Hopes, worries, and fears, and when I'd face up to it, thoughts about her, about me, about our marriage.

Through sheer willpower I'd nearly always succeed in suppressing such thoughts. But never for very long. I needed to trust my wife, but there was no reason to suppose that just because I was locked in a prison cell her pattern would change.

When sleep did come, it was often troubled.

This was my routine.

Fortunately, for our sanity, there were variations.

About once a week we were given a small cube of meat, usually thumbnail size. This was our sole meat ration, and we looked forward to it with a longing out of all proportion to what we actually received. We were starved for fats. There was margarine available from the prison commissary, but it didn't satisfy the body's craving.

Also about once a week the doctor or nurse came around to see how we were feeling, asking if we needed pills for constipation or aspirin for headaches. Oddly enough, the nurses were known as "Sisters," a lingering vestige of more religious days.

Zigurd told me a story relating to these visits. A former cellmate, a young boy arrested for painting posters satirizing Soviet leaders, had developed a crush on one of the nurses. There was no indication that his feelings were reciprocated, but he talked of nothing else, counting the days, hours, minutes, until her next visit. One day, while Zigurd was napping, he tore apart his tin plate and swallowed the pieces, knowing the doctors would have to operate to remove them and that he would remain in the hospital, within sight of her, while recuperating.

Sensing my skepticism, Zigurd assured me the story was true. When the guard took the boy out, Zigurd said he could hear the tin pieces rattling in his stomach as he walked.

It wasn't long before I accepted such stories as fact, the incredible all too soon becoming, if not acceptable, understandable. Many prisoners committed suicide. Others went mad. One, whether insane or merely feigning it to be transferred to a mental hospital, painted the walls of his cell with his excreta. Believing that he was faking his insanity, the prison officials left him in his own filth.

During his time at Vladimir, Zigurd had had several cellmates. Often he told me stories about them. Also, from shortly after his arrival, he had kept a journal. Sometimes he read me passages. Through him I was able to put together a comprehensive picture of prison life in Russia. And, I suspect, one much more honest than my captors wished me to have.

About once a month all prisoners were visited by a representative of the KGB, at first a major, later a colonel, who asked us if we needed anything, had any complaints or questions. Major Yakovlov was the political commissar for Vladimir, and it was apparent from his questions that "the people in Moscow" were anxious that their well-publicized American convict have as good an impression of Russia as possible, under the circumstances.

Why? Again it seemed to be evidence that I might be released shortly.

We requested books. There was a prison library, but none of its volumes were in English. There were English books available from Moscow University library, and Major Yakovlov arranged for them to send some. It took about a week to ten days before the first ones arrived.

Our greatest need was work. Zigurd asked the Little Major if there was anything we could do. All that was then available was a device for making fishnet-type shopping bags. Having made them previously, Zigurd showed me how. It was a complicated procedure, involving tying tight knots in cotton string, then pulling them together with a wooden shuttle. The cheap string filled the air with lint and dust. When after several days we began coughing up the lint, we started worrying about the effect on our lungs. Fortunately, by this time other work was available. The guard brought in paper, a pattern, glue, and a sharp knife, and we set to work making envelopes. Because paper was in short supply, we'd ration it, making only a certain number at a time in order to have work left for the following day. Aside from the few we used ourselves, I never learned what happened to the envelopes we made. Perhaps they helped fulfill some Five Year Plan.

At first the guard took the knife away each night. Later, apparently more sure of us, he allowed us to keep it in the cell.

With the envelope-making we could keep busy about an hour each morning and afternoon.

Still, time hung heavy. Zigurd did his best to lighten it. One day, reading a copy of *O. Henry's Short Stories*, one of the paperbacks I'd brought from Moscow, he came across the word "snoozer" and asked what it meant. I told him. That afternoon when I woke up from my nap there was a hand-lettered sign on my chest: "Biggest Snoozer South of the Arctic Circle."

I still thank God he had a sense of humor.

During his long imprisonment Zigurd had developed good study habits. I hadn't. Often, out of boredom, or just to escape having to memorize the Russian words, I'd look out the window. The guard didn't seem to mind when we peeked through the crack, but if we attempted to stand on the bed and look out the top, he'd either bang on the door or come in. One afternoon while looking out I had a surprise. A group of women was escorted through the gate. For some reason I had never imagined there were female prisoners here. Wearing black shawls, dresses that reached nearly to the ground, and felt boots, they were nearly all very old. Most, Zigurd told me, had been imprisoned as "religious fanatics." In a godless country, that category, I supposed, was a most comprehensive one. A they went through the gate, many of the women would cross themselves. I wondered if they were former nuns.

There was no difference between days of the week, with one exception. On Sundays the work camp was closed and the prisoners didn't march by. Yet we anticipated several other occasions far more than any holiday.

Every five days we were allowed to change our underwear, socks, and sheets. And every ten days was shower day.

On shower day, the usually strict security was relaxed somewhat. The bathhouse was located in the same building that housed the kitchen, on the other side of the gate, to the left as you walked toward the administration building. We were taken there at the same time as five to seven of the work-camp prisoners. There were several guards. And conversation was supposedly forbidden. But it went on anyway.

Each man was locked in a separate shower stall. The water was scalding hot, and the guards let you soak in it almost as long as you wanted.

There were several washbasins, and since hot water was available, which was not so with the sinks in our cellblock, the prisoners often used this opportunity to shave. Some, like Zigurd, had small pieces of mirror. One man had taken a regular double-edged razor blade and fastened it onto a stick with a bent nail. He shaved with it as deftly as if it were a straight razor.

The only other time we were taken outside our cells, other than for walks or to go to the toilet, was when we received a package. My first from the American Embassy in Moscow arrived on the twenty-fifth of September, and from then on, with one notable exception, the package came every month.

Escorted downstairs to the office of the building superintendent, we had to open the container in the presence of prison officials. On top were various magazines—*Time, Newsweek, Life.* These were placed in a stack to the side. *Zahpretne.* Unfavorable to the USSR. Not allowed. But, with scarcely a glance at their titles, books were allowed. As were the writing tablets, pen and pencil set, cigarettes, toothpaste, soap, deodorant, Chapstick; several items of clothing; and food.

We could now not only vary our menu somewhat—there were six cans of meat, four cans of fish, one jar of pickles, one jar of mustard, and nine boxes of cookies—but for breakfast we could have instant coffee, complete with sugar and Pream.

Zigurd also received one package a month, from his parents, usually containing some kind of smoked meat. The two package days became major events in our lives.

There were other, unexpected variations in our routine, not always pleasant.

Occasionally the lights would go off, power failures being fairly common in our part of Russia. If this happened at night it was a startling experience. We were accustomed to a light twenty-four hours a day, and it was amazing how dark the dark was. The only thing similar I had experienced was a spelunking expedition while in college, when a friend and I had become lost in a cave and turned out the flashlight—very briefly—to conserve the batteries.

At such times the guard would go from cell to cell distributing candles. Blowing them out, I was informed, was a punishment-cell offense.

I'd seen the outside of the punishment cells, located in the basement of the building between the administration building and the work-camp barracks, but had never seen inside one. Zigurd—whether from personal knowledge or hearsay, I never knew—said they were located half-underground, with a single window at the top for light and air. The furnishings consisted of one wooden bench. No blankets. And there were no sanitary facilities.

Late one night, within several weeks after my arrival at Vladimir, I discovered the one thing a prisoner fears more than any other.

Zigurd was already asleep. As usual, I was restlessly tossing and turning, when I caught the first acrid whiff.

"*Zigurd*," I cried; "*something's on fire!*"

Whatever it was, it wasn't in our cell. As the smoke smell grew stronger, we could hear running feet; that sound was soon drowned out by prisoners in other cells yelling or banging on their doors.

I had never known pure panic before. Not even when I thought I was trapped in the falling U-2 matched what I felt then. The building was old, the floors wood, we were locked in with no way to get out.

After a while the acrid smell diminished, and finally the cellblock became quiet again.

The next morning, although sure he already knew the answer, Zigurd asked the guard what had happened.

One of the prisoners had gone mad and set his mattress on fire.

Even though I was not allowed American newspapers or news magazines, we could obtain, fairly regularly, *Pravda* and the French Communist newspaper *L'Humanité*, and, occasionally, the American *Worker* and the British *Daily Worker*.

Of the last two, I preferred the British version. Though it had just as much propaganda, it also contained straight news dispatches from Reuters.

As for the other two papers, they played special roles in our lives.

Although Russian cigarettes could be purchased from the commissary, and I obtained American cigarettes in my embassy package, once a week each prisoner was issued a few ounces of coarse tobacco, made from ground-up tobacco stalks, for roll-your-owns.

There was a saying in the prison: *Pravda* best for cigarette paper, *L'Humanité* for toilet tissue.

Communist propaganda does have its uses.

Eleven

On September 21 I was told I would be allowed to write four letters per month. I decided, initially, to write two to Barbara, one to my parents, then, on different months, to alternate the remaining one among my sisters.

Unlike at Lubyanka, there was no attempt to dictate contents, nor were the letters edited, then rewritten. They were read, however, and we left the envelopes unsealed for that purpose.

As yet I hadn't received any mail from home. Though the move from Moscow had probably delayed it, it still concerned me. Zigurd suggested that in the future I do what he did. Work up an arrangement with my correspondents to number our letters. That way we could tell if any were missing.

I tried to make my letters as cheery as possible. This took some imagination, and even then didn't always come off. For example, in my first letter I noted, "Don't worry about me. Where I am there is very little that can happen to me. I am safer here than in an airplane. Think of it that way."

I neglected to add that, given a choice, I'd pick the sky.

Airplanes were very much on my mind, particularly after I had discovered that jets would occasionally pass overhead. Apparently we were near a letdown pattern. Several times, on our walks, I recognized MIG 17s and 15s.

Because to me flying had always been a form of freedom, the sound and sight of those MIGs filled me with special longing.

Although there was no evidence that our cell was bugged, we automatically presumed this to be the case, and by unspoken agreement saved certain topics of conversation for our walks. Escape was one.

We didn't admit it was impossible. To do so would have been to surrender one of our few hopes. But, considered realistically, we had to face the fact that our prospects were less than good.

Sawing bars and dropping two stories to the ground was out. We couldn't even reach the bars, without first breaking several windows.

The guards inside the prison had no guns. But those in the towers did. No prisoner ever crossed the yard alone. Even service personnel—cooks and others—were escorted. Seeing a prisoner without escort, guards were under orders to shoot.

I tried to remember some notable POW escapes during World War II. Most had involved digging tunnels. We weren't near any ground. The walk area was asphalt. And we were watched every minute.

During the war POWs were usually housed in barracks, in large groups. Thus they could plan, assign duties, establish cover, create diversions. Except for shower day, when there were guards present, we had no contact whatsoever with other prisoners. There was never a time, not even in the toilet, that we weren't subject to surveillance.

On October 1 I received three letters, two from my parents, one from my sister Jessie. The dates—September 13, 17, 19—indicated a delay of twelve to eighteen days.

The first letter from Barbara did not arrive until a week later. It was dated September 10, and had taken twenty-seven days.

She had answered two of mine with one of hers. Unless some letters were missing, this was the first time she had written since the trial, and that bothered me. Her news wasn't good. Neither Khrushchev nor Brezhnev had acknowledged receiving the appeals.

Yet just receiving mail made the day an occasion. And to top it off, that afternoon I saw my first movie.

The theater was located in the work-camp barracks; about forty prisoners were already in the small auditorium, seated on wooden benches, when we arrived. We weren't allowed to join them. My cellmate and I, plus a guard, shared a bench in the projection room, watching the movie through a small glass window. Here, as elsewhere, the "politicals" were strictly segregated, not only from other prisoners but also from each other. No more than one or two attended each showing.

Between reels the lights would come on, and the work-camp

inmates would turn around in their seats to stare up at us in frank curiosity. I was equally curious about them.

We were forbidden to talk to the projectionists, who were also prisoners. However, you don't need words to convey a feeling of mutual sympathy.

The movie was about deep-sea diving. Zigurd translated enough for me to follow the plot. It wasn't particularly good, but the change was most welcome.

Sometimes, Zigurd told me, there would be a movie almost every week. At other times, months would pass before the prison received a print. Too, it was a privilege revocable at any time, on whim of the authorities. During one period the Soviets had attempted to make Vladimir a "showcase prison," even allowing TV. That phase had quickly passed. Now it was like any other, a place apart from the main current of life; yet, not quite. There were political commissars, to make sure prisoners were indoctrinated in each change of party line. And whenever there was a food shortage in the Soviet Union, prisoners were among the first to feel it.

On October 13 I received some good news: although I could write only four letters each month, I could receive as many as were sent me. I wrote Barbara to this effect, adding something else that had been on my mind: "This is grasping at straws, I know, but have you heard anything at all about the possibility of an exchange of prisoners? Maybe you could get the lawyers who accompanied you to Moscow to check into this and maybe accomplish something in this direction. If it isn't pushed, it will probably be forgotten. I realize there are probably more important people they would rather exchange for; but I can hope."

By the lawyers, I of course meant the CIA.

Diary, October 15: "Saw my second movie—about a quarrel on a collective farm. Not real good."

After that I'd rarely have to ask Zigurd to explain the plot. All too often it was the same one: boy tractor driver meets girl tractor driver; they fall in love and drive tractors together.

Occasionally the singing was good. The acting was something else.

The next diary entry was October 20: "First snow. Pretty cold." With it began my first winter in Russia.

Winter was early this year, the guard said, the earliest in seventy years, meaning it would be long and hard.

Our radiator was the old-fashioned type. When the wind was blowing from the west, or opposite, side of the building, the cell was nice and warm. When it came from the east, however, our teeth chattered.

When the temperature dropped below freezing, we were allowed to divide our walk time, so as to have one hour in the morning, the other in the afternoon. Even then we rarely wanted to stay out the full hour. We would walk steadily, stopping only to feed the pigeons.

As the days grew shorter, daylight did not come until eight in the morning, and getting up at six became more difficult. I no longer looked forward to the morning trip to the bathroom. Now, with the window open, the temperature inside was the same as out. It was something to be endured.

Winter brought some advantages. The milk didn't spoil. And the dead-air space between the two windows became a freezer where we could store what meat Zigurd's parents sent, permitting us to ration it out for a longer period.

Diary, October 23, 1960: "Saw a movie about a poet and artist in prerevolutionary days. Good, though I didn't understand it enough to enjoy it thoroughly."

October 29: "Saw another movie about construction of a railroad bridge in Siberia. Fair."

The diary entries were brief, for two reasons. There was very little to write about, and it was so cold in the cell now that we had to wear gloves.

Letter to Barbara, October 31: "Winter has definitely set in here. It has snowed almost every day since the twentieth. The temperature has been freezing or below for about three weeks now. . . .

"I suppose you have read about the American tourist who was sentenced to seven years for spying and who was released when he appealed to the Presidium. I heard about it on the Moscow News and was very surprised. He was convicted under the same article as I was, but then, his case was much different from mine.

"I am tempted to write an appeal, although I am sure it would do no good. One doesn't know until one tries, though. Many things that have happened here have surprised me. Last May I didn't think I would be alive in October, but here I am. I guess I should be satisfied, but I still hope for some miracle to happen."

It was an up-and-down cycle. There were all-right days, and bad ones.

Diary, November 1: "Usual day of prison life. Have now been in prison for six months. I am sure I will never stay for ten years. Will do something drastic first."

November 4: "People from Moscow KGB visited me today."

The visit, which came as a surprise, was my first real interrogation since the trial. Obviously aeronautical experts had been studying the remains of the U-2, since all questions concerned the aircraft. Handing me photographs, they would ask: Why does the drive shaft in this electrical motor turn this way instead of that? Why do the flaps move up as well as down? There was nothing in this to fall into the realm of security or to give them any sort of technical advantage, yet I had resisted their questioning for so long that it was an ingrained habit. I answered all the obvious ones, replying to the others that when a pilot flips a switch he knows only that certain things are supposed to happen; he doesn't necessarily know the engineering sequence involved.

Early in October, deciding to follow Zigurd's example and keep a journal, I had ordered a bound notebook from Moscow. It finally arrived, and on November 4 I made my first entry.

The purpose of my journal, I decided, would be to put down everything I could remember about the May 1 flight and events following. If I didn't do this, I'd probably forget many details, and there were some in which, I was sure, the CIA would be most interested. Like the diary, however, the journal posed two problems: when I was released, I might not be allowed to take it with me: and, in the interim, my jailers might read or copy it while we were outside the cell. Therefore I would have to continue to maintain all the fictions: this had been my first overflight; I had learned I was to make it only a few hours before takeoff; and so on. When it came to touchy matters, I decided to use a memory code, words or phrases to serve as reminders of things I didn't wish to have read. Even should they keep both the journal and the diary, the two would have served one positive function—giving me something to do. But since I did want to keep them, I took out some insurance. Here and there I'd add a phrase such as "No brainwashing here . . ." or "Have never seen a prisoner mistreated . . .," the kind of thing they would be anxious to have publicized. I didn't know if it would help, but it wouldn't hurt.

Before leaving Moscow, Barbara had been unable to find some of the winter clothing I needed. One of the KGB officials had told her that they wouldn't hold too strictly to the one-package rule; she could send the remainder upon her return to the United States. On November 5 the package arrived, containing some much-needed winter long johns, an extra pair of shoes, a puzzle and a bridge game, and various other items. Its value was declared at sixty-seven dollars, the postage $49.54, and the customs duty twelve hundred rubles. There wasn't anything I needed that much, I decided.

Except possibly a letter. Although I searched the package, there wasn't one. It had been nearly a month since I had received her last.

Representatives of the KGB came about every two weeks. I told them bluntly, "I'm not getting all my mail. The letters from my wife aren't coming through. You must be stopping them."

"No," they insisted, "we aren't. But we'll check and see."

They seemed very disturbed that I would even think they would do such a thing.

During the trial I had stated that I felt no animosity toward the Russian people. This was true. Although I had no fondness for my interrogators at Lubyanka, and I harbored only contempt for the trial team of Rudenko-Grinev, the majority of the people I had met in Russia, from the farmers who captured me in the field to my guards at Vladimir, were friendly and without malice. Ordinary people, they were as curious about me as I about them. Apparently each of us had been led to believe the other monstrous; the discovery that this wasn't true was a pleasant surprise. A few of the guards had been surly, but they were surly to everyone. By contrast, the Little Major seemed jolly whatever the occasion.

I could honestly say that while an uninvited house guest of the Russians, I had never met anyone I really hated.

On November 6 I met the exception.

That day Zigurd and I were taken to the theater to watch a concert put on by some of the work-camp prisoners. There was a comedy skit—the comedian easily recognizable by his long nose; several of the prisoners were quite talented musicians; and one, a large dark man known as "Gypsy," did fabulous cossack dances.

While we were sitting on the bench in the projection room, the prison commander walked in. I glanced at him briefly—I had seen him only once previously, on the day of my arrival—then returned my attention to the show.

Angrily, with Zigurd acting as a reluctant interpreter, he demanded that I stand at attention.

All prisoners were required to stand in the presence of the prison commander, he bellowed. No one had told me this. When someone came into the cell, we stood automatically, out of simple politeness, but I'd never given it any thought.

For a good ten minutes he cursed me, and the United States, with the vilest epithets he could muster, only a portion of which Zigurd repeated.

It was a small incident, certainly nothing compared to what some prisoners undergo at the hands of their captors, but I reacted strongly.

Revenge is sweet, and I desperately needed some of that sweetening. But, considering our relative circumstances, I could see no way to accomplish it. Until, that evening, when the time came to write in my diary.

Zigurd and I were unsure whether our cell was searched when we were out. Several times, before leaving for walks or a movie, we had set traps—a thread stretched between the beds, a drawer open a fraction of an inch. But, on our return, they were undisturbed. I didn't know whether my diary was being read. But this was one time I fervently hoped it would be.

For my entry that day I wrote: "Went to a concert put on by prisoners in barracks number 3. Liked it. Whole day spoiled by prison commander. First *S.O.B.* I have seen in Russia."

S.O.B. was in bold black letters and underlined.

I could visualize the prison commander asking a translator, "What is an S.O.B.?"

And I could picture the translator trying to explain it to him.

A daydream, of course. But most satisfying.

Diary, November 7: "Big holiday here. Sundays and holidays are bad in prison. A person knows other people are celebrating and feels lonely. The radio told of the celebration in Moscow. Twenty-gun salute, fireworks, etc."

In Russia it was the forty-third anniversary of the Bolshevik Revolution. Tomorrow it would be election day in the United States and I was eagerly awaiting word of the outcome. Although limited in my news sources, I had followed this election with far greater interest than any previous one.

From my father's letters I had received the distinct impression that the Eisenhower administration was anxious to sweep the U-2 incident under the rug. This had come across with some bitterness, since my father, an iconoclast in just about everything, was one of those rare creatures, a Virginia Republican. Shortly after my capture, his attorney, Carl McAfee, had tried to see the President. Failing in this, he had talked to Vice-President Nixon, who assured him that everything that could be done would be done. Perhaps needless to say, my father did not believe this was the case.

There was one lingering reminder of the U-2 episode. My presence in a Russian prison. For a time I had hoped that Eisenhower would attempt to remedy this before leaving office. Knowing the stand he had already taken, I was sure he would never apologize to Khrushchev for the overflights, but I had hoped that some understanding could be reached wherein both sides could save face. I was far less confident now. Politics being politics, the time to do this would have been before the election, when the Republicans could have derived some political benefit. Now, it seemed, they didn't want to be reminded.

According to the highly slanted Russian interpretation of the news, the two candidates differed only in degree, both being committed to continuing the arms race. I knew little as to the issues of the campaign. I did know, however, that Kennedy had said earlier that had he been President when the incident occurred, he would have apologized to Khrushchev; that following my trial he had pronounced the sentence "extremely harsh," stating that the testimony made clear that Powers "was only carrying out his duty." And I had heard a little about the Kennedy-Nixon debates. I observed in my journal: "Nixon said that the next President should be a man who was not afraid to stand up to Khrushchev. I don't know what Kennedy replied to this, but I do know my own opinion. I think we need a man as President who would try to get along with people and not go around with a chip on his shoulder saying 'I'm not afraid of you.' We need a man who would try to settle and ease the tension in the world. We definitely do not need a man who thinks he has to stand up to another man and prove to the world that he isn't afraid, even if he kills half the population of his country proving it."

I hoped Kennedy had won. I added, pointedly, that my opinions were formed solely on the limited, edited news available to me. "If I had heard all of the speeches, etc., my opinions might be different."

My sentence, I felt sure, could be terminated only by an easing of tensions between the East and the West. I now had a highly personal stake in world peace.

During the trial Grinev had made a big point of my being apolitical, never having voted in an American election. I was not proud of this fact. I had been away from home since turning twenty-one; while stationed at various Air Force bases and while overseas I had always intended to write home for an absentee ballot, but had never gotten around to it.

Now, one way of the other, my future could very well depend on the outcome of the balloting.

I vowed that if —*when*—I returned to the United States, never again would I miss an opportunity to cast my vote.

Something had been on my mind since long before the trial. Now, awaiting the election results and knowing that whichever way the balloting went that the Eisenhower years were coming to an end, I gave it more thought.

I asked myself why, with the Summit so close, had Eisenhower approved my flight?

I tried to assemble the pieces of the puzzle, those few I possessed. I knew there had been no overflights for months and then suddenly two in close succession. The pilots believed the resumption of the flights was due at least in part to the agency's fear that Russia was now close to solving her missile-guidance problem. I knew that my particular flight had been authorized on the highest level because my take-off had been delayed until White House approval had been received.

I also knew the intelligence objectives of both flights were important—but important enough to take this risk at this time?

One possible explanation occurred to me. At first it seemed farfetched; yet, the more I thought about it, the more sense it made.

Could Eisenhower have *wanted* Khrushchev to know of the flights?

We knew that the Russians had radar-tracked most if not all of the overflights, so the chances were that these last two U-2 flights would not have gone undetected. Might Eisenhower or his advisers have felt it to be to our advantage, psychologically, to have Khrushchev know, to have this very much on his mind when he arrived in Paris for the talks?

Had the flight gone off as planned, it would not have been mentioned. The two men sitting across the table from each other: Eisenhower smug in the knowledge that we could overfly Russia at will, and Khrushchev not able to do a thing about it; Khrushchev inwardly raging but unable to protest, because to do so would be to admit that his country did not have missiles capable of reaching the planes.

What a perfect setting for reopening discussions of Eisenhower's Open Skies Plan!

In agreeing to what was already the status quo, Khrushchev would have had far more to gain than lose. And Eisenhower would climax his last year in office with a spectacular accomplishment, a major step toward disarmament.

It was all speculation. And in a sense moot, because the flight had not gone off as scheduled. Yet it interested me. This was one of a number of puzzles I hoped to solve on my return to the United States.

There was no U.S. election news on the eighth. On the ninth Moscow Radio said the results were uncertain: Kennedy was ahead, but the count was still not final.

Diary, November 10: "Very glad to hear that Kennedy will be the new President of the U.S. Hope he goes all out for peace."

Now all I could do was what I had been doing: wait and see.

Diary, November 11: "Nothing much happened today. Managed to miss studying Russian. Kept my cellmate talking, and he forgot."

I didn't talk to Zigurd just to avoid studying. He had lived a fascinating life, and whenever he seemed in the mood, I encouraged him to tell me about it. He was as sparing with the details of his underground experiences as I was with my CIA flights. Without ever spelling it out, we respected the fact that some areas would always remain off limits, no matter how much we might trust each other. It was other things, often casually revealed, accidentally glimpsed, that gave me the clearest insights into Zigurd's character. We were together constantly; one of us was never out of the cell without the other; yet it was a long time before I began to feel I really knew him.

One morning while we were washing I noticed two small scars on his shoulder. How had he got them? I asked. Later, during one of our walks, he told me. When the Germans conscripted soldiers from occupied countries, they tattooed numbers on their shoulders, to identify them if they deserted. In fleeing from the Germans to the Allied side, Zigurd had realized that this evidence could cost him his life or be detrimental to his ever obtaining employment. Heating a piece of metal red hot, he had applied it directly to the tattoos, in an attempt to burn them off. He wasn't completely successful. The numbers were obliterated, but the scars remained as evidence.

Yet there was a deeply sensitive side to him too, that came across when he described the retreat from Latvia—frozen bodies piled like cordwood alongside the roads, and how the sight affected him;

or when he talked about the girl from the displaced persons' camp. They had fallen in love and they had almost married, but Zigurd had hesitated. Too long. Relatives were found abroad who offered to sponsor her. She was now either in the United States or Canada, he was not sure which. He thought of her often, with guilt, knowing that because of him they had lost their chance for happiness. The more he thought about it, the more he realized how he must have hurt her. And now suffered himself because of it.

In prison such thoughts and feelings have a way of assuming monstrous proportions, until they dwarf all else.

Gradually, as I began to know Zigurd better, I came to trust him. If a "plant," he had a most unenviable job, living the life of a prisoner. Though always interested in my stories about flying, he never inquired into details. Only once did he touch on something of a sensitive nature—asking how high the U-2 flew. This is the first question people usually ask even today. I suspect I could have told him ten thousand feet and he would have been impressed.

The memory of the girl haunted Zigurd. But something even deeper troubled him. I knew only that in some way it concerned his parents. But a long time passed before he told me about it.

Once a year each prisoner was photographed, and the pictures were sent to his relatives as evidence that he was neither dead nor being mistreated. Our turn came in November. There was a regular photographic studio in one of the barracks, and although there was no "birdie," we were told to smile, so the people back home could see how happy we were. I tried but was less than successful.

While at Adana I had worn my hair fairly short. In prison I'd let it grow, intending to comb it back. Instead it just stood straight up. With only a small piece of mirror, I didn't realize how funny it looked, until seeing the prints.

But Zigurd was immensely proud of his new head of hair. And only then did he stop wearing the beret.

Diary entry: "Barbara's birthday. One year I have no gift for her. Wrote a letter this morning, at least started it, wishing her a happy birthday. Will mail it later in the month. Got books from the library, had already read two. Read *The Iron Heel* by Jack London."

As a boy I'd read many of London's books, but none of his socialist works. It gave me an entirely different perspective on the man.

November 18: "Still no mail from the U.S. Temperature this morning −24°C. Have put on long underwear. Must remember to thank Barbara for the clothes she sent. Cabbage for supper."

Something was definitely wrong with our radiator. Even wearing all the clothes we had, fur cap with ear flaps down, we were literally freezing. For days we had complained to the guard; he'd feel the radiator, look puzzled, tell us the radiators in all the other cells were working, then, as if that settled the matter, do nothing. Except to bring in a thermometer, which only made us feel the cold all the more. On the morning of November 21 he checked it; the reading in our cell was below zero Centigrade. With that, something was done. Later in the day workmen arrived and installed an electrical outlet near the door. And the following day the Little Major personally delivered the electric heater from his office, an act of kindness I'll never forget.

November 23: "Still no mail from the U.S. today. Prison officials (KGB) checking for me on this end." Again potatoes for supper, but with roast meat and apples Zigurd's parents had sent, which made all the difference.

Zigurd's parents had a small plot of land with an orchard. In season they sent apples, onions, and garlic. Zigurd would take the garlic and put it in the meat, not for flavoring but because he had read somewhere that garlic would preserve meat. Whether it did or didn't, I wasn't sure. By the time we received the apples they had usually begun to rot. But what we could eat tasted marvelous. They were the only fruit we received.

In the order of their frequency of appearance, I dreamed of: desserts—banana splits, coconut-cream pie, anything made with eggs or ice cream; meat—all kinds, but hamburgers especially; and greens—I'd never known how much you could miss a salad.

November 25: "Still no letters. Mailed two today, one to Barbara and one to Mother. Russian studies going very slowly. Can't get in the studying mood. Potatoes two times today."

In my letter to Barbara I told her my reaction to the election: "I am glad that Kennedy won. I sincerely hope he turns out to be a good President and puts the good of the people above all other considerations." I asked her to send newspaper clippings of any of his speeches relating to foreign policy. I was particularly anxious to obtain a copy of his forthcoming inaugural speech, as soon after he made it as possible. I wanted to see if there were any indications of his attitude toward Russia.

November 26: "Wind blowing this morning. Makes it seem very cold. One letter from Mother. Took thirty-four days to arrive. Something wrong. Started trying to read a Russian story. Constant use of dictionary and many questions."

Boredom was the greatest problem. It was compounded when we lacked books, but even when we had them I was often restless. I could read for only an hour or two at a time. Then I'd put the book aside and work on envelopes for another hour. Then read awhile again, then pace the cell awhile. I'd do a few pushups, a little exercise, as much as space would permit, careful to make as little noise as possible, so as not to disturb Zigurd if he was reading. I'd try reading some more, or, if we both felt like it, talk.

After a while we developed a sensitivity to each other's moods. Respecting the need for silence was important. Equally important at times, and there were many such, was realizing when the other needed cheering up.

Zigurd was involved in one activity I wasn't. Before my arrival he had made several carpets. He'd been working on one when I arrived, but only after we had exhausted all the obvious subjects of discussion had he taken it up again. Watching him work, I asked questions, as much to make conversation as from curiosity. To me needlework had always seemed a woman's occupation. But in Latvia, on long winter nights, with little else to do, whole families engaged in handicraft. Zigurd had turned to rugmaking only after being sent to Vladimir, however. One of the Latvian magazines his mother sent contained some patterns. Drawing vertical lines over the pages of a ruled notebook, he had made graph paper, then transferred the pattern onto it. His mother had sent burlap bags, wool and needles. And from there he had found his own way.

As the pattern of the rug began to emerge, my interest grew. At least it was something to occupy the time. Finally I asked if he had an extra sack. Yes, and we could order more wool and needles from Moscow.

Picking out a pattern, I followed his example, transposing it onto paper, then onto the sack. When the wool arrived, it was too thin to use. I had to stretch it out the length of the cell about five times, then double it and twist it to get the desired thickness.

November 29: "Started making a small carpet today. May send it to Barbara as an anniversary present."

I was extremely depressed about Barbara. I hadn't received a letter from her in fifty-three days.

I considered every possibility. She was sick and unable to write.

Unlikely; surely her mother or someone else would have informed me. The KGB was withholding my mail, in an attempt to break me. This was also improbable: as far as I could tell, they appeared to believe that I had told them everything I knew; too, they seemed honestly concerned about my failure to receive letters. The mail was being delayed, or some letters had been lost. Both were possible.

There was one other alternative. She simply wasn't bothering to write.

There were several reasons why this might be true. I tried not to think of them. I was not proud of how I had handled Barbara's and my marriage, her various problems. I was spending many long hours wondering and worrying about her. What more could I have done to help? Well, it was too late to do anything now. That was certain. What I really wanted, I realized, was a connection with the outside world. I was hanging on to anything familiar to keep my sanity. I needed reassurance that things would remain the same while I was in prison. I needed a letter from her to prove that life was going on as usual on the outside, that it was a life I knew and understood, that it was one I could become part of once again when I was free.

December 1: "Started *War and Peace.* Very good. Cabbage for supper."

December 7: "Talked with the KGB colonel."

It was an odd interview. He asked me if I felt I was being treated well. I replied, much better than I had expected, although I was sure no prison was enjoyable. How did I like the movies? Not wishing to appear ungrateful for what was a most welcome break in our monotonous routine, I told him they were "interesting." But he persisted: How did they compare with American films? Well, since he seemed to want a frank answer, I told him: They ranked about the same as some of our B-grade westerns.

My reply appeared to upset him very much. The Russians, he said, had pioneered the art of film making. They made the finest motion pictures in the world. Then why, I inquired, weren't the prisoners shown any of them? Because, he replied, they preferred the kind of movie we were being shown.

He remained disturbed by my reaction. If they could arrange to bring one of their classic motion pictures to the prison, would I like to see it?

Of course, I replied.

After he left, Zigurd and I talked about the exchange, coming to the same conclusion. It seemed a good omen.

On December 10 there was a letter from Barbara, the first in sixty-three days. Knowing that she was well was a tremendous relief. Most of the letter, postmarked November 26, was in answer to my questions about the possibility of a prisoner exchange. The United States had only two prisoners of comparable importance: Morton Sobell, convicted of espionage in the aftermath of the Rosenberg case, and Colonel Rudolf Abel, the Soviet spy convicted of espionage in 1957, now serving a thirty-year sentence at the federal penitentiary in Atlanta. It was doubtful if Sobell, an American who continued to maintain his innocence, would be interested, while the Soviet Union had never recognized Abel as one of their own. There had been much conjecture in the press about a possible Abel-Powers swap, however, especially immediately after my capture, though there had been no mention of it of late. If I felt it might help, Barbara said she would try to see Abel at Atlanta.

I asked Zigurd what he knew about Abel. He had never heard of him. This, I learned, was true throughout the Soviet Union, where there had been no radio, TV, or press mention of either his arrest or conviction. He was a "blown" spy. Russia didn't claim him.

In reply to her letter I wrote, "There is no need for you to attempt to see that Colonel Rudolf Abel. Just forget about that. We can only let nature take its course. I feel that the only thing which could improve my situation would be better relations between the two countries. I don't know that this would help, but I am sure it would do no harm. . . .

"It is odd how I keep hoping a miracle will happen and someday someone will walk in and say that I am going home. I don't believe in miracles, but I am always hoping and waiting for something to happen. I try to interpret each little variation of the routine as having some special meaning. This is all silly, but one never loses hope. It is very good in a way. If I knew definitely that I would have to spend the entire ten years here, I think I would do something drastic. But as it is, I keep thinking that maybe next month or the one after that, etc., will be the one I am waiting for. As long as I do not lose hope, everything will be all right. I haven't lost hope yet."

Again I asked her to be sure to send me a copy of Kennedy's inaugural address.

Barbara hadn't started numbering her letters, so there was no way I could tell whether some were being lost or if she simply hadn't written between September 23 and November 26.

December 13: "Bath today. No glue, so cannot make envelopes. Millet for breakfast, millet soup and potatoes for dinner, a type of potato salad for supper. Wrote letter to wife. Have no idea what she is doing or where she is living. Sent it care of her mother in Milledgeville."

December 14: "Received seven letters today!"

There was one from Barbara, another from her mother, with whom she was living I now learned, the rest from my sisters and parents. My mother's letters always moved me because they evoked home: "Daddy went up to the high knob to try to get a deer this morning." Her own health wasn't very good, but I wasn't to worry. She closed, "I can't enjoy coffee, not knowing if you have a cup or not."

The health of both my parents concerned me. On his return from Russia, my father had discovered that he had diabetes. Yet he was still "pestering" the people in Washington, especially the State Department, trying to get them to initiate some action in my case.

Barbara's letter bothered me also. I knew she was under a tremendous strain, that all of this must seem like a horrible nightmare to her, yet reading her letter I had the feeling that she was bored and just writing to fill the pages, not really thinking about what she was saying. For example, she asked about my job in the mail room, which meant she hadn't read my letter about the envelope making very carefully. And she asked if they observed Thanksgiving in the Soviet Union. But, I told myself, everything that happens in prison assumes an importance and magnitude all out of proportion to reality.

December 15: "Fed pigeons during walk. Am partial to a white pigeon and try to feed him more than the others. He is too shy and lets the other pigeons take his food. No glue, so no envelopes made today. Potatoes for supper."

The embassy had included a jar of peanut butter in my last package. Together with the jelly, obtained from the prison commissary, Zigurd got his first peanut-butter-and-jelly sandwich. From his initial look, I decided this must be an acquired taste.

On December 18 the KGB colonel and an interpreter arrived with the print of a classic Russian film, *Soldashka*, and Zigurd and I were given a private showing. Beautifully made, the film depicted an ancient conquest of Russia by barbarians and their eventual defeat.

But even here they couldn't resist propagandizing. The message was tacked on to the end, to the effect that: "Come to Russia as a friend, you will be welcomed. Come as an enemy, you will be met with a sword."

Or a rocket.

Actually the movie itself impressed me less than their going to the trouble to bring it all the way from Moscow for a private screening. All this concern with giving me the best impression of Russia had to be for some reason. And the only possible reason I could see was that they intended to release me soon. I tried not to draw too much hope from the incident, but despite my resolve, I did.

Zigurd agreed. It was a very good omen.

December 19: "Has been a long day. Two visits by Major Dimitri. He is going on leave tomorrow. Our contact will be Major Yakovlov. A good man. Will soon finish *Anna Karenina*. Someone pulled the tail feathers out of one of the pigeons. He flies like a duck now." Another common trick was to tie a pigeon's legs together, which gave him a sort of Charlie Chaplin walk. In a way, I could understand why such things were done—they were antidotes to boredom—yet such senseless cruelty greatly disturbed me.

Often, through the hole in our cell window, I'd study the prisoners as they went through the gate. Before long I began to type them. The political prisoners were usually quiet, studious. Going from one place to another, they often carried a book along. It was as if they realized they had a certain amount of time to serve and were determined to use it to best advantage. They seemed to avoid causing trouble.

It was different with the work-camp prisoners, many of whom were rowdy, constantly breaking rules, getting into arguments with each other or with the guards.

It was an interesting generalization, except for one thing. There were several rowdies in our building also. They would yell out the windows. Or try to catch the pigeons. Or throw things from their windows.

Zigurd explained the seeming discrepancy. Fights were common in the work camp. One prisoner might steal another's bread, while someone else got knifed for it. Occasionally, to escape vendetta, a prisoner would try to obtain a transfer. There were two ways to do this: hurt himself so badly he would have to be hospitalized; or become a political prisoner. The latter was fairly easily accomplished. He need only mock Khrushchev or write anti-Soviet slogans on the wall. Taken before a judge and resentenced as a political prisoner, he would be reassigned to building number 2. This meant time added on to his sentence and the loss of some privileges, but it was preferable to being stabbed.

Occasionally Zigurd and I would get into arguments, albeit friendly ones. During one of our bull sessions I mentioned that it was an established fact that north of the equator whirlpools move in a clockwise direction, while south of the equator they move counterclockwise.

He doubted this, and said so.

Finally, after some thought, we came up with a scheme to prove or disprove at least half the theory. The next time we went to the toilet we would stop up the washbasin with a sheet of paper and fill it full of water. Then, very carefully, we'd pull the paper out and watch which way the water went. Since we were obviously north of the equator, the motion should be clockwise.

The trouble was, when we pulled out the paper it made waves, confusing everything. We had tried this a half-dozen times, getting water all over ourselves and the floor, when the guard looked in. He was not at all sure what we were up to, but whatever it was, we were to stop.

On the subject of whirlpools, Zigurd remained a skeptic.

December 21: "Dad's birthday. Had potatoes for supper, as usual. But with meat!"

The meat, roast pork, had arrived in a package from Zigurd's parents. To preserve it, Zigurd's mother had packed the meat in lard in which she had previously cooked onions. This gave it a strong onion taste. By smearing the lard on bread we made some of the most delicious sandwiches I had ever tasted.

My diary entries now contained no mention of my Russian lessons. For good reason. I was trying to forget them. For me, prison was not conducive to studying. Working on the carpet gave me an excuse to skip memorizing the long lists of words Zigurd supplied. After missing one day it became easier to miss the next, until it gradually slipped out of the routine. Also, since the prospect of release seemed to be even brighter—the significance of the special movie had now become almost a certainty—it seemed useless to persist in learning the language.

December 23: "Package from American Embassy with coffee, cigarettes, razor blades, candy, etc. Was told today that starting in January I would be given *The National Geographic, Popular*

Science, and *Nation* magazines. Can be bought in Russia. Two walks today; made envelopes. Potatoes for supper; didn't take any."

December 25: "Christmas Day. Had manna for breakfast, soup and plate of noodles for dinner, and a plate of mashed potatoes for supper. Typical Sunday here but no movie this weekend. Took one walk and took a nap in the afternoon. All that made this Christmas Day was my knowing it was. Am pretty homesick. Worked on carpet quite a lot today."

December 26: "Only took one walk today. Made 250 envelopes. Finished a play by Gorky, *Lower Depths.* Worked on carpet. Had potatoes for supper; didn't take any."

December 27: "Four letters today. Two from Barbara, one from Mom and Dad, and one from Jessie. Jessie's and Barbara's had pictures in them."

December 31: "New Year's Eve—a very lonely day with lots of reminiscences. Spent several hours writing in the history of my stay here [the journal]. Thinking very much of my wife. Hope I can go to sleep tonight."

Twelve

On New Year's Day I was startled to hear my own voice on the radio. It was a year-end wrap-up of significant events of 1960, and parts of the trial were rebroadcast.

I asked Zigurd if there was any mention of the RB-47 pilots, but on this the news was curiously silent. So far as I knew, they had yet to be brought to trial. However, on the off-chance they had been sent to Vladimir, I had resumed whistling American songs during our walks, in hope of making contact.

My diary entries for 1961 started off with a humorous note.

January 1: "Just opened a package that I thought was cookies. Turned out to be Cocktail Dainties! Why in the world is the American Embassy sending me cocktail snacks when they know I don't have and can't get cocktails?"

On January 2, regular programming was interrupted for Khrushchev's New Year's toast. Greatly excited, Zigurd translated it for me. Khrushchev had said that with the passing of the old year and the old government of the United States, Russia was willing to forget the U-2 incident and start 1961 fresh!

Diary: "Surely they can't forget about it with me in prison? Much hope."

Zigurd shared it. He had maintained, from the very start, that I would not serve my full sentence.

That same day something else occurred to make me hope he was right.

With the Little Major on leave, Major Yakovlov brought the mail. Just before leaving, he told us we needed haircuts.

Journal: "This is very strange, for no one has ever mentioned our needing haircuts before, even though they were certainly needed."

To a prisoner, anything out of the ordinary, no matter how seemingly unimportant, takes on significance.

First there was Khrushchev's toast, then Major Yakovlov's remark about haircuts. If they were going to release me, they would want me to look presentable. It all fitted.

Of course, I reminded myself, we did need haircuts. It could be coincidence.

I didn't believe that. Nor for a moment.

Following the excitement, reaction set in.

Diary, January 3: "Having a sinking spell in my thoughts. I suppose my chances of being released soon are better than they were, but I am too unimportant a person for anyone to worry about me. My release depends on the whims of men who could not care less what happens to me or to any single person. They think in millions, not in ones. Made over five-hundred envelopes today."

Using up my two-hundred-and-fifty-envelope quota was a nervous response. I paid for it immediately.

January 4: "Ran out of paper for making envelopes today. No more available, so can't make any."

January 5: "Has been a very bad day for me. Have been very depressed most of the day. Took bath and was supposed to get a haircut, but barber didn't show up."

Journal: "A prisoner never gives up hope. He is always waiting for some miracle to happen. There would probably be a lot more trouble in prisons if this were not so. . . . A person would go completely crazy in prison if there wasn't, in the back of his mind, this hope of getting out, some way or the other."

We got the haircuts on the seventh.

On the ninth we were visited again by the major. I asked outright how my chances looked. He replied that things would go well for me if Kennedy made a policy of having better relations with the USSR.

This time I didn't try to hide my excitement. One thing I had learned about the Communists, particularly the KGB, was that no one ever ventured a personal opinion. Every statement was prefaced by the collective *we*: "We think . . ." We feel . . .," I was never told anything that Moscow hadn't approved, that wasn't the official line. The major wouldn't have ventured this much unless he had some assurance that prospects were good.

January 11: "I don't think I have mentioned it before, but ever since May 1 I have had a constant high-frequency ringing in my ears. It was lower than usual this evening."

January 13: "Excellent news today. The colonel (regional KGB, from Vladimir) told me that my release from prison depended wholly upon how Kennedy reacted to the toast of Khrushchev on New Year's Eve. I certainly hope that Kennedy in his speech on the twentieth will come out very strong for good relations and easing the tension in the world. Hope he repeats what he said during the campaign, about apologizing for the flight, etc."

January 15: "Started reading *Ben-Hur*. I finished all I can do to the carpet this morning. I hope I am able to deliver it in person to the States soon. I feel fairly certain that February will see me free, but there is always the possibility of it not happening. I refuse to think about that. Potatoes for supper."

I was rather proud of the carpet. It measured twenty-one by twenty-eight inches; had six colors in the pattern—light and dark green, tan, red, pink, and black; and contained over thirteen-thousand crosses, each cross formed by pushing the needle through four times. I estimated it had taken about three hundred hours. At least I would have something to show for the time I had spent in Russia.

Letter to Barbara, January 16: "I have great hope of something very important happening soon. I don't want to build up your hopes, but it is entirely possible that I could be released in the near future. I am placing much hope on the attitude of Kennedy toward better relations with the Soviet Union, which I think he will try to improve. If his attitude is favorable, then my chances are very good."

Citing Khrushchev's toast and his intention to pass over the incident, I noted, "in order for the incident to pass and be forgotten, it would be necessary for me to leave prison. I hope they haven't forgotten that part of the incident and the fact that I am still here. . . .

"These are optimistic hopes, and are far from certainties. I hope they aren't too optimistic, and I hope by the time this letter reaches you that we both will have heard something or, better still, will have seen each other on that side of the Atlantic. If we haven't heard by that time, then these were only wishful thoughts."

After mentioning that I had finished her anniversary gift, and hoped to deliver it in person, I closed with some pessimistic thoughts: "In a way I suppose it is very stupid of me to have any hopes of being released soon. If it doesn't happen, I will be extremely disappointed, so I should not allow myself to get into the position of being disappointed."

Diary, January 18: "About −20°C. My cellmate and I only take one walk when it is this cold. It is almost impossible to crumble bread for the pigeons at this temperature. The hands get numb after a few seconds. One can not stand still, either, or the feet freeze."

January 19: "Tomorrow—the day of Kennedy's speech. I won't find out about it until twenty-first, twenty-second, or twenty-third. My fate depends on what he says."

January 20: "Long-awaited day. Hope Kennedy comes out with some positive statements in my favor. He can certainly do me much good if only he sincerely tries to lessen tension. . . ."

January 22: "Part of Kennedy's speech was in today's *Pravda*. My cellmate said it couldn't be better for me. Also he said that Khrushchev had gone to visit Ambassador Thompson which could be a good omen. Potatoes for supper."

January 23: "Kennedy failed to say anything about the U-2 flights, etc. It could help me very much if he took a favorable attitude on this question. I am sure he will have to commit himself soon, probably at his first press conference. Potatoes."

The following day brought a big surprise: ninety-two Christmas cards!

Nearly all were from the San Francisco Bay area. On December 12, San Francisco *Chronicle* columnist Herb Caen had written: "While you're making out your Christmas cards, you might remember to send one to Francis Gary Powers, c/o American Embassy, Moscow, USSR. Let him know that U-2 haven't forgotten."

This was my real Christmas. For the first time I received mail that hadn't been opened and read. The sheer volume had apparently caused the censor to mutter the Russian equivalent of "To hell with it"; more than half the letters had been passed on unopened.

Several teachers had asked their classes to write me; the compositions were extremely moving. One class had sent a little package of various odds and ends from their pockets which they wanted to share with me. Included were several pieces of bubblegum.

Zigurd, who had never seen bubblegum, watched in amazement as I popped a huge bubble. Try as he might, however, he was unable to do it himself. We used all the pieces in the attempt.

On January 26, when I had just awakened and was getting out of bed, the news came over the radio: the two RB-47 pilots had been freed!

I was tremendously happy, for them and for what this portended for me. According to the Soviet account, the pilots had been released in return for Kennedy's promise there would be no more overflights.

Finally that fear could be put aside.

Diary, same day: "I have much hope. Visited by KGB colonel from region of Vladimir. Wanted to know if I had any questions and said that my position was much better than before. Said he was very optimistic. Cabbage for supper."

Writing to Barbara, I asked her to send a thank-you letter to Herb Caen, "if you can spare the time." I also noted that perhaps it was unwise for us to get our hopes up. After all, the RB-47 boys had never been brought to trial and sentenced while I had.

Diary, January 27: "More news about the release of the other two, but not one word about me."

On the twenty-eighth, Radio Moscow reported that President Kennedy had been on hand to meet the two fliers on their arrival at Andrews Air Force Base.

January 31: "Last day of my ninth month. This has been a month full of expectations and disappointments. The world situation has improved, and as a result I am sure my situation has also improved, but it isn't noticeable yet. Seems I should have heard something by now. . . ."

I finished a letter to Barbara, to be mailed the following day, since I had exhausted my quota of letters for January. It was an angry letter. While I had heard a brief summary of Kennedy's first press conference, which appeared most encouraging, some of the reaction to the release of the RB-47 pilots disturbed me greatly.

"Two of the people, who made statements should be shot as far as I am concerned. You probably read about them in the papers on the twenty-sixth and twenty-seventh. They are Representative William Avery and Senator Aiken. Aiken said: 'The nation might gain the impression that the President is thankful to Russia for releasing the two pilots.'

"I personally hope that not only the President but the whole nation is thankful. As far as I am concerned, it is no disgrace to be thankful for something that means so much to so many people. I am proud of Kennedy for being thankful, and if I ever have the opportunity, I will tell the two men what I think of people who would rather have the two RB-47 boys stay in prison because their being free places the United States 'in an embarrassing position,' as Avery said.

"What would they have said if it had been their sons or relatives? Would they have said the same thing? If not, then they had no right to say it in this situation. I am perfectly willing to let one or both of them come and spend the remainder of my sentence in my place if they think someone should remain in a Russian prison, although the treatment I am receiving is much better than they deserve."

In the back of my mind was the sickening realization that if Kennedy was under political pressure for this, my chances were suddenly less than bright.

In closing, I gave way to my real feelings:

"Barbara, I don't know what to think. I have tried to figure out what is in store for me, but I am completely baffled. Everything looks good, but I am still here. Has the Soviet Union decided that two people are enough? If so, it looks as if their gesture was a half-gesture, and they are keeping an ace in the hole (me).

"Oh, well, they didn't invite me to come, and I don't suppose I have any reason to complain. But they didn't invite the other boys either. I am quite dizzy from trying to reason out what is going on. It would have been best if I had heard nothing about it at all. I am constantly hoping that each day will bring me some news, and each day I am disappointed when it does not arrive.

"My chances are still much better than I first thought, but each day that nothing happens probably lessens them a little. Maybe this is just pessimism on my part. It is entirely possible that things are being done for my release right now and that it takes time to do this. My impression of Khrushchev is that he is a person who doesn't do things halfway, but there is much more involved than I know about.

"It would certainly help me a lot to know something definite even if it were bad. It is the unknown that bothers me so much. . . ."

After cursory entries on the first and second of February, I stopped writing in the diary. It was too much a reminder that nothing was happening.

There were a few bright spots during the month.

Among the American magazines the authorities purchased for me in Moscow was the January *National Geographic*. There was a large color spread on Mamie Eisenhower's farewell tour of the White House. One Sunday afternoon, when the guard and the cleaning woman expressed interest in seeing the pictures, we opened the magazine on the shelf of the feeding-port door and, with Zigurd translating, I told them about the history of the White House and its significance to Americans. When we finished with the magazines, we showed each other pictures of our families.

That afternoon one little bit of the Iron Curtain ceased to exist. That was a bright spot.

Another was beating Zigurd at chess, an occasion rare enough to be memorable.

Upon my arrival at Vladimir, one of Zigurd's first questions was: did I play chess? My affirmative reply pleased him immensely. It was only much later, after we had come to know each other well enough to say such things, that he admitted his disappointment after our first game. I knew how to move the pieces, but as for the philosophy behind the game, I knew next to nothing. Chess was big in Latvia, as in the Soviet Union. Newspapers carried chess problems, and Moscow Radio reported notable matches with all the excitement of an American sportscaster describing a no-hitter baseball game. One day Zigurd mentioned beating an opponent blindfolded. This time it was my turn to be skeptical. To prove it, he had trounced me soundly, sitting all the way across the cell with his back turned. Gradually, under his tutelage, I became a better player, but the occasions when I beat him were few and far between.

The *National Geographic* episode and the chess game were two bright spots. There weren't many during that month of February.

My disappointment was gradual, but cumulative. As each day passed with no word, I became increasingly despondent. I couldn't shake the feeling that I had been let down, abandoned; that had Ambassador Thompson brought up my case with Khrushchev at the same time as he has the RB-47 pilots, I would have been released. My captors had given every indication they were prepared to let me go. I was happy for the RB-47 boys, yet in my darker moments I couldn't help thinking that if they hadn't been here, I might have been released.

Time passed slowly. Movies were now about a month apart, occasionally less often. We had stopped making envelopes because paper was unavailable. I had started another carpet, having mailed the first one to Barbara, but ran out of wool and was waiting to see if Zigurd's mother was able to find the right colors in Latvia. I knew I should take up my Russian again, but didn't. Perhaps unconsciously I felt that to do so would be to admit I would be staying. Nor was reading any longer an escape. One evening I discovered I was staring at a blank page: the words were no longer there. My peripheral vision was normal, but my central vision was gone. My eyes were just tired, I decided, putting the book aside. When I picked it up later, everything was fine. But the following day there was the blank spot again. And it kept returning, with increasing frequency. Two things frighten a pilot more than any others: heart and eye trouble. The heart palpitations remained— they had never completely left me since May 1, 1960—and now this. I discussed it with Zigurd, and we decided it might be a vitamin deficiency due to our poor diet. Vitamins were not available through the prison commissary, but Zigurd wrote to his parents asking them to send some. They had done this for him on a previous occasion. However, there would be at least a month before they arrived. Meantime, the problem remained.

That, however, was not my major worry. One thing now concerned me almost to the exclusion of all else.

Barbara had again stopped writing. Her last letter, written January 9, had arrived on the twenty-sixth of that month. After that, nothing.

I was annoyed at myself for letting this business with Barbara's letters upset me so. I knew she was undependable. But emotionally, I needed to hear from her about the world I knew. Contact with Barbara was contact with home, contact with life.

On February 22 the KGB colonel made his regular visit. Through Zigurd I tried to engage him in conversation, to determine if he had heard anything, but he was very brisk and businesslike. His manner seemed to indicate that something had changed. However, it was not until two days later that I received confirmation. As I wrote in the journal on the twenty-fifth, "The major came yesterday and said the relations between the two countries had not gotten any worse, but they also were not better, and they couldn't see them getting better in the near future. This is the same as saying I won't be released in the near future."

Still no letter from Barbara, although other mail was coming through. Mother: "It hurt real bad to see the other two boys arrive back here and you not with them, but I'm happy for them and their families."

On February 28 something odd occurred which took my thoughts, temporarily, off my growing concern. Because of its nature, I couldn't trust it to my diary or journal, except for a coded reminder.

Earlier Zigurd had told me that prisoners sometimes exchanged messages by wadding them in bread and throwing them when the guard wasn't looking.

While I was walking in the exercise yard, a ball of bread, apparently tossed from one of the second-floor cell windows, landed at my feet. Making sure the guard had his back turned, I quickly scooped it up and palmed it. Not until we were back in our cell did I take out the message and read it.

It was in English, but strangely worded: "Dear Friend! You will live by and by. In that glorie land below the sky . . . but you must live so interestly, that you would be able to say something to your grandmother, when you return home. I can . . . if you are the man."

I puzzled over it for hours. By "grandmother" did the writer mean "Uncle Sam," and was he trying to say he had information for him?

I didn't, and still don't, know. No further attempt at contact was made. Separated as we were from the other prisoners, Zigurd and I had no idea whether any of them could speak or write English. Occasionally some of them would yell a word or two from their windows, but it was always "Hello" or something equally simple, repeated several times as though it were the only word they knew.

The need to communicate can lead one to all sorts of extremes. Once, when I was looking out the window, I saw a pigeon carrying a message. Literally. A prisoner had tied a string about two feet long to the pigeon's leg; at the other end a letter, in a regular envelope. I could even see the postage stamp.

The sight was both comical and sad, sad because one of the guards saw it too and brought the pigeon down with one shot.

That was the only time, in either Lubyanka or Vladimir prison, that I heard a shot fired.

It was no longer easy to make excuses for Barbara's failure to write—yet I continued to do so in spite of the fact that she didn't have a job and lived with her mother, receiving a monthly check from the agency, leaving her few responsibilities. I not only thought of every possible excuse, I even reached way out for improbable explanations, wondering for example, if some of her letters were on a plane I heard had just crashed in Belgium.

I couldn't write to my parents, asking them to inquire. Relations between them and my wife were strained enough without letting them know that she wasn't writing to me. All I could do was wait.

By the end of February, thirty-three days had passed since Barbara's last letter, and thoughts of her had become an obsession. Coinciding as it did with my disappointment over not being released, it was as if in addition to the government abandoning me, my wife had done so also.

I suppose there exists in every prisoner's mind doubts about those he loves, no mater how blameless they may be. The mere fact that they are free, and you aren't, builds resentments. But such doubts can be overcome where trust exists. I was denied that. I couldn't trust Barbara. And without trust love begins to die, not fast but slowly and painfully.

Some of the agony I was going through was poured into the diary and journal. Even more remained bottled up inside. . . . "I can never have a future with her, because the past will always be between us. . . . Although in principle I'm opposed to it, there seems no other way than a divorce when I return to the States. It should have been done in 1957. . . . I thought at the time I loved her too much to let her go, that I wouldn't admit failure, but now I don't know. . . . I am at my wit's end as to what to do. That is the worst thing about prison life. The helplessness, the not knowing. All you can do is sit and wait and think, which, in my case, is very bad. . . ."

On March 8 I requested and received permission to write a letter to the American Embassy, asking them to make inquiries to see if my wife were ill or had been in an accident.

Diary, March 9: "Today, after an afternoon nap, I started working on a carpet, and while I was working I became very nervous and my whole body was tense. My hands shook so badly my cellmate wanted to call the doctor, but I wouldn't let him. It only lasted thirty minutes. . . . If this keeps up, I think it could drive me crazy. . . ."

Some weeks earlier I had mailed the first carpet to Barbara, hoping it would arrive in time for our anniversary, also hoping that its arrival would result in a letter. The package was now returned, refused by U.S. Customs. The significance of this wasn't lost on me.

March 11: "I received a letter from my wife, which was written on February 21 and mailed on February 22. She offered no explanation as to why she hasn't written between January 9 and February 21. Except that she has been visiting relatives in North Carolina. . . ."

The letter did nothing to ease my mind. It was either very insensitive or carefully contrived. Barbara didn't bother with the pretext, used in the past, that some of her letters had apparently gone astray; though unnumbered, the letter contained the newspaper copy of Kennedy's inaugural address I had asked for, dated January 21. The tone of the letter was as though she was bored, and performing some unpleasant task.

Two problems, however, had been resolved, both thanks to Zigurd's mother. She had sent vitamins, and after several days my eyesight returned to normal. She had also sent wool, enabling us to resume our carpet-making. Examining it, I found that it was dyed. Apparently she had been unable to find the colors that we had requested, and had gone to the trouble of dyeing it herself, thoughtfulness that moved me very much. She also provided one of our few laughs during this dark period. Earlier she had sent a package containing what Zigurd asserted was rabbit. It had an unusually long neck, and I marveled at how different rabbits in Latvia were from those in the United States. The meat was very good, though different from all the rabbit I has tasted, and Zigurd wrote thanking her for us both. In a very humorours reply, she informed us that our rabbit had been a goose.

Gradually, with a great deal of help from Zigurd, I began to emerge from my long depression. The world's chess championship was being held in Moscow, and as the radio broadcast the moves we would copy them down and reconstruct the games on our board. The new carpet progressed well; I again took up my Russian studies. There were also other developments.

Diary, March 31: "Have received two very nice letters from Barbara. She still does not say a word about why she did not write for such a long time. It is surprising how much her letters ease my mind and make me feel better."

This was true even though the news they contained was not hopeful. Kennedy, appearing on *Meet the Press*, had been asked why I hadn't been released with the RB-47 pilots. He had replied, "That is a different situation." Asked what was being done to negotiate my release, he said, "The time has not come yet."

Now all my thoughts were on May 1. If the Russians were to release me, this seemed the most logical time. A national holiday—the traditional time for amnesties. The anniversary of my capture. Again hope began to build. But this time world events dashed it before it got out of hand.

On April 18 Premier Khrushchev announced over Radio Moscow

that on the previous day, troops, "trained, equipped, and armed in the United States of America," had launched an unsuccessful attempt to invade Cuba.

With the Bay of Pigs disaster, I gave up any hopes for clemency.

Thirteen

I t snowed a little on May 1, the uncelebrated anniversary of my first year in Russia, but spring was very much on my mind. I remembered how one year ago, flying over the Urals, I'd looked down and noticed first signs of the changing season. Even more poignant were thoughts of home. "Everything is getting green now around the place," my mother had written. "The apple tree isn't in bloom yet, but you can begin to see a little of the green leaves around the bloom buds. The peach blossoms have about gone."

"I certainly do miss grass and trees," I wrote in one letter. "I haven't seen a tree since last September, when I came here from Moscow. Sometimes, when the wind is blowing right, it seems we can smell the forests, but it may be only imagination. I have no idea how far it is to the nearest woods."

Zigurd felt the change as much as I. Often now he talked of Latvia.

During the long dark period of receiving no mail from Barbara, I had been obsessed with my problems to the point that I never considered the possibility of Zigurd having his own. But he did. Only now did he bring out some of the things bothering him.

His parents were old, at an age when he felt he should be supporting them. Instead they were helping him. This worried him a great deal. Each package was a reminder of his obligation. To do what he could to make up for their sacrifices, he had vowed that following his release he would return home and take care of them as long as they lived.

He was the most unselfish person I had ever met, a trait that came across in a thousand big and little ways. At Christmas my parents had sent me a box of homemade candy. I offered it to him. After taking one or two pieces, he refused more, implying he really didn't like it. But I could tell he did. He simply wanted me to have it. Only by threatening to throw the candy away, and then by dividing it into equal portions, could I persuade him to eat more.

When he had moved to our cell a few days before my arrival, he had taken the bed on the right. On moving in, I presumed he had done so because the bed was more comfortable. Only after a time did it occur to me he had chosen the least pleasant side, that near the bucket.

Realizing that I would be facing a difficult time, not only as a prisoner but as a foreigner, he had done this—just as he did many other things, without comment or fuss—to make the adjustment easier.

That was the kind of person he was.

Though his parents were elderly, they had to carry all their water into the house from a well in the yard. This was something Zigurd hoped someday to remedy, although he was not sure how.

We set to work solving the problem. Our cell was littered with drawings of rejected ideas, some of which would have done Rube Goldberg proud. Finally, after many hours of debate, we came up with one which seemed workable: a thousand-gallon tank in the attic, to be filled from the well by a simple pump arrangement. We even planned to position it next to the chimney, in order that the water not freeze in winter.

Across the back of the envelope my father had printed in large letters: REMEMBER WHAT PATRICK HENRY SAID!

Inside was a clipping from the *Washington Post*, dated April 12, 1961:

SOVIET TO FREE POWERS MAY 1, PAPER SAYS

LONDON, April 12 [Wednesday]—The London *Daily Mail* said today U-2 pilot Francis Gary Powers will be freed from a Soviet prison in the next few weeks and will choose to stay in Russia.

The *Mail's* Moscow correspondent, John Mossman, said Powers probably will be freed May 1—exactly a year after his reconnaissance plane was shot down.

And the newspaper quoted Mrs. Powers as saying in New York:

"I would love to go to Moscow to join my husband. I will go out to him if possible even if he decided to stay on after his release."

Mossman quoted no Russian source for his story, but reported:

"He [Powers] is believed to be in Vladimir Prison, near Moscow. His release is planned as a demonstration of increased goodwill between the Soviet Union and America."

In Washington, a State Department spokesman said "We haven't heard anything about it."

I read it several times, with increasing anger.

Who was this Mossman, and why would he print such a lie? Had he made it up, just to have a story to write, or, if he had a source, who was it, and what did he and they hope to accomplish?

My father claimed he didn't believe the story. Yet the message on the envelope seemed to indicate otherwise. And if my own father gave it credence, what about others?

"I am a citizen of the United States and am proud to be one," I wrote him. "Don't worry about my doing anything or giving any cause for my country to doubt me. It looks as if this British correspondent is trying, for reasons I can't guess, to make people believe I have renounced my country. I would never do this. Even if I were offered an immediate release on condition that I remain in the Soviet Union. I would refuse. Not because I don't think I could live here, but because I am an American and will always be an American.

"I cannot imagine where this Mossman got his information unless he invented it himself. You may rest assured that I will return home, where I belong and where I want to be, as soon as I am released. Remaining here has never entered my mind.

"If I were free, I would demand that his sources be revealed, and if it was his own fabrication, then I would sue him (the only way to make him realize that there are other people who may be hurt by his lies). I am sure that he has not even considered how his lies will affect my reputation in the future.

"One thing that bothers me very much is that many people who read it will believe the article. To some of them I will appear a traitor even though there is no truth to the article whatsoever."

In reference to my father's remark about Patrick Henry, I observed, "He is remembered, much to his credit, for what he said. It looks as if I will be remembered, much to my discredit, for what some correspondent writes, even though there is not a word of truth in what he wrote.

"I was born an American and intend to die an American. In the States, I hope."

As for the reliability of another portion of Mossman's story, I noted that it was now May 3, two days after my promised release, and I was "still occupying the same cell in the same prison."

I wrote a similar letter to Barbara, also asking what she had been doing in New York City, "or is that a lie also?"

It was a lie, according to a letter from her on the eighth. Enclosing a clipping of the Mossman story, she explained that he had not talked to her—nor had she been in New York. The article, however, had been given wide circulation by the news services, as a result of which her phone had been ringing constantly with interview requests.

Barbara's affinity for publicity bothered me. Earlier she had released several of my letters to a magazine, not even bothering to inform me she had done so. She had explained that interviews were the only way to keep the case in public consciousness, and while I couldn't disagree with that, I did wish she would devote just a portion of the time thus expended to letter writing.

When Zigurd and I went to the office to receive my monthly embassy package, there was a new man on duty. Unfamiliar with the rules, he let me have the magazines, including four copies of *Time*. This was the first time since being in Russia that I had been allowed an American news magazine, and I read each issue avidly, trying to form a picture of the world outside.

There was one mention of my case. And it puzzled me.

"Should we be alarmed by the difference between the behavior of Airman Powers and of Nathan Hale?" asked Fund-for-the-Republic President Robert Maynard Hutchins. He did not wait for an answer. He has already seen dark "signs that the moral character of America is changing," and has ordered the fund's Center for the Study of Democratic Institutions to take a two-year look at the problem. With an assist from such men as Supreme Court Justice William O. Douglas, University of California President Clark Kerr, and Jesuit Philosopher John Courtney Murray, Hutchins hopes to turn up "various viewpoints on what the Good Life shall be in America," to reach "dependable conclusions about our national strength and weakness."

"I wonder what in the world he is talking about?" I wrote Barbara, "I hope I am not being accused of changing the moral character of America."

Though I treated it flippantly in my letter, the item disturbed me. Was this due to the Mossman lie? Or, for some reason unknown to me, was I being criticized in the United States, and my family keeping it from me?

It was the first time that possibility had occurred to me.

By mid-May I had heard that Kennedy and Khrushchev would be meeting in early June for disarmament talks. I tried to remain pessimistic. Journal: "It is very hard to conceive that the two countries will agree on doing away with nuclear weapons when they cannot even agree officially to do away with nuclear tests. I am afraid that if my being released depends on disarmament talks, then there is no hope at all. I like to think it doesn't depend on politics, but I'm afraid it does."

By the twenty-sixth I was still trying to maintain my skepticism. Writing Barbara about the meeting, I said, "It will probably be over by the time you receive this letter. I suppose it could result in my being released, but I don't think I had better make any plans. . . . Even if the meeting does not affect me at all, I certainly hope they settle some important problems and try to make this world a better place to live in."

But by now the pattern was set. Periods of despondency, followed by resignation, in turn followed by rapidly mounting hope, then back to the first.

Although I knew better, I couldn't help anticipating.

The talks were held June 3 and 4, in Vienna. Diary, June 5: "It looks as if the meeting between K. and K. ended pretty well. There has been no official announcement of what transpired and probably will not be, but it looks good from my position. It could be that sometime this month I might be released. . . .

"If I am lucky enough to get out this month, I will be very happy, though I will feel bad about leaving my cellmate in prison. . . . He is one of the finest people I have ever known. . . . I sincerely hope he does not have to serve his full sentence. He has about nine more years to go.

"I just finished a book of short stories by Pushkin, *The Tales of Ivan Belken.* I liked it very much. It is the first I have read by him, and I would like to read more, especially *Evgeni Onegin.*"

The last was a coded reminder, for my return to the United States, about a story Zigurd had told me regarding a former cellmate, Evgeni Brick.

During World War II great numbers of people had fled from Russia and its satellites. When the war ended the Soviet Union had declared an amnesty, promising them freedom if they returned.

Zigurd had distrusted the offer. One who hadn't was a man named Evgeni Brick. Approached by American intelligence in West Germany, Brick had agreed to return to the USSR and spy for the United States. The moment he walked down the ramp from the airplane, the Russians had taken him into custody.

I had made a note of the name "Evgeni," as I was sure the CIA would be interested in the fate of their former agent, just as I was sure British intelligence would be interested in learning what had happened to Zigurd.

The June 5, 1961, entry was the last in my diary.

Letter to Barbara, June 15: "I am sorry I wrote that I might be released after the meeting between K. and K. I cannot help reaching for each little ray of hope and trying to turn it into a beacon of optimism. . . . One thing that makes me pretty sad is—if nothing happens as a result of the meeting, then I have very little chance of being released at all. If a meeting between K. and K. will not do it, then what will?"

By this time I had heard the news. Asked by the press what Khrushchev had said regarding the Powers case, Kennedy had replied, "The matter wasn't even discussed."

Winter had turned to summer with only a glimpse of spring in between: a row of flowers the work-camp prisoners had planted outside their barracks.

"The weather is getting hot here," I wrote home. "We haven't had any rain for several weeks, and most of the days are clear and sunny. I have already got a good suntan by taking my shirt off during my walks. Not everyone can spend a couple of hours each day sunbathing."

There was very little else to write home about.

I was again persisting in my study of Russian, but with minimal progress; by the time I'd finish translating an article in *Pravda* it was no longer news, but ancient history. Having run out of the right colors of wool, I'd had to leave the second carpet uncompleted, and was now well into a third, this one larger and more ambitious than the first, measuring 25½ by 31½ inches and with seven colors—gold, black, brown, yellow, and light, medium, and dark blue. Reading material was no longer quite so scarce. Barbara had sent thirty paperbacks, including Robert Lewis Taylor's *The Travels of Jaimie McPheeters* and James Michener's *Hawaii.* In addition, I systematically devoured the English books in Moscow University library: *The Adventures of Peregrine Pickle* and *The Adventures of Roderick Random* by Tobias Smollett; *The Apple Cart* by George Bernard Shaw; *Arrowsmith, Babbitt, Main Street, Elmer Gantry,* and *Kingsblood Royal* by Sinclair Lewis; *Candide* by Voltaire; *Bleak House, Little Dorrit, Great Expectations, Heartbreak House, Nicholas Nickleby* by Charles Dickens; *The Forsyte Saga* by John Galsworthy; *Henry Esmond* by William Makepeace Thackeray; *Tom Jones— A Foundling, The History of the Adventures of Joseph Andrews and His Friend Mr. Abraham Adams* by Henry Fielding; *Jude the Obscure* by Thomas Hardy; *The Jungle Book* by Rudyard Kipling; the complete works of William Shakespeare; the continuation of Mikhail Sholokhov's Don novels, *Seeds of Tomorrow* and *Harvest on the Don; War and Peace* and *Anna Karenina* by Leo Tolstoy; *Octopus* by Frank Norris; *The Prince and the Pauper* by Mark Twain; *The Store* by T. S. Stribling; *The Titan* by Theodore Dreiser; *Typee* by Herman Melville; and *Wuthering Heights* by Emily Bronte.

Even visits to the dentist became memorable breaks from the routine. I lost a filling, which had to be replaced, not once but several times. It finally stayed, but became badly discolored. The dentist's equipment was extremely primitive. Even here were those jars of leeches. By this time I had no doubt as to how they were used, having seen doctors applying them to people's backs in the prison movies. But I never could understand why the dentist had them. Fortunately, I never found out.

"Well you heat it and it bursts, and becomes a big, white, fluffy, soft—"

Finally I gave up. How do you explain popcorn to a man who has never seen or tasted it?

A pigeon flew through the top of the window and got caught between the panes of glass. I climbed on to the cabinet and got it out, bringing it back into the cell with me. But I'd been spotted. Hearing a rush of feet up the stairs, I released it before the cell door opened.

Did they think we were going to try to cook it and eat it, or use it to send a message?

Actually, I'd hoped to have it for a pet for a little while. Yet I knew that even if we could manage to hide its presence from the guard—a nearly impossible feat—I wouldn't have been able to keep it long. I could never have made it a prisoner too.

We were never sure whether our cell was bugged. Occasionally, out of boredom and curiosity, we would voice the most fantastic lies, or denounce the Soviet authorities in the vilest possible terms, hoping for someone to come in and reprimand us. Then we'd know. No one ever did. Somehow this was in itself depressing, knowing that no one really cared that much.

When starting my journal I had been careful to include only things which would not irritate my captors, hoping in this way to ensure their letting me take the journal with me upon release. Now I no longer bothered to censor myself. Many pages were devoted to the lack of freedom of expression in the Soviet Union; the prevalence of one viewpoint and one viewpoint only, the "correct" one; the use of lies which, through constant reiteration, became credible truth. Listening to Radio Moscow one day, I heard an American Communist denounce the United States as a place where there is no freedom. "Of course the Russian people believe this," I wrote. "They do not stop to think that this man is going to return to the country where he knows no freedom, and that once there he won't be sent to prison for what he has said. While here he would be tried and convicted of uttering anti-Soviet propaganda." Yet the Russian people believed this, just as they believed their leaders alone were for peace, that only the United States stood in the way of disarmament.

In my opinion, I noted, the controlled press, as found in the Soviet Union, is as insidious a form of brainwashing as exists.

This one-sided interpretation of the news bothered me greatly, not only because of its obvious effect on the thinking of the Russians but also because I realized a man subjected to it for a long period, denied comparisons, other sources, would almost inevitably emerge thinking like a Communist.

How long would it take? I wasn't sure. But I suspected that by the end of ten years the process would be fairly complete.

July 4 was a particularly bad day. But all holidays were, as I'm sure is true with prisoners everywhere, whatever their sentences or crimes. When you lock up a man, you lock up his memories too.

There were few periods of excitement or elation now. Only mail affected my mood.

With one exception, my outgoing letters from Vladimir were not censored in the sense of words being crossed out or letters returned for rewriting, though every letter was read, which in itself imposes a subtle form of censorship on the writer. The exception was a letter in which I mentioned my cellmate's name and sentence. This was not permitted, and I had to rewrite the letter, deleting this information. Also, as far as I could determine, I had received every letter written by my wife or parents, and none of these had been censored.

Therefore I was surprised when, in early July, I received a letter from my father, dated June 14, in which a number of words were inked out. Reading to the end, however, I discovered a P.S. in my father's handwriting: "I blocked out a few names that I didn't want to mention in this letter. We are still doing our best to help you. Will continue. Your Pop."

My father wouldn't have made a good spy. Holding the letter up to the light, I was able to guess at a few of the deletions. The edited portion read: "I could not find out what was discussed at the K.K. meeting June 3, but I did have a call from _____ [Abel's?] lawyer in N.Y. He is in touch with _____ [Abel's wife in?] East Germany and _____ is working for a _____ release from that end and Mr. Donovan _____ this end. Just how much good it will do is yet to be seen. I was told I would receive a letter from _____ in E. Germany. I have not received it yet but will soon, I know."

What was this all about? As far as I could determine, my father was attempting to arrange something with Abel's wife and this Mr. Donovan, who I assumed was Abel's attorney. As far as I was concerned, he was wasting his time, and I wrote him to that effect.

In early August I received a letter from Barbara in which she mentioned that the New York *Herald Tribune* had recently published an article speculating on an Abel-Powers swap, the two men to be released to live in a neutral country.

I wouldn't agree to that, I wrote her. To accomplish this, I would have to ask for political asylum and, as far as I was concerned, this was tantamount to renouncing my country. I was an American, and I wanted to come home, very badly. "I know nothing will come of the negotiations, because as far as I know Abel is not a Soviet citizen, and why should the Soviet Union agree to exchange for a noncitizen? It is just that my father is grasping at straws."

A day or two later I received a letter from my father which dumbfounded me. I read it over and over, in disbelief.

According to my father, he and his attorney, Carl McAfee, had attempted to see President Kennedy shortly before he left for Vienna, but had been told that Kennedy wanted two hundred dollars for an interview. My father, not being able to afford it, had been forced to drop the interview plans.

I couldn't believe it! I knew little of Presidential protocol, but that a President of the United States could charge a citizen for his time was incredible. Kennedy certainly didn't need the money. Although to my father two hundred dollars was a great deal of money, to Kennedy it was nothing.

It seemed far more likely that one of Kennedy's aides was using his privileged position to line his own pockets, even if it meant profit at the suffering of a grieving parent. I decided upon my return to the United States to determine whether there was any truth to the story and, if so, to do everything in my power to make it public. I was sure that the American people wouldn't stand for such a thing.

This callous heartlessness greatly shocked me. I tried to convince myself it simply couldn't happen. Yet, in my isolation, anything seemed conceivable.

I had stopped writing in the journal in March. In September, when I started again, more than a little of my bitterness remained, spilling over onto the pages: "I am afraid I will never be a Kennedy supporter in the future. . . . It seems to me that Kennedy would have tried to get me released. I don't expect him to go out of his way to help me, but I feel that I would have been released long before now if he had made the slightest effort when he met with Khrushchev. . . . I don't mean to complain or bemoan my fate. I did as good a job as I could for them, and in return they should try to aid me. . . .

"Before I was captured I had a great tendency to accept things as they were, not questioning the policies of the United States, since I knew we had intelligent people in our government whose job it was to make decisions for the benefit of the country as a whole. I realized that they were more intelligent than I, and if they did something I thought strange, it was only because I did not know all the reasons for the action, and I accepted it as right and proper.

"But now I realize there is more to it all than I saw at first. . . ."

The Mossman article, Hutchins' remarks as reported in *Time*, the neutral-country story, my father's letter—all continued to bother me, as did the thought that upon my return to the United States I might not again be trusted with a responsible position. Even if people didn't believe the lies about my defection, they could always say I had been "brainwashed" or "exposed to Communism." As I wrote in one letter, "I try to tell myself that things will be all right in the future, sometime, but I can't eliminate the present. I am even afraid of what the future will bring. I have had strong feelings it may not turn out as I would like. In fact, it scares me sometimes to think about it."

Barbara was doing nothing to help my state of mind. After a spurt of letters—four in one month—they had again become infrequent. I knew I was receiving all she sent, since, at my insistence, she was now numbering them. On August 17, my thirty-second birthday, she had given a reporter a long interview, a copy of which my parents had sent me. In it she stated that as soon as I was transferred to a work camp she would come to Russia, to live near me. But she hadn't thought to write me this, although that news, if true, would have meant a great deal to me. She had also told the reporter she had just finished a long birthday letter to me. As I noted in my journal, apparently talking about the letter so exhausted her that she didn't get around to writing it. She hadn't bothered to send a birthday card.

Fourteen

I n late September we heard that two junior officers in the Dutch Merchant Marine, Ewert Reidon, thirty, and Lou de Yaher, twenty-five, had been arrested and charged with spying in the Soviet Union for NATO. The pair had been arrested near the Czechoslovakian border following a month-long auto trip through the Ukraine. Brought to trial in Kiev in early October, they had been given thirteen years, an indication that Russia was currently pursuing a hard line.

Shortly afterward they arrived at Vladimir. Peeping through the crack in the window, I spotted them being escorted through the gate, each carrying a bag. They looked very young and very forlorn. I wished there was some way to contact them, but I doubted if I would have an opportunity, and in this I was right. In the way that prisons have of swallowing up people, I never saw them again.

Letter from my father, dated September 16, received October 10: "The letter I have been expecting has not come through yet. I was

told by Mr. Donovan that I would hear from her [Mrs. Abel?]. . . .
Carl and I are going to Washington to see about a few things. . . .
I have also written to Khrushchev."

Included was a clipping. I had never thought I would be happy
to find myself considered unimportant. But this time I was.

FREE POWERS, NIKITA HINTS

NEW YORK (AP)—Soviet Premier Nikita Khrushchev says Francis Gary Powers may be released before his 10-year sentence
is up, but international tension makes it impossible to free
the U-2 pilot from his Soviet prison right now.

Khrushchev told C. L. Sulzberger of *The New York Times*
in an interview published today that "Powers himself is not
of such value that we would consider it necessary to make
him serve his full sentence."

Powers was shot down over the Soviet city of Sverdlovsk
May 1, 1960, and subsequently convicted as a spy.

Although the time obviously wasn't yet right, I found the news
encouraging. And my mood was helped by a letter from Barbara,
the first in a long time.

The feeling did not last long. On Friday, October 13, an unlucky
day if ever there was one, I received a letter from Barbara's mother.
She did not know how to tell me this, writing it to me pained her
greatly, but on September 22, following a family conference and
on the advice of doctors, she had been forced to have Barbara
committed to a mental institution.

The news came as a tremendous shock. Barbara's last letter had
been written on September 18, just four days before the commitment, and, though brief, as usual, there had been no indication
she was ill.

Now, for the first time, I had an inkling as to why Barbara had
done some of the things she had: the incidents in Florida, Athens,
Tripoli; her conflicting stories; and, since I'd been in Russia, her
erratic letter writing. She was ill and had been for a long time. The
news, in a way, was almost a relief. It helped explain so much.
And now, maybe, under the proper medical treatment, she would
get well. God, I hoped and prayed for that! But I needed to
know more.

My mother-in-law's letter was short on details. All she said was
that Barbara had been drinking heavily and that the doctors said

she was emotionally disturbed. There was no mention of the names of her doctors, or of the hospital.

Immediately I wrote letters to Barbara's mother, her sister, and her brother, an Air Force chaplain, asking for more information.

My feelings were a mélange of concern, helplessness, guilt, and understanding. Coupled with the terrible uncertainty was the realization that there was nothing, absolutely nothing, I could do. If I weren't in prison, this probably wouldn't have happened to Barbara. If I had been firmer with her about her drinking, when I first realized it was a problem, maybe this could have been avoided. If it hadn't been for the frequent separations. . . . These recriminations changed nothing, yet I could not stop blaming myself.

Journal, October 14: "I am very upset and cannot get it out of my mind. If only I knew exactly what is going on, I think I would feel much better. I am sure that a great deal is my fault. . . ."

Not for another thirteen days did I receive a letter. In the interim, in my desperation, I exhausted the possibilities. As I wrote in the journal, "I have even conceived the crazy idea of writing to the Supreme Soviet of the USSR to ask them to let me go home for a short while to see if I can help in any way. . . . I would promise to return. I realize it is a crazy idea, but it might work, because they could get a lot of favorable publicity from it.

"I know it is stupid, but I am grasping at straws. If I have no mail by early next week, I will try it."

The next letter, from Barbara's sister, was more detailed. Barbara's drinking had gotten completely out of control. It had reached the point where her mother was no longer able to remain in the house with her because of the fights that resulted. Under these circumstances they had felt the best thing for her was medical help, and she had been committed to the Psychiatric Center of Augusta's University Hospital. She had an excellent doctor, Corbett H. Thigpen, author of the book *The Three Faces of Eve*, and was receiving the best care possible. They were sorry they hadn't been able to contact me first, but because of her condition they felt it best for Barbara if they acted promptly.

It was a very considerate letter, and it relieved my fears somewhat to know she was being helped. But I had the feeling they were withholding something; I wrote, begging for more information, asking that they not treat me as a child but tell me exactly what was happening. I pointed out that my imagination would create fears far worse than anything they could write.

On November 1 I received two letters. One was from Barbara.

Although written October 7, she made no mention of being in the hospital. The other was from Barbara's brother, the Air Force chaplain, who had handled the details of the commitment and who had been appointed Barbara's legal guardian in my absence. He stated that she was now free to leave the hospital at any time she wished.

Another letter from Barbara arrived November 5, this one, written October 15, explaining that she hadn't told me about being in the hospital in her earlier letter because she had not wanted me to worry. There was no mention of drinking; tension was given as the reason for her being there. She had high praise for Dr. Thigpen, although she complained about his strictness; he wouldn't even let her have matches.

Although I was already well over my monthly quota for outgoing letters, I wrote Dr. Thigpen, as well as Barbara's own doctor in Milledgeville, asking for more information. I hoped the Russians would let them go through.

Because of the delay between the time a letter was written and the time I received it, I was unsure whether Barbara was still in the hospital. The thought that she might be better, might even have been released, made living from day to day a little easier. That sort of hospital must be very like a prison, I thought, and I wouldn't wish that on anybody.

Too, I now had something else to think about, which, though not unrelated, concerned me very much.

Following my conviction, I had been told that on completion of one half of my three-year prison sentence—or eighteen months—I could apply for an early transfer to a work camp, where the remaining years of my sentence were to be served. Such requests were by no means granted automatically but at the discretion of the court. My conduct as a prisoner had been good, so I couldn't see this hindering the application. November 1 had marked the completion of my eighteenth month.

Yet, as I observed in the journal: "This camp business has me worried. Here in the prison I have been relatively isolated. I have contact only with my cellmate. In a camp it is my understanding that all prisoners are free to mingle, and they more or less govern themselves. Of course, there are guards outside. It is my impression that they are set up somewhat like concentration camps during the war. I have heard that there are fights, and groups who oppose each other, and I do not know how I will fit into such a situation, since I cannot speak the language. I don't fear any harm to myself, because I don't think the Soviet government would want to cause an international incident by exposing a citizen of the United States to conditions which could result in his being harmed. It would be hard for them to explain why they could not protect their prisoners if word were to get out that something had happened to me."

Then, too, there were some privileges I enjoyed in prison that might be revoked if I transferred to a work camp, such as my receiving the embassy packages, books, and unlimited amounts of mail. Also keeping my hair.

Zigurd tried in every way he could to keep me from getting my hopes up. He was sure the request would never be granted. The Soviets couldn't risk the chance of having me killed by some patriot anxious to make a name for himself.

But there was one important factor in favor of work camp. I had heard that prisoners there were allowed to have their wives visit them for ten days every three months. If Barbara could come to Russia, even for a short time, perhaps we could discuss and resolve some of our difficulties.

On November 15 I submitted my application for a transfer.

Journal, November 21: "Last Saturday the colonel came to have a talk with me about the application to the work camp. He asked a few questions about why I wanted to transfer there, and then he said he would come back later with information about the questions I asked him concerning visiting privileges and the granting of a visa to Barbara. When I mentioned that it would probably be a long time before I heard anything from the application, he said it might be sooner than I think. I feel certain he knew much more about their plans for me than he let on. . . ."

Journal: "Today is Tuesday, November 28. I expected some mail today but didn't receive any. It has been over two weeks since I received my last letter, and over three weeks since I have had one from Barbara. Is the cure progressing as it should?

"I also have not received my monthly package from the embassy. It is almost two weeks late. I wonder if there is any connection between the missing package and the missing mail?

"Another thing that seems odd, since this is the first time it has happened, is that for about five days I have not received the *Daily Worker.* When it did arrive there were several issues missing, ranging from about the fourth to the ninth of November. (I do not remember the exact dates, because I thought very little of it at the time.) Yesterday I received the November 23 issue, but November

22 was missing. This is very odd, because I have been receiving this newspaper for many months and I have never missed getting an issue. They are often late but always come."

Little things, but the mind fits them into a pattern.

"Today for the first time I realized there might be a connection between the missing newspapers and the absence of mail. The mail I should be receiving now and for the past week would have been sent from the United States about the same time the missing papers were printed. Could it be that something has happened to my wife or other members of my family and that mention of it was made in the papers and also in the letters? If so, it must be very serious to be withheld from me."

I didn't commit my worst fears to paper, not wishing to give them that much reality.

An explanation for the missing embassy package occurred to me. Maybe the money in my account had run out, and Barbara, being in the hospital, had been unable to replace it. The thought that the embassy would stop the package for this reason did nothing to help my frame of mind. But this still didn't explain the absence of mail and the missing newspapers.

I put a request through the authorities to check, to see if they could learn what had happened.

The November embassy package never did arrive for a simple reason: Somebody had forgotten to send it.

I felt more relief than anger. Like my hopes, my fears were constructed of little pieces of circumstantial evidence. There was now one less piece.

On December 8 I received two letters from Barbara, one having taken thirty-five days to arrive and the other thirty-eight. In the last, dated October 25, she said she was ready to go home, only Dr. Thigpen didn't agree. She was now assigned to a private room in an open ward; however, still not allowed matches.

Knowing that Barbara was alive, even if still in the hospital, was a great relief. And at least there she would be properly cared for.

On December 11 the colonel brought me the bad news. Journal: "There will be no work camp for me. I was told that a law or decree had been passed by the Presidium in the early part of May, 1961, in which the sentence of several crimes, mine included, naturally, cannot be mitigated by any court, but only by a pardon from the Presidium of the Supreme Soviet itself. This decree has been in effect since May and was approved on the fifth of December, twenty days after my application was tendered.

"The only chance I have of getting a mitigation of my sentence is by a pardon from the Presidium of the Supreme Soviet. This is very unlikely, because they have not even bothered to answer the pleas that my wife and parents submitted to them in my behalf more than a year ago."

Secretly, in the back of my mind, I had hoped for more from the work-camp application than I had confided in the journal. There was always the possibility—although admittedly remote—that in reviewing my sentence the court might decide to extend clemency. Thus my disappointment was compounded.

However, the colonel's attitude wasn't entirely negative. He wasn't sure it could be arranged—he would have to check further— but it was possible that if I did have visitors from the United States that provision might be made for my being allowed to spend a longer period of time with them.

I grabbed onto this as if it were a life raft. Even if it could only be a short visit, just a few days, perhaps Barbara and I could solve some of our problems, one way or the other. I wrote her to this effect, urging her to consider making the trip.

That same day I heard from Barbara's mother that Barbara had been released from the hospital late in October. However, she had gone back several days later with a bad case of flu.

There was a single letter from Barbara on December 21, written November 19, when she was still in the hospital. There was no mention of what her plans were once she was released, except that because of the conflicts with her mother she would have to find a place by herself. I wasn't too happy about that. There would be no one to look after her.

My second Christmas in the Soviet Union was even rougher than my first. There were few cards; people have a tendency to forget. There were several presents, including a beautiful pair of woolen mittens knitted for me by Zigurd's mother. But there was little in the way of encouraging news. With what seemed my last hope frustrated, and no prospect of release in sight, I slipped into a deep lethargy. Though he tried his best, Zigurd was unable to pull me out of it. For hours I would sit staring at the floor, saying nothing. Nor did a letter I received on December 27 from one of Barbara's relatives do anything to brighten the holiday season, even though it contained the news that she was now out of the hospital.

Earlier I had written asking for details about her illness, and how her commitment had come about. I had wanted to know everything. Now I was almost sorry I had asked.

Written late in November, the letter stated: "Truthfully, her trouble is loneliness, guilt, and nerves. She is still drinking, and of course I can understand your feelings, for she has not been all that she should have been, or should be."

"... *guilt* ... *not all she should have been, or should be* ..."

I was left with the words and with whatever implications my imagination could put to them.

Now the memories came back. And no effect of will would exorcise them. I could no longer suppress the truth, or make excuses to avoid facing it.

Shortly after our marriage I had been sent on temporary duty to Eglin AFB, Florida, for gunnery training. To celebrate our third-month anniversary—July 2, 1955—Barbara was going to drive down and join me. The second was the Saturday of the long July Fourth weekend, and only after considerable effort had I been able to obtain a motel reservation. She was to arrive late Saturday afternoon, the drive taking three to five hours. She didn't arrive until the following afternoon, with the excuse that she had stopped and visited some girl friends at a cabin on the beach and they had persuaded her to stay overnight.

I knew Barbara well enough to sense when she was lying, and I sensed it then. Yet, not knowing the girls, there was no way to check her story. Nor, to be frank, did I wish to. At that point I had only a suspicion, and because I loved her, it was not one I wanted to pursue.

The residue was doubt, a small seed, but, together with others, enough to make me think twice about accepting the job with the CIA, because of the long separation it entailed. Prior to our marriage, we had broken our engagement several times, usually following arguments when I found Barbara dating others.

When Barbara arrived in Greece in the fall of 1956 I was very pleased. That she was determined we be together, even if only on occasional weekends, was a hopeful sign. This feeling did not last long, however. On my visits to Athens there were "incidents." But again only suspicions, nothing definite. Unexplained telephone calls. Looks and remarks exchanged in bars. Obvious contradictions in stories she told me. Arguments often resulted.

Not long after this, Richard Bissell, the CIA's deputy director of plans, and one of the key figures behind the overflight program, visited Adana. Barbara would have to leave Greece, he told me. Her presence there, when other pilots weren't allowed to bring their wives over, wasn't good for morale. This, at least, was the excuse he gave. Having talked to other pilots, knowing that none at that time planned to bring over their families, I felt there was something more Bissell wasn't telling me, that perhaps something was going on in Athens that I didn't know about. Since Barbara did not wish to return to the United States, and only a short period of time remained on my contract, a job was found for her at Wheelus AFB, Tripoli, Libya.

This meant I could see her far less often. There were, however, unscheduled flights, ferrying T-33s over for repairs. I picked up these whenever the schedule permitted.

My unexpected, and unplanned, arrival late one afternoon turned some of my suspicions into certainties. Going to the women's quarters, where Barbara was staying, I asked one of the girls if she was there. Yes, she replied, but I had better not go up to her room as she was getting ready to go out, and her date had already arrived.

I went up. And hastened her date's departure. In the argument that followed, I noticed that Barbara was trying to conceal a letter sticking out of her purse. Aware that I'd noticed it, she grabbed it and ran into another room, locking the door behind her. I kicked down the door and took the letter from her. It was from an Air Force officer in Athens, informing her he had decided to divorce his wife, and could she arrange to divorce me they could be married.

By the time I had finished reading it, the Air Police arrived and placed me under arrest. When Barbara attempted to retrieve the letter, they confiscated it. Taken before the base authorities, we had no choice but to explain the whole mess. After some remarks on my temper, it was suggested that if we wished to resume our argument we do so off base, and I was released. Although Barbara demanded that they return the letter to her, it was handed to me.

Tearfully Barbara explained that the letter was as much a surprise to her as to me. Though she had had dinner with the man on several occasions, and had provided a listening ear for his marital problems, he had given no indication of his real feelings for her.

I wanted very much to believe Barbara.

Yet, on my return to Adana, I began to have misgivings. In all fairness to her, she could be telling the truth. Unable to live with such uncertainty, at the first opportunity I flew to Athens. Knowing some of the places Barbara had frequented, I asked questions. And received answers, more than I had anticipated, and not at all those I wanted to hear.

In August, 1957, I took Barbara back to the United States, with the idea of obtaining a divorce.

It is difficult to explain, especially to oneself, why one tries to save a marriage when it has obviously gone bad. In our case, although there were no children, there were several complicating factors. One was an earlier divorce in my family, which had determined me never to go through anything similar. Another was my feeling that I was more than a little responsible for the situation, leaving Barbara alone so often. From almost the start of our marriage there had been a series of separations, necessitated at first by Air Force assignments, later by my work for the agency. When the agency decided to extend the overflight program, and, as incentive for the pilots to renew their contracts, permitted families to be brought to Adana, I decided that if we were together and not separated *maybe* we could salvage our marriage.

Maybe. I was not at all sure. It was not a matter of forgetting. I knew I could never do that. But, with a sincere effort on Barbara's part, and with the separations behind us, perhaps we could make a fresh start, a new beginning. It wouldn't be easy, I knew.

I had never confronted her with what I had learned in Athens. Perhaps that had been a mistake. If so, it was not the only one. Another was underestimating the extent of the problem, believing it could be so simply solved. At Adana there had been more incidents—nothing definite enough to precipitate a break, only strong suspicions, but enough of these to leave the marriage very shaky, even if it hadn't been for the increasing problem of her drinking.

This was the situation when I took off from Peshawar, Pakistan, on May 1, 1960.

It was time I grew up and faced the truth I'd avoided much too long. I had hoped that with her hospitalization everything would change. But obviously nothing had. With her release she had begun drinking again, and stopped writing.

There was only one alternative now. To end it, for the sake of both of us. But in my present situation there was no way to do that. Again my utter helplessness overwhelmed me. It was compounded by still another realization. I had clung to the marriage for so long, hoping to save it, when all evidence indicated it was beyond saving. I'd done the same thing with each and every prospect of early release, when all evidence indicated there was little hope.

Had I deceived myself about being released too?

January 1, 1962. Although I dutifully wrote in my journal that I was hopeful the new year would see me free I saw little likelihood of that happening. Tensions were building over the Berlin question. In the past I had foolishly drawn hope from all sorts of unlikely circumstances, but I was not now optimistic enough to believe that I had a chance if my release depended on the settlement of the Berlin issue.

Occasionally there would be days when my depression would dissipate temporarily. More often than not it was due to Zigurd, who understood what I was going through and did his best to help.

One day we had an argument. Zigurd maintained that people can dream in color. I insisted they couldn't. At least I could never remember dreaming in anything except black and white.

But I was wrong. That night I dreamed of a large banquet. The colors of the food and wines were as vivid as any could be.

Unfortunately, I awoke before I ate or drank a mouthful.

She was quite plain: I was sure her interest in me was professional, nothing more; yet I realized I was counting the days between the nurse's visits.

Powers, you're being a fool, I told myself. Zigurd warned you, when he told you about his cellmate. Yet now you're letting the same thing happen to you.

Once I recognized the symptoms, the attraction vanished. But the story of the boy who ate his tin plate no longer seemed incredible.

Journal, January 28: "I have written Barbara only once this month, because I am trying to stick to the resolution I made to write only when she writes. . . . I must admit I am becoming more and more afraid of what the future holds for me. Am I man enough to face all the things I may have to face, including a divorce? Divorce, much as I hate the idea of it, is fast becoming the only answer to Barbara's and my problems. I must truly admit I do not know how well I will face up to things. I hope it works out so that I am proven wrong in all my thoughts. But that hope is slim."

When I took up the journal again on January 31, 1962, the subject was the same. There was still no letter from Barbara. She had written once in mid-December, then nothing after that. And there was no news, of any sort, from which I could draw even the slightest hope of release.

I closed the entry: "I am a nervous wreck because of this, and as hard as I try, I cannot keep from thinking about it. *I need help badly! But who can help?*"

Those were the last words I wrote in the journal.

Fifteen

At about 7:30 on the evening of Wednesday, February 7, 1962, Zigurd and I were just returning from our evening trip to the toilet when we noticed the KGB colonel from Vladimir and the interpreter walking down the corridor ahead of us. They stopped outside our cell. It was an odd time for a visit, enough in itself to alert us that something out of the ordinary had happened.

Following us inside our cell, the colonel asked me, "How would you like to go to Moscow tomorrow morning?"

"Fine," I replied, still unsure.

"Without guards," he added.

Then I knew. But I couldn't be positive. My hopes had been aroused so often, only to have them wither and die, that I couldn't face the prospect of another disappointment. "Why?" I asked. "What's happening?" But he would tell me nothing more.

Zigurd was exuberant. It could mean only one thing. Hadn't he told me from the start that I wouldn't have to serve the full ten years?

Not until the guard brought in two suitcases and informed me I should spend the evening packing did I really believe it.

I was going home!

Yet my excitement was saddened by the realization that Zigurd was not, that he still had eight of his fifteen years to serve, with his earliest chance of parole nearly three years away. But he was as happy as if it had been his own release.

Having few possessions, it took me only a short time to pack. I made a large parcel of the three carpets, the only product of my imprisonment, except for memories. In between the carpets I slipped the diary and journal, hoping the Russians would overlook them. Anything I felt he could use, such as books, pipes, tobacco, I gave to Zigurd.

We couldn't sleep, but talked all night. We promised to write, to visit each other someday, although, I'm sure, we both realized the likelihood was remote. We exchanged home addresses and photographs. Across the back of a photo of himself taken some years earlier in Germany he wrote, "To my friend and cellmate 9-9-60, 8-2-62. Zigurd Kruminsh."

September 9, 1960—February 8, 1962. I had been in Vladimir for seventeen months.

Shortly after six A.M. the guard brought the items which had been held for me, including my wedding ring. I hadn't been allowed to wear it in either prison.

With the arrival of my escorts, we said our good-byes. Because it was not easy, we made them brief. I felt as if I was leaving a part of myself behind. And in a sense I was, for Zigurd was now speaking with a pronounced Virginia accent.

Walking across the courtyard to the gate, I looked at the window of cell number 31.

Contrary to rules, Zigurd was standing on the cabinet, looking down at me from the window at the top.

Emerging from the other side of the administration building, I climbed into an automobile with the colonel, the interpreter, and a driver, and we rode away from Vladimir Prison. I didn't look back.

The colonel kept his promise. When we reached the railroad station and boarded the train, there were no guards. We had the whole compartment to ourselves, until, at one of the many stops, two peasant women got on, sitting toward the end of the car. But they paid no attention to me, and, I must admit, I was little interested in them, spending most of my time staring out the window at all the open space. It was a beautiful day, there was still snow everywhere, and finally, trees. Trees!

But it was the slowest train I had ever ridden. I thought perhaps it was my imagination, until the interpreter explained that winter thaws were causing the ground to shift, and we had to travel slowly for safety's sake.

I tried to question the colonel, but apparently he was under orders to tell me as little as possible. Thus far, no one had actually stated that I was to be released. But I would permit no other thoughts to enter my mind.

It was late afternoon when we reached Moscow. A car was waiting at the station. I had guessed I would be driven directly to the American Embassy and turned over to officials there, but I guessed wrong. Instead the car followed a familiar route, one I had not been anxious to retrace.

Once again I drove through the gates of Lubyanka Prison.

I was taken to my old cellblock, to a cell two doors from the one I had formerly occupied. I was now able to confirm one of my suspicions: there were beds softer than the torture rack they had originally given me. This one had two mattresses.

Only then did the colonel inform me that we were going to East Germany the following morning.

I had about one hundred dollars in my prison account, he said. They couldn't give it to me in dollars, only rubles, and I couldn't spend them outside the USSR, so what did I want to do with them? I asked if the money could be credited to Zigurd's account; I was told no, and so I asked if I could spend it on souvenirs to take home. I also wanted to obtain a phonograph record. When at Vladimir I had heard a girl singer on Radio Moscow. She had one of the most beautiful voices I had ever heard, and I had developed something of a crush on her. Phonetically her name sounded like Savancova. The record I liked most was her version of Grieg's *Solveig's Song*. They promised to try to get it.

The mention of my being unable to spend rubles outside the USSR was the closest anyone had come to saying I was to be freed.

Following a bath, a luxury, since I wasn't "due" for one for another five days, the colonel explained we had arrived too late for supper. However, since I had money, they could send out for food. Was there something I especially wanted?

"Meat," I replied, "and a martini."

Laughing, the colonel said they probably couldn't manage the martini. However, when the meal arrived—two breaded veal cutlets, the most meat I had been given by the Russians—there was a tin cup with it, half full of brandy. It was good and potent, and having had nothing to drink for twenty-one months, I slept well that night.

Early the next morning, Friday, February 9, the three of us were driven to the airport. En route the interpreter informed me they had purchased souvenirs, but had been unable to find the phonograph record I wanted, which surprised me, since the singer was apparently one of the most popular in the Soviet Union. At the airport a plane was waiting, the only other occupants the two pilots. I'd spent so much time dreaming about escape that the thought pattern was hard to break; I wasn't checked out on this type of aircraft, but I was sure I could manage it in about one minute, after disposing of the two pilots. Later, when one of them came back and made conversation through the interpreter, I was thankful he hadn't been able to read my thoughts.

We were going in the right direction—west.

Everything was precisely arranged. When we landed in East Germany, a car was waiting. Without any delays we were driven directly into East Berlin. February in Germany is bleak. There was no snow, the leaves were gone from the trees, the grass was dead. Our destination was a "safe" house, but unlike the agency, they made no attempt to make their residences inconspicuous. There were guards all around the outside, patrolling with submachine guns. Every time I looked out a window I could see one. The house, apparently once a private home, was luxuriously fitted. I guessed that it was used for top Russian Communist-party functionaries on their visits to East Berlin. That night supper was served with crystal and silver.

Earlier the colonel had asked me if there was anything I especially wanted. I observed that I'd like a little more of the brandy. When we sat down at the table, he produced a bottle that either was Hennessey Four Star or an exact imitation. I began to sip my drink, but he said that since I was with Russians I should drink the way they did, and, following his example, I swallowed the whole drink in one gulp. The colonel corked the bottle, saying that we would save the remainder for the next morning.

"If everything goes well," he said through the interpreter, "you will be released tomorrow morning and will have a reason to celebrate."

It was now official, "if everything goes well." Curious, I asked why I was being released at this time. He replied that it was a gesture of goodwill. "We wish to show the world how humane the Soviets can be." I suspected there was more to it, but said nothing.

The interpreter and I had beds in a room on the second floor. Following dinner, we played several games of chess. I hadn't realized how much Zigurd had taught me. I beat him several times.

There was no light in the room. But the door was left open, and there was a light in the hall. There was a guard downstairs, in addition to those outside. The bed was comfortable, but I was so tense that I slept little, dozing off only a few times. So much depended on the next morning. Although the situation looked good, far better than ever before, I kept reminding myself that anything could happen.

Saturday, February 10, 1962. Up very early, we had the brandy with breakfast. The car arrived shortly after five A.M., and a long drive followed. I noticed that we seemed to be leaving the city and returning to the country. That worried me. I was afraid we were headed back to the airport. I wanted to stay as close to West Berlin as possible. Eventually, however, we drove into what I later learned was the Potsdam section, and after circling one block several times, stopped.

A well-dressed man, who looked and talked like an American, but I later learned was Ivan A. Schischkin, Soviet consular representative in East Berlin, got into the car and explained the procedure. We were to drive directly to Glienicker Bridge, which spanned Lake Wannsee, separating Potsdam from West Berlin. At 8:20 A.M. we would walk onto the bridge, at the same time a group of Americans approached from the other side. About ten yards from the white line in the center, both groups would stop. Part of our group would then go forward to meet part of their group; we were to remain behind. If all was satisfactory, I would then be escorted forward and across the white line marking the border between East and West.

"However," he added with some firmness, "if anything goes wrong on the bridge, you are to return with us. Do you understand that?"

I nodded. But I decided then that should something of that sort occur, I would run for it. Even if it meant a bullet, I wasn't coming back.

It was a cold, dark day, the sky overcast. Even with my heavy coat and Russian fur cap, I felt chilly. We reached our end of the bridge about eight A.M. It was painted a dull green color. Under any other circumstances I probably would have found it ugly, but at that moment it was one of the most beautiful things I had ever seen.

At about 8:15 we got out of the car. The colonel who had accompanied me from Vladimir shook my hand. It was the first such gesture since my capture. We walked onto the bridge, which was devoid of traffic. I carried my suitcases, one of the KGB men the box of souvenirs and rug parcel. I could see, too far away for any of them to be clearly recognizable, a group of men approaching from the other side.

Following the plan, both groups stopped about ten yards from the center, three men from our side, two from the other going forward to the line. I remained behind, between the colonel and another KGB man. A short distance behind us were armed guards. It would be a long run, and they would have ample time to shoot. That didn't shake my resolve. I wasn't going back.

After a few minutes the colonel left me and walked across the line. At the same time, one of the men from the other side also crossed and walked up to me, grinning broadly. I recognized him as a former acquaintance in the U-2 program. His was the first familiar face I had seen in a very long time.

"Gee, it's good to see you," I exclaimed, shaking hands.

"You know who I am, don't you?" he asked.

"You're Bill."

He looked surprised, then laughed. "No, I'm Murphy. Bill was my boss. You've got our names confused." He was right.

"What was the name of your high-school football coach?" he asked.

It was my turn to look puzzled. Then I remembered the Air Force form I had filled out more than ten years ago, with questions to be used in case I had to be identified. The agency had gone to all the trouble of digging it out of my service records.

For the life of me I couldn't think of the name. In the excitement, my mind went blank.

I did better with the names of my wife, my mother, my dog.

"You're Francis Gary Powers," he finally said, bringing the agency's little guessing game to an end. He had known, of course, who I was all the time. Recrossing the white line, he relayed this information to the others: Identification positive.

At the same time, the KGB colonel also recrossed the line and rejoined me. I wondered what he had been up to.

There followed a long delay. Apparently the negotiators were awaiting some word from the other end of the bridge. As minute after minute slowly passed, the distance to the center of the span seemed to grow greater. Glancing over the side of the bridge, I spotted two men in a small boat, on the West German side of the river. Each man was carrying a shotgun, and was dressed like a duck hunter. Their hunting clothes appeared straight out of Abercrombie & Fitch. I was certain they were agency men, and I added another possibility: diving off the bridge and swimming to the boat.

While we were waiting, Schischkin, the Soviet consular representative, remarked, "The next time you come to see us, come as a friend."

"Next time," I answered, "I'll come as a tourist."

With a smile, Schischkin replied, "I didn't say as a tourist. I said as a friend."

Suddenly there was a yell from the other end. The negotiators huddled briefly, then nodded to the colonel, who pushed me forward. As I walked toward the line, another man—thin, gaunt, middle-aged—approached from the other side. We crossed at the same time.

It was 8:52 A.M. on Saturday, February 10, 1962. One year, nine months, and ten days after my capture by the Russians.

I was again a free man.

Murphy ran up and slapped me on the back. "You know who that was, don't you?" he asked, indicating the other man.

"No," I replied.

"Abel, Colonel Rudolf Abel, the Soviet spy."

It was the first time I realized that my release had been part of an exchange. The KGB colonel from Vladimir, I now realized, had crossed the line to identify Abel. I wondered if they were friends, and if Abel had remembered the name of his high-school football coach.

While Abel and the Soviets stood in precise military formation on their side of the border, concluding the negotiations with their counterparts, Murphy and I walked over to the edge of the bridge and began talking with the excitement of two kids.

I couldn't help noticing the contrast. The Americans, friendly, excited, making no attempt to hide their feelings; the Russians, rigid, emotionless, totally businesslike.

Much handshaking followed, everyone talking at the same time, as the American delegation joined us. Getting into a car at the end of the bridge, I was introduced to James Donovan, Abel's American attorney, who I now learned had arranged the trade. I also learned the reason for the delay on the bridge. They had been awaiting confirmation of the release at "Checkpoint Charlie" of Frederick L. Pryor, a Yale student arrested on espionage charges in East Germany six months earlier.

Two Americans for one Russian seemed to me an excellent bargain.

Asking about my wife and parents, I was told they were well and would be greeting me before long. They didn't know about my release, but would be notified as soon as word was relayed to the President.

It all seemed very unreal.

We drove rapidly to Tempelhof Airport, where we were hustled onto a C-47 cargo plane. Destination Wiesbaden. Minutes after we were airborne, a flight surgeon examined me. The air corridor was bumpy, however, and his attempts to extract blood from my arm left it black and blue for weeks. The blood samples were necessary to determine whether I had been drugged. This seemed to be the first question of almost everyone to whom I talked: had I been drugged? They seemed almost disappointed when I told them I hadn't.

All my gear had been loaded aboard the plane. My suitcases, a box, and the parcel with the rugs. Checking the latter, I was pleased to find both my diary and journal intact.

Murphy asked what was in the box. I explained about the souvenirs, mentioning that I hadn't yet had a chance to look at them.

It occurred to someone, or maybe several people at the same time, that perhaps we had better examine the box, to make sure the Russians hadn't planted a bomb. Although I felt this somewhat unlikely, I was as cautious as the others when it was opened. Packed inside were plaster of paris desk sets and paperweights commemorating Sputnik; wood carvings of various animals—horses, dogs, and a frog on a lily pad; a University of Moscow ashtray; dolls that came apart with ever-smaller dolls inside; small figurines, including a ballet dancer; and a very charming beautifully carved little troika. There was no bomb.

On landing at Wiesbaden, one of the Air force officers gave me a coat to throw over mine, so I wouldn't attract attention. We quickly walked over to a Lockheed Constellation, belonging to the commanding general of USAF Europe. In less than fifteen minutes we were airborne. The destination this time—the United States.

As soon as we leveled off, a white-jacketed flight steward asked whether we wanted anything to drink. Donovan ordered a double scotch, I a martini.

This was my first opportunity to talk to Donovan at any length. I asked him how the exchange had come about.

He told me that when Abel was sentenced in 1957, he had argued against giving him the death sentence, on grounds that someday the United States might find it advantageous to exchange him for an American. The actual exchange for me, however, had been *my father's* idea. He had written a letter to Abel at the federal penitentiary at Atlanta as early as June 2, 1960, one month and one day after my capture, broaching the idea of a swap.

DEAR COLONEL ABEL:

I am the father of Francis Gary Powers, who is connected with the U-2 plane incident of several weeks ago. I am quite sure that you are familiar with this international incident and also the fact that my son is being currently held by the Soviet Union on an espionage charge.

You can readily understand the concern that a father would have for his son and my strong desire to have my son released and brought home. My present feeling is that I would be more than happy to approach the State Department and the President of the United States for an exchange for the release of my son. By this I mean that I would urge and do everything possible to have my government release you and return you to your country if the powers in your country would release my son and let him return home to me. If you are inclined to go along with this arrangement, I would appreciate your so advising the powers in your country along these lines.

I would appreciate hearing from you in this regard as soon as possible.

Very truly yours,
Oliver Powers

Again I had underrated my dad.

Abel had contacted Donovan, who had obtained permission from the State Department to explore the possibility. It was not until hearing from a woman in East Germany who purported herself to be Abel's wife that the actual negotiations had begun. Even after Donovan's arrival in Berlin on February 2, the negotiations had nearly broken off several times, the most recent incident occurring when the Soviets had tried to go back on the original deal, deciding they would release only Pryor for Abel, and keep me. Donovan had refused to go along with this, for which I was very thankful.

After several more drinks, dinner was served. It consisted of a green salad; a beautiful steak, medium rare; and a potato. I had thought I would never be able to look at a potato again. But this one was baked instead of boiled and was served with butter. It made all the difference.

One of the pilots came back and told us that word of my release had just been made public in the United States, the radio carrying the official White House announcement shortly after three A.M., EST. That meant my wife and family had been notified. For a long time I thought about their reactions.

Shortly after Donovan went to bed, the pilot came back to ask if I would like to visit the cockpit. The sight of the instrument panel was in the nature of a homecoming. With a grin, the co-pilot indicated the wheel, saying "Why don't you take it for awhile, just to see if you remember how?" I was tempted but declined. I spent some time talking to them. I hadn't realized how much I had missed pilots' small talk.

When we landed at the Azores for refueling, nearly everyone else got out to stretch their legs and get a sandwich. I had to stay aboard the plane so as not to be spotted by reporters.

It was a sample of things to come. Elaborate security precautions had been put into effect for our arrival in the United States, which were explained to me when we took off again. I was back in the world of cloak-and-dagger operations.

About six hours later, as we approached the eastern seaboard, I saw the first lights of the United States. Having so few hours before been a prisoner on the other side of the Iron Curtain, they seemed unreal. I still couldn't comprehend that after twenty-one months of captivity I was once again a free man.

Which was perhaps best, for, though I was yet to realize it, I wasn't quite free, not yet. In a sense, I had been released by the Russians to become a *de facto* prisoner of the CIA.

FOUR

USA

One

Reporters were watching all the major airports, but particularly Andrews Air Force Base, outside Washington, D.C. Possibly this was because it was here that President Kennedy had met the two RB-47 pilots, though I strongly suspect the CIA had also planted a rumor the plane would be landing there.

It did. Only it stopped first at Dover, Delaware, where Murphy and I alighted. Then it went on to Andrews, where Donovan and a man of my approximate height and build evaded pursuit by immediately taking off in a helicopter.

My welcoming committee consisted of agency security men; my first steps on American soil—the runway at Dover—were on a run, from plane to waiting automobile. Though a reporter had been assigned to Dover, one of the agency representatives invited him into base operations for a cup of coffee. By the time he had finished it, we were off the base and en route to a "safe" house on Maryland's eastern shore.

Why the tight security? They replied, without elaboration, that the agency wanted to debrief me before exposure to the press.

That was fine with me. For more months than I cared to remember, I had lived by a set routine. The sudden change, coupled with all the excitement, was exhausting. I looked forward to a couple of days of privacy and rest.

I didn't know then that the "couple of days" would end in being over three weeks, and that few of those days would be restful.

We arrived at the "safe" house, Ashford Farms, a private estate near Oxford, Maryland, about five A.M. After several hours' sleep I awoke to a pleasant realization. My irregular heartbeat had disappeared. Thinking back, I realized I hadn't noticed it since crossing the bridge.

Other discoveries followed. The bathroom had hot and cold running water. And a toilet with a seat. And a mirror. And all sorts of other marvelous conveniences, including a scale. From the tight fit of my pants I had assumed that, despite the limited diet, I'd gained weight in prison. Before my capture I'd weighed between 175 and 180 pounds. Stepping onto the scale, I found I now weighed 152. A loss of twenty-three to twenty-eight pounds; the extra two inches around the middle was due solely to lack of exercise.

Following a large breakfast, only a small portion of which I could eat, photographs were taken, for release to the press. This time there was no need to tell me to smile. I grinned all over the place. Then I saw another doctor—a psychiatrist. Had the Russians drugged me? No, not to my knowledge. Had I been brainwashed? No, at least not in the sense that we usually define brainwashing. How was I feeling now? Extremely nervous. I had felt so since learning I would see Barbara and my parents after lunch. He gave me some tranquilizers, the first I had ever taken. They helped.

My mother and father arrived first. It was a very emotional, though jubilant scene. While in prison I had often wondered whether I would see either of them again. They looked very much the same as when I had seen them in Moscow, although worry had obviously aged them. Our conversation was dominated by family news, everyone so busy asking questions that there was hardly time to listen to the replies.

Barbara and her brother, the Air Force chaplain, arrived shortly afterward. I had anticipated and feared this moment. At Vladimir, during the last long period when Barbara hadn't written, I had reached a decision: to obtain a divorce upon my return to the United States. It was as firm as any decision could be, yet I knew that seeing her again, in entirely different circumstances, my resolve might be shaken.

She had changed most of all. Bloated, her face puffy, her eyes heavily lidded, at least thirty pounds overweight, she was almost unrecognizable. Despite thick makeup, it was apparent her dissipation had taken a terrible toll.

I had loved Barbara, and, at times, I had hated her too. Now both emotions were gone. All I felt was pity, and all I wanted was to help her, if she would let me. I had no illusions. Our marriage was dead. It had died while I was in Vladimir Prison. Only the form remained.

We talked a long time that night. She was vague as to the details of her life while I had been in prison, her only explanation for the absence of letters that there had been nothing to write about. Her main complaint was that she had not been warned that I was going to be released. I wondered why she felt a warning necessary, and started to ask, but then stopped myself. In that way lay more pain. And I'd had more than enough of that. The questions, and the answers, could wait until both of us were strong enough for them.

I did learn a few things, one especially surprising. Upon return to the United States, following my trial, she had been interrogated by the CIA. Their first question: "Mrs. Powers, are you sure the man you saw in Moscow was your husband?"

Although assuring them he was, she still sensed their skepticism.

I could see them covering all possibilities. But this, as far as I was concerned, was nothing more than wishful thinking on their part.

It was not to be the last time I was to encounter evidence of this reluctance to accept obvious facts.

I awoke once during the night, panicked by the blackness. Then I remembered where I was and gratefully slipped back into sleep. With this, as with other things, I had anticipated a long adjustment, but after that, sleeping without a light never bothered me again.

It was like a series of aftershocks following a major earthquake. All at once I realized: I have all kinds of room! I can go outside whenever I want to! I'm not limited to a walk area of twenty by twenty-five feet!

Perhaps a taste of freedom whets the appetite, making you want more.

Barbara was permitted to stay at the farm, but her brother left the same day he arrived. The second morning my parents returned to The Pound. Soon after they left, Murphy and I took a walk around the yard in front of the house. Ashford Farms was a large estate, at least sixty acres, surrounded by a high wire fence guarded by German shepherds and, I presumed, more than a few agency employees. Like the house itself—a two-story, beautifully furnished Georgian structure—the estate was roomy but secure. Aside from my family, everyone I came in contact with was agency. Even the meals were cooked by one of the agency men.

"Murph," I said, as we tramped through the snow, "I get the impression that I'm almost a prisoner here. Tell me something. If I wanted to leave right now—just pack my bag and walk out— could I do it?"

After a moment of quiet thought, he replied, "I don't think so."

I didn't know how they could stop me. But at that time I wasn't particularly anxious to find out. Extremely nervous, still trying to adjust to my changed situation, I wasn't in any hurry to face the world, especially the press, not quite yet. I became even less so after reading American newspapers and watching TV for the first time in twenty-one months. The exchange dominated the news. Much of what was said stunned me.

While imprisoned I had been protected by my isolation and my correspondents. I had seen no American newspapers, and in the letters I received there was no hint of censure. More than that, I had often drawn strength from the knowledge that the American people were behind me, that they understood what I was going through.

The criticism hit me with a sledgehammer blow.

"A HERO OR A MAN WHO FAILED HIS MISSION?" read the headline on the New York Sunday *Herald Tribune.*

The American people demanded answers to certain questions, the paper said. Among them:

"Why, knowing that neither he nor the U-2 should fall into unfriendly hands, didn't he blow himself up, and the plane?

"Why didn't Powers use the poison needle he had on hand? Or the pistol he had with him?"

Apparently a great many people were under the impression that I had been under orders to kill myself, come what may. But, as I had attempted to make clear in the trial, I had no such orders. I was to use the destruct device—which wouldn't have destroyed the plane, only a portion of the equipment—if possible. Under the circumstances, it had not been possible. I could understand why, not having been in the cockpit with me, some people might doubt my story. But when it came to the poison needle, there shouldn't have been any doubt. Since carrying it was optional, suicide was obviously optional too.

Now I understood what was behind the Hutchins remark in *Time* about Nathan Hale and me.

It bothered me that this criticism was apparently long-standing, and that the CIA—although it would have been very easy to do so, without in any way jeopardizing security—had made no attempt to set the record straight by stating exactly what my instructions were. Instead they had let this misapprehension, damning as it was, continue undisputed.

Much was made of the fact that Abel had not testified during his trial, while I had. But no one pointed out that our law gave Abel the right to remain silent, while under Soviet law I had been denied that luxury, the refusal to testify in itself being considered incriminating.

Five words from my trial testimony had been emphasized almost to the exclusion of all others: "deeply repentant and profoundly sorry." At the time, I had been sure the American people would understand that this was the only defense I had. But obviously they hadn't. Those words were emphasized throughout all accounts of the trial.

The criticism went far beyond that, however. Comparisons were made between my conduct and Abel's following capture, the implication being that while Abel had revealed nothing about his mission, I had "spilled my guts," "told everything."

I knew better. The other pilots knew better. As did the agency, the President, the Secretary of State, and, I presumed, quite a few others. I could see why this particular misapprehension hadn't been corrected. To do so, while I was still in prison, would have placed me in additional jeopardy. Also it would have made the Russians reconsider everything I had told them, and quite possibly give them clues to what I hadn't told. Although obviously disturbed by the implication that I was some kind of traitor, I felt sure that now I was no longer in Russian hands, the truth would out.

Yet some of the information I had withheld was so sensitive as to make me wonder if it could ever be made public. And, thinking about this, I became vaguely uneasy.

One story, featured in all the papers and on TV, bothered me more than any other. "U.S. 'UNWISE' IN SPY SWAP," read the headlines. "RUSSIANS GOT BEST OF DEAL, SAYS LAWYER."

William F. Tompkins, a former assistant U.S. attorney general, and the prosecutor of Abel, was quoted as saying: "It's like trading Mickey Mantle for an average ballplayer. We gave them an extremely valuable man and got back an airplane driver."

That made me angry. Not because I put a high value on myself, but because it ignored the fact that the United States had gained the release of two Americans by freeing one Russian. (Actually, the count rose to three. Later, Marvin Makinen, a University of Pennsylvania student serving an eight-year sentence for espionage in a Soviet prison in Kiev, was released as a result of negotiations begun by Donovan.) To my mind, this was the same kind of irresponsible criticism that followed President Kennedy's statement that he was "grateful" for the release of the two RB-47 pilots.

Too, although Abel had once been an important Soviet agent, of what intelligence value was he now, either to us or the Russians? If he hadn't betrayed his espionage apparatus after nearly five years of imprisonment, it seemed unlikely he would do so in the future. And should he still possess secrets he had not yet communicated to his government, they would be equally dated. Apparently Tompkins wanted him to serve his full thirty-year sentence, as fit punishment for his crime. A perfect example of a prosecutor's mentality, of which I'd had more than enough in Russia.

I was pleased to discover that Tompkins' attitude wasn't quite universal. Asked about the swap, former President Harry Truman had said, "I guess that's a fair trade."

Several of the TV news programs reviewed the U-2 incident, from May 1, 1960, through the exchange. Watching them, I learned for the first time many details of what had happened following my capture.

From talking to an agency friend I had known in Turkey, I learned something else I had wondered about: what had happened in Adana when word was received I hadn't arrived in Bödo.

The party for the communications chief who was returning to the States had gone on as scheduled.

I had figured as much. Once one of those parties got started, only an act of God could stop it. This one, I now learned, had lasted three days.

What I couldn't have guessed, however, was that the 10-10 detachment hadn't pulled out until August. As inconceivable as it seemed, despite Khrushchev's charges, my letters, the statements from my interrogations, the photographs the Soviets had released, the agency was apparently not totally convinced that I had actually been captured and was still alive—until the Russians brought me to trial!

Aside from a brief statement that I was in the United States, appeared to be in good physical condition, had seen my family, and was undergoing questioning at an undisclosed location, the White House remained silent about the exchange. That day, however, there was a report in *The New York Times* which said that following my interrogation a board of inquiry would be convened by the Central Intelligence Agency "to investigate the circumstances of the capture of Francis Gary Powers by the Soviet Union and the crash of his U-2 reconnaissance plane in the Ural Mountains."

I asked one of the agency men what that meant. Don't worry, he told me. That's just to get the press off our backs.

When will the debriefing start? I was anxious to get it done. It would begin the following day, he said, and would take place at Ashford Farms.

Despite reassurances from Murphy and others, I couldn't shake the feeling that all at once I was on trial again.

The debriefing didn't take place at Ashford Farms. Late that night,

Monday, February 12, one of the agents received a telephone call. Hanging up the phone, he said: "Some reporter's on to our location. We're going to have to move. Better get packed."

Although there was a blizzard outside, we climbed into several cars and, with more speed than caution, drove off the estate. Later I learned that reporters had succeeded in following us for a few miles but lost us in the snow. There were, in the papers, two different accounts of how Ashford Farms had been compromised. One was that an astute Associated Press stringer, suspicious, since its recent sale, of the estate's new tenants, had put it under surveillance. Another had it that the draperies in the background of the photos released by the CIA were identified by someone who had visited Ashford Farms on a previous occasion.

Our destination was another of the agency's "safe" houses, this one near Gettysburg, Pennsylvania. It wasn't an easy trip. Barbara was desperate for a drink. I'd tried to get her to talk to the doctor at Ashford Farms, but she had refused to do so. I'd then tried to keep her from drinking, but she had begged so pathetically that I'd let her have beer. It tore me apart to see her suffer. It was obvious that she was sick and needed help. This she vehemently denied. Contrary to what I might have heard from the rumormongers, she said, she did not have a drinking problem. It was nerves, she went on, that was all. Given a couple of days, she would pull herself together and be fine.

Debriefings started the next afternoon. Present in addition to agency representatives was Clarence L. "Kelly" Johnson, designer of the U-2. I had seen Johnson on one previous occasion, at Lockheed early in the program, but had never met him.

"Before we start," Johnson said, "I want to tell Mr. Powers something. No matter what happens as a result of this investigation, I want you to know that if you ever need a job, you have one at Lockheed."

That vote of confidence meant more to me than I could ever say.

With that the debriefings began. Johnson had the first question: "What happened to my plane?"

I told him, describing the orange flash, the slight acceleration, and the erratic manner in which the aircraft behaved after that. He asked a number of technical questions. After I had answered, he stated his satisfaction with my explanation.

From Johnson I learned of another Khrushchev trap. Following his announcement that he had the pilot and the plane, the Soviet premier had released a photograph of "the captured U-2," a mass of twisted wreckage. To the casual viewer, it seemed inconceivable that the pilot could have survived the crash. But Johnson was not a casual viewer. He knew every rivet in the U-2, and after studying the photograph, announced that the plane just wasn't made right, a judgment confirmed when the real wreckage was put on display in Gorky Park.

What had Khrushchev intended with the fake photo? The most likely possibility was that he hoped to convince Eisenhower the pilot was dead, meaning there could be little actual proof of espionage, and thereby baiting him into yet another public lie.

The Russians had set still another trap, I later learned from people in the agency. Immediately after my disappearance, there was a report of a strange plane with an incredibly long wingspan being seen parked off the runway at Svedlovsk, undamaged and intact. Still later, there were reports that a man resembling me had been seen drinking, carousing with assorted females, and otherwise living it up in various Communist cities. The purpose, apparently, was to make the United States think I had landed my plane and defected.

When Johnson had finished his questions, the agency men began asking theirs. The first session lasted several hours.

At night, after the debriefings, I'd read the papers and watch TV. I didn't want to. Yet I had to know what was going on.

"Powers served his country badly," Martin B. McKneally, national commander of the American Legion, told the press. "We are left with the impression that there was more of the mercenary in him than the patriot."

John Wickers, another American Legion official, said: "I view the exchange with astonishment and disgust. Powers was a cowardly American who evidently valued his own skin far more than the welfare of the nation that was paying him so handsomely."

It was easy to dismiss such statements as the product of ignorance, which they were, for none of these people was aware of what my orders were, or that I had, on my own initiative, gone far beyond them. But it didn't make such remarks sting any the less.

Led by Tompkins, the lynching bee ranged from a syndicated sob sister who described me as a "tower of jelly . . . who will, when the chips are down, go to any length to save his own neck" and who offered the unsolicited advice that Powers should "save his money and find a nice, pleasant spot outside the U.S. in which eventually to live and spend it," to Senator Stephen Young, Democrat, Ohio, who said, "I wish that this pilot—who was being paid thirty thousand dollars a year—had shown only ten percent of the spirit and courage of Nathan Hale. If it is up to me, I am going to make sure that he never flies for the U.S. government again."

Much of the criticism focused on the amount of my pay, the argument apparently being that I had been paid this "fantastically high amount" to kill myself before capture, which I had failed to do. Under the subhead "Mercenary," one paper reported, authoritatively, that in addition to my twenty-five-hundred-dollar monthly salary, I had received a ten-thousand-dollar tax-free bonus for every flight. Had this been true, and had my major concern been money, I would have been quite happily retired long before May 1, 1960.

None of the accounts mentioned that twenty-five hundred dollars per month was less than the captain of a commercial airliner received for considerably less hazardous work; that the mechanics in the U-2 project and the technical representatives of the various companies which supplied cameras, film, and so forth ended up earning nearly as much, and in some cases more, than the pilots. The pilots were government employees, and as such subject to both federal and state income taxes. The mechanics and technical representatives were not federal employees. If they remained outside the country eighteen months or more, as most of them did, they paid no taxes, greatly increasing their take-home pay. Nor did they mention that the pilots who never made an overflight were paid exactly the same amount as those who did.

It was my "fifty-thousand-dollar" back pay that concerned them most, however. Should I be allowed to receive it?

"Our recommendation would be no," *Newsday* editorialized. "He was hired to do a job, and he flopped at that job. He left his U-2 behind, substantially undamaged, so the Reds could copy or improve upon it. Under the circumstances, back pay would be laughable. He is lucky to be home again. Anything he can contribute about the Russians will be willingly received. But he is no hero, and he should not be regarded as one. The White House is eminently right in not bringing him in for a meeting with the President. . . ."

Actually, to set the record straight, the amount of my back pay was not $50,000, but approximately $52,500, or $2,500 per month for twenty-one months.

Again unmentioned was that a total of $10,500 or five hundred dollars per month, had already been paid to Barbara while I was in prison. And that the walloping tax bite would further reduce the amount to less than half the total—or about twenty-two thousand dollars.

In addition, because there was no provision for accumulating it in my contract, I also lost the money ordinarily paid for unused leave time. Fortunately I still had my savings, from the earlier portion of the program.

According to newspapers, one of the major reasons for holding the board of inquiry was to determine whether I should receive my back pay. This was not true. Arrangements regarding payments had been made in my contract, and no one from the agency had indicated differently.

The papers didn't stop at twisting the "facts" to make their case. In more than one instance, they manufactured them.

"The life of pilot Powers is important," said an editorial in the *Dallas Morning News,* which I saw sometime later, "but so are the many lives which may have been lost as a result of his failure to follow orders."

As far as I knew, no deaths had resulted from the U-2 incident.

"It has been reported," the editorial continued, "that at least two U-2 pilots blew themselves and their planes up when they ran into trouble. These are the real U-2 heroes, and Powers should not be allowed to join them until he has given a good explanation of why he failed to do the same."

This too was a complete lie. A number of pilots—including close personal friends—had lost their lives in U-2 crashes. But not one had involved the destruct device, which was carried only on missions over hostile territory. To this date—and over the years I have remained in contact with several people involved with the U-2— the destruct device, for all the publicity it has received, has never been used. Not once.

Yet surely some who read that editorial believed it, felt I was not only a traitor but also a murderer.

After reading such nonsense, I was thankful the agency was keeping me from a face-to-face encounter with the press. It might have made headlines of a different sort.

Not all the fictions were a result of "imaginative reporting." Some person or persons in the government had been responsible for the dissemination of more than a few. One was the story which had bothered me so much in Russia. I now learned that the editor of an aviation journal had stated on an NBC-TV White Paper on the U-2 that he had been assured by totally reliable government sources that the U-2 had not been hit at sixty-eight-thousand feet but, suffering an engine flameout, had descended to thirty-thousand feet, at which point it was shot down. U.S. intelligence knew this, he said, because (1) I had radioed this information; and (2) the entire flight had been tracked on radar. The story was certainly a nice plug for the effectiveness of our radio and radar. The only trouble was, both claims were not only not true, they were also not possible.

My early suspicions were not certainties. There were some people in the government absolutely refusing to accept the fact that Russia had surface-to-air missiles capable of hitting high-flying aircraft.

It wasn't until much later, in 1965, with the publication of President Eisenhower's memoirs, that I was to learn how far up the chain of command this misapprehension apparently extended.

"HERO OR BUM?" asked one newspaper. "Many questions need answering, not the least of which involve Powers' own conduct," noted another. "Should he, like Nathan Hale, have died for his country?" queried *Newsweek*.

I stopped reading the newspapers and news magazines. Yet it wasn't that easy. For by this time I had heard, from several people in the agency something even more disturbing. Negotiations for the Abel-Powers trade had begun under William P. Rogers, Eisenhower's attorney general. The current attorney general, Robert F. Kennedy, had opposed the trade. Moreover, he had said that upon my return to the United States he personally intended to try me for treason.

For God's sake, why? I asked the people from the agency. As the President's brother, he was certainly aware of the true facts of the case, including the importance of the information withheld.

There was no clear-cut answer, only conjecture. Rumor had it that, reacting to criticism of his appointment as attorney general when he had never actually practiced law, Robert Kennedy had wanted to "prove himself" with a spectacular trial.

I felt there must be more to it than that.

They were the experts. They knew what was important and what wasn't. Yet as the debriefings continued—we had by this time moved to a third "safe" house, near McLean, Virginia, not far from Hickory Hill, the Kennedy estate—I couldn't help feeling disappointed by their lack of thoroughness, the questioning being neither so intensive nor the queries so probing as I had anticipated.

It seemed to me that some of the information I possessed—concerning what I had observed on the May 1 flight and subsequently during my interrogations, trial, and imprisonment—was of intelligence value. For example, that the KGB had asked me some questions and not others seemed significant, as did whether the question was general or specific, was in the nature of a "fishing expedition" or indicated prior detailed knowledge. Such things, I felt, were important clues as to how good their intelligence was, and, though only bits and pieces, might be helpful in constructing a composite picture of the extent of their knowledge.

But the agency apparently felt otherwise. In this, as with other areas I thought important, they showed little interest.

They were far more concerned about what I had told the Russians regarding some of their other clandestine operations, and greatly surprised to discover that quite often I knew little or nothing about them.

There were many questions I felt should have been asked—but weren't. Yet when I attempted to volunteer information, often as not it wasn't appreciated. For example, while being questioned about the KGB officials with whom I had come into contact, I was shown a photograph of Shelepin, head of the KGB, and asked if I could identify him. But when I volunteered that it was Rudenko, not Shelepin, who appeared to be the "big wheel" in the interrogations, the man to whom the others deferred, they quickly passed on to something else. Maybe this wasn't important. Yet, for a comparable example, if in the interrogations of a Soviet spy FBI Director J. Edgar Hoover played a superior role to Attorney General Robert Kennedy, I suspect the KGB would have been greatly interested in that fact.

One of the reasons I had kept the journal was to record things I felt might later be of use to the agency. When I told them about the journal, however, they expressed no desire to see it. I had assumed they would be interested in the fate of their former agent Evgeni Brick. From their reactions I got the distinct impression that they couldn't have cared less. I had presumed they would communicate my information regarding Zigurd Kruminsh to the British, since he had been a British agent. If they did, there was no follow-up.

From the start, it was obvious they believed my story. The "Collins" message had gotten through. As had the repeated references to my altitude. And, from the simple fact that certain things hadn't happened which would have happened had I told the Russians about the "special" missions, they realized I hadn't told everything. I was pleased that they believed me. Yet I remained disappointed in the debriefings. It may be that the information I possessed was worthless. The only way to determine that, however, was to find out what I did know, then evaluate its importance or lack of it. Instead they seemed to have decided in advance what they were interested in, which—to me, at least—seemed a rather faulty intelligence practice. And considering the questions, I couldn't help discerning an obvious pattern behind them: that the agency was not really interested in what I had to tell them; their primary concern was to get the CIA off the hook.

Two

I f true, this was not the first attempt to pass the buck, to pin the blame elsewhere. Shortly after my return, on coming into contact with several former participants in Operation Overflight, I heard a most disturbing story.

When I had failed to appear at Bodö, Norway, the ramifications had hit Washington like a burst of flack. I had gone down somewhere in Russia: there could be no other explanation. Yet, because number 360 had a fuel-tank problem, this didn't necessarily mean I had been shot down, and, since Russia was a very large country, it could be that the plane wouldn't be found. In any event, it was unlikely the pilot was still alive.

A contingency plan was hastily drawn up, for use in the event the Russians should have the wreckage of the plane and decide to make an issue of it.

The plan was quite simple. One of the higher-ranking agency representatives at Adana, a man whom we'll call Rick Newman, would confess to overzealously taking it upon himself to order me to make the flight, with no authorization whatsoever. Thus, by blaming a "gung-ho" underling, the President and the CIA could evade admission of responsibility.

The reason for their settling on Newman and not Colonel Shelton was obvious: they needed a civilian, so the Russians couldn't term it a military operation.

As preparation for putting the plan into effect, Newman was secretly flown from Turkey to Germany and hidden in the basement of the house of our agency liaison there, to make sure he couldn't be reached by reporters.

The plan, however, had one basic flaw: it presumed that I was dead. Alive, with no prior knowledge of the cover story, anything I said would in all likelihood contradict their version.

With Khrushchev's announcement on May 7 that the pilot was "alive and kicking," it should have been obvious the plan would have to be scrapped. Yet at six P.M. on the seventh, some dozen hours after word reached the United States of Khrushchev's speech, the State Department released the cover story, approved by the President, that although a U-2 had probably made an intelligence-gathering flight over the Soviet Union, no authorization for such a flight had been given by authorities in Washington.

The first three paragraphs of James Reston's lead story on the front page of The New York Times, May 8, 1960, give the details:

WASHINGTON, May 7—The United States admitted tonight that one of the country's planes equipped for intelligence purposes had "probably" flown over Soviet territory.

An official statement stressed, however, that "there was no authorization for any such flight" from authorities in Washington.

As to who might have authorized the flight, officials refused to comment. If this particular flight of the U-2 was not authorized here, it could only be assumed that someone in the chain of command in the Middle East or Europe had given the order.

Eventually, of course, the plan was abandoned, with President Eisenhower's unprecedented admission that he had personally authorized the overflights, but not before several alternate plans had been considered, including Central Intelligence Agency Director Allen Dulles' offer to resign and assume the blame.

I heard the story from several people in the agency. One was Newman himself, who laughed as he recounted how he had hidden in that basement for several days.

Newman had a wife and three children. Although presumably there would have been some financial compensation—perhaps his retirement with a better pension than otherwise—they would have had to live the rest of their lives under the stigma that he had recklessly precipitated an action which wrecked the Summit Conference and conceivably could have launched a nuclear war.

It was not an easy laugh.

Nor did I laugh in return. For, in a sense, the plan called for two scapegoats, as the flight could not have taken place without my concurrence.

On hearing the story, I was glad, for the sake of everyone concerned, that the plan had been abandoned.

What I didn't realize, until much later, was that this was only half-true.

According to the newspapers, retired Federal Appeals Court Judge E. Barrett Prettyman had been chosen to conduct the board of inquiry. The hearing would be held "in-house," closed to the press and public, in CIA headquarters in Washington.

A few days earlier, I was taken to 2430 E Street to meet Allen Dulles. By this time Dulles had been replaced as Director of Central Intelligence (DCI) by Kennedy appointee John A. McCone. He was still in the process of moving out of his office, however.

It was an odd meeting. Dulles greeted me with a bemused look. We shook hands. He commented wryly that he had heard quite a bit about me. I told him how pleased I was to be back in the United States. He replied that he had read the debriefing reports: "We are proud of what you have done."

Later, wondering why the meeting had taken place, I guessed it was simply because Dulles wanted to meet the spy who had given him so many headaches.

I had a problem, which became clearly obvious just as I was to appear before the board of inquiry. With few exceptions, most agency personnel I had come into contact with since my return home were people I had never met previously. Most of them—such as the security men who kept me in "protective custody" at the "safe" houses—had no connection with the U-2 program. This meant that they were not cleared for such information, and I couldn't discuss the more sensitive aspects of the operation with them.

I knew nothing about Prettyman himself. It had been reiterated, a number of times, that the hearing was merely a formality, in order to give something to the press, that, insofar as the agency itself was concerned, I had already been completely "cleared." Obviously it would help my case, put me in a far more favorable light, if I could reveal exactly what I had withheld from the Russians. Yet some of it, such as that portion pertaining to the "special" missions, no hint of which had ever appeared publicly, was still political dynamite. Any leak, even at this late date, could have tremendous international repercussions.

"How much should I tell Prettyman?" I asked one of the agency representatives. His suggestion: "Use your own discretion." It was not exactly a carte-blanche reply.

Obviously the "special" missions were not to be mentioned: those missions that began on September 27, 1956, in Turkey, when Colonel Perry instructed me to fly over the Mediterranean, watch for and photograph any concentration of two or more ships.

The assignment, the first of many such "special" missions, gave me an increased respect for the effectiveness of American intelligence. In July, 1956, Egypt had seized the Suez Canal. In late September, a full month before the first shot was fired in the Sinai, the United States was aware not only that Israel intended to invade Egypt but also that preparations were being made for France and Great Britain to come to her aid.

The ships U.S. intelligence was looking for were British, French, and Israeli.

I flew the mission, going as far as the island of Malta, and returning, caught sight of several ships and photographed them. From the air I could not identify the registry; however, later, when the photographs had been developed and studied, I was told the mission had been successful. Although I was in a very real sense spying on the vessels of three friendly nations, I felt no compunctions about my action. In our atomic age, any war, no matter how isolated, how small, how seemingly insignificant, could blossom into a nuclear holocaust. It seemed to me then—and still does— far more important that we know exactly what was going on and do nothing about it, as in this case, than plunge in and try to do something, with no real idea of what was happening, as had been the case on more than a few other occasions.

After that the "special" missions became frequent occurrences. Because I had done so well in navigation during my training at Watertown, Colonel Perry assigned me many of these flights. A great number of them during this period were over Israel and Egypt. On such missions I would usually first overfly Cyprus, at that time still under British rule, with cameras on, primarily to see if a fleet was being assembled there, then on to Egypt and Israel. One does not realize, until seeing it from the air, just how small Israel is. A few passes, a few miles apart, and it could be photographed in its entirety. By comparison, Egypt is a mammoth presence.

On these missions several places merited special attention. The

Suez Canal, of course, was one. Another was the Gulf of 'Aqaba, then as now a source of contention. Here, in close proximity, Israel, Jordan, Saudi Arabia, and Egypt all had ports, Israel's port being its only link with the Red Sea. Another was the Sinai Peninsula. There are few more desolate places than the Sinai. Against it, the deserts of the American Southwest look like oases. For miles and miles there is absolutely nothing but bleakness.

Yet, on a flight on October 30, 1956, I looked down and spotted something. Black puffs of smoke—what must have been the first shots fired in the first daytime battle of the Sinai campaign.

With the outbreak of the war, flights were stepped up, photo interpreters on the alert at Adana to process and study films the moment a plane returned. It would be safe to say that American intelligence probably possessed a clearer overview of the entire war than many of the battlefront commanders. Within hours we could verify or disprove the intelligence reports of the combatants.

After the war, flights continued, but on a random basis, chiefly to watch for new military buildups along the borders.

Nor were we interested only in Egypt and Israel. If there was a trouble spot in the Middle East, the U-2s observed it. If a spot turned hot, we'd overfly it, frequently. Once it had cooled down, there would be only occasional missions, to watch for unusual activity. We checked on Syria, whether there was an outbreak of hostilities or not, to keep an eye on its critical oil pipelines. Iraq, another trouble spot, received periodic attention, as did Jordan. Saudi Arabia was of lesser interest. However, since it was along the way, we overflew it also, our route taking us over both the capital, Riyadh, and Mecca. Skirmishes between the Greek and Turkish Cypriots were silently witnessed, as was the heavy fighting between Lebanese Army troops and Moslem rebel forces in 1958. During 1959, when disorders broke out in Yemen, I flew a mission there. It was a memorable flight, not only for the distance covered—it was about as far from Turkey as the U-2 could fly and return—but also because I encountered several varieties of trouble en route. One was a violent thunderstorm, the worst I had ever seen, which obscured our objective. For a while I was unaware whether I could fly above it, it extended so high. The other occurred on the way down. My flight line called for me to remain over the land side of the Arabian coast; on looking in my mirror, however, I saw condensation trails behind the aircraft, until that time unheard of at our altitude. Realizing I could be spotted from the ground, I moved out over the Red Sea, over what I presumed could be claimed as international waters.

Then, by slowing down, I managed to climb a little higher to see if the contrails would go away. To my relief, they did.

These were the "special" missions. They began in the fall of 1956 and continued into 1960. If any of the U-2 flights merited the label "milk runs," it was these. Such flights lacked the tension of the overflights. No one was shooting at us. Presumably no one was aware of our presence. Had we been forced to crash-land, we could always explain that we had been flying over the Mediterranean and had come down in the closest place, a believable story so long as the equipment and photographic films weren't examined. Fortunately, there were no crash landings.

The primary mission of the U-2s was overflying Russia. This was the enemy, the greatest threat to our existence. In importance, the overflights—infrequent as they were—outranked anything else we did, and were the major reason for our presence in Turkey. The border surveillance and the atomic sampling, though vital, were secondary. Although they made up the bulk of our flying, in intelligence value the "special" missions took last place.

In terms of propaganda value to the Russians, however, the order was exactly reversed. We were fairly sure they knew about most if not all of the overflights. What they had no knowledge of were the "special" missions. Of all the information I withheld, this was the most dangerous, because of what the Russians could do with it.

It requires little imagination to conceive the devastating effect on America's foreign relations had Khrushchev been able to reveal that the United States was spying not only on most of the countries in the Middle East but also on her own allies.

After considerable thought, I decided that unless Prettyman worded his questions in such a way as to indicate prior knowledge of the subject, I would mention neither this nor other sensitive matters.

This was part of the problem. The other part was psychological. The debriefings had been informal, held in the "safe" houses with people I knew had been cleared by the agency. During these, I had been completely honest in my replies, withholding nothing; yet, even then, I had often found myself hesitating before giving answers. For twenty-one months my interrogators had been the Enemy. Almost automatically, a question put me on the defensive. Although the board of inquiry was held in a conference room in CIA headquarters with several friends, including Colonel Shelton and another pilot, among the dozen or so persons in attendance, the semiofficial nature of the proceedings put me once more in this frame of mind. It was a hard habit to break.

After the first several questions I found myself disliking Prettyman; since he was a not unkindly-looking, white-haired old gentleman, this was probably due in large part to my preconditioning. I wasn't evasive. When asked why I had told the Russians my altitude, I answered that sixty-eight-thousand feet wasn't my correct altitude, told him what my actual altitude was, and explained what I had hoped to accomplish with the lie. But then neither did I go out of my way to educate him in all aspects of the U-2 program.

I've often wondered, in the years since, whether I made the right choice.

Prettyman, on the other hand, did nothing to put me at ease. Some of his questions bordered on the accusative. Several times he indicated, less in actual words than manner, that he had doubts about my responses. On one of these occasions, after some question so minor I've now forgotten it, I finally reacted angrily, bellowing, "If you don't believe me, I'll be glad to take a lie-detector test!"

Even before the words were out of my mouth, I regretted saying them, I had sworn, after the first polygraph examination, that I would never take another.

"Would you be willing to take a lie-detector test on everything you have testified here?"

I knew that I'd been trapped. From the way he quickly snapped up my offer, I felt sure that he had purposely goaded me into making it.

What could I reply? I wanted very much to say no, as emphatically as possible. But to do so would be the same as admitting I had been lying. Which was not true.

"Yes," I replied, most reluctantly.

Shortly after that the hearing was concluded. It had lasted only part of a day, but had accomplished what I was now sure was its principal objective. The agency could tell the press that Powers had volunteered to take a lie-detector test.

That evening the agency brought Colonel Shelton and the other pilot out to the "safe" house for dinner. It was a jolly time, with lots of reminiscences.

I apologized to Shelton for using his name so freely, explaining that I had wanted to minimize the number of people compromised.

He said he had realized what I was up to when he learned he was running the detachment all by himself. Still I could not help feeling sorry for having placed the burden on him, especially when he described the desolate base to which he had been ostracized.

It was an easy, relaxed evening, in a sense the first such since my return to the United States.

The polygraph test was no easier the second time around. If anything, it was worse, because you anticipated. Still, some of the questions caught me off guard:

"Do you have any funds deposited in a numbered Swiss bank account?"

"Did anything happen in Russia for which you could be blackmailed?"

"Are you a double agent?"

Fortunately, the polygraph operator—the same man who had given me my initial test in the hotel room in 1956—was an expert. He could tell the difference between a reaction activated by anger and one caused by a lie. Because I did react, strongly, to the implications behind such questions.

Excepting only breaks for coffee and lunch, I was "on the box" the full day. When the last electrode came off, I made no vows. I'd done that once. Superstitiously, I wasn't going to make that mistake again.

As before, I wasn't told whether or not I had "passed."

Since my return there had been mounting pressure for a public hearing before Congress. I had hoped the Prettyman report, when released, would clear up all doubts, but realistically I knew it wouldn't. Having been subjected to a series of official cover stories, which, one after another, had been exposed as fiction, the American people would not be inclined to accept the CIA's assurances that I was "clean." Therefore I wasn't too surprised when I was told that arrangements had been made for me to appear in an open hearing before the Committee on Armed Services of the United States Senate on March 6. The Prettyman report would be made public shortly before this. In addition, the DCI, John McCone, would appear before the committee, in closed-door session prior to my appearance, to brief the senators on those aspects of the incident which were still classified. The President had already stated that I would reveal only that information "in the national interest to give."

Nervous as I was before crowds, I was not looking forward to the hearing, except that it would mean the end of my ordeal and, hopefully, the slanders, which I knew deeply hurt my family. They had been forced to live through the stigma of having people brand me a traitor. Barbara, however, had no intention of staying for my "vindication" or whatever might result. She wanted to go home to Georgia. Over the past several weeks she had grown increasingly restless. The reason was obvious—my insistence that she cut down her drinking, and the security measures in effect at the "safe" house, made it impossible for her to get all the liquor she wanted. Against my better judgment, I agreed to the trip, promising to meet her in Milledgeville after the Senate hearing and a brief homecoming visit to The Pound.

The latter was to include a community-wide celebration, during which I was to be awarded the American Citizenship Medal by the Veterans of Foreign Wars. That this had been planned long before the people of Virginia knew whether I had or hadn't been cleared was a welcome vote of confidence.

"STATEMENT CONCERNING FRANCIS GARY POWERS."

Released to the press just prior to the Senate hearing, my "clearance" consisted of eleven typewritten pages. It began: "Since his return from imprisonment in Soviet Russia, Francis Gary Powers has undergone a most intensive debriefing by CIA and other intelligence specialists, aeronautical technicians, and other experts concerned with various aspects of his mission and subsequent capture by the Soviets. This was followed by a complete review by a board of inquiry presided over by Judge E. Barrett Prettyman to determine if Powers complied with the terms of his employment and his obligation as an American. The board has submitted its report to the director of Central Intelligence.

"Certain basic points should be kept in mind in connection with this case. The pilots involved in the U-2 program were selected on the basis of aviation proficiency, physical stamina, emotional stability, and, of course, personal security. They were not selected or trained as espionage agents, and the whole nature of the mission was far removed from the traditional espionage scene. Their job was to fly the plane, and it was so demanding an assignment that on completion of a mission, physical fatigue was a hazard on landing."

It took the CIA just two paragraphs to get itself off the hook, to gloss over the fact that we were almost totally unprepared for the possibility that one of the U-2s might go down in Russia.

What followed interested me greatly.

"The pilots' contracts provided that they perform such services as might be required and follow such instructions and briefings in connection therewith as were given to them by their superiors. The guidance was as follows:

"a. If evasion is not feasible and capture appears imminent, pilots should surrender without resistance and adopt a cooperative attitude toward their captors.

"b. At all times while in the custody of their captors, pilots will conduct themselves with dignity and maintain a respectful attitude toward their superiors.

"c. Pilots will be instructed that they are perfectly free to tell the full truth about their mission with the exception of certain specifications of the aircraft. They will be advised to represent themselves as civilians, to admit previous Air Force affiliation, to admit current CIA employment, and to make no attempt to deny the nature of their mission.

"They were instructed, therefore, to be cooperative with their captors within limitations, to use their own judgment of what they should attempt to withhold, and not to subject themselves to strenuous hostile interrogation. It has been established that Mr. Powers had been briefed in accordance with this policy and so understood his guidance."

My actual instructions, obtained only after I had brought the issue to the fore, were much more concise: "You may as well tell them everything, because they're going to get it out of you anyway."

There was no indication in the wording that I had failed to heed this suggestion or gone far beyond what I was required to do.

"In regard to the poison needle," the statement continued, "it should be emphasized that this was intended for use primarily if the pilot were subjected to torture or other circumstances which in his discretion warranted the taking of his own life. There were no instructions that he should commit suicide and no expectation that he would do so except in those situations just described, and I emphasize that even taking the needle with him in the plane was not mandatory; it was his option."

I was glad to have that on record. And I was not displeased by what followed.

"Mr. Powers' performance on prior missions has been reviewed, and it is clear that he was one of the outstanding pilots of the whole

U-2 program. He was proficient both as a flyer and as a navigator and showed himself calm in emergency situations. His security background has been exhaustively reviewed, and any circumstances which might conceivably have led to pressure from or defection to the Russians have also been exhaustively reviewed, and no evidence has been found to support any theory that failure of his flight might be laid to Soviet espionage activities."

Though I was unaware of it at the time, that last statement was open to question. As will be noted, there did exist some rather astonishing circumstantial evidence which indicated that my flight may have been betrayed before I even lifted off the ground.

As for the exhaustive review of my background, I had learned of this during the debriefings, from one of the men conducting the investigation. "I'll bet we know more about you than you know about yourself," he remarked, adding, "The amazing thing is how clean you came out. I've been doing this sort of thing for a long time, and you're the closest to Jack Armstrong, the All-American Boy, I've seen." I think he meant that as a compliment.

The statement then reviewed at some length the details of my May 1, 1960, flight, concluding: "In connection with Powers' efforts to operate the destruct switches, it should be noted that the basic weight limitations kept the explosive charge to two and a half pounds and the purpose of the destruct mechanism was to render inoperable the precision camera and other equipment, not to destroy them and the film."

That was a bit vaguer than I would have liked. Since there was so much criticism on this point, I'd hoped that the agency would make it very clear that even had I activated the switches, the plane itself would not have been totally destroyed.

The statement then concluded that the one hypodermic injection I had been given probably wasn't truth serum but a general immunization shot; that despite repeated requests to contact the American Embassy or my family, I had been held incommunicado and interrogated for about one hundred days. Paraphrasing me, it observed: "He states that the interrogation was not intense in the sense of physical violence or severe hostile methods, and that in some respects he was able to resist answering specific questions. As an example, his interrogators were interested in the names of people participating in the project, and he states that he tried to anticipate what names would become known and gave those, such as the names of his commanding officer and certain other personnel at his home base in Adana, Turkey, who would probably be known in any case to the Russians. However, they asked him for names of other pilots, and he states that he refused to give these on the grounds that they were his friends and comrades and if he gave their names they would lose their jobs and, therefore, he could not do so. He states they accepted this position. It is his stated belief, therefore, that the information he gave was that which in all probability would be known in any case to his captors."

That bothered me. All the emphasis was on those few questions I had refused to answer. Of far greater importance were the many questions I *had* answered—*incorrectly*. The doors I had closed with a simple "I don't know," the blind alleys up which I had led them when it looked as if they were getting too close to the truth.

Except for the single example of the names of the pilots, there was no indication that I had withheld information from the Russians.

I could understand why the information I held back couldn't be specified. If mention was made that I had lied about the altitude of the U-2, for example, the Russians might reexamine the whole subject and possibly—through radar plots of this and other flights—determine what the actual altitude had been, thus, conceivably, someday placing the life of another pilot in jeopardy. It was the same with the number of overflights and their targets, my atomic-weapons training, the "special" missions, and so on.

Nothing would have been compromised by making the simple statement: "In the opinion of the experts who debriefed him, Powers withheld information vital to the security of the United States." Just that and nothing more would have made all the difference.

I was not interested in being proclaimed a hero. I had done only what I felt was right. But then, neither did I like the implication left by this vague, evasive wording. As a "clearance," it was smudged, equivocal.

I read on, as the report now approached its summary judgment:

"All the facts concerning Mr. Powers' mission, the descent of his plane, his capture, and his subsequent actions, have been subjected to intensive study. In the first place, Powers was interrogated for many days consecutively by a debriefing team of experienced interrogators, one of whose duties was to evaluate Powers' credibility. They expressed the unanimous view that Powers was truthful in his account. Secondly, an intensive inquiry was made by government officials into the background, life history, education, conduct, and character of Powers. This team included doctors, specialists in psychiatry and psychology, personnel officers, his former colleagues in the Air Force and on the U-2 project. All these persons were of the view that Powers is inherently and by practice a truthful man. Thirdly, Powers appeared before a board of inquiry and testified at length, both directly and under cross-examination. The board agreed that in his appearance he appeared to be truthful, frank, straightforward, and without any indicated attempt to evade questions or color what he was saying. In the board's judgment, he reflected an attitude of complete candor. In the fourth place, when during his examination before the board a question was raised as to the accuracy of one of his statements, he volunteered with some vehemence that, although he disliked the process of the polygraph, he would like to undergo a polygraph test."

The word "like" was definitely an exaggeration.

"That test was subsequently duly administered by an expert, and in it he was examined on all of the factual phases which the board considered critical in this inquiry. The report by the polygraph operator is that he displayed no indications of deviation from the truth in the course of that examination. In the fifth place, a study of the photograph of the debris of the plane and other information concerning the plane revealed, in the opinion of experts making the study, no condition which suggested an inconsistency with Powers' account of what had transpired. The board noted the testimony of Russian witnesses at the trial in Moscow which dealt with the descent and capture of Powers and with technical features of the plane and the incident.

"The testimony was consistent with the account given by Powers. Powers was able to identify a spot near a small village where he thought he had landed. This location checked with prior testimony given by Powers as to physical features, directions, and distances, and also corresponded with earlier independent information not known to Powers that certain of the persons who captured him lived in this same small village. Some information from confidential sources was available. Some of it corroborated Powers and some of it was inconsistent in parts with Powers' story, but that which was inconsistent was in part contradictory with itself and subject to various interpretations. Some of this information was the basis for considerable speculation shortly after the 1 May episode and subsequent stories in the press that Powers' plane had descended gradually from its extreme altitude and had been shot down by a Russian fighter at medium altitude. On careful analysis, it appears that the information on which these stories were based was erroneous or was susceptible of varying interpretations. The board came to the conclusion that it could not accept a doubtful interpretation in this regard which was inconsistent with all the other known facts and consequently rejected these newspaper stories as not founded in fact."

Finally the bogus story was laid to rest. Yet there was not a hint as to who had perpetrated this fiction in the first place. Or why.

The final paragraph of the statement read:

"On all the information available, therefore, it is the conclusion of the board of inquiry which reviewed Mr. Powers' case and of the director of Central Intelligence, who has carefully studied the board's report and has discussed it with the board, that Mr. Powers lived up to the terms of his employment and instructions in connection with his mission and in his obligations as an American under the circumstances in which he found himself. It should be noted that competent aerodynamicists and aeronautical engineers have carefully studied Powers' description of his experience and have concluded on the basis of scientific analysis that a U-2 plane damaged as he described would perform in its descent in about the manner he stated. Accordingly, the amount due Mr. Powers under the terms of his contract will be paid to him."

"POWERS CLEARED BY CIA," the headlines would read.

Yet I wondered.

Three

There's been a change in plans," one of the agents informed me excitedly. "You're going to the White House before you go to the Senate. You have an appointment with the President."

Nervous enough before, I was doubly so now. The newspapers had made much of President Kennedy's greeting the two RB-47 pilots but "snubbing Powers." This meeting, I realized, could do much to allay the criticism. It also meant that the attorney general had apparently gotten the message. The likelihood of my actually being brought to trial was, I felt, quite remote. Still, that it had even been considered bothered me.

We were awaiting the arrival of the limousines to take us to 1600 Pennsylvania Avenue, when another message came through. One of the agents gave me the news. "The White House called. The appointment has been canceled."

Why? He didn't know; there had been no explanation.

With my appearance before the Senate to begin in just a couple of hours, I hadn't the time to worry about it. To mask my disappointment, I told myself that maybe it had been postponed until after the hearing. But I didn't really believe that. Something had happened.

I wished they hadn't brought it up in the first place.

Thoughtfully, the chairman of the Committee on Armed Services, Richard B. Russell of Georgia, had provided the agency with a list of questions he would ask me at the start, to put me at ease. Then I would be asked to describe exactly what had happened on my May 1 flight. Beyond that I'd be on my own; the committee members were free to ask whatever questions they wished.

CIA Director McCone had given his closed-door testimony that morning, at the same time the chairmen of the House and Senate Armed Forces committees had jointly released my CIA clearance, thus providing groundwork for my testimony.

As we drove to the Old Senate Office Building, I scanned the list. What part of Virginia are you from? Where did you attend grammar and high school? Where did you go to college? I was admittedly shy; the mere thought of appearing before a large crowd frightened me. This little bit of prebriefing was helpful, and I was thankful to Russell for being so considerate.

We made it out of the automobile and into the building without being spotted. But as we were walking down the corridor to the Senate caucus room, one of the TV reporters recognized me. Within seconds the cameras were focused and questions were coming from every direction.

I thought: This is the first time I've ever been on TV! But, before I could panic, I remembered: No, it isn't. There was Moscow. You should be a seasoned performer by now.

Powers can't make any statement at this time, my escort insisted, trying to hurry me past. Would I talk to them after the hearing ended? I promised to do so.

There were about four hundred people in the Senate caucus room. Including Chairman Russell, fourteen senators were present: Harry Flood Byrd, Virginia; John Stennis, Mississippi; Stuart Symington, Missouri; Henry M. Jackson, Washington; Sam J. Ervin, Jr., North Carolina; Strom Thurmond, South Carolina; Robert C. Byrd, West Virginia; Leverett Saltonstall, Massachusetts; Margaret Chase Smith, Maine; Francis Case, South Dakota; Prescott Bush, Connecticut; J. Glenn Beall, Maryland; and Barry Goldwater, Arizona.

As I sat down at a table, facing them, someone handed me a

model of the U-2, and I held it while the flash bulbs snapped. Promptly at two P.M. the chairman called the hearing to order.

Chairman Russell began: "That will be all for those cameras. I will ask the officers to see that rule is enforced and that no further pictures are taken. If you need any additional policemen for that purpose, we will summon them.

"The Armed Services Committee, through the Central Intelligence Agency, has extended to Mr. Francis Gary Powers an invitation to appear in open session this afternoon.

"Before we hear from Mr. Powers, the Chair would like to make a very short statement concerning the circumstances of this hearing.

"The Chair believes it can be fairly stated that this committee and its subcommittees have attempted to deal with subjects involving the Central Intelligence Agency and, indeed, all matters affecting the national security, in an unspectacular manner.

"Accordingly, to some, it may appear that this hearing in the caucus room, under these circumstances, is somewhat uncharacteristic of the proceedings of this committee.

"In this instance, however, the correction of some erroneous impressions and an opportunity for Mr. Powers to reveal as much of his experience as is consistent with security requirements make it apparent that a hearing of this type at this time is not only in the national interest, but is in the interest of fair play for Mr. Powers. . . .

"Mr. Powers, after having been subjected to a public trial in Moscow, you should feel no trepidation whatever in appearing before a group of your fellow citizens and elected representatives. I hope that you feel just as much at ease as you possibly can.

"I understand from Senator Byrd that you are a Virginia boy. What part of Virginia are you from?"

After the initial questions, Chairman Russell asked me to tell, in my own words, exactly what had happened on May 1. I did, describing the prebreathing, the last check of the maps, my final instructions from Colonel Shelton, and the delayed takeoff—but omitting mention that this had been occasioned because we were awaiting White House approval. Then I described the flight itself, seeing the jet contrails below and realizing I had been radar-tracked, the autopilot trouble, the route—but again omitting certain things, such as how I made my radio fixes, that this would be the first time a U-2 had overflown Sverdlovsk. Although I was accompanied by Lawrence Houston, general counsel for the Central Intelligence Agency, there had been no prior briefing by the agency on what I should or should not say. Apparently by this time it was presumed I knew what was and wasn't sensitive. All I could do was guess, hoping some of these matters had been earlier covered by McCone.

Interrupted only for occasional clarification by Russell, I then described in considerable detail the orange flash and what had followed, up to my final unsuccessful attempt to activate the destruct switches. From the faces of the senators I couldn't tell whether or not they believed me. All I knew was that I was telling the truth.

I went on to tell of my descent and capture, the trip to Sverdlovsk, the bringing in of my maps and assorted wreckage, the questioning, my decision to admit that I was employed by the CIA, the trip to Moscow, Lubyanka Prison, and the interrogations. Realizing that I had been talking for what seemed a very long time, I paused and observed that they probably had many questions.

Russell had several. I had been vague as to time. Didn't I have a wristwatch? No, I replied, explaining that because of the difficulty of putting it on over the pressure suit, I didn't wear one. Had I ever experienced a jet-plane flameout? Yes, and there was no comparison.

CHAIRMAN RUSSELL: Has there ever been any other occasion when you were in an airplane and were the target of a ground-to-air missile or explosive or shell of any kind?

POWERS: Not that I know of.

CHAIRMAN RUSSELL: You have never seen any ground-to-air missile explode?

I replied that I hadn't, although I had seen motion pictures of such happenings, adding, "I am sure that nothing hit this aircraft. If something did hit it, I am sure I would have felt it."

I'd had twenty-one months to think about this question and was convinced—as were "Kelly" Johnson and others—that the plane must have been disabled by the shock waves from a near-miss. Had it been a direct hit, I doubted seriously whether I would be here testifying before the Senate.

While I was talking, one of the Senate pages handed me a white envelope. I slipped it into my pocket and promptly forgot it.

CHAIRMAN RUSSELL: I wish you would clear up the matter of the needle, Mr. Powers. Were you under any obligation to destroy yourself if you were captured?

POWERS: Oh, no. I don't remember exactly who gave me the needle that morning, but they told me, "You can take it if you want to." They said, "If something does happen, you may be tortured. Maybe you could conceal this on your person in some way, and if you see that you cannot withstand the torture, you might want to use it." And that is the reason I took the needle. But I could have left it. I wasn't told to take it.

CHAIRMAN RUSSELL: Do you have the instructions that you received that morning and that you usually received before you—

Russell stopped abruptly, realizing he had almost mentioned my other overflights.

He was referring to the three paragraphs in the CIA clearance regarding what I was to do in the event of capture. On his instructions, I read them into the record.

Russell then questioned me about the red-and-white parachute I had seen. Earlier, when this had been brought up during the debriefings, one of the agency intelligence men had told me there was evidence indicating that in their attempt to get me the Russians had also shot down one of their own planes. I wasn't told the source of this information, only that from contacts within Russia they had learned about the funeral of a fighter pilot who presumably had piloted the aircraft.

This fit in with what I had suspected.

However, since this was an area which might be sensitive— involving, as it did, our intelligence apparatus within Russia—and because, too, my information on this was secondhand, I didn't mention it to the committee. I did observe that the second chute was not a part of my equipment.

We came now to my treatment after capture.

CHAIRMAN RUSSELL: Did they threaten you at any time when they were examining you?

POWERS: There were no definite threats, but they didn't let me forget that this crime was punishable by death. Anytime they would mention it was seven to fifteen years or death, and they wouldn't let me forget that.

CHAIRMAN RUSSELL: Did you ever manifest any reluctance in answering the questions that they asked you, or did you answer them immediately?

POWERS: I refused to answer several of their questions. I showed reluctance on many.

CHAIRMAN RUSSELL: Pardon?

POWERS: I showed reluctance on many, some that I couldn't see how they could be of any interest to them at all, but I was just reluctant in answering all questions.

I was caught in a trap, and not one of my own making. I wanted to say more, but couldn't. I had no idea how much McCone had told the committee. I could only hope he had made clear that important information had been withheld.

CHAIRMAN RUSSELL: That was not exactly in conformity with your instructions there to cooperate with your captors, was it?

POWERS: Well, you shouldn't go overboard with this cooperation. . . .

CHAIRMAN RUSSELL: You were quoted in the press as having stated at your trial that you had made a terrible mistake in flying over Russia and apologized to the Russian people and would never do it again. Was that a misquotation, or did you make that statement at your trial?

POWERS: No, that wasn't a misquotation. I made this statement on the advice of my defense counsel, and also because it was easy to say I was sorry, because what I meant by saying that, and what I wanted them to think I meant, were quite different. My main sorrow was that the mission failed, and I was sorry that I was there, and it was causing a lot of adverse publicity in the States. But, of course, some of these things I couldn't say in that statement.

Russell then questioned me at some length about my imprisonment, the food, whether I felt my cellmate was a plant, how I was treated generally.

CHAIRMAN RUSSELL: I can't refrain from saying that the Russians were much more gentle with you than I would ever have expected they would have been to one who was taken under those circumstances.

POWERS: It surprised me also. I expected much worse treatment than I received.

CHAIRMAN RUSSELL: I rather think you got off somewhat better than a Russian spy would in this country under the same circumstances.

POWERS: I really don't know.

CHAIRMAN RUSSELL: It might depend on where he happened to land. Undoubtedly he would have a rough time in the section of the country from which I come.

Russell then turned the questioning over to the other senators. White-haired Senator Saltonstall from Massachusetts, looking every bit the formidable New Englander, led off.

SENATOR SALTONSTALL: Mr. Chairman, Mr. Powers, I think I only have one or two questions. I have listened with interest to what you have said. I have listened to what Mr. McCone has told us, what he has given out in unclassified information, and I have listened to the chairman. My question would be this: Did I understand you correctly that when you were coming down in the parachute you threw away your instructions and threw away your map?

POWERS: No, I had no written instructions with me, but I did have a map, and I tore that up in very small pieces and scattered it out in the air as I was coming down.

SENATOR SALTONSTALL: So that your instructions were in your head, so to speak?

POWERS: Yes.

SENATOR SALTONSTALL: Now, did you have a briefcase or something else in which these other things, your special food, and these other things, were that they looked through afterward?

POWERS: Yes, I had what we call a seat pack. In this seat pack was a collapsible life raft, some food, some water, matches, several other items necessary to, say, live off the land or survive in an unpopulated area.

SENATOR SALTONSTALL: In other words, nothing except survival kit?

POWERS: Yes. There were also some cloth maps for escape and evasion.

I was anticipating another question, and what came next caught me completely off guard.

SENATOR SALTONSTALL: Mr. Powers, I will just say this: After listening to Mr. McCone and after listening to you, I commend you as a courageous, fine young American citizen who lived up to your instructions and who did the best you could under very difficult circumstances.

I managed to say "Thank you very much," but my voice choked. I was deeply moved by his response. Excepting only the private remarks of Allen Dulles, this was the first commendation I had received since my return.

CHAIRMAN RUSSELL: Senator Byrd?

SENATOR BYRD: The chairman has very ably covered the ground, and I will not ask any questions. I do want to join with Senator Saltonstall in expressing my opinion that this witness, Mr. Powers, has made an excellent presentation. He has been frank, and I am also very much gratified that Mr. McCone has testified before the committee that so far as he knows no action has been taken by you which was contrary to your instructions or contrary to the interests of this country.

CHAIRMAN RUSSELL: Senator Smith?

SENATOR SMITH: Mr. Chairman, my questions have been covered, thank you.

Senator Stennis then questioned me regarding Grinev, my defense counsel, inquiring: "He rendered you a valuable service, did he?"

POWERS: Well, I really don't know. I never did trust him any more than the rest of them.

SENATOR STENNIS: I mean by that he gave you information and talked to you, and you think you were better off at the trial than you would have been without his aid. What about that?

POWERS: I really don't know.

SENATOR STENNIS: You have understood, I suppose, that at the time this occurred there was some publicity here, not a great deal, but some, that was not altogether favorable to you. Did you know about that?

POWERS: I have heard about this since I—

SENATOR STENNIS: This is just a prelude for my saying this—that it is with satisfaction that I learn that you have been fully exonerated by the men who most know how to judge what you did, what the facts were, by your superiors and those who employed you. Not only that, but they found that you have discharged all of your obligations to your country, and it is with satisfaction to us here, and I think to the American people, to learn that, to know it is true. I know it makes you feel mighty good.

POWERS: There was one thing that I always remembered while I was there and that was that "I am an American."

SENATOR STENNIS: You are an American.

POWERS: Right.

SENATOR STENNIS: And proud of it?

POWERS: Right.

There was a spontaneous burst of applause from the audience which lasted several minutes. It more than made up for the applause that had greeted my ten-year prison sentence in Moscow.

After asking several questions about the wreckage of the plane, Senator Case brought up the subject of the timing of the flight. I was hoping the senators could enlighten me on this, for I was as curious as anyone else as to why approval had been given so close to the Summit. But, aside from my bringing out that weather conditions had determined the particular day, we got no closer to an answer.

Senator Symington, who had once visited Incirlik but had been denied information on Detachment 10-10 because he lacked the proper "need-to-know" approval (a refusal that greatly impressed him with our security), followed with a number of technical questions about the explosion. What did I think caused it, the former Secretary of the Air Force asked. I observed that the Russians had "stressed many, many times that they got me on the very first shot of a rocket, but they stressed it so much that I tend to disbelieve it."

I had been told, during the debriefings, that intelligence sources within Russia had claimed a total of fourteen rockets had been fired at me. Whether this was true or not, I didn't know. I did suspect, however, that there had been more than one.

SENATOR SYMINGTON: Is there any possibility that you were hit twice, once at a higher altitude, say, a near-miss, and again at a lower altitude?

POWERS: No.

I made that "No" as emphatic as possible.

SENATOR SYMINGTON: You did your best to destroy the plane, but, because of the gs on you at the time, you were just unable to reach the controls; is that correct?

POWERS: Yes, that is right.

SENATOR SYMINGTON: Mr. Chairman, I would like to join you and other members of the committee in commending Mr. Powers for the way he handled himself in this unfortunate episode. I have no further questions.

SENATOR BUSH: Mr. Chairman, I have no questions, but I also would like to say, having heard Mr. McCone's reports today and having listened to Mr. Powers' remarkable story, that I am satisfied he has conducted himself in exemplary fashion and in accordance with the highest traditions of service to one's country, and I congratulate him upon his conduct in captivity and his safe return to the United States.

Senator Jackson then asked me whether the Russians had attempted to indoctrinate me in Communism. I replied that there had been no direct attempt as such, but that the only news I received came from Communist sources. He also asked me to describe my release, which I did, noting that not until I had stepped across the line did I learn that it was an exchange, with Abel involved.

SENATOR JACKSON: Mr. Chairman, I want to conclude by saying that I associate myself with the remarks previously made here. I think it is quite clear from what we have heard this morning and now that Mr. Powers has lived up to his contract.

CHAIRMAN RUSSELL: Senator Beall?

SENATOR BEALL: Mr. Chairman, I have no questions. I do want to associate myself with you and the balance of the committee in commending Mr. Powers for the very intelligent way he has handled himself. I was at the hearings this morning, and I am convinced that he has been very frank with us, and I congratulate him.

CHAIRMAN RUSSELL: Senator Thurmond?

SENATOR THURMOND: No questions, Mr. Chairman.

CHAIRMAN RUSSELL: Senator Goldwater?

SENATOR GOLDWATER: I have no questions.

Following some queries regarding Soviet justice and the absence of the jury system in Russia, Chairman Russell asked: "Any further questions by any member of the committee?" There were none.

Of the fourteen senators present, seven—Saltonstall, Byrd of Virginia, Stennis, Symington, Bush, Jackson, and Beall—had gone on record as stating their belief that I had lived up to my obligations, both insofar as my CIA contract was concerned and as an American. Chairman Russell, though he had made no statement, had indicated his agreement by the manner of his questioning. (Following the hearing, he told reporters that he agreed I had lived up to the terms of my contract.) Whatever the personal opinions of the remaining senators—Smith of Maine, Thurmond, Ervin, Byrd of West Virginia, Case, and Goldwater—they had declined to state them publicly. Later, however, on opening the envelope handed to me during the hearing, I found a Senate memorandum. Written in pencil, it read: "You did a good job for your country. Thanks. Barry Goldwater."

CHAIRMAN RUSSELL: I will ask all the policemen to please see that Mr. Powers and his CIA escort are able to get out before the rush. Will all of you please keep your seats.

They disobeyed his instructions, however, bringing the hearing to an end with a standing ovation.

Looking at my watch, I realized the hearing had lasted only ninety minutes. It had seemed much longer.

As my two escorts and I were attempting to make our way through the crowd of well-wishers, Senator Saltonstall brought over two of my sisters. They were the only members of my family who had been able to attend the hearing; this was the first time I had seen them since my return to the United States. Our reunion was brief, however. The moment we reached the hall, a bevy of reporters descended upon us.

"What are you going to do with your back pay, Mr. Powers?"

"Spend it."

"How?"

"Slowly."

Before I could answer any more questions, or talk further with my sisters, my escort rushed me out of the building.

As for what followed, *Time* summed it up concisely: "Then he disappeared into a waiting government car—leaving behind him a persistent feeling that some of his story remained untold."

Following the Senate hearing, I checked into Georgetown University Hospital for rest and a complete physical examination. With little else to do, I resumed reading the newspapers. With few exceptions—Wallace Carroll of *The New York Times*, for example, wittily described the hearing as "hominy all the way," glossing over the fact that it was not a Southerner but a Yankee, Saltonstall of Massachusetts, who had taken the lead in commending me—accounts of the Senate hearing were mostly favorable.

I had the feeling it had turned out much better than some people—possibly including President Kennedy—had anticipated.

What was behind the canceled meeting with the President? By now it was obviously a cancellation, not a postponement because some urgent matter had taken priority. Perhaps the President had not wanted to steal the Senate's thunder, as he would have done by greeting me prior to the hearing. Yet, if that were the case, why had the appointment been scheduled in the first place? It was more likely that the decision to cancel the meeting was political: not sure which way the hearing would go, perhaps Kennedy had not wanted to risk identifying himself with what might have turned out to be the losing side.

Personally, I was pleased with the hearing, not so much because I had been "vindicated," but because it was now over and I could resume my life. Yet I knew the committee's response wouldn't satisfy everyone. The senators had been briefed by McCone; the public hadn't. They didn't know what was being withheld, if anything. Until such time as the whole truth could be told, doubts would remain, and the hearing itself would appear to some to be a "whitewash."

I had been looking forward to the time in the hospital, since it would give me a chance to think about my future. Now that I had the chance, however, I found it difficult to make plans. Despite the threat of Senator Young, I had learned there would be no difficulty about my returning to the Air Force. Yet I didn't want to go back in immediately, at least not until after the publicity had died down and I could slip back into the routine as just another pilot. I briefly considered Kelly Johnson's offer; but I had no idea what my job would be, nor did I know how serious his offer had been. The agency had suggested that, until making up my mind, I could work in the new CIA headquarters at Langley, Virginia. My duties were unspecified, except that I would probably be spending a portion of my time in the training section. That appealed to me for one reason: I had been almost totally unprepared for capture. If I could help others to better equip themselves for what they might encounter in similar circumstances, the experience wouldn't have been wasted. The drawback, however, was that I would be grounded. And I doubted if I could ever be happy in anything other than a flying job.

And there was my marriage. That too called for a decision. I evaded that, also, by telling myself I couldn't leave Barbara now, not when she seemed to need me most. Had I faced the facts squarely, I would have been forced to admit that the continual arguments comprising most of our time together were helping neither of us.

My problems were by no means unique. Like any returning veteran, I needed time to adjust, wasn't anxious to make any big decisions, at least not yet.

I left the hospital with all my problems intact. As for the checkup, it had only revealed what I already knew, that one souvenir of my sojourn in Russia was a bad stomach condition which I would probably have for the rest of my life.

Ironically, most of the foods I had dreamed about eating while I was in prison in Russia, I now couldn't have.

This particular souvenir caused me trouble until 1968, at which time—after Lovelace Clinic and others had failed to alleviate the condition—a private physician prescribed medication that immediately relieved the pain. Only during the past two years have I been able to eat salads, corn, and sundry other foods I so missed. The condition remains, however; one day off the pills, and the symptoms come back. Imprisonment may be an effective method of diet, but I don't recommend it.

Two men from the agency drove me to The Pound. I had expected they would remain, but to my surprise they returned to Washington. I was finally on my own.

Lonely I was not. My sisters, their husbands and their children, plus more relatives than I knew I had, attended the homecoming. Some eight-hundred people crowded into the National Guard Armory at Big Stone Gap, Virginia, to witness the VFW award ceremony. There were two high-school bands. Beside me on the platform sat my mother and father. This was really their day. More than any other single person, my father could claim credit for effecting my release, by first suggesting the trade for Abel. I was immensely proud to see him receive his due.

On my own initiative, rather than instructions from the agency, I had decided if possible to avoid the press. However, when it's raining, the roads have turned to mud, and cars are stuck outside your front door with no one else to help pull them out, what can you do? Too, they had gone to the trouble of driving all the way to The Pound, and it seemed unfair not to see them. One, Jim Clarke of radio station WGH, Newport News, Virginia, arrived about eleven o'clock the night of the award ceremony. Most of the family had already gone to bed exhausted. After some persuasion, I consented to tape an interview which was broadcast a few days later. As with the other reporters, I told him little more than I had told the Senate. Although Clarke was pleasant and did his best to put me at ease, his interview had one bad aftereffect. At one point I stated I "thought" I had seventy seconds on the destruct device. As mentioned earlier, not all of the timers worked uniformly, some with a variance of as much as five seconds either way. Tired after the long emotional day, my mind blanked. I couldn't remember exactly how accurate this particular timer might have been.

Later, at least one reporter picked up that qualifying word and used it to resurrect the whole conspiracy theory first proposed by the Soviets, that is, that the pilots weren't sure they had a full seventy seconds; they were afraid the CIA had rigged the device to explode prematurely, killing them too.

After that I refused all interview requests. I felt—with some justification, I believe—no small amount of resentment toward at least some members of the fourth estate, particularly those who had presumed to try me in absentia before all the facts were in and when there was no way I could defend myself.

While in The Pound I saw McAfee, my father's attorney, and asked him about the two-hundred-dollar fee demanded for an interview with Kennedy. McAfee refused to identify the person, however. He would say only that it was someone in the White House. I had no choice but to leave it at that.

From The Pound I went to Milledgeville, Georgia, to pick up Barbara. By this time I had decided to accept the CIA's offer, at least until such time as I could make up my mind as to what I wanted to do.

I had been in Milledgeville only a short time before I sensed a strong hostility toward Barbara there. She explained it was because she was a "celebrity"; people resented her fame. But I felt something else on coming into contact with residents: pity, not for Barbara but for me. It was as if everyone knew something I didn't and felt sorry for me. I didn't like that a bit. Fortunately, our stay was brief. On returning to Washington, we found an apartment in Alexandria and I went back to work for the CIA, grounded in the first nine to five job I've ever had in my life.

Since my return I had received a great deal of mail, some sent in care of my parents, but much of it directed to me at the CIA. Of several hundred letters, only a few were critical. Most were warmly congratulatory. I heard from friends not seen since boyhood, pilots I'd last seen in the service. The majority, however, were from people I had never met, many from mothers who had prayed for my release. And there were some surprises, among them a letter from Cardinal Spellman, thanking me for coming to his defense during my trial.

As surprising were the large number of offers to buy the rights to my story. On reporting to work at the agency there was a whole sheaf of telegrams and urgent telephone messages. One book publisher, wasting no time on preliminaries, offered a flat $150,000 advance.

Thus far my side of the story hadn't been told. Because of national security, I realized it might be years before some aspects could be made public. However, there was much that could—no, *should*—be known, if for no other reason than to avoid repeating the same mistakes in the future. For mistakes had been made, bad ones. The U-2 incident was an almost classic textbook case of unpreparedness. Too, the story told the American people was heavy with lies and distortions. This seemed a good way to set the record straight. I made inquiries within the agency as to whether there would be any objection to my writing a book about my experiences. I realized it would take some time for the request to travel up the chain of command, but was prepared to wait.

At the same time, I also asked if I could write to my former cellmate. The answer came back quite promptly. Negative. It would look bad if anyone found out you were writing someone inside Russia.

Though I abided by the decision, it was less for this reason than another. I didn't want to cause Zigurd any trouble. And there was just a chance that by writing to him I might do so.

Admittedly, my previous experience with the agency had spoiled me. I had been part of a select, smoothly functioning team of experts who had a job to do and did it, with a minimum of fuss. As such, I had seen only glimpses of the actual organizational structure of the CIA. They were enough, however, to convince me that things had now changed.

By this time both Dulles and Bissell had left, the latter offering his resignation as deputy director of plans just seven days after my release. Bissell had survived the U-2 episode, but not the Bay of Pigs, becoming just one of the scapegoats for that tragic fiasco. Controversy over it was still raging within the agency. The plan had been good but poorly executed. It never would have worked. Kennedy was responsible for its failure by withdrawing air support. Kennedy had never authorized air support in the first place, therefore couldn't have withdrawn it. So the arguments went.

Although a year had passed, everyone still seemed to be searching for someone else on whom to pin the blame.

Maybe I was naïve. Maybe it had always existed without my noticing it. But politics now seemed to dominate the agency, almost to the exclusion of its primary function, collecting intelligence. Everything had to be justified, especially in the light of how it might appear in the press. Decisions were avoided because of possible backlash if they proved wrong (though this was not new to me with my military background). Concern appeared to be less with what the facts were than with how such information would be accepted. And it takes little insight to realize that when intelligence is shaped to be what its recipients want to hear, it ceases to be intelligence.

In part, I was witnessing a vast organizational shake-up, due to President Kennedy's vow to restructure the agency following the failure of the Cuban invasion. In a world of secrets, the least kept was that John McCone, although an astute businessman—according to the General Accounting office, his California shipbuilding company had turned a hundred-thousand-dollar investment into forty-four million dollars during World War II—knew little about intelligence. He was a political appointee, and, I now learned, Robert Kennedy's personal choice as successor to Dulles. According to rumor, he was not the first choice. Although I found it difficult to believe—it has since been brought out in other accounts—Robert Kennedy had apparently wanted to take over as director of Central Intelligence, in addition to being attorney general, the idea being scotched because it would have lent fuel to the argument that the Kennedys were attempting to create a dynasty.

If true, it would provide another possible explanation for the story that he had wanted to try me. Powers could be made a symbol of the failure of the old order.

Maybe the shake-up was long overdue. Maybe the CIA had acquired too much independent power and needed to be brought under closer control of the President. I only knew what I saw— bureaucratic chaos. Divided loyalties. Jockeying for favor. A half-dozen people doing jobs previously done by one. Paperwork increasing at such a rate that one suspected the task of collecting intelligence could be dropped, with the paperwork alone sufficient to keep everyone occupied.

Undoubtedly only a portion of this was due to McCone. Perhaps what I was witnessing was simply that the CIA, having outgrown its youthful exuberance, was suffering the middle-age spread that seems to be the lot of most government agencies.

Admittedly I saw only part of the whole picture. But it bothered me.

Another thing also bothered me. Even within the agency many people were unsure of my exact status: had Powers been cleared, or hadn't he? The people at the top knew, but hadn't let the word filter down. I encountered no animosity, but I did find a great deal of puzzlement. The CIA clearance, with its evasive wording, had raised almost as many doubts as it had laid to rest.

My attitude toward this remains today much as it was then. I knew what I had and hadn't done. I did not feel I had to clear my name. Nor did I feel I had to justify my conduct to anyone. People would have to accept me as is. Those who couldn't, I wasn't interested in having for friends. Fortunately, over the years the former have predominated.

Yet this did not mean that I was happy at having been placed in this position.

I enjoyed my work with the training section because I felt it was important. The tricks the Russians used in their interrogations, the difficulty of improvising a workable cover story, the decision of how much to tell and how much to withhold, how to avoid being trapped in a lie, how best to cope with incarceration—these were only a few of the problems we explored. I also read the accounts of other prisoners, pointing out where my experiences differed or were the same. And I consulted with the people in psychological testing to give them clues as to what to look for in screening certain covert personnel.

It was satisfying work—later I learned that a number of my suggestions had been incorporated into the training program for certain personnel—but I was also aware that it was temporary, something to do until such time as I could make some decisions. Not all of them concerning my future employment.

Nothing had changed with Barbara, except to grow worse. Again there were the suspicions: unexplained absences from the apartment; charges on the phone bill for long-distance calls I thought were in error but had been made to an unfamiliar number in Georgia; constant pleading to be allowed to go back there for a visit, although, estranged from her mother, she could never provide a good explanation for the necessity of such a trip. And the certainties: bottles under the bed, in closets, in dresser drawers. One night in April, following a familiar argument, in which I insisted that if she couldn't stop drinking by herself she would have to have medical aid, she swallowed a whole bottle of sleeping pills. I rushed her to the hospital, just in time.

Following her recovery, I tried to get her to remain in the hospital for treatment of her alcoholism. But she refused; she still would not admit she was an alcoholic. I had hoped this close call would bring her to her senses, make her realize she needed competent help. It didn't. Upon her release the situation remained unchanged. In May she simply packed a bag and returned to Georgia.

On returning from a trip to the West Coast, I stopped in Phoenix to see some friends. While deplaning I was paged to contact TWA for a message. Few people knew my itinerary; so I knew it was something out of the ordinary. Checking with TWA, I was given a local number to call; on calling it, I was given still another number, this one in Washington, D.C. The CIA agent who answered informed me that Barbara and a male companion had been in some kind of trouble at a drive-in restaurant in Milledgeville. Refusing to leave when asked to do so by the management, they had caused such a scene that police had to be called. By some means, word of the incident had reached the CIA. The situation had been resolved, but the agency felt I should know what had happened.

On arriving in Milledgeville, I laid down the law. She had to have medical help, had to leave Milledgeville, and had to stop seeing certain people, including her male companion. I was going back to Washington, I told her; if she wanted to accompany me, it would have to be under those conditions. Otherwise I was going alone and would take whatever action I deemed necessary. Believing this was just another empty threat, Barbara chose to stay in Milledgeville.

In August I returned to The Pound, ostensibly for a visit but really to think things through. When I did, I was forced to admit there was no helping Barbara, not without her agreement; that in continuing the marriage I was only holding onto the shell of what was and what might have been; all else was ashes—had been for a long time. Before returning to Washington, I took off my wedding ring.

Georgia was still my legal residence. Not long after this I returned to Milledgeville to consult an attorney. While there I asked the questions avoided since my return. The answers confirmed my worst suspicions while in prison. But now it no longer mattered. I filed suit for divorce. The decree became final in January, 1963.

In May, 1962, I was given verbal permission to write the book. I was not informed as to who made the decision, but I was sure the request had gone all the way up to McCone, since no one else would be willing to take such responsibility.

Consulting with an attorney, I went through the offers, finally deciding on a joint proposal advanced by the publishing firm Holt, Rinehart and Winston and the *Saturday Evening Post*. Negotiations began and had reached the contract stage when, in early July, I was informed, again verbally, that upon reconsideration it had been decided that a book at this time would not be advantageous either to me or to the agency. While they could not forbid me to publish the book, they strongly suggested that I not do so.

Word had filtered down through several levels. However, it was clear that the decision to grant permission had been vetoed by someone higher up than McCone. That left few possibilities.

A good amount of time and money had been spent on the negotiations, and a number of people inconvenienced. I didn't like that. Neither did I appreciate the implication that I might be adversely affected if the truth were told.

Yet I also felt something else, something perhaps only a person who has spent time in prison can fully comprehend. I was deeply grateful to the agency and to the government for effecting my release. They could just as easily have left me in prison until May 1,

1970, had I lived that long. In a sense, each day of my freedom before that time I owed to them.

That that freedom was to be qualified, however, that silence was the price I would have to pay for it, was not a pleasant realization. Especially when I suspected that the chief motivation behind the decision was political, the fear that what I had to say might embarrass the agency.

I spent the weekend of the Fourth of July trying to decide what to do.

On July 6 I wrote the following letter:

Dear Mr. McCone:

Recently there has been communicated to me your views concerning my intention to publish an account of my personal experiences preceding, during, and after my imprisonment by the Russian government.

While you have been correctly informed that I have been negotiating with interested publishers with a view toward publishing my personal account, I wish again to dispel any doubts concerning my initiating these negotiations without prior consultation. The invitations to discuss the publishing of my experiences were received from various publishers both before and immediately upon my return to the United States. These invitations were directed not only to me but to various agency officials, including yourself. I made no effort to discuss these offers until I had been advised that there was no objection on the part of the agency or the government to my doing so. While I did not expect any encouragement in this matter, I am distressed that I was misled in believing there was no objection.

I understand now that you are of the opinion that in view of the public acceptance of the presentation of my account to the Senate Armed Services Committee, any further effort by me to comment in extenuation of my experiences would only result in possible injury to the agency and to myself.

I will, therefore, accept your feeling on this subject, and although I am not persuaded by the logic thereof, I will abide by your desires not to publish a book on my experiences at this time. I would be less than candid if I left the impression that I am taking these steps willingly. I am not, however, unmindful of the great effort which was made by the government to obtain my release from imprisonment, and am most grateful for this interest in my behalf. Accordingly, I am advising those publishers with whom I have been negotiating and who have shown an active interest in publishing my experiences that I will not entertain any further consideration of their offers.

Very truly yours,
Francis Gary Powers

I had been muzzled. It was only then that I began to have doubts whether the story would ever be told.

Four

My decision to leave the Central Intelligence Agency was motivated by three factors:

1. Suppression of the book, to which I had reluctantly acquiesced. Already one book, the first of several on the U-2 incident, had appeared, its authors, so far as I knew, having made no attempt to contact me.

2. The obvious fact that I was just killing time. Though I had my own office, with the implication that I could stay on at the agency as long as I wished, I had run out of meaningful work.

3. I was itching to fly.

With nearly twelve years of service, and only a little more than eight to go until retirement, I couldn't afford not to go back into the Air Force. Yet I still wasn't ready to lead a regimented life: I wanted to be able to go where I pleased, do what I wanted to do. On checking with the Air Force, I was told there was no hurry as to a decision; I could take my time.

One of my friends at the agency knew "Kelly" Johnson and offered to call him to see if the job at Lockheed was still open. Johnson suggested I fly out to California and talk to him. In September, 1962, I did so.

I was about ready to say I was interested only in a flying job when he asked: Would you like to be a test pilot?

I suspect that at one time or another this has been almost every pilot's ambition: I knew it was mine. I said I would.

Flying U-2s?

The answer was written across my face in a big grin.

On returning to Washington, I submitted my resignation to the CIA, and reported to work at Lockheed on October 15, 1962.

By this time the U-2 had proven itself again. While at the agency, I had kept abreast of developments in the program, and was aware that Air Force pilots, under the command of SAC, were making overflights of Cuba. I also knew that late in August a U-2 had spotted a number of Soviets SAMs, probably similar to the one that brought me down. What no one knew for certain, however, until a U-2 returned from its overflight along the western edge of Cuba on October 14 and its photographs had been processed and studied, was that sites were being built for medium-range ballistic missiles capable of reaching targets in the United States.

We were to pay a high price for our intelligence on the Cuban missile crisis. While overflying Cuba, USAF Major Rudolph Anderson was shot down by a Soviet SAM.

With his death, no one could any longer doubt that Russian missiles were capable of reaching the U-2's altitude.

My work at Lockheed was as an engineering test pilot. This consisted of test-flying the planes whenever there was a modification, a new piece of equipment installed, or the return of an aircraft for maintenance.

Getting back into the tight pressure suit was an odd sensation—uncomfortable as ever. But there was one improvement. It had been found that an hour of prebreathing prior to flight would suffice. Again I was back in the high altitudes. Perhaps needless to say, my insurance premiums rose even more astronomically.

Except for a few close calls, I thoroughly enjoyed the work. Two times hatch covers blew out. One knocked a hole in the wing and in the tail. The other jammed the canopy so I couldn't get out. But each time I managed to make it back. And, while I was working at high altitudes, where the aircraft was most temperamental, there were, I'll frankly admit, occasions when I was scared. But my confidence in the U-2 remains unshaken. It was and still is a remarkable aircraft, one of a kind.

I only wish there were more of them around.

In 1963 I received the first of what was to be a number of rude awakenings.

You're going to have to make up your mind, Powers, the general said. If you want to go back into the Air Force, you'll have to do it soon.

With nearly twelve years toward retirement—

Five and a half, he corrected me. Your time in the CIA won't count.

On joining the U-2 program in 1956 I had signed a document, cosigned by Secretary of the Air Force Donald A. Quarles, promising me that upon completion of service with the agency I could return to the Air Force with no loss of time in grade or toward retirement, my rank to correspond with that of my contemporaries. This had been a major factor in my accepting employment with the CIA. The same was true of the other pilots, all of whom had signed the same document. A number of them had already returned to the Air Force under those conditions.

The general knew this. But there had been too much publicity about my case. Although they would let me reenlist at comparable rank—an old captain, or a new major—they would have to renege on their promise regarding my CIA service counting as time toward retirement.

I was being penalized for doing my duty, for having spent twenty-one months in a Russian prison!

He was sorry, but that was the way things were.

I could have fought it, I suppose. However, as with my agency contract and numerous other documents I had signed, the CIA retained the only copy. To contest this, I would have to use other pilots as witnesses. Some of them, I was quite sure, wouldn't lie. But it would be damn rough on them. My attempt to obtain what I had been "guaranteed in writing" might mean the Air Force would penalize them, too.

The agency knew me well, perhaps too well. They were gambling on my not causing a fuss, for just this reason. And, in this instance, they read me right.

The general also informed me that for the same reason I wouldn't be allowed to receive the Distinguished Flying Cross, awarded to me in 1957.

The second disillusionment came in April. Compared to the broken promise regarding my Air Force service, it was decidedly minor. (Many of my contemporaries in the program have retired or will become eligible for retirement in 1970 as lieutenant-colonels or better, at six to seven hundred dollars a month for life.) Yet, indicative of a pattern, it was in its own way decidedly important.

On April 20, 1963, at a secret ceremony which took place in the Los Angeles area, a number of the pilots who had participated in the U-2 program were awarded the Intelligence Star, one of the Central Intelligence Agency's highest decorations.

There was one exception. Francis Gary Powers hadn't been invited.

"Kelly" Johnson and a couple other people who worked with me attended. They were very secretive about it, however, because they had been instructed not to let me know what was going on. I knew all the time, from pilot friends with whom I had kept in contact.

It was more than a slight, more than the failure to receive an award. It was confirmation of what I had half-suspected for some time, but didn't really want to admit. I was, to borrow from John LeCarré, the spy who was to stay out in the cold. Things began fitting into place: the agency's failure to clear up the misconceptions regarding my orders, and by so doing lending credence to the criticism; the canceled White House visit; the smudged clearance.

It wasn't too difficult to deduce the reasoning behind it. I could almost hear the discussion:

The public is already down on Powers because they think he told more than he should. We can't divulge what he withheld. Since he's already been made the scapegoat, why not leave it at that? Otherwise there will be questions. The agency has been under enough fire already. This will divert the criticism.

Conjecture, of course, but I suspect it's fairly close to what happened.

As to who made the decision, I have only suspicions. As to when it occurred, it must have been sometime prior to the issuance of the clearance. That the Senate hearing went as favorably as it did was, I believe, a surprise to almost everyone concerned.

I was to be the scapegoat.

And there was absolutely nothing I could do about it.

Ironically, not all of the pilots who received the award had made an overflight of Russia.

While working at Langley I had met a very attractive and intelligent agency employee named Claudia Edwards Downey. Sue, as she was known to her friends, had been one of the agency people with initial doubts about Francis Gary Powers. She managed to overcome them. One of my earliest impressions of her wasn't exactly favorable: she had spilled a cup of hot coffee on me. Our romance blossomed over the wires of the Bell System. My monthly telephone bill had grown so large, in fact, that we decided there was only one way to reduce it. On October 21, 1963, Sue resigned from the agency and we were married October 26, in Catlett, Virginia. It was the beginning, without qualification, of the happiest part of my life.

After spending about six months in an apartment, we purchased a home in the Verdugo Mountains, its panoramic view including Burbank airport's north-south runway. This meant that I was only five minutes from work and Sue could watch my takeoffs and landings. The same day we made the down payment, I was informed that Lockheed was moving its testing facilities to Van Nuys airport.

But we liked the house—and have been especially fortunate in having neighbors who have become good friends.

On August 17, 1960, the Russians had given me a trial for my thirty-first birthday present. On my thirty-fifth birthday, in 1964, the California courts granted me permission to adopt Claudia Dee, Sue's seven-year-old daughter by a previous marriage. I've never had a nicer birthday present.

And on June 5, 1965, we celebrated the birth of a son, Francis Gary Powers, II.

Fame—fortunately, as far as I'm concerned—is a fleeting thing. People forget the face first, then the name. There were still occasional requests for interviews; but thanks to the public-relations department at Lockheed, I was able to fend them off. While it was never possible to forget completely all that had happened, Sue and I were able to build a new life independent of the past.

But there were occasional reminders.

Two worth noting occurred in 1964, one very disappointing, the other not.

I had a great deal of respect for James B. Donovan, the New York attorney who had arranged my exchange for Abel. Not only was I indebted to him for my release, I was tremendously impressed when shortly afterward he successfully negotiated the release of 9,700—yes, *9,700*—Cubans and Americans from Castro's Cuba. Since my return we had had little contact. I had sent him a sugar-cured Virginia ham; over cocktails on the plane taking me home after my release, we had, in jest, agreed that a Virginia ham would be the "fee" for his services. We had also exchanged Christmas cards. Beyond that, however, I'd heard nothing until publication of his book on the Abel case in 1964.

In describing our conversation on that plane ride, Donovan observed: "Powers was a special type, I thought. People at home had been critical of his performance when downed and later when tried in Moscow. Yet, in charity, suppose you wished to recruit an American to sail a shaky espionage glider over the heart of hostile Russia at 75,000 feet [incorrect] from Turkey to Norway. Powers was a man who, for adequate pay, would do it, and as he passed over Minsk would calmly reach for a salami sandwich. We are all different, and it is a little unfair to expect every virtue in any one of us."

I might not like that—and of course didn't—but if that happened to be Donovan's impression of me, I couldn't fault him for saying it. I could, however, for the sizable number of errors in his story. Two of these bothered me very much, both concerning that same return flight.

"I went up to the cockpit," Donovan writes, met the colonel piloting the plane, and heard American news broadcasts about the exchange on Glienicker Bridge. . . . The colonel and his crew shook my hand and were more than friendly. I noticed they avoided Powers."

Inviting me up to the cockpit and asking whether I wanted to fly the plane wasn't exactly avoiding me. In fairness to Donovan, he had gone to bed before this happened, and possibly wasn't aware of what occurred, but he must have been aware that we exchanged friendly remarks at various other times during the flight.

I didn't appreciate the picture he was painting. And there was more.

In relating portions of our conversation, he quoted me as saying: "I thought more about politics and international things than I ever did before. For example, it just doesn't make sense to me that we don't recognize Red China and let her into the United Nations." To which Donovan adds the comment, "It did not seem a proper occasion on which to discuss the point."

The implication was obvious. Powers came back spouting Communist propaganda.

My recollections of the conversation differ somewhat, and I think that Murphy and others present will bear me out on this.

Donovan had been entertaining us with details of his negotiations with a KGB official. At one point the official had told Donovan, "You should study Russian." Donovan replied, "In my country only the optimists study Russian. The pessimists study Chinese." The KGB official, he said, didn't perceive the humor.

We did, however, and laughed appreciatively. Donovan then asked me whether the Russians had ever discussed the Red Chinese with me. I replied that they had never brought up the subject in conversation; in reading the *Daily Worker*, however, and on listening to radio news as translated by my cellmate, I had heard them occasionally bemoan the unfairness of excluding China from the UN. However, I added, both my cellmate and I agreed that that was probably the last thing in the world the Russians wanted.

In the same spirit of charity extended to me by Donovan, I will only say that his recollections of our conversation are hazy.

Later there was a letter. Negotiating to sell his book to Hollywood, he was willing to offer me twenty-five hundred dollars for use of my name and story. Permission wasn't necessary, he said, but he had personally arranged this for me. As an extra added incentive, he might also be able to arrange for me to play myself in the movie, should I so desire.

I was tempted to reply that since the mercenary Powers had passed up sixty times that amount by deciding not to write his book, he was placing a rather high price on my vanity.

But I didn't.

I was, and remain, grateful to him for the part he played in my release. But I also want to keep the record straight.

My first meeting with former CIA Director Allen Dulles seemed preordained, one of those meetings decreed by fate. The second meeting, while not a surprise, did catch me off guard.

In March, 1964, the Lockheed Management Club hosted a dinner at the Beverly Hilton Hotel. Chief speaker was Dulles. Sue and I were there, to hear our former boss. We entered the room just behind Mr. and Mrs. Johnson, who were escorting Mr. and Mrs. Dulles. Spotting me, Mrs. Johnson said, "Oh, Mr. Dulles, I believe you know Francis Gary Powers."

It was not a name he was likely to forget.

His greeting was most cordial, as was mine. I had never considered Dulles responsible for the role into which I had been placed; that decision, I believe, had occurred during the reign of his successor.

After acknowledging his introduction, Dulles departed from his prepared speech: "I want to say, too, as I start, that I am gratified that I can be here for another reason, because I would like to say to all of you, as I have said from time to time when the opportunity presented, that I think one of your number—Francis Gary Powers— who has been criticized from time to time, I believe unjustly, deserves well of his country. He performed his duty in a very dangerous mission and he performed it well, and I think I know more about that than some of his detractors and critics know, and I am glad to say that to him tonight."

Dulles' talk was taped. Later "Kelly" Johnson had his remarks transcribed and a copy sent to me.

In April, 1965, I was asked to come back to Washington to be awarded the Intelligence Star.

My first reaction, quite frankly and quite bluntly, was to suggest they shove it.

We made the trip, however, for several reasons. It was less than two months before the birth of Gary, and would be the last opportunity to visit our families for some time. Following the ceremony, there was to be a dinner at Normandie Farms, Maryland, with a number of friends from the early days of the U-2 program in attendance, many of whom, including Bissell, I hadn't seen in years.

I'm not sure why, having once declined the opportunity, it was decided to make the presentation in 1965. By this time McCone had submitted his resignation, and a Johnson appointee, retired Vice Admiral William F. Raborn Jr., was scheduled to be sworn in as DCI in little more than a week. Perhaps it was felt that this was a bit of leftover business to be gotten out of the way before the new DCI took over. At any rate, although the ceremony was impressive, it was cheapened for me not only by what had preceded it, but by the realization that the presentation was worded in such a way as to commend me for my "courageous action" and "valor" prior to 1960. Apparently it was felt the Virginia hillbilly wouldn't catch such a subtlety, or notice, when I examined the scroll accompanying the medal, that the date on it was that of the earlier ceremony, April 20, 1963.

Word of the secret ceremony leaked to the press. The accounts were wrong in one particular, however. Instead of the actual April date, they said it occurred on May 1, 1965, the fifth anniversary of my flight.

That was, I'm quite sure, the last thing the agency wished to commemorate.

As is probably obvious from my account, I'm patient, unusually so, and always have been. While some might consider this a virtue,

I think of it as a fault. But it's the way I am, and try as I might, I haven't been able to change it.

For a time I put thoughts of the book aside. My work, my family, our friends, were more than enough to fill my time. Too, more than a few of my recollections were not pleasant. I was not anxious to relive them.

And no man, even in the privacy of his innermost thoughts, likes to admit he has been used.

Meanwhile, other books dealing with the U-2 incident continued to appear, among them Allen Dulles' *The Craft of Intelligence,* Harper & Row, 1963, which related the story of the exposure of the Russian bomber hoax; and Ronald Seth's *The Anatomy of Espionage,* E. P. Dutton, 1963, which considered the U-2 flights in relation to the whole broad spectrum of intelligence-gathering.

In his chapter on the U-2 story, Seth did something a great number of others hadn't. He studied the trial testimony, concluding: "Indeed, throughout the whole of his trial, [Powers] comported himself with a dignity and spirit which might have been found lacking in many another. All the way down the line, Powers was badly served—by his President and others who ought to have known better, by faulty intelligence which led him to believe that he was invulnerable, and by attempts just before the trial to accuse the Russians of having brainwashed or drugged him."

One book of special interest was Lyman B. Kirkpatrick's *The Real CIA,* Macmillan, 1968, for its glimpse of what happened in the inner chambers of the agency when realization dawned that I hadn't made it to Bodö. It caused, according to Kirkpatrick, former executive director of the Central Intelligence Agency, "one of the most momentous flaps that I witnessed during my time in the federal government."

Kirkpatrick's account is not wholly uncritical of the handling of the affair. With remarkable understatement, he notes: "It was fairly obvious that the unit of the CIA that was responsible for the cover story had not thought the matter through very carefully." He continues: "To my knowledge nobody has ever yet devised a method for quickly destroying a tightly rolled package of hundreds of feet of film. Even if Francis Powers had succeeded in pressing the 'destruction button,' which would have blown the plane and the camera apart, the odds would still have been quite good that careful Soviet search would have found the rolls of film."

Yet this mistaken assumption—that the plane would have been

totally obliterated, all evidence of espionage destroyed—apparently was believed at the highest level, by the President himself.

Kirkpatrick was in California at the time of Khrushchev's shattering announcement. Cornered by reporters, his single comment was, "No comment." He notes: "Later I was pleased to learn that one of the newscasters, in commenting upon the episode, characterized my statement as the only intelligent one made by the government during the event." With that I am inclined to agree. From a strictly selfish viewpoint, my interrogations would have gone easier had there been a little less talk.

Kirkpatrick concludes: "The development and use of the U-2 was a remarkable accomplishment, and the fact that it came to the end of its starring role over Russia on May 1, 1960, should not dim the achievements of the men who made it possible. . . . Francis Powers, and the others who flew the plane, also deserve full credit for their courage and ability. Powers conducted himself with dignity during his interrogation and trial and revealed nothing to the Russians that they did not already know. Upon his return to the United States in 1962, after he was exchanged for Rudolf Abel, a review board headed by Federal Judge E. B. Prettyman went into the minute details of his conduct while a prisoner and found that he had conducted himself in accordance with instructions. He was decorated by the CIA."

You could write a whole book between some of the sentences of that paragraph.

The most surprising account, however, appeared in 1965: *Waging Peace: The White House Years 1956–1961*, Doubleday, its author former President Dwight D. Eisenhower.

In the chapter entitled "The Summit That Never Was," Eisenhower describes how he received the news on May 1. By way of preface to this astonishing paragraph, Brigadier General Andrew J. Goodpaster was White House staff secretary, and served as liaison between the President and the CIA:

"On the afternoon of May 1, 1960, General Goodpaster telephoned me: 'One of our reconnaissance planes,' he said, 'on a scheduled flight from its base in Adana, Turkey, is overdue and possibly lost.' I knew instantly that this was one of our U-2 planes, probably over Russia. Early the next morning he came into my office, his face an etching of bad news. He plunged to the point at once. 'Mr. President, I have received word from the CIA that the U-2 reconnaissance plane I mentioned yesterday is still missing.

The pilot reported an engine flameout at a position about three hundred miles inside Russia and has not been heard from since. With the amount of fuel he had on board, there is not a chance of his still being aloft.' "

I had never an engine flameout nor did I radio back to the base. And the CIA certainly knew this.

It was now obvious why this particular story had received such widespread acceptance. Apparently even the President believed it.

There remains the possibility that the account is in error. One problem with memoirs of heads of state is that they are often the work of a number of people. Recollections differ, time clouds detail. I was told, in this particular instance, however, that a man from the agency was given a leave of absence to help prepare material for the chapter on the U-2 incident. That this slipped past him, if it did, is all the more astonishing.

It may be that General Goodpaster misunderstood the message; it is also possible that someone in the agency, not wanting to accept hard realities, speculated that this *might* have been what happened. If so, it should have been presented to the President that way, as pure speculation. Conveyed as straight intelligence, with the addition "the pilot reported" for authenticity, it constitutes a serious breach of trust.

There are indications throughout the Eisenhower account that he was not informed on all developments in Operation Overflight.

"A final important characteristic of the plane was its fragile construction," Eisenhower writes. "This led to the assumption (insisted upon by the CIA and the Joint Chiefs) that in the event of mishap the plane would virtually disintegrate. It would be impossible, if things should go wrong, they said, for the Soviets to come in possession of the equipment intact—or, unfortunately, of a live pilot. This was a cruel assumption, but I was assured that the young pilots undertaking these missions were doing so with their eyes wide open and motivated by a high degree of patriotism, a swashbuckling bravado, and certain material inducements."

Our feeling that the plane was too fragile to last was, as noted, strong at the start of the program. By 1957, however, with the stepping up of the flights, we knew better. Nor did we by that time believe that in the event of accident at high altitudes the plane would disintegrate. The tragic death of Lockheed test pilot Robert L. Sieker in April, 1957, had dispelled this notion. The crash which killed Sieker had left his plane virtually intact. It was so mangled as to be beyond repair, but all the parts were there.

Later Eisenhower stated: "There was, to be sure, reason for deep concern and sadness over the probable loss of the pilot, but not for immediate alarm about the equipment. I had been assured that if a plane were to go down it would be destroyed either in the air or on impact, so that proof of espionage would be lacking. Self-destroying mechanisms were built in."

If Eisenhower was told this, he was deceived. Had we been carrying ten times the two-and-a-half-pound explosive charge, there would have been no guarantee that the entire plane and all its contents would have been destroyed. Nor was the single mechanism "self-destroying." It had to be activated by the pilot.

Eisenhower's astonishment following Khrushchev's announcement was undoubtedly genuine: "On that afternoon, Friday, May 6 [Saturday, May 7], Mr. Khrushchev, appearing before the Supreme Soviet once more, announced what to me was unbelievable. The uninjured pilot of our reconnaissance plane, along with much of his equipment intact, was in Soviet hands."

The evidence strongly suggests that although the President was consulted for authorization of the flight packages, no effort was made to brief him on the many changes in the situation. For example, nowhere in his account is there any mention that we were worried about Soviet SAMs and had been for a long time, or that we realized it was only a matter of time before the Russians would solve their missile-guidance problem.

Again, this is only a personal opinion—possibly erroneous, as I do not know all the facts—but I am inclined to feel that since permission for the flights was so difficult to obtain, the President simply was not informed of the many dangers involved, lest he consider the advisability of discontinuing the overflight program entirely.

I also get the impression throughout his account, though it is only obliquely implied, that Eisenhower believed the pilots had been ordered to kill themselves rather than submit to capture.

Yet I find it difficult to believe the President of the United States would approve a kimikaze-type operation.

The one question I had been hoping would be answered with his book wasn't. Why was this particular flight scheduled so close to the Summit?

But there are clues. And they would seem to bear out my earlier suspicion that the flight on May 1, 1960, was intended not only for the intelligence data we could have obtained—although that was unquestionably important—but also to give Eisenhower a better bargaining position at the conference table.

Eisenhower admits: "Almost from the very beginning, we learned that the Soviets knew of the flights. . . . " Being aware of this, he must have been aware that it was unlikely this particular flight would have gone undetected. My guess that Eisenhower wanted Khrushchev to know we were still making the flights, in the hope he could use this as leverage in reintroducing the Open Skies Plan in Paris, may not have been too wild a guess. Although I was uninformed of this while in Russia, in his opening remarks at the abortive Summit Conference he stated:

"I have come to Paris to seek agreements with the Soviet Union which would eliminate the necessity for all forms of espionage, including overflights. I see no reason to use this incident to disrupt the conference.

"Should it prove impossible, because of the Soviet attitude, to come to grips here in Paris with this problem and the other vital issues threatening world peace, I am planning in the near future to submit to the United Nations a proposal for the creation of a United Nations aerial surveillance to detect preparations for attack. This plan I had intended to place before this conference. This surveillance system would operate in the territories of all nations prepared to accept such inspection. For its part, the United States is prepared not only to accept United Nations aerial surveillance, but to do everything in its power to contribute to the rapid organization and successful operation of such international surveillance."*

If Eisenhower's intention was that Khrushchev learn of the flight, it must be said that, whatever else may have happened, he was certainly successful in that.

Some mysteries remain. Eisenhower's reason for authorizing the flight is one.

Even more fascinating in some ways is another: Was the May 1, 1960, flight of the U-2 "betrayed?"

The CIA has said it wasn't. But again there are clues. Although the evidence is by no means conclusive, three separate—and seemingly

*Grateful acknowledgment is made to Doubleday and Company, Inc., for permission to quote from *Waging Peace: The White House Years 1956–1961*, by President Dwight D. Eisenhower.

unrelated—incidents indicate that this *might* have been the case. They are presented here strictly for purposes of speculation.

In July, 1960, William Hamilton Martin and Bernon Ferguson Mitchell, two cryptologists employed by the National Security Agency, "disappeared." On September 6, 1960, they surfaced in Moscow, at a press conference, where they revealed a great deal of information they claimed to have learned while working for the secret agency. One of their claims was that the NSA was monitoring the codes of some forty nations, including many friendly to the United States, even to the extent of intercepting communications of the various governments to their delegations at the United Nations.

I was informed of their defection by the Soviets a day or two after this—shortly before I was to be transferred from Lubyanka to Vladimir. At the time, however, I was unaware whether the story was simply a ruse designed by my captors to trap me into some admission, or whether the defection and press conference had actually taken place.

Not until my return to the United States did I learn the particulars of the case—that Martin and Mitchell, both alleged homosexuals, had gone to work for the National Security Agency early in 1957; in February, 1958, for reasons known only to themselves, they had joined the Communist party and begun transmitting secret information to the Russians.

The full extent of this information has never been made public by either side. That the two men knew of the U-2 overflights, however, there can be no question. Obviously acting under instructions from Moscow, but posing as concerned civil servants, they called on Representative Wayne Hays, Democrat, Ohio, to protest the overflights, apparently in the hope he would apply congressional pressure to have them stopped. (That the Soviets would thus risk exposing two such well-placed agents is indicative of how desperately they wanted to stop the overflights.)

The National Security Agency was well aware of the overflights, because, as has since been made public, the NSA was involved in processing and studying electronic data received from the U-2 flights.

Both men were still working for the NSA at the time my last mission was scheduled. Whether in the course of their duties they learned of it and gave this information to their Communist contact is one of those questions which remains unanswered.

Among the people I talked to following my return to the United States was an agency man who had worked in the communications section at Adana. His position was supervisorial; he knew what was going on. Curious, I asked him about the delayed Presidential approval on this particular flight.

This was only one of two things which distinguished this flight from those which preceded it, he told me. The other, a mistake that should never have been made, was the result of a breakdown of communications between Germany and Turkey.

The overflight orders were conveyed from the United States to Germany, and from Germany to Turkey, via radio code. From Turkey they were then transmitted to the crew in Pakistan, by similar means. The night prior to the flight, having worked around the clock several days awaiting transmission of Presidential approval, the communications man had gone to bed for a few hours, leaving an assistant in charge. During his absence, radio communications between Germany and Turkey broke down. When the approval did come through, the agent in Germany relayed it to Adana over an open telephone line—something absolutely forbidden in any circumstance. The assistant had then relayed it to Peshawar.

The communications man learned of this only the next morning, on arriving at work. Had he been on duty when the message came in, he swore, he never would had sent it further, the risk of the call's having been monitored being so great.

Thus there is a possibility that the Russians knew I would be taking off even before I did.

More than one writer has suggested that the CIA itself betrayed the flight, as a part of some vast conspiracy to wreck the Summit. Lest in mentioning the above I encourage further exploitation of this wild fantasy, it should be stated that the best—and most conclusive—evidence against this theory is the simplest: the agency's total lack of preparedness for the crash possibility, and the "monumental flap" that ensued.

The third bit of "evidence" poses far more questions than it answers. Yet it is, in its own way, by far the most intriguing. It concerns the possibility of the altitude of the U-2 having been betrayed.

When the U-2's altitude is referred to as "secret," that term is qualified. In addition to those personally involved in U-2 flights, a number of others, by the nature of their duties, had access to this information. These included air-traffic controllers and at least some of the radar personnel at the bases where U-2s were stationed.

In 1957 the U-2s were based in a new location, Atsugi, Japan.

In September of that year a seventeen-year-old Marine Corps private was assigned to Marine Air Control Squadron No. 1 (MACS-1), based at Atsugi. MACS-1 was a radar unit whose duties included scouting for incoming foreign aircraft. Its equipment included height-finding radar. The private, a trained radar operator, had access to this equipment.

He remained in Japan until November, 1958, at which time he was returned to the United States and assigned to Marine Air Control Squadron No. 9 (MACS-9) at the Marine Corps Air Station at El Toro, California. El Toro was not a U-2 base, but U-2s frequently flew over this portion of Southern California. At El Toro he had access not only to radar and radio codes but also to the new MPS 16 height-finding radar gear.

In September, 1959, he obtained a "hardship discharge" from the U.S. Marine Corps.

The following month he defected to the Soviet Union.

On October 31 he appeared in the American Embassy in Moscow to state his intention of renouncing his U.S. citizenship. According to Richard E. Snyder, the second secretary and senior consular official, and John A. McVickar, Snyder's assistant, who was also present, during the course of the conversation he mentioned that he had already offered to tell the Russians everything he knew about the Marine Corps and his specialty, radar operation. He also intimated that he might know something of "special interest."

His name was Lee Harvey Oswald.

Six months later my U-2 was shot down.

Oswald's familiarity with MPS 16 height-finding radar gear and radar and radio codes (the latter were changed following his defection) are mentioned in the testimony of John E. Donovan, a former first lieutenant assigned to the same El Toro radar unit as Oswald, on page 298 of Volume 8 of the *Warren Commission Hearings.* According to Donovan, Oswald "had the access to the location of all bases in the west coast area, all radio frequencies for all squadrons, all tactical call signs, and the relative strength of all squadrons, number and type of aircraft in a squadron, who was the commanding officer, the authentication code of entering and exiting the ADIZ, which stands for Air Defense Identification Zone. He knew the range of our radar. He knew the range of our radio. And he knew the range of the surrounding units' radio and radar."

Oswald's conversation with Snyder is mentioned at least three times in the *Report of the Warren Commission on the Assassination of President Kennedy* (page references are to *The New York Times* edition, published by McGraw-Hill, October, 1964):

Page 618: "Oswald told him that he had already offered to tell a Soviet official what he had learned as a radar operator in the Marines."

Page 665: "Oswald stated to Snyder that he had voluntarily told Soviet officials that he would make known to them all information concerning the Marine Corps and his specialty therein, radar operations, as he possessed."

Page 369: "He stated that he had volunteered to give Soviet officials any information that he had concerning Marine Corps operations, and intimated that he might know something of special interest."

During the six months following the October 31, 1959, embassy meeting, there were only two overflights of the USSR. The one which occurred on April 9, 1960, was uneventful. The one which followed, on May 1, 1960, wasn't.

Here the trail ends, except for one tantalizing lead, discovered during the research for this volume.

Among the Warren Commission Documents in the National Archives in Washington, D.C., is one numbered 931, dated May 13, 1964, CIA National Security Classification Secret.

In response to an inquiry, Mark G. Eckhoff, director, Legislative, Judicial, and Diplomatic Records Division, National Archives, in a letter dated October 13, 1969, stated: "Commission Document 931 is still classified and withheld from research."

The title of Document No. 931 is "Oswald's Access to Information About the U-2."

The former President could write about the U-2 episode; retired agency officials—Dulles, Kirkpatrick—could write about it, as could others in no way connected with the program. The man most directly involved could not.

In August, 1967, I again requested permission to write a book concerning my experiences.

I was more hopeful this time. Raborn had been replaced by Richard Helms, a man who had worked his way up through the ranks of the CIA and undoubtedly knew more about intelligence than any other director since Dulles. There were also indications that intelligence, not politics, was Helms' primary concern.

I was told that the request would be made of the "big man" at what seemed "the most opportune moment."

"This isn't the right time to bring it up," I was told in a telephone call a couple of weeks later.

Nor was the moment opportune the next time they called. For in the interim the "spy ship" *Pueblo* had been captured by the North Koreans, and the last thing the government wanted, I was told, was more publicity.

With the seizure of the *Pueblo,* interest in the U-2 story was reactivated. Although the two events differed in at least one important particular—the *Pueblo* was outside the territorial waters of North Korea, I had intruded right into the heart of Russia—there were obvious parallels. And some not so obvious, because they involved that portion of the U-2 story which had never been made public. I wondered how many *Pueblo* episodes would have to occur before we accepted the basic lessons we should have learned from the U-2 crisis.

This was one factor in my decision to go ahead with the book. There were others. My job was not risk-free; if anything happened to me, chances were the story would never be told. Too, and this was not the least of my considerations, in a few years my children would be reading about the U-2 incident in school. I wanted them to know the truth.

In the fall of 1968 I was contacted by John Dodds, editor-in-chief of Holt, Rinehart and Winston, Inc. Dodds was aware of the earlier negotiations for the book, and was anxious to publish my story if I was ready to write it. I was more than ready.

Sue and I flew to New York and talked to him. On our return to California I informed the agency of the Holt offer and, for the last time, asked permission to publish my account.

After waiting several weeks, my patience finally came to an end. Since they had helped perpetuate the Francis Gary Powers mercenary label, I'd play the part. Sarcastically I wrote to them that I was going to write the book, and while entertaining bids, and since they had been so anxious to suppress it, I'd be glad to consider their best offer.

It was, in its own way, my declaration of independence.

To my surprise, I did receive an answer, in the form of a telephone call asking me if I would be willing to come to Washington to discuss the matter. I did, informing them at the outset that I intended to accept the offer made by Holt, Rinehart and Winston.

Only then was I told the agency had no objection to my writing the book. While they, of course, couldn't give such permission in writing, they did want me to know that they would be glad to do anything possible to assist me.

Although not ungrateful for their offer, I politely declined it. Undoubtedly access to their records would shed light on some of the more puzzling aspects of the U-2 episode. On the other hand, such cooperation would carry with it an unspoken obligation. This was to be my version of the story, not the agency's. I was determined to tell it as I had lived it, and this, to the best of my ability, I have done.

As the writing of the book progressed, I made an interesting discovery. Although this may also sound like sarcasm, it isn't. In suppressing the book for nearly eight years, the agency did me a favor. I could now tell the story far more fully and frankly than would have been possible in 1962.

I have omitted only a few particulars, and in fairness to the reader I will state their nature.

I have not included the actual altitude of the U-2. By now it may be presumed that Russia, Cuba, and Communist China all know it. Yet, just on the chance that it isn't known and that the life of a pilot might be placed in jeopardy, it will go unmentioned.

I have not itemized the number of overflights, nor related what intelligence information was received. My reasoning on this matter remains the same as when I first withheld this information from the Russians. Having held it back through many hours of interrogation, I have no intention of giving it to them now for the price of a book.

I have not mentioned certain phases of my training, both in the Air Force and in the agency, which might still be in use and thus beneficial to an enemy.

I have not included the names of other pilots, agency personnel, or representatives of Lockheed and the many other companies involved in the U-2 program. It is not my business to "blow their cover."

And I have omitted some matters which I feel could affect present national security.

These are the only things excluded.

In the fall of 1969, as the book was nearing completion, I did something else I had wanted to do for a very long time. I wrote a letter.

Dear Zigurd:

It's been a long time since I last saw you standing in the window at Vladimir as I was being led away. As happy as I was to be leaving, there was a great sadness in me that you were remaining behind those bleak walls.

I'm sure you've heard that I was exchanged for Soviet spy Colonel Rudolf Abel. You probably have not heard much of what transpired after my release.

One of the things happening to me now is that I am writing my life story, to be published in the spring of next year. The research and reviewing of my journal and diary brought back memories, many of which I have tried to forget.

I am sending this letter to you in care of your parents, at the address you gave me the night before I left Vladimir. If you are allowed to correspond, I would like very much to hear from you. If the above-mentioned proves to be a good address, I will send you a copy of my book as soon as it is published. It will bring you up to date on the many things that have happened since I last saw you.

I hope your parents are well and happy. It would please me if you would convey to them my best wishes and my sincerest appreciation for the aid and kindness they showed me while we were at Vladimir.

Sincerely yours,
Francis Gary Powers

Some weeks later I received the return receipt I had requested. The handwriting was familiar; it was signed by Zigurd. Although to date there has been no reply, I am immensely relieved to know that he is alive and apparently no longer in prison.

FIVE

LOS ANGELES, CALIFORNIA JANUARY, 1970

Asked during a television interview what lessons for the future could be drawn from the U-2 crisis, James Hagerty, President Eisenhower's press secretary, replied, "Don't get caught."

Similarly questioned during an appearance before the Senate Foreign Relations Committee, Secretary of State Christian Herter phrased his response only slightly differently, "Not to have accidents."

While not wishing to contradict such eminent spokesmen, I would like to respectfully submit that if these are the only lessons we've learned, we're in trouble.

On May 1, 1970, a decade will have passed since "the incident over Sverdlovsk." Ten years. That's a long time to avoid facing the truth. For better or worse, the decade has been one of change, sometimes peacefully effected, often otherwise. Scarcely a government in the world remains the same as in 1960. During this period the national administration of the United States has changed four times, the directorship of the Central Intelligence Agency an equal number. It is no longer possible to suppress the facts of the U-2 episode with the excuse that they are still classified, not when time has made it all too apparent that in this case "classified" is only a synonym for "politically embarrassing," and even that excuse has lost validity.

Hopefully, the passage of time has given us some perspective. Hopefully, too, we've matured enough in our attitudes to accept a few hard realities.

One is that we blundered, and badly, not only during the U-2 "crisis," but long before it became a crisis.

We were unprepared for the possibility that a plane might go down in Russia. Yet that possibility had existed from the start of the program. A rocket wasn't needed. A simple malfunction could have done it. That possibility should have been taken into consideration. It wasn't.

We used a plane of which almost every part carried some indication of national identity. We loaded it with equipment which, should even a portion be discovered, would constitute conclusive proof of espionage intent. And we placed aboard it an explosive device insufficient to the task of destroying all evidence.

If the intention was simply to render inoperative certain parts of the equipment, fine. But in this case the agency should have kept those limitations in mind. It should also have considered the possibility that in some situations even this might not be possible. Instead, if President Eisenhower's memoirs are correct, even the President was led to believe that "in the event of mishap the plane would virtually disintegrate."

A lesson learned? According to accounts of the *Pueblo's* seizure, it carried "hundreds of pounds" of classified documents, with no simple means of destroying them in an emergency. In the case of the *Pueblo,* however, there was at least the excuse of a reason for complacency—that the ship was to remain supposedly invulnerable in international waters. With the U-2, we lacked that excuse.

We manned the U-2 with pilots who had never been adequately briefed on what to do if captured. The word "capture" did not appear in their contracts, it did not come up in their discussions. As for me, it was mentioned only once in a briefing, and then only after I had made a number of flights over Russia and only because I had brought it up. We should have talked about it, *planned* for it as for any other possible eventuality. Ignoring a problem does not solve it.

Perhaps it was felt best, psychologically, that such fears never arise. If so, apparently both the occupant of the White House and many in the upper echelons of the CIA succumbed to this psychological conditioning also, inasmuch as they were as unprepared as the pilots.

And remained so, even while evidence accumulated that the day was rapidly approaching when we would no longer be invulnerable to missiles at our altitude.

It is a bad intelligence practice to fail to consider all available evidence. Yet, throughout the U-2 crisis, there are indications that this is exactly what happened, not once, but again and again.

If the pilots were under orders to kill themselves to evade capture—as so many, including even the President, apparently believed—then the pilots should have been apprised of this fact. In which case, we should have been required to carry the needle, not given a choice in the matter; and use should have been declared mandatory, not optional, the briefing officer making definite exactly what was expected of us. While I can only speak for one of the pilots, I know that had I been told this I would have been ready to obey those orders, or never taken the flight.

As pilots, we were not only unprepared for capture, we were *ill*-prepared, in many ways a much worse situation. The advice "You may as well tell them everything, because they're going to get it out of you anyway" was, under the circumstances, bad. Perhaps the agency couldn't have foreseen this. Brainwashing, drugs, and torture having been the lot of prisoners in the past, it may have been wise to prepare us for the worst. All I know, however, is that had I followed these instructions, the damage to the United States would have been monumental.

Even more serious, in many ways, were the misconceptions I carried with me. From the American press, from my Air Force indoctrinations, from the attitude adopted by the agency, I had been led to believe that Russian intelligence was nearly omnipotent, that the KGB had agents everywhere, that "they probably know more about you than you know about yourself."

These misconceptions, as it turned out, were far more dangerous than the advice I had been given. Because I believed the Russians knew a great deal more than they probably did, I may well have told them far more than was necessary. That it was a great deal less than our orders called for does not minimize its seriousness. Overrating an enemy can be as much a mistake as underrating him.

At no point in my agency training was I instructed on how to handle myself during an interrogation. In my CIA "clearance" the agency justified this with the explanation that we were hired as pilots, not espionage agents. This was true. But it ignores the fact that, though pilots, we were potentially in as much danger of capture as any covert agent. We should have been briefed—as to what tricks to expect, as to tricks we could in turn use to avoid answering a question, as to how best to withstand hour after hour of continuous interrogation. While such briefings, I realize, wouldn't have prepared me for all eventualities, they would have helped immensely, if only to give me a realistic idea of what was possible under the right conditions. Instead, I had to improvise. It worked out better than I expected. But it could have gone very badly.

Much has been written about the mistakes made in pulling from the files a cover story which did not fit the facts, then maintaining it even when it was obviously discredited. In all this criticism, one very serious error has never been brought out. And that is that the pilots themselves were never informed as to what the cover story would be. I not only hadn't been briefed, I wasn't even sure a cover story would be issued. It may well be that no cover story would have been adequate to the situation; the one I improvised fell apart the moment my maps and rolls of film were brought in. But it would have helped to have some idea about the story being told in the world outside.

While we overrated the Russians in many ways, we also underrated them in the one area in which they are undisputed masters: propaganda.

In *Waging Peace,* President Eisenhower wrote: "Of those concerned, I was the only principal who consistently expressed a conviction that if ever one of the planes fell in Soviet territory a wave of excitement amounting almost to panic would sweep the world, inspired by the standard Soviet claim of injustice, unfairness, aggression, and ruthlessness. The others, except for my own immediate staff and Mr. Bissell, disagreed. Secretary Dulles, for instance, would say laughingly, 'If the Soviets ever capture one of these planes, I'm sure they will never admit it. To do so would make it necessary for them to admit also that for years we had been carrying on flights over their territory while they, the Soviets, had been helpless to do anything about the matter.'"

Secretary Dulles made a bad guess. But he could have been right. The worst mistake is not that he guessed wrongly, but that we were unprepared for any other possibility. Not only that, but even after the receipt of contrary evidence, we ignored it because it did not fit our preconceptions. Instead, we engaged in wishful thinking, as if wishing would make it so.

There were, I'm quite sure, many in Washington who hoped that the pilot was dead. That is, I realize, a strong assertion, but after ten years it seems foolish any longer to deny the obvious. The cover story, and our whole official attitude in the week of May 1 through May 7, was predicated upon this assumption. Yet, from the beginning, the possibility that I was alive existed and was ignored.

I was amazed to discover, on my return to the United States, that on May 5—*two days* before Khrushchev's announcement of my capture—the State Department received a telegram from Ambassador Thompson in Moscow warning of a rumor that the pilot was alive and a captive of the Russians. It was an unconfirmed report, the drunken bragging of a Soviet official at a diplomatic reception. But surely someone in our intelligence apparatus should have been alerted. Instead we continued to embellish the cover story, walking blindly into Khrushchev's trap.

It was a decidedly one-sided chess game, Khrushchev calling the moves, the U.S. ignoring the pieces on the board.

I now believe that the story that I had descended to a lower altitude was a controlled leak. I also believe that some person or persons within the agency, desperate to justify the decision to make the flight, helped perpetuate it. If the aircraft had descended to a lower altitude and then was shot down, it would have been bad luck, therefore, no one in the agency could be blamed.

The tenacity with which human beings, and governments, can stick to a fixed notion, even in the face of overwhelming proof to the contrary, is quite incredible. It is especially so when manifesting itself in an organization whose task includes the collection and evaluation of intelligence.

Even after I was brought to trial there were those in the agency who continued to hope that it wasn't Powers but someone else who had stood in that prisoner's dock.

Looking back, I now suspect that the decision to make me a scapegoat was due, at least in part, to someone's pique that, by being alive, I had proven them wrong.

There were other reasons, and although I am admittedly less than an impartial spectator, I think those reasons should be examined for whatever insight they may give into the U-2 episode.

Though the phrase was not coined until a much later date and under a different set of circumstances, in a very real sense the "credibility gap" was born of the contradictory official statements which appeared after the downing of the U-2.

The gap between what the government knew and what it told the American public had, of course, existed for a long time. But for the first time the American people realized they had been lied to, had been intentionally deceived by their own government. Even worse, the government had been caught in those lies, and made to seem a fool in the eyes of the world. One lingering after-effect was a distrust of government pronouncements, as evidenced by the public's refusal to accept the Warren Commission Report, statements on the Vietnam war, the official version of the Green Berets' case.

The most immediate result, however, was anger; and that anger needed an outlet, someone to blame.

Many criticized President Eisenhower for making the unprecedented admission that he had authorized espionage. Boxed into a corner by Khrushchev, given a choice between this and the admission he was not in charge of his own government, he really had little opportunity to do otherwise. Yet I personally feel it says much for the President that he chose this alternative to one of the "easy outs," such as making Allen Dulles or "Newman" and Powers the scapegoats.

Others found another target. Following the lead of the Russians, they made the pilot the symbol. It was far easier to fix the blame on a single individual, as did Representative Cannon when he suggested the fault might lie in "some psychological defect" in the pilot, than to accept the unpleasant fact that the blame would have to be shared by a great many people.

The impression that I had "told everything," the belief that I had gone against orders by refusing to kill myself, my statement during the trial that I was "sorry," added weight to the censure.

There were good and valid reasons why the CIA did nothing to clear up these impressions during my imprisonment.

It was otherwise when I returned home.

A scapegoat, by dictionary definition, is one made to bear the blame for others or to suffer in their place.

The making of scapegoats is also an excuse to avoid facing the truth.

These, to my mind, were some of the mistakes made during the U-2 incident. I state them here neither to justify my own conduct nor to engage in Monday-morning quarterbacking (it is rather late for that, thanks to the eight-year suppression of this story). Nor is it my intention to join those who would make the Central Intelligence Agency a repository of all our national ills. This simplistic attitude is only another manifestation of scapegoatism. I believe in the value of accurate, properly evaluated intelligence. Its lack, I feel strongly, is one of the greatest dangers our system of government faces in this thermonuclear age. The CIA is a major part of our intelligence apparatus. I have no desire to subvert it.

But this does not mean I wouldn't like to see it function better. Although these are strong criticisms, I feel they are both constructive and fair. They should come as no surprise to the CIA; they are much the same complaints I made in the debriefings upon my return, in my work with the training section. Perhaps unrealistically, I had hoped that by now some of these lessons would have been learned.

Having stated this, I also wish to make it clear that I do not approve of everything the CIA has done. While the lack of accurate intelligence may be one of the greatest threats to our national survival, it is not the only one. Sometimes in our rush to achieve an objective we overlook our reason for pursuing it. It would be tragic if, in the process of trying to protect our government, we forgot that it was founded upon the concept of the worth of the individual.

These are some of the negative aspects of the U-2 incident. There is, I believe, a more positive side to the whole affair.

There are many turning points in history; the U-2 incident was one. Never again would we look at the world in quite the same way. Never again would we be quite so innocent.

When my U-2 was shot down, a number of our most cherished illusions went crashing down with it: that the United States was too honorable to use the deplorable enemy tactics of espionage; that we were incapable of acting in our own defense, until after being attacked.

I'm not too sure the loss was all that great.

As a people, we Americans grew up a little in May, 1960, and during the days that followed. As with any growing process, it was at times a painful experience.

Yet I suspect that, for more than a few persons, reaction to the disclosure that we were keeping our eyes on Russia must have been similar to what I first felt in 1956 on learning of Operation Overflight; pride that the United States could conceive and carry out an intelligence operation of such boldness and importance; relief that we weren't asleep, weren't totally unprepared.

I'm also inclined to agree with Philip M. Wagner, when he wrote in the June, 1962, *Harper's* that President Eisenhower's admission that the United States was engaged in espionage "had a number of wholesome effects."

"For one thing, it invoked a sudden respect for American intelligence work which had not been general in Europe. In invoked that same respect in Russia. It also caused abrupt revision of estimates of American military strength, and such estimates are important influences on the course of diplomacy. If we had been able to keep that secret, what other secrets were we perhaps keeping? Were we as weak as many had been saying? Possibly not. It caused other revisions of judgment. U-2 was damning commentary on the supposed invulnerability of Russian air defense."

Also, I'm not too sure some of those negative aspects mightn't prove to be of positive value. It isn't necessarily bad that we've become suspicious of the motives behind some of our governmental pronouncements, that we question whether certain information is being withheld from the public because of "national security" or for strictly political reasons, that our elected leaders are on occasion called upon to justify their actions to the people they represent, that we demand—though we don't always obtain—a greater honesty from our officials.

The alternative is the kind of government to be found in the Soviet Union, Hungary, Czechoslovakia, Communist China, and elsewhere.

Following the U-2 incident, espionage attained an acceptance in the United States reaching the dimensions of a popular fad. Beginning with America's discovery of Ian Fleming's James Bond novels and the popularity of such TV shows as *I Spy* it progressed to the much more realistic novels of John LeCarré and others.

In 1960, in the earliest cover stories following the downing of the U-2, the United States denied its engagement in anything so distasteful as espionage.

In 1968, with the capture of the *Pueblo,* the United States was frank from the outset in admitting that the ship's mission was intelligence-gathering.

In my trial in August, 1960, when, acting on the advice of counsel, I stated that I was "deeply repentant and profoundly sorry," many in the U.S. damned me for doing so.

In December, 1968, when a representative of the United States government signed a document admitting that the *Pueblo* had invaded North Korean waters, at the same time stating that this was a lie, done only to effect the release of the crew, there was little criticism of his action.

For better or worse, we've grown up to accept some of the realities of our times, unpleasant though they may be.

But then, we're not the only ones who've done so. In 1960 the Soviet Union was still denying that it used spies. In 1962 the release of Powers and Abel was not an exchange, for Abel was not one of theirs; it was simply a gesture of Soviet humaneness, on behalf of the families of the two men (which, presumably out of modesty, they did not bother to announce in the USSR). It was therefore with more than a little amusement that I read a wire-service report in November, 1969, describing an event in East Berlin. One of that city's streets was being renamed for Richard Sorge, the remarkable agent who stole German and Japanese secrets for the Russians. Present for the dedication ceremony, according to the account from behind the Iron Curtain, were Russia's most famous spies, including one Rudolf Abel.

In 1970 the U-2 will celebrate its fifteenth birthday. Those few which remain, that is.

Of the original aircraft, less than one-third survive. None died of old age. None were junked for parts. All met violent ends. Communist China accounted for at least four, Cuba two, Russia one. Communist China has released a photograph of four it downed. The actual number may be higher. These particular planes are owned and piloted by Nationalist China. In addition to the crash which killed Major Anderson, another went down while returning from a Cuban overflight.

Ironically, the aircraft which made so many headlines during the sixties was never produced during that decade. Production ceased in the late fifties.

It's no secret that the U-2, manned by USAF pilots, again proved its value over Vietnam. Elsewhere, its primary use today is for high-altitude air sampling to detect and measure radio-activity. Not too long ago the U-2 also played a major role in a program to obtain data on high-level turbulence, to determine its effect on super-sonic transports.

Some have the impression that the U-2 became obsolete with the advent of the space satellite, just as the covert agent was supposedly superseded by the spy flight. Neither example is true, and I believe it is dangerous if we deceive ourselves into thinking this is so. Each had, and continues to have, its uses and can obtain information which the other can't. As far as I know, a satellite can't fly over a country at any time of the day or night and photograph exactly what it chooses. Nor can it fly slow enough to monitor radio and radar messages in their entirety. Too, for all the claims made by both Russia and the United States, I've still to see any photographic evidence that its cameras can pick out troops in the field or even smaller objects. Someday maybe. But at present I remain unconvinced.

Yet the fact remains that as an aircraft the U-2 is a vanishing species.

When I began working at Lockheed I had about six hundred hours' flight time in the U-2. Today I have in excess of two thousand. I know and respect the plane, and would like to see its life extended. Of a number of possible uses which have occurred to me, two may merit mention. One is the possibility that NASA, or possibly one of the larger universities, obtain one of the Air Force U-2s and adapt it for installation of a telescope for use in astronomy. Since it flies above ninety percent of the earth's atmosphere, the photographs would be exceptionally clear. The other possibility would be for a TV network to purchase several for transmission of weather pictures. Thus, before leaving for work in the morning, the viewer could not only see the weather picture over the area where he lived and worked, he could also follow the course of storm fronts as they moved in and know what was coming up. Only someone who has flown in a U-2 can realize how graphic such an overview can be.

There are, I'm sure, other possibilities such as map making, particularly of heretofore uncharted areas. And in wanting to prolong the usefulness of the U-2, my motives, I must admit, are not entirely unselfish. For the year 1970 will probably mark the end of my association with the U-2. In October, 1969, as this book was in its final stages, I was informed by "Kelly" Johnson that, U-2 test work being scarce, as of early 1970 my services would no longer be required at Lockheed.

As I write this, it's possible I've already made my last U-2 flight.

Regrets? Yes, I have a few. My greatest is not that I made the flight on May 1, 1960; rather the opposite—that we did not do more when we had the chance. We had the opportunity, the pilots, the planes, and, I sincerely believe, the need. Yet from the very start of the program in 1956 we made far fewer overflights of Russia than were possible. Moreover, from early 1958 until April, 1960, we made almost none. If the program was important to our survival in 1956 and 1957—and I'm convinced it was because of the single flight which exposed the Russian bomber hoax and alerted us to the USSR's emphasis on missiles, then in itself it alone was worth the cost of the whole program, saving not only millions of dollars but, possibly, millions of lives. The overflights became even more important as Russia's missile development progressed. We could have done much more than we did. I regret that we did not. I only hope that time won't prove this to have been one of our costliest mistakes.

This is my most serious regret. I have others, of course. But my participation in Operation Overflight isn't one of them. I'm very proud of that. While I might wish that many of the things that followed had never happened, I have the satisfaction of knowing that I served my country—and, I believe, well.

That is no small satisfaction.

On that day when all men and all nations agree, there will be no more need for U-2s, RB-47s, EC-121s, spy ships, and surveillance satellites, and their successors.

Until such time, it is almost inevitable that there will be more "incidents."

But that doesn't mean that we can't learn from our mistakes.

by Francis Gary Powers, Jr.*

The Cold War lasted for another thirty-one years after my father was shot down over the Soviet Union. The U-2 Incident forced the U.S. government to admit publicly that a worldwide intelligence network operated by the CIA was able to penetrate the Soviet Union. This effort, in the words of President Eisenhower, was a "vital but distasteful necessity in order to avert another Pearl Harbor."

Although my father's flight—the twenty-fourth over the Soviet Union—was the last to overfly that country, U-2s operated by the CIA continued to fly reconnaissance missions over Cuba, the Middle East, China, Southeast Asia, and other areas. And more U-2s were shot down by SA-2 missiles, the same weapon that downed my father's aircraft on May Day 1960. The CIA operated the U-2 until 1974, when the agency's surviving U-2s were transferred to the U.S. Air Force.

After his return to the United States, my father worked briefly at CIA headquarters in Langley, Virginia, near Washington, D.C., training agents on how to conduct themselves if captured and subjected to interrogation. One day, as my father turned a hallway corner, he bumped into an attractive woman. Coffee was spilled. He offered to buy Sue Downey another cup and, with his car in the shop, managed from the subsequent conversation to get a ride to work from her. In repayment, he asked her out to lunch. She accepted that invitation and soon lunch turned into dinner, and dinner into romance. My father and his first wife, Barbara, were separated. That marriage, rocky from the start, didn't survive the shootdown, his imprisonment, and the subsequent press coverage. They divorced officially in January 1963.

*I wish to acknowledge the help of Norman Polmar in preparing the afterword.

Dad tired of the desk job at CIA. Upon his return from the Soviet Union, Dad had been told by Kelly Johnson, who had designed the U-2, that he could work at Lockheed anytime he needed a job. In the fall of 1962, Dad took Johnson up on the offer. After he passed the physical and psychological examinations and was requalified in the U-2, Dad moved to California to work for Johnson at the Lockheed Skunk Works. In the meantime, not content with his long-distance relationship with Sue Downey, Dad invited her to Los Angeles for a visit. He proposed marriage to her a few weeks later. She received two diamonds, one for each year that they had known each other. They married and started a family, which included my sister, Claudia, a daughter from Mom's previous marriage. I came along in 1965.

In 1969, Dad started working on his autobiography. Shortly before *Operation Overflight* was published in early 1970, Kelly Johnson called him into his office at Burbank to inform my father that there was no more work for him at Lockheed. Kelly also told him that the CIA had been paying his salary directly to Lockheed for his work as a U-2 test pilot. (The U-2s were being transferred to the Air Force at the time.) The agency, it appeared, was willing to pay Dad's salary so long as he kept quiet about the U-2 Incident, but the book's publication had ruffled some feathers at Langley, so Lockheed had to let him go.

In 1972, after two years of promoting the book and appearing on the lecture and talk show circuit, my father found a pilot's job, in this case reporting on weather, traffic, and news for KGIL Radio Station in Los Angeles. In 1976, he became a helicopter traffic pilot-reporter for KNBC News Channel 4. On August 1, 1977, while conducting a traffic report over Los Angeles, his helicopter crashed, killing him and George Spears, his cameraman.

The events between that day in August and weeks later, when I started junior high school, are a little blurred. Everything was in a whirlwind. A friend's dad had driven me home from summer school. It was about 1:15 p.m. No sooner had I set foot inside our home than Mom dragged me out again to catch a quick meal at a local restaurant and to pick up some groceries. We missed the breaking news about my dad's fatal crash because the car radio was broken. When we arrived home, two close family friends, Mrs. Neff and Mrs. Marlow, greeted us. Mrs. Marlow was the wife of Jess Marlow, who was the anchorman and my dad's colleague at KNBC. Mrs. Neff said, "Sue, you had better sit down." In reply, Mom asked her to help with the groceries and they would talk in a minute. Again Mrs. Neff said, "Sue, you had better sit down." Suddenly my mom's expression changed; she looked as if she had seen a ghost. As the groceries dropped, I heard my mother say, "Oh my God, it's Frank. If he is alive, take me to him; if he is dead let me know." All the two women could do was shake their heads and shrug their shoulders because they didn't know yet or weren't telling.

I found myself in my room staring out the window thinking that Dad had been in an accident and had broken an arm or a leg. Mrs. Neff talked with me a bit, nothing that I remember other than being asked if there were a friend I would like to go visit. My automatic response was Chris Conrad, a life long friend and son of actor Robert Conrad of "Wild, Wild West" and "Baa Baa Black Sheep" fame. Chris and I had met in the second grade and grown up together.

After a telephone call to Chris, Mrs. Neff drove me to the Conrad home in Encino. About the time we arrived, Mrs. Conrad came home and asked Mrs. Neff why we were there. Mrs. Neff explained that there had been an accident and that my father had been injured. They talked alone for a while in whispers as Chris and I poked each other. When Mrs. Conrad gave me a huge bear hug, my eyes started to water and I wiped away the tears that were forming, not realizing why I was crying and trying not to cry in front of one of my friends.

Within a half-hour after Mrs. Neff had left, the phone rang at the Conrad's home. Mrs. Conrad answered and I heard her say, "Yes, I know, Gary is here now." With that she asked me to come to the phone because "Duke," as Bob Conrad was known, wanted to speak with me. Mr. Conrad gave me a pep talk and told me how much my father meant to a lot of people and some other remarks that were meant to comfort and console me. I remember him saying that my father was a great man, a true American hero, and that I should be proud to carry his name.

I think I spent the night at the Conrad's house. I returned home to find a large number of people there, including another good friend of my dad's, Gregg Anderson, who was coordinating the phone calls, burial plans, airline reservations, hotel reservations, and the press. For the next several hours different people arrived and departed, with more friends and family arriving over the next several days. A memorial service was held and I heard that Barbara, my dad's first wife, attended, although I do not remember her. I remember riding to the service with my mother, sister, and aunts, and gazing out of the window as we pulled up to the church, which overflowed with people. The limousine doors opened and many of my friends and their parents greeted me. I also saw a gaggle of news reporters with cameras and microphones extended toward us. As we entered the church, Mom whispered to me that I should not say a word.

Jess Marlow gave the eulogy. I heard a lot of sobbing. It seemed to end as quickly as it had begun and we exited the side door only to be met by an onslaught of news reporters with their cameras and microphones. I remember wanting to jump out and step on a microphone that was being held inches from me. Mother reminded me not to say a word and to do nothing as we walked directly towards the waiting car. The sea of reporters parted as black doors opened and we made our way home.

The wake lasted into the early hours of the morning. I remember being downstairs in the TV room and peeking around the corner as people watched the evening news. I saw Jess Marlow give an overview of the service and I remember that he started to cry when he said that Frank would be missed by all at KNBC.

General Leo P. Gerry, who had been the Air Force project officer for the U-2, was at the wake; he pulled me aside and said that my father had been issued the Distinguished Flying Cross and that he would make certain we received it. Some nine years passed before, in 1986, we received Dad's medal at an informal ceremony during a U-2 reunion in Las Vegas.

My father's burial plans remained unsettled. Dad had told Gregg Anderson that in the event of his death he was not to let my mother attempt to bury him at Arlington National Cemetery. He felt that too many people in the CIA and government would oppose it. Every time Gregg asked Mom where Frank was to be buried she would say Arlington. Once when Gregg asked if there was an alternative, she said, "No"—only Arlington.

Gregg called CIA headquarters in Langley, Virginia, to gauge the agency's attitude. He told me later that it was the oddest experience that he had ever had. Every time he called, the line would pick up but no one would say anything until Gregg spoke first. As soon as Gregg identified himself and said he was calling on behalf of the Francis Gary Powers family, the person on the other end would reply and the conversation would start. The details are not clear, but in the end Mom had her way, though she and Gregg needed the help of a congressman who assisted us in getting President Carter to authorize Dad's interment at Arlington. While waiting in the airport lounge at the start of the trip to Washington, Mom excused herself to, as she said, check on Dad. Only years later did I learn that she had gone to look in the coffin before it was placed in the airplane.

Subsequently, at the cemetery prior to the burial, Mom told me that my father was being buried in a section of Arlington that was off the beaten path. It was a spot on top of a hill that the tour buses didn't visit. She also said that it was the section of Arlington where several CIA heroes were buried. At the funeral a man walked up to me and put a coin in my hand. He said that "Zigurd" wanted me to have this. Zigurd had been my Dad's cellmate in prison in the Soviet Union. I turned around to show my mom, saying, look what this man gave me. She asked, "What man?" When I turned around to point him out he had disappeared into the crowd.

On the flight back to California, as I was looking out the window in a clear blue sky there was one dark cloud in the distance. As we flew by the dark cloud took on the shape of a silent U-2 floating in the sky. Several minutes passed, and I asked Mom if she had seen what I had seen. She nodded her head yes, and fought to hold back tears. I said, "Mom, don't cry. It's Dad's way of letting us know it will be all right."

CPSIA information can be obtained at www.ICGtesting.com
Printed in the USA
LVOW06s0544051215

465429LV00007B/10/P

9 781574 884227